Managing Change in Organizations

Fifth edition

Managing Change in Organizations

Colin A. Carnall

Warwick Business School
The University of Warwick

FT Prentice Hall
FINANCIAL TIMES

An imprint of **Pearson Education**

Harlow, England • London • New York • Boston • San Francisco • Toronto • Sydney • Singapore • Hong Kong
Tokyo • Seoul • Taipei • New Delhi • Cape Town • Madrid • Mexico City • Amsterdam • Munich • Paris • Milan

Pearson Education Limited

Edinburgh Gate
Harlow
Essex CM20 2JE
England

and Associated Companies throughout the world

Visit us on the World Wide Web at:
www.pearsoned.co.uk

———————————

First published 1990
Second edition published 1995
Third edition published 1999
Fourth edition published 2003
Fifth edition published 2007

ISBN: 978-0-273-70414-0

British Library Cataloguing-in-Publication Data
A catalogue record for this book is available from the British Library

10 9 8 7 6 5 4 3 2 1
10 09 08 07

Typeset in 9.5/12.5pt Stone Serif by 71
Printed and bound by Ashford Colour Press., Gosport

The publisher's policy is to use paper manufactured from sustainable forests.

Brief contents

Preface   xv
Acknowledgements   xvii

Part I   The challenge of organization change   **1**

1   The challenge of change   3
2   Organization structures: choice and leadership   12
3   The transformation perspective   37

Part II   Theories of organization change   **61**

4   Theories of change: traditional models   63
5   Theories of change: critical perspectives   78
6   Theories of change: strategic management models   93

Part III   Themes and issues in organization change   **105**

7   Organizations in the twenty-first century:
   the value-added organization   107
8   Sustaining organizational effectiveness   120
9   Leadership in practice   148
10   The learning organization   160
11   Strategies for change   172

Part IV   Change management techniques   **187**

12   Diagnosing change   189
13   Managing major changes   224
14   Change architecture   254
15   A strategy for organizational effectiveness   280

Part V   Strategic change   **293**

16   Learning from change   295
17   Culture models and organization change   307
18   Strategic convergence: a new model for organizational change   326
19   Strategies for corporate transformation   340

References   345
Index   355

Contents

Preface   xv
Acknowledgements   xvii

Part I The challenge of organization change

1 The challenge of change   3

Introduction   3
The profile of ambition   5
Implementation   7
Change architecture   8
Conclusion   11
Exercises   11

2 Organization structures: choice and leadership   12

Introduction   12
Management structures and management in action   13
    The entrepreneurial structure   13
    The functional structure   14
    The product structure   14
    The divisional structure   14
    The matrix structure   15
    The federal structure   16
    Management in action   16
The dilemmas of organization   18
    Centralization versus decentralization   18
      For centralization   19
      For decentralization   19
    Global versus local   21
    Efficiency versus effectiveness   21
    Professionals versus line management   22
    From control to commitment   24
    Change versus stability   27
Leadership and 'excellence'   27
    Strategy and structure   29
    Managerial performance   34
Conclusion   35
Exercises   36

3 The transformation perspective   37

Introduction   37
New 'rules for the organizational game'   38
Changing organizations   41
Transforming the organization   46
The value-added organization   49
The network organization   58
Conclusion   60
Exercises   60

Part II Theories of organization change

4 Theories of change: traditional models   63

Introduction   63
The 'clinical' approach   67
Linear approaches   68
Systems theory   72
Emergent approaches to change   73
Conclusion   77
Exercises   77

5 Theories of change: critical perspectives   78

Introduction   78
Emerging thinking about organizational change   81
    Critical theory   81
    Postmodernism   83
    Complexity theory   84
Experience-based design   89
Social movements and large-scale change   89
The evolution of theory about organization change   91
Conclusion   92
Exercises   92

6 Theories of change: strategic management models 93

Introduction   93
Strategic management: the resource-based view   93
The level of ambition   95
Radical or transformational change   97
Conclusion   103
Exercises   104

Part III Themes and issues in organization change

7 Organizations in the twenty-first century: the value-added organization

Introduction	107
Changing the rules of the game	108
Techniques for a value-added organization	109
Stage A1: Business capability profile	110
Stage A2: Value-added metric	112
Stage B: Process design – mapping the value flow	114
1 Value-added design	114
2 Estimate value-added problems of 'command and control' mode	114
3 Value-added clusters	114
4 Value-added contributions	114
Stage C: The 'balanced scorecard'	116
The workshop activity	118
Selecting the measures	118
Creating an implementation plan	118
Conclusion	118
Exercises	119

8 Sustaining organizational effectiveness

Introduction	120
Blocks to problem solving and change	120
Perceptual blocks	121
Emotional blocks	121
Cultural blocks	122
Environmental blocks	123
Cognitive blocks	123
Working through the blocks	123
Limits to problem solving	124
Organizations and rationality	126
An example: organization and counter-rational behaviour	129
Contingency, choice and organizational environments	136
Organization design, resources and complexity	138
Criticisms of the contingency approach	140
The innovative organization	144
Conclusion	146
Exercises	147

9 Leadership in practice   148

Introduction   148
All things to all men!   149
Leadership, vision and strategy   150
Leaders and situations   151
The context of leadership   154
Managers and leadership   156
Leadership and 'human scale'   158
Conclusion   159
Exercises   159

10 The learning organization   160

Introduction   160
Changing perceptions of organization   161
Disciplines for the learning organization   164
Convergence and the learning organization   167
Competence development in handling change   169
Conclusion   170
Exercises   171

11 Strategies for change   172

Introduction   172
Management performance and learning   182
  Effective team work   182
  Effective organizational structures and systems   182
  Organizational change   183
  Learning from changing   183
Conclusion   184
Exercises   185

Part IV Change management techniques

12 Diagnosing change   189

Introduction   189
Monitoring performance, measuring effectiveness   190
Efficiency and effectiveness   191
Techniques for assessment   194
  Assessing organizational effectiveness: exercise   194
    Part 1: Functional analysis   195
    Part 2: Organizational diagnosis   201
Understanding the 'human' dimension of change   206
  'Rational–economic man'   207
  'Social man'   208

'Self-actualizing man'   208
'Complex man'   209
The change equation   210
Authenticity in diagnosis   221
  Insightful organizational diagnosis   222
  Effective change architecture   223
  Adaptive culture   223
Conclusion   223
Exercises   223

13 Managing major changes   224

Introduction   224
Managerial skills for effective organizational change   225
  Managing transitions   225
  Dealing with organizational culture: a major financial institution   229
    The organizational culture: a major financial institution   230
    Managing in different cultures   231
    Implementation   232
  The politics of organizational change   232
    Managing change   234
  Coping with organizational change   235
    Rebuilding self-esteem   236
  Coping with change   238
  The coping cycle   240
    Stage 1: Denial   240
    Stage 2: Defence   242
    Stage 3: Discarding   242
    Stage 4: Adaptation   243
    Stage 5: Internalization   243
Coping with the process of change   244
  Coping with change: issues to be faced   244
    Know yourself   244
    Know your situation   246
    Know others who can help   247
    Working on self-esteem   248
Crafting change for the individual   249
Providing information   250
Give people time   251
Involving people   251
  Advantages and disadvantages of involving people   252
    Advantages   252
    Disadvantages   252
Conclusion   253
Exercises   253

14 Change architecture   254

Introduction   254
Cycles of change   255
  Awareness   255
  Capability   256
  Inclusion   256
    Stage 1: Beginnings   256
    Stage 2: Focusing   256
    Stage 3: Inclusion   257
Learning and change   258
Programmes of change   261
  Learning   265
    Central management   269
    Local management   270
Change architecture: blocks   272
  Step 1: Creating a guiding coalition   276
  Step 2: Visioning the future   276
  Step 3: Identifying gaps   276
  Step 4: Mapping   276
  Step 5: Modelling the dynamics of the vision   276
Conclusion   278
Exercises   279

15 A strategy for organizational effectiveness   280

Introduction   280
Force field analysis   280
The implementation exercise (checklists 1 and 2)   281
  Problems and solutions   281
    Checklist 1: Readiness for change   281
    Checklist 2: Managing change   286
The self-assessment exercise (checklist 3)   288
Conclusion   290
Exercises   291

Part V Strategic change

16 Learning from change   295

Introduction   295
Managing change for management development   299
The management of crisis and turnaround   301
Conclusion   306
Exercises   306

17 Culture models and organization change   307

Introduction   307
What is organization culture?   308
Models of organizational culture   311
    Hofstede   311
    Deal and Kennedy   311
    Handy   312
    The work of Ed Schein   313
    Trompenars   313
    Goffee and Jones   314
Managing corporate politics   316
Leadership and corporate politics   319
Coping with conflict   320
    Some things that managers cannot do much about   320
        Decision making is neither a rational nor an orderly process   320
        Conflicting demands   322
        Uncertainty   322
        Bias   322
        External forces   322
Some things that top and middle managers can do   322
    Set and sustain values   323
    Support problem solving and risk   323
    Design systems to support action   323
    Focus on the manageable   323
    In an uncertain world managers cannot be everywhere   323
    Spend time on the problem/project   323
    Interpret the traditions of the organization around the new systems,
    procedures and solutions   324
    Manage the timing effectively   324
Managing corporate politics   324
Conclusion   325
Exercises   325

18 Strategic convergence: a new model for organization change   326

Introduction   326
Ambition in change   328
Components of change architecture   329
Performance characteristics of change architecture   330
Ensuring appropriate structure   331
Resonance   331
Change culture   332
Change leadership   333
Accelerator effect   334

A framework for assessing capability to change   335
Conclusion   336
Appendix: The change capability framework   336

19 Strategies for corporate transformation   340

Introduction   340
'Market-induced' change   340
Learning as a transformational resource   342
Strategy for corporate transformation   342
Conclusion   344
Exercises   344

References   345
Index   355

Supporting resources

Visit **www.pearsoned.co.uk/carnall** to find valuable online resources

For instructors
- Complete, downloadable Instructor's Manual
- PowerPoint slides that can be downloaded and used for presentations

For more information please contact your local Pearson Education sales representative or visit **www.pearsoned.co.uk/carnall**

Preface

This edition includes a number of significant changes. First, I have organized the book into five parts to help the reader navigate the text more easily. Second, I have added a more substantial coverage of the underpinning theoretical material on change. I have responded to feedback from academic colleagues and others that there is value in doing so. The new material includes wholly new chapters on traditional and critical theory models of change, and substantially revised and extended chapters on strategic management models of change and of culture change.

There is one further key departure from previous editions. Hitherto I have sought mainly to select from existing theory by looking only at what seemed to me to be the most practical and relevant. I made clear that I made no claim to be developing new models. In this edition I have both included a fuller treatment of current theory and presented a new strategic change model derived from my own work in the field.

This is a strategic convergence model and seeks to fill gaps in the existing treatment of change in the literature. Not least the model starts from the proposition that no model of strategic change can be adequate unless it takes account of the reality that in modern organizations we are often making hundreds of changes at the same time. Multiplicity of change initiatives combined with multiplicity of change activities associated with any particular change initiative is a current reality. The model seeks to address that reality. Based on the idea of change architecture introduced in the third edition, the model is now developed sufficiently to feature in most of my own work with organizations, in both the public and private sectors.

As before I acknowledge the ideas and stimulus of many executives and others with whom I work and the perspective of my wife, Ruth, a successful practitioner and leader of change. All errors are my sole responsibility.

Colin Carnall
Westerham, Kent; November 2006

Acknowledgements

We are grateful to the following for permission to reproduce copyright material:

Colin Hastings for our Figure 2.1 entitled 'The new and old organizational cultures' from Hastings, C. (1993) *The New Organization*, London: McGraw-Hill; Harvard Business School Publishing for our Table 2.1 entitled 'Management models' from Walton, R.E. (1985) 'From control to commitment: transforming workforce management in the USA', in Clark, K., Hayes, R.H., and Lorenz, C. (eds) *The Uneasy Alliance: Managing the productivity-technology dilemma*, Boston, MA: Harvard Business School Publishing; the Center for Leadership Studies for our Figure 9.2 entitled 'Situational Leadership® theory' from Hersey, P., Blanchard, K. and Johnson, D. (2000) *Management of Organizational Behavior: Leading Human Resources*, 8th edition, Upper Saddle River, NJ: Prentice Hall, © Copyright 2006 Reprinted with permission of the Center for Leadership Studies, Inc., Ecscondido, CA 92025, All rights reserved; John Wiley & Sons Limited for our Table 14.1 entitled 'Cycles of management' from Juch, B. (1983) *Personal Development*, Chichester, West Sussex: © John Wiley & Sons Limited, Reproduced with permission; John Wiley & Sons, Inc., for our Table 16.1 entitled 'Organizational syndromes' from Miller, D. and de Vries, K., (1984) *The Neurotic Organization,* New York: Jossey-Bass, Copyright © and Reprinted with permission of John Wiley & Sons, Inc.

In some instances we have been unable to trace the owners of copyright material, and we would appreciate any information that would enable us to do so.

Part I

THE CHALLENGE OF ORGANIZATION CHANGE

1   The challenge of change

2   Organization structures: choice and leadership

3   The transformation perspective

1 The challenge of change

Introduction

Everyone says that change is difficult. Difficult to conceive because one must inevitably deal with people issues and an uncertain future. The more so to implement because consequences can be difficult to predict, harder to track and therefore can create a dynamic all of their own. In particular, everyone claims that major change is hard because of the so-called 'soft' or people issues. Is this really so? Does the reader know of any organization or institution which has not experienced change in the last decade or so? Would anyone seriously argue that we are not living in a period of rapid change? Is it not true that we are also living in an era through which dramatic changes of productivity, technology, brand, image and reputation are commonplace?

Some will say 'yes' to these questions but then question the longer-term consequences. What kind of society are we creating? Do we devote enough attention to the long-term consequences of what we do? Fair enough, but that is to shift the argument. The fact is that more and more change is being delivered. Organizations are engaged in delivering higher productivity, higher levels of activity and customer satisfaction and so on. This is not to say that all is well nor that all are successful. Rather it is to note that organizations have grown volumes, activity and profitability during a period in which ever more complex demands (for customer satisfaction and business ethics) have been added in the increasingly complex and diverse environments in which we operate. The challenge facing the senior executive has grown and yet more change is being achieved.

So we must be getting something right! It may be possible to see change as demanding and tiring but not as necessarily inherently difficult. This argument partly turns on the idea of 'resistance to change'. Some argue that people are inherently resistant to change. Whether for personal or institutional reasons, strategic change can be beset by opposition from key stakeholders, whether key professionals, other vested interests, unions and the like. Although this is true and I do not seek to diminish the importance of this point, it is a partial truth. Much of what we refer to as 'resistance to change' is really 'resistance to uncertainty'. Thus the resistance derives from the process of handling and managing change, not from the change as such.

If people understand what is to be achieved, why, how and by whom, this can help. If they understand the impact on themselves, even more so. This is not to argue that all resistance disappears. Indeed you can argue that more information provided to those who do seek to obstruct change because their interests are threatened may help them in their obstruction. But that is a matter of stakeholder handling, timing and tactics. My point is that the arguments of many behavioural scientists writing about change are overwhelmingly partial and, at least in part, misleading. Rapidly skating over the issue of what ought to be changed, much of the writing I refer to deals in employee attitudes, satisfactions, beliefs and so on. Not that this is unimportant, but it is not the whole story. Much of an employee's response to any proposal for change lies in its perceived relevance, credibility and likely success. If someone argues that something should change and presents a credible plan which we feel is likely to succeed, then we are more likely to agree with it. But we will search the organization change literature in vain for ways of measuring 'implementability'. Nor will we find any attempt to identify the 'degree of ambition' in any proposals for change. The literature takes the content of change as a given – a 'black box'. There is some material on risk analysis which clearly is relevant but even so most of the literature ignores even this material.

This book, therefore, seeks to depart from much of the existing literature by tackling three problems in an integrated fashion:

1 What we can say about how to identify what should change and how to judge how ambitious the change plans are.

2 What assessment we can make of the likelihood of these changes being capable of implementation and what kinds of change architectures can be developed to enhance the likelihood of implementation.

3 What the people and organizational issues of strategic change are and how they can best be tackled.

The first two are inevitably linked. Part of the issue of how ambitious any set of proposals are lies in how ready the organization is to adopt them and/or whether an effective change plan can be adopted. Thus risk analysis and a sense of how capable of implementation proposals are in the given organization at the relevant moment in its life and in the economic, competitive or other relevant context is a necessary condition for success.

In seeking to get to grips with the first problem we will examine ideas about strategy formulation and new models of organization sufficiently to shape an outline of how this problem can be formulated and considered, although our purpose is not to write a book on strategy formulation but rather to show how an understanding of how that discipline can help us. We then turn to a review of the main theoretical models of organization change. These provide a conceptual basis for thinking about how best to understand and manage change in organizations as well as providing a means of understanding what happens in organizations as change is underway.

We then go on to look at the second problem. To do so we will deploy and examine concepts such as change architecture, learning organizations and knowledge management. These ideas we will draw together to develop the concept of a change readiness index – a measure of how likely it is that a given set of changes can be implemented. Our purpose here is to enable some analysis to be brought to bear on the question of how ambitious we can and should be when considering proposals for change.

Finally, with regard to problem 3, we will look at a range of individual, team and organizational issues relevant to any understanding of change management. Here we will look at change diagnosis, at leadership, at the change coping cycle model and much more. We will also seek to show how the various issues implicated by problems 1 and 2 form part of the context of people's attitudes and how behaviour is formed in any given change setting. Ultimately our objective is to show what we understand of how to make change. We seek to go beyond the bounds of doubt that we often see when practitioners discuss major changes. Here we seek to focus on what we know and on what we can reasonably infer from experience. Much still remains uncertain and difficult to predict but our view is that we should build on what we know so we can make changes with greater confidence sustained by the thought that we can learn more from the experience of doing so.

The profile of ambition

How then can business leaders conceive ambitious strategic change? What does ambition mean in this context? Clearly competitiveness is key, just as clearly understanding the assets on which competitiveness can be based is also important. But we must also beware naive assumptions. As Hampden-Turner (1996) demonstrates, a focus on a single factor can bring immediate success and longer-term failure. But Kay (1993) probably lays the most appropriate foundation. For him the differentiator on which market power is based is known as 'distinctive capability'. In turn this is based on the following:

- *Reputation*:   essentially the market perception of product/service offerings in terms of tangible attributes – linked to brands.
- *Architecture*:   the relationship of resources including knowledge and flexibility – i.e. internal, external and networks – which the firm can bring to bear.
- *Innovation*:   the capacity to change.

For distinctive capability to be a source of competitive advantage, however, it must be *sustainable*. Here the truth is that nothing is ultimately sustainable as the fortunes over time of many a major corporate demonstrate all too clearly. Scale and market share help but Kay (1993) infers that the management of public policy might be just as important (e.g. Microsoft). All of this points to the need to understand how to create and maintain value-added as the foundation of corporate success, the argument as presented by Kay (1993).

Value-based management is a watchword of current management. It means different things to different observers. For some it is about economic value added, shareholder value and the like. For others the key is social capital (Fukuyama, 1995). Taking this latter view, others see value-based management as more than simply a matter of value-added. Mission, purposes and strategy require or imply a statement of corporate values. Managing a business as if values matter then attracts our attention. Herein lies the argument about *alignment*. Success will come to those whose strategic architecture aligns vision, mission, values, strategy, structure, etc.

A recent proponent of this view is Markides (2000), for whom sustaining advantage is achieved by:

1 Organizing its various activities into 'tight' systems which support and reinforce each other. In essence the advantage is sustained because, while imitators may adopt various ideas and techniques, the ability to manage interfaces really well is difficult to copy.

2 Creating an underlying organization environment of culture, structure, incentives and people, which is also difficult to copy.

Both describe alignment, but Markides goes on to argue that success now often comes precisely by avoiding the tendency to copy. Instead of competing head-to-head with an existing set of competitors, each with well-protected positions, the key is to create a new strategic position by changing the rules of the game. Examples include Body Shop, CNN, Dell, Direct Line Insurance, easyJet, Federal Express, Ikea and Swatch among others. Markides offers a useful framework for considering strategic innovation which, summarized, goes as follows:

Question the status quo and scan the environment – for sector and your business.

Does this lead to a potentially new strategic position?

If you adopt this position, can you find synergies with existing business?

The Kay view takes the idea of *core competence* as a part of strategic architecture. Grunig and Kuhn (2001) develop these ideas into a clearer analytical framework. For them the evaluation of success potential for strategy (building on Ohmae, 1982) requires the assessment of market and competitive strength at three levels:

1 *Market position*	Market attractiveness Competitive intensity Market share Growth/decline of share
2 *Market offers*	Scope and range Quality and service Add-ons Price Speed Including measures relative to competitors
3 *Resources*	Sustainability of competitive advantage (rarity, unitability, substitution)

Following through with the *resource-based* view of strategy these authors note that it is possible to adopt either an 'outside-in' approach to assessing success potential (the market-based view) or an 'inside-out' approach (the resource-based view). However, they regard the latter as being the exception rather than the norm. Nevertheless what is interesting in their formulation is the way they track from assessing success potential through to the concept of the balanced scorecard (following Kaplan and Norton, 1996) and on into the definition of implementation measures, for which they propose a two-by-two matrix looking at motivation and knowledge and competencies on one dimension, and change drivers and obstacles on the other dimension.

Implementation

This leads on to an outline of the whole question of implementation and the idea of an index of change readiness. But what dimensions to include in such an index? In short, implementation could be defined as those processes needed for designing and organizing the process of change to be effective. So how can we judge the effectiveness of change?

Why do some change programmes succeed and others fail? Why can some companies achieve change quickly and others not at all? Why do more and more companies see leadership and culture as defining issues in success or failure? Why are we most concerned to establish the process of change properly? Why do changing organizations concern themselves about values and benchmarking? Is not the central issue for successful change that of 'reading' the environment right and putting in place a competitive business model? Is there not a case for saying that in many strategic changes the most important thing is to define the right business model and replicate it accurately? Are we really convinced with the 'no one best way' argument? This has it that any of a range of business models can be appropriate, and therefore one should concern oneself mostly with the human-centred model.

Throughout my working career in the business school world I have often met this dilemma. Managers are often seen as unable or unwilling to take the human-centred view seriously. Could it be that in reality some of this is about people arguing for the adoption of the human-centred view and not considering the 'task-centred' view seriously enough? Might there not in fact be 'one best way', or at least only a few variants of 'one best way'? If so, getting managers to focus only on the so-called human issues is unlikely to be meaningful.

The socio-technical systems school was an early attempt to resolve this issue. It held that joint optimization was the relevant goal but then principally focused on work-group organization as a prime work organization design innovation. Any examination of outcomes from change projects based on this concept demonstrates that the increased flexibility arising is often a source of significantly enhanced performance. Employee satisfaction often also improves. And this leads to a further dilemma. Why do academic observers and consultants so often perceive attempts at change to be failures? Boonstra (2004) makes this very point. In the USA by far the majority of attempts to redesign business processes fail. The development of new strategies runs aground in 75 per cent of cases. Research in The Netherlands indicates that 70 per cent or more of change programmes lead to 'insufficient results'.

And yet this perception surely flies in the face of the evidence. Industries and sectors have been transformed in recent years. We re-engineer hospitals, government itself and the great companies of the world. Ford was very different in the year 2000 compared with, say, 1960. Is anyone seriously arguing that the privatized British Telecommunications plc of today's world has not gone through dramatic change since privatization? Or British Airways?

Pfeffer (1998) argues the case that you can 'build profits by putting people first', as does Gratton (2000). In each case these authors cite evidence which appears to show that strategic change is regularly achieved. The literature on lean manufacturing does much the same. However, from my own experience working with organizations engaged in making major change, it is clear that many executives see the process of change as problematic. It is difficult to engage stakeholders. The human-centred approach is of value but not often used. Very little attempt is made to learn from experience and so on.

Change architecture

Only recently have observers begun to examine how change programmes are constructed. This may be called change architecture. And yet the principal concern of the work published so far is that of participation and involvement. This is an important but only partial approach. Nevertheless some interesting work has been published.

Thus Emery and Purser (1996) discuss the role of 'search conferences' and Bunker and Alban (1996) look at processes for engaging the 'whole system' for rapid change. Jacobs (1994) identifies three sequential processes as being required to achieve strategic change:

- Building a common database.
- Discovering the future in diverse perspectives.
- Creating commitment to action plans.

The first is particularly interesting. What does it mean? Is it what many often refer to as the process of building acceptance of the need for change? No it is not. Rather it is a process of building credible and valid measures of performance focused on understanding how well we are doing, how we compare to competitors (benchmarking) and what else is changing in the environment. Thus the key element of the first process is about measurement. Here balanced scorecards (Kaplan and Norton, 1996), benchmarking (Watson, 1993) and ideas such as 360° appraisal all play into this element. Not least the concern is about measurement, accountability, transparency and access to outcome measures. Value-added is a key metaphor for this process. Increasingly we see a need to balance between focus on issues such as cost and scale on the one hand with those of product/service development, customer service enhancement and growth on the other.

The second and third issues require dialogue, reflection and sharing and therefore processes are needed to engage key stakeholders. Bruch and Sattelberger (2001), reporting work at Lufthansa, show how processes such as strategy forums, open-space events and learning maps utilizing data from the above but assessed and discussed from various perspectives (of internal and external stakeholders) can be utilized to build new 'mental models' for the business. Learning is a key issue here and this requires 'valid knowledge' and processes for reflection and dialogue. Interestingly enough there is evidence emerging about the need to combine dialogue with a focus on action and follow-through. Thus Norlton (1998) noted that workshop evaluations very early on show how those involved seek closure, direction and future plans and targets – thus providing a vital process in which people both engage in dialogue and in creating new plans – a genuinely problem-oriented process. Much the same emerged in Greenly and Carnall (2001).

All of this suggests that the statement so often articulated, 'the most important resource of this business is its people', is increasingly meaningful not merely as rhetoric but also in practice. If we depend more and more on fewer people and if the loyalty of those people, particularly managers, can no longer be assumed but rather must be earned and retained, then clearly we need to be concerned about how we utilize them, develop them and resource them and about the opportunities for rewards, promotion and success which we provide. If changes depend on the people who implement them then one must be concerned to ensure that those people possess the necessary skills. If those same people are motivated by challenge and opportunity then we must provide that as well. But if the latter will only follow if changes are successful then the introduction of changes which our people view as being credible, as likely to succeed, becomes a paramount issue.

So ultimately what do we mean by change architecture? Not least we mean that set of arrangements, systems, resources and processes through which we engage people in 'productive reasoning' focused on creating a new future. The principles through which the various techniques (strategy forum, communication cascades, 'town meetings', 'open-space events', balanced scorecards and much more) are designed together are as follows:

1 We seek to clarify *governance* and *accountability* for strategic change.
2 We seek to *engage* key stakeholders in appropriate ways.
3 We seek to secure *alignment* for all or at least a critical mass of key stakeholders in ways supportive of success, however defined.
4 We seek effective, credible and accessible *performance measures* provided on a relatively *transparent* basis.
5 We need a balanced set of performance measures (i.e. covering finance, activity, quality, adaptability, markets, customer and employee satisfaction, etc.) presented on a *common platform*.
6 We seek to acquire or develop the *new skills and capabilities* and to *mobilize commitment and resources*.
7 We seek to leverage *knowledge* of relevance to the future out of the way we operate and capture the results of our use of the techniques we apply, i.e. we seek to use strategic change as a *learning* process.

CASE STUDY

KPMG

Thornbury (1999) relates how the global accounting and consulting firm KPMG implemented a major culture change programme as part of its globalization process. As it became global, KPMG utilized organization design and restructuring approaches as a means of reconciling what is often ultimately problematic – the issue of organizing around disciplines, functions, clients, regions, sectors and so on.

$\rightarrow$

Creating a KPMG which looked and acted like a single global firm was a real challenge, not least because it was not so in terms of structure. Thornbury argued that to achieve this aim, the organization needed 'glue' to hold it together. This was to be sought via four initiatives:

■ creating a shared set of values;

■ aligning what was on offer to create a consistent core service offering;

■ developing common and consistent business processes;

■ creating a common infrastructure.

At the heart of this, clearly, are the shared values but, arguably, the other initiatives are vital to moving the organization in a common direction and they therefore play a role in defining and then living up to shared values.

For us the key issue relates to the strategy for change. It must deal with a number of contextual factors:

■ the remnants of old structures;

■ the 'not invented here' syndrome;

■ the primacy of the client in the sense that those with good client track records are often influential internationally over issues about which they know little or nothing;

■ a tradition of intellectualism which often means that changes are debated rather than implemented.

To overcome these barriers, not least to encourage the engagement of KPMG people, had to be a key element of the strategy.

A three-phase process was established:

1 *Phase 1*   (a)   Diagnosis – researching the culture using surveys and focus groups.
          (b)   Launching the values via an international council workshop (involving the 35–40 leaders of the firm).
          (c)   Revision of the KPMG mission statement.

2 *Phase 2*   (a)   Defining the desired culture via a series of development programmes and the 1997 KPMG international partners conference.
          (b)   Refining the values at the Asia Pacific conference.
          (c)   Finalizing the values statement at the March 1998 meeting of the international council.

3 *Phase 3*   (a)   Developing an implementation toolkit to be used in practices around the world – guidelines, workbooks, questionnaires, workshop designs and exercises which could be used by local 'change agents' – including a board-game to be used by workshop participants, known as the values game.
          (b)   Built into the implementation toolkit is material on leadership alignment, personal and team development, communications, managing the process as well as the culture change content listed above.

And a crucial piece of learning! A real key is the word 'integration'. While initially you may run with the culture change concept as a separate activity, the more you integrate with other initiatives and programmes the better.

Source: Thornbury (1999)

Conclusion

In this chapter I have sought to introduce the themes of this book. I argue strategic change is both an intellectual challenge and a process for handling people and uncertainty. A recent book links these two as in effect the same challenge – that of finding ever more ingenious solutions to age-old problems of markets, competitiveness, technology, etc. (Homer-Dixon, 2000). I think the challenge is to do both well and propose to explore that point in the chapters that follow. Thus making change successfully is indeed an intellectual task. It is much more than about being 'good with people'. It is capable of being understood more thoroughly and should not be consigned to the 'mystery' surrounding behavioural science theory and often attached to the use of psychometric tests. It is a challenge for management and leadership teams. It is not a task or set of tasks to be shunned or to be passed on to the new 'wizards' of organization design. But the various professional and academic disciplines can and do help – our task is to better understand how.

EXERCISES

1 What change architecture can you identify in the KPMG case study?

2 What mechanisms have you seen used to ensure that learning and development forms part of a change programme?

3 How might we seek to learn from a failure in organization change?

2 Organization structures: choice and leadership

Introduction

Organization structures allow us to organize and deploy resources. They allow us to define job activities, responsibilities and accountabilities. They provide for decision making and information flows. They help to establish the power structure for the organization. They influence the identity and corporate image of the organization. They establish people's attitudes, at least in part.

The weekend before writing this chapter for the first edition of this book I was running a management development workshop for a large investment bank. The bank had made losses but to no greater extent than other, competing institutions. Yet the financial press had been critical of it and not of others. Moreover, its parent institution (a large bank which wholly owned the investment bank) had replaced a number of key senior managers and was engaged in a review of the investment bank. Meanwhile, the attitudes of staff, middle and senior managers were very problematic, not surprisingly.

Why was that? Well, there had been the stock market fall in autumn 1987. But the bank's competitors had experienced the same fall. Much discussion and debate at the workshop was concluded with the view that the strategy and structure developed by the investment bank when it was founded was unclear. Many grand statements of objectives had been made but it was much less clear whether the structure established provided the right balance of information, power and resources to support the various activities within the organization in achieving those objectives. Moreover, it was felt that the main deficiency had been in professional management. There had been over-reliance on 'market makers'. Such people may well be able to exploit market opportunities but had they the skill to create and sustain a large investment bank? Some of their main competitors had been managed more closely by parent organizations, they argued, giving them the advantages of both professional management and 'market makers'; a better balance had been struck between control from the 'parent' and autonomy of the subsidiary.

Was the structure of the investment bank appropriate to the tasks and opportunities it faced? Was the relationship and structure between it and the 'parent' appropriate? To what extent had the weaknesses in organizational structure left it vulnerable to the 'autumn crash'? To what extent had weaknesses of strategy, structure and control, the impact of the 'crash' and subsequent losses under-mined the confidence of employees, including senior management? To what extent had its corporate image been 'dented', leaving it open to the attention of the financial press? Well, we cannot answer all these questions here, much as the managers in the workshop could only debate them without drawing final con-clusions. However, one thing is clear. Organizational structures can be an influ-ential element in whether or not an organization can be effective.

Management structures and management in action

It is conventional to establish and describe various management structures. Broadly speaking there are six alternative 'model' structures:

1 The simple or entrepreneurial structure.
2 The functional structure.
3 The product structure.
4 The divisional structure.
5 The matrix structure.
6 The federal structure.

However, we shall see that it is not as simple as this; nevertheless let us quickly review these six structures.

The entrepreneurial structure

This is the simplest of these model structures. Everything typically depends on the entrepreneur or owner of the business. They make the decisions. They under-take much of the work. Other employees are taken on to carry out specific tasks. Little or no identifiable departmental structuring exists. These are flexible organ-izations. Trading companies are often structured in this flexible way. Partnerships are typically a variant of this structure.

Growth and geographical dispersion, and the need for outside investment, can create pressures to change from this structure. For example, in the property industry many estate agency partnerships have either been acquired by financial institu-tions or, having generated internal growth, have established divisional structures. Increased competition and, more importantly, business opportunity are creating the pressure for change. The managing director of a holding company now owning some 300 estate agency outlets, organized into geographical divisions, recently made two compelling points about this industry. First, for every £1 profit he could make selling property in the domestic market he could make £7 if he could sell an endowment policy linked to a mortgage. This opportunity was attracting financial institutions into the market. Second, the public image of estate agents was low. Organizing the industry could help to improve the service it provided by improved information provision to clients. It might also allow the industry to improve its image by developing and enforcing codes of practice. Whatever the truth of these predictions, the pressures for change are self-evident.

■ The functional structure

Growth often leads to the development of a functional structure. Here similar activities are grouped into departments: personnel, marketing, finance, operations and so on. Coordination is achieved through a board of directors or management committee, overseen by a managing director or general manager. If the organization is not too large the functional structure provides three main advantages:

1 It allows for the development of particular kinds of expertise, engineering, technology, finance, personnel, etc.

2 It provides career paths for professional staff who work with and then manage people from a similar background.

3 It provides for the effective utilization of personnel across various departments.

However, further growth, geographical dispersion or product/service diversification can create pressures on this form of organizational structure.

■ The product structure

Managers operating within a functional structure are unlikely to devote the necessary time and commitment to each of a range of products/services or markets. It will be difficult to establish criteria by which priorities are to be established. Individuals need to be accountable for products/services or markets if they are to attract appropriate resources. The functional structure provides us with a good basis for achieving internal efficiency of functions and coordination. It does not provide us with a good basis for product/service/market growth in a competitive environment. In practice, it turns out to be difficult to allocate resources to the different products/services on any rational basis.

In the product structure, activity is grouped around products/services/markets. Each group will have its own specialists, at least from disciplines which are best organized at product level (say, for example, engineering and marketing). Typically, finance and personnel may remain functionally organized, reporting directly to the management committee or board, alongside the product groups. This structure brings with it two key advantages:

1 The product groups are better equipped to respond to market demands for growth or change to products/services. They do not need to compete for resources unless the rate of growth is such that the resources allocated to them must be expanded.

2 The work of the various specialists (engineers, marketing) becomes directly related to the market. The likelihood is that in this structure people can and will become 'closer to the customer'.

However, growth or decline in a product/service can be difficult to handle. The former leads to a demand for more resources, the latter for the reassignment of staff between product groups.

■ The divisional structure

Further growth can create pressure on senior management, who will become 'swamped' by day-to-day matters. This means that either senior management tend to ignore broader matters and corporate planning *or* they tend to ignore the operational matters, creating a managerial 'vacuum' within which coordination may become difficult. Divisionalization involves breaking the organization down into relatively autonomous units called divisions. Each division might serve a particular product or a particular market; each will have its own divisional chief executive and management committee or board; each might be organized on functional, product or even matrix lines (see below); each may have a different structure.

This structure creates the following four advantages:

1 Cost and profit performance are matters for the divisional managers. The group chief executive need not be concerned with these issues ordinarily.

2 The main functions of a group are overall financial planning and management, strategic planning, business development and management development. However, clearly, divisional managers need to be involved and much care needs to be given to establishing the involvement of the divisions. Various options are feasible.

3 Each division is free to respond to the demands of its own markets within a framework created by overall strategic plans and budgets.

4 This structure allows accountability to be 'pushed' down the organization, providing a balance between corporate development and control and local, market autonomy. However, striking the balance can be difficult in practice.

The matrix structure

The various structures I have described are attempts to combine market and functional focus to organizational work. The matrix structure is one in which both foci are given importance throughout the organizational structure. Indeed, the structure gives each equal importance. However, beware: as we shall see, structure is not everything. Matrix structures are often found on large construction, aerospace or computer software development projects. Where an organization deals with more than one complex project there is a need to coordinate and develop project and various specialist activities. As the demand for various specialist inputs is variable over the life of a product we need a structure which promotes both effective deployment on a project when needed and adaptability over time so that resources can be easily switched between projects. The matrix structure identifies project management structures, accountable for the project, and functional structures, accountable for each discipline, say engineering, operations and so on.

Matrix structures have three advantages:

1 They allow for the development of cohesive and effective teams of specialists working towards the objectives of a key project.

2 They provide for the professional and career development of specialist staff.

3 They provide for the flexible use of specialist staff.

However, the difficulty of handling a matrix structure can lie in the problem of reconciling the need for flexibility with the need for project coordination and control. This reconciliation implies good working relationships between project and functional management which may, in practice, be difficult to establish.

The federal structure

This structure carries the decentralization of the divisional structure a stage further. The group establishes strategic business units for each product market and controls them from the centre without an intervening divisional structure. This reflects the fact that, in practice, further growth often means that divisions operate more than one unit, firm or plant.

Accountability could readily become confused between group, division and firm levels. The three advantages of the federal structure are as follows:

1 Accountability is clear and defined at unit level.

2 Resources are not expended at divisional level.

3 Groups can achieve growth or divestment quickly to suit corporate strategies.

However, the emergence of the 'federal structure' can recreate the pressures on senior management which the divisional structure once removed. Effective reporting systems, information systems and decentralization are three keys to the solution of this problem.

Management in action

In practice, organizations implement variants of the above structures. Many large organizations in both the public and private sectors operate divisional structures alongside some element of matrix management. Thus an international oil company and a large hospital group I know are both organized into divisions; both have a finance function separate from the divisions (divisional directors and the finance director both being on the executive committee or board) but both assign finance staff to each division.

At local level, people interpret the demands of the tasks in hand, alongside ideas of good financial management practice and standing orders, rules and regulations, in ways which allow them to get on with their work as they see it. In practice, the task of senior management is to establish priorities and to achieve both control and adaptability. The reality is that, at all levels of management, there is considerable discretion on a day-to-day basis. Top management attempts to exert complete control are generally counterproductive. They discourage initiative and encourage ritual or even ineffective behaviour, and take time and money to exert.

People have long distinguished the formal from the informal structure of organizations. The formal structure is that defined by organizational charts, job descriptions and so on. The informal structure is that which emerges from and around the formal structure.

For centuries observers and leaders have remarked on the distinctions between expected and unexpected behaviour in organizations. The fact that the distinctions continue to be made under various names points to an apparently universal condition. From at least the time of Augustus Caesar, these dissimilarities were recognized and incorporated in the terms de jure (by right) and de facto (in fact), which are roughly equivalent to legal or official, and actual but unofficial. In industry and business today one repeatedly hears the same

general meaning phrased as 'administration versus politics', 'theory versus practice', 'red tape versus working relations'.

Dalton (1959) page 219

Dalton defines formal or official as 'that which is planned and agreed upon' and informal or unofficial as 'the spontaneous and flexible ties among members, guided by feelings and personal interests indispensable for the operation of the formal, but too fluid to be entirely contained by it'. Thus the informal system is a system of mutual help and adjustment. For example, a piecework system may require that a supervisor only issues a new job to an operator when the previously issued job is finished, exchanging the old job card for the new card. The operators might wish to accumulate a number of cards because this provides them with a reserve of 'time' that they may use should problems hinder the completion of a job. In such a situation the accumulated time may be booked in and average bonus maintained. Supervisors and operatives must work together and both may ignore the formal requirements of the system, the supervisor being prepared to issue a new job without demanding the previous job card, the operators 'accumulating' cards to use in the event of problems, and so on.

Informal communication may arise from work-related or social reasons. Most work just cannot be done without some informal communication. Many studies show that managers of all kinds prefer informal and verbal communication to documents and that they spend around 45 per cent of their time communicating outside the formal authority structure. Regular channels are often slow and unreliable. The information that a manager obtains from outside the formal system is often qualitative but it is rich with meaning. A manager walking through a department 'sensing' an uneasy or tense atmosphere would be short-sighted to prefer the formal evidence that this is an efficient department. Will it continue to be efficient? Should changes in work patterns or methods need to be introduced; can this be achieved effectively? In fact most managers bypass the formal systems of communication (now increasingly known as the management information system, MIS) and build their own networks of informal contacts (Mintzberg, 1973).

The second reason for the existence of informal communication in organizations is social. People need to relate to each other. Moreover, people may bypass the formal system in order to advance their own personal ambitions or needs. They 'leak' sensitive information to outsiders, or they hold information back. It is worth noting that informal communication can be vital to the success of an organization, particularly where employees work in a hostile or unsafe environment.

The importance of informal systems has been shown in many studies, notably by Strauss (1963) in studies of purchasing departments. He found that the most effective and high-status purchasing officers favoured mutual adjustment over direct supervision and standardization. To resolve conflict with other departments (e.g. engineering departments) they were reluctant to appeal to the purchasing manager, to rely on the rules or to require written agreements; rather, they relied on friendships, the exchange of favours and their own informal political power. They tended to 'oil the wheels' of the formal system. If we are to understand behaviour in organizations we must understand both the formal and the informal.

Authority and communication are facilitating processes for the two basic flow processes: work flow and decision making. Decisions include much else besides what we normally understand as objectivity, rationality and purpose. When making decisions people are constrained by past decisions and by the culture of the organization. Many individual and group inputs are made in a decision process, and the outcome may be a decision that nobody particularly supports or feels committed to.

Decisions are often based on inadequate, and even conflicting, information. Moreover, decisions are sequential rather than once and for all processes. Commitment and support for the implementation of a decision are crucial factors. Decisions are not complete until the necessary resources are applied in the appropriate manner. Delay or scaling down of resources may change a decision subsequent to the meeting where the decision was apparently taken. These are issues to which we shall be returning in a later chapter.

The dilemmas of organization

For all these reasons, too much concentration on the management structure itself can be misleading. Managers are often designing and redesigning the management structure, assigning different responsibilities and resources to divisions and departments. Decisions about the management structure pose a number of dilemmas which must be resolved if organizations are to be managed effectively. But by 'resolved' we do not mean once and for all. We mean resolved in the internal and external circumstances of the organization at any point in time. There are six main dilemmas, as follows:

1 Centralization *vs* decentralization.
2 Global *vs* local.
3 Efficiency *vs* effectiveness.
4 Professionals *vs* line management.
5 Control *vs* commitment.
6 Change *vs* stability.

Centralization versus decentralization

Once upon a time it was not relevant to ask managers 'Is your organization centralized or decentralized?' but, rather, 'In what direction is it going this year?' There seemed to be a cyclical process at work. In good times when markets were growing, organizations decentralized to encourage local initiative in what might be varied local markets and circumstances. In tougher periods when markets were 'tight' and income generation a problem, organizations centralized in order to gain greater control over expenditure, employment policies and so forth. However, the picture is complicated by the growth of organizations. Growth from the small entrepreneurial business to the large and diversified conglomerate seems to impose patterns of organizational design. There seem to be distinct phases in the growth of an organization, each with its own tensions and its own distinctive organizational solution, albeit not necessarily applied in pure form in any particular case. We have already examined these in the various management structures considered earlier in this chapter, each discussed in the context of the growth of organizations. And I said there that currently, in many organizations, managers are creating structures which both centralize and decentralize; namely, to centralize key issues such as finance, business development, acquisition, corporate strategy and management development, but to decentralize operational/profit accountability to the unit, whether a business unit or some other unit (a school, hospital, police force, etc.).

As will be clear already, there are arguments for and against centralization and these depend on the circumstances. These issues are addressed at length by Brooke (1984) and are summarized by Child (1984) as follows.

For centralization

1 Coordination is more straightforward if decisions are made at clearly recognized points within the organizational structure.

2 Senior management have a broader perspective on developments within the organization and maintain conformity with established policies. They are more likely to keep up to date with recent developments throughout the industrial sector.

3 Centralization of control and procedures provides a way of assisting the various functional areas in the organization – research and development, production, personnel, finance and administration – to maintain an appropriate balance. This occurs by centralizing decisions on resource allocation, functional policies, targets and human resource matters.

4 Centralization can allow rationalization of managerial overheads by avoiding duplication of activities or resources where similar activities are being carried out independently in divisions or subunits.

5 Top managers are seen to have proved themselves by the time they reach a senior position. Although a point in favour of centralization, there is a danger that management can adopt the attitude that purely because they are at the top, they are right.

6 Crises often require strong leadership to cope with external and internal pressures. Centralization of power and control of procedures focus on a key person or group. Thus arises the opportunity for speedy decision making and control over communication and coordination.

For decentralization

1 Delegation can reduce the amount of stress and overload experienced by senior management, especially when operating in large-scale, complex organizations. When senior management become overloaded, the exercise of control is diminished. Delegation can remove some of the burden from senior management allowing them to spend more time on policy issues and long-term planning.

2 Many believe that the motivation of employees will increase with the higher degree of discretion and control that they can apply to their work. The opportunity to make decisions and be involved can help to provide personal satisfaction and commitment for the individual. It is assumed that individual goals will broadly be in line with those of the corporate organization. In situations of delegated power, the matching of personal goals and corporate goals is more likely to be possible, but delegation can be severely tested in situations where people work independently of each other. The problem here is to motivate people sufficiently to coordinate their activities without too much central direction.

3 Large or growing organizations need managers who are able to cope with uncertainty because of the volume of complex tasks that have to be performed. It is impossible for one person, or small groups of people, to supervise such complex activities simultaneously. Delegation can therefore assist management development by widening the on-the-job skills of managers and hence provide a number of people who are capable of undertaking senior management positions.

4 Delegation generally allows for greater flexibility by providing for less rigid response to problems at the operative levels in the organization. Decisions do not have to be referred up the hierarchy.

5 By establishing relatively independent subunits within an organization, where middle management are held responsible for operations, delegation can result in improved controls and performance measurements. Accountability can be identified.

Decisions on the level of centralization and decentralization are neither simple nor final. They depend on the circumstances and may need reviewing as circumstances change. Criteria to be considered over and above the points made above are as follows:

■ The objectives, strategy and technology of the organization.

■ The ability of senior management to develop and implement a new management structure.

■ Timing, particularly taking account of other changes in the environment or within the organization.

■ The skills and attitudes of employees and their commitment to the organization.

■ The size of the organization, including size of divisions and/or units.

■ The geographic dispersion of the organization.

■ Time scales and decision making. Technological, safety or other reasons can mean that some decisions must be made quickly and locally, although organizations can still establish procedures, policies and guidelines to provide a decision framework.

■ Relevant external issues such as legislation or central/local government requirements.

Thus it is that in practice these are complex criteria that are central to the question of how responsive and adaptable organizations can become.

Global versus local

This is a variant of the centralization versus decentralization dilemma but in a sense more important because of the scale factor. Once a company has begun to operate internationally establishing manufacturing, marketing and/or distribution/after-sales support operations around the world, it faces this dilemma of how to balance the need to motivate managers to operate successfully within a given local market with its particular demands and characteristics against the demand for global development and coherence. Thus we may need to develop and leverage a particular technology across the globe, in the way that drug companies such as Novartis are so skilled at doing. Additionally, concern to develop an integrated capability, coherence in culture and an integrated logistics chain can create pressures on local needs.

Efficiency versus effectiveness

The third dilemma is that between efficiency and effectiveness. This will be examined more thoroughly in the next chapter but for the moment suffice it to say that efficiency may be defined as achieving stated goals (say the manufacture, sale and distribution of a given product or service) within given resource constraints. Effectiveness includes efficiency *and* adaptability to future circumstances. The effective organization balances immediate efficiency with the ability to deploy new products and services for the future. The dilemma emerges in all sorts of practical ways. When cuts in budgets are needed it may seem relatively easy to cut training and research and development (R&D). Both may incur cost but not generate income and seem, therefore, to be more likely candidates for cuts than are operational activities. Yet both might be important to the future of the organization.

It should, however, be noted that both training and R&D are services which can be sold externally, thus generating income. Thus the dilemma is not between today's figures and activities which focus on the future but create cost in today's 'bottom line'; rather, it is between adopting an *internal* or an *external focus* to activities.

The efficient organization focuses on internal efficiency and control. The effective organization constantly strives to ensure that all its activities pass externally imposed criteria. These may be the ability to generate income by sales, or income by grant-aid (e.g. by obtaining research contracts), or by other external reference points. To be effective an organization must adapt to changing external circumstances.

There are various practical ways of overcoming this dilemma between efficiency and effectiveness. They all depend on achieving a better understanding of the necessity for change and adaptability. This may be achieved in a variety of ways:

- Job rotation can be utilized to give people a broader perspective of the organization's work.
- Following the first point, selection and training of people can emphasize a broader background.
- Intensive use may be made of all available methods of communication in order to create a better degree of shared understanding of the organization's tasks, resources, opportunities, etc.

- An organizational climate can be created which supports experiment and risk taking (see below).

- Participation may be increased in planning, both generally and by specific approaches such as quality circles.

- Innovation should always be on agendas for strategic planning, management development activities and workshops/conferences.

- Project groups can be established to resolve specific tasks and problems. Such groups should be recruited from all the departments involved, creating broader perspectives and quicker acceptance of new ideas.

- Product champions should be identified, along with organizational champions whose task is to create resources and time for new activities to be proved and to integrate the emerging new products/services or systems with existing corporate strategy.

In various ways these ideas are designed to open up the way in which we think about our organization. They aim at helping people to take a broader and more flexible look at what they do and at what they might do. Adaptability and innovation are reinforced by making them an explicit part of the work people do. Of course, it is not easy to do these things. Moreover, we need to act within a coherent framework of management strategy. For the moment we leave these ideas as a starting point. I return to them later in the book and within a broader strategy for change.

■ Professionals versus line management

The fourth dilemma is the extent to which organizations rely on professional expertise or the 'street-wise' approach of the line manager. The professional brings the technical input and ideas which have been applied in other situations. The line manager has knowledge of the specific local circumstances. With the ever-increasing specialization within occupations, combined with the growth of organizations, we often either employ specialists and/or contract for their services with outside organizations (e.g. management consulting firms, universities, etc.).

Take information technology as an example. Can or should development be in the hands of professional information technology staff or of line managers? The former understand the technology, the latter understand the business and local needs. This is a simplification of course, but the plain fact is that many large organizations appear to have gone through at least three phases of development, partly to do with this dilemma and partly to do with technological factors. The first phase saw the introduction of computers under the control of data processing specialists. Systems development took time and often users found the results were elaborate, unwieldy and not particularly helpful. The development of smaller computers (desktops, personal computers, etc.) led many users to develop their own local systems. These often proved to be useful locally but were incapable of integration into broader organization-wide systems and databases. Thus information technology specialists attempt to re-establish their influence by providing advice and support to users. In the third phase, projects are explicitly project managed, often by users and not specialists.

Such problems are common throughout the various professions. Achieving the right balance often turns out to be a question of creating the right systems within which to manage the professionals (be they engineers, accountants, lawyers, doctors or whatever).

Professionals have a knowledge base and a set of values which distinguish them from other groups of employees. This knowledge base comprises the skills and techniques which their training has equipped them to deploy. It is worth noting that many people question attempts by professionals to monopolize the application of specific knowledge and techniques. Nevertheless, we know that organizations use professionals – engineers, accountants and lawyers – as well as what we might call quasi-professionals – personnel specialists, marketing specialists, and so on (quasi-professional only because the relevant professional bodies have yet to gain the status and control of the profession achieved by, say, the accounting institutions). Our purpose here is not to define 'professional' but, rather, to examine how organizations seem to manage professionals. Increasingly, organizations manage professionals on the following principles:

- *Emphasize decentralization*: managers depend on the contribution, effort and skills of the professional employee. Thus motivation and control are sensitive issues and too much direction can be counterproductive. Managers tend to share responsibility and the professional has to learn to take responsibility for management decisions and how to communicate with management. Examples include the growing input into management of doctors in the healthcare field and of data processing specialists and marketing specialists in corporate management.

- *Depend less on 'rational' controls*: too much concern and reliance on quantitative measures can lead to unintended consequences (see Chapter 13). That does not mean that less monitoring and planning is needed. Quite the opposite. However, performance review is carried out with, rather than on, professionals. Involvement is important because judgement in handling a range of quantitative and qualitative measures becomes important.

- *Place greater emphasis on intrinsic motivation*: in particular, career development seems to be of great importance and attention must therefore be paid to delegation, challenge, training and development as well as to motivators such as pay, status, etc.

- *Place greater emphasis on team working*: different professional groups will hold and argue strongly for their own diverse views. Thus professional organizations must handle conflict. People skills and team-building skills are therefore of great importance.

- *Place more emphasis on conflict management*: the conflict referred to above needs to be managed. Uncertainty and complex tasks create the conditions for conflict, along with the previous point. Management need to keep in close touch with the various professional groups and use team building and involvement to communicate decisions quickly and effectively. All these are means of handling conflict constructively.

- *Use matrix management and project structures*: there is a real need to create structures which place primary emphasis on the work to be done and on how to provide for the contribution of different professional groups to that work. These structures emphasize task or team cultures. The various professional groups will be interdependent, thus emphasizing the need for matrix or project (taskforce) approaches to planning and to management.

■ *Place more emphasis on trust*: trust is difficult to establish. Managers, other employees and clients place trust in professionals. This creates great pressure for consistency and fairness in the management of organizations; without it some stakeholders may become dissatisfied. There will still be organizational politics but for these to be constructively managed they need to be surrounded by a reasonable degree of openness.

■ *Place more emphasis on values and ethics*: top management devote considerable time and energy to articulating the organization's mission, values and ethics. They cannot control professionals directly and thus codes of behaviour conducive to trusting relationships are very important. This should be a joint management and professional task. Often it is neglected because it does not solve everyday issues and problems. Nevertheless, longer-run success seems to depend on greater self-regulation within professional organizations.

■ From control to commitment

The improvement of organizational effectiveness involved depends on our ability to diagnose the organization's problems, to identify solutions and to adopt and adapt these solutions to organizational life. One approach to these various challenges has been described by Walton (1985). This approach is based on the assumption that managers have generally relied on inadequate models for managing their employees. They expect and accept much less from employees than is potentially available. Management has failed to motivate employees or to develop their latent capacities (and thus has failed to develop 'invisible assets' – see Chapter 13).

Walton refers to this traditional model as the control model. In this model, work is divided into specialized tasks. Performance expectations are defined as 'standards' that define the minimum acceptable performance. Both expectations and standards are the lowest common denominators. No attempt is made to establish maximum or potential performance.

Two developments prompted movement away from this model. Changing employee attitudes and expectations meant that attempts to gain control created a dissatisfied and low-performing workforce which, in turn, meant that control and efficiency was undermined. Intensified competition was a second development. The control model seems to produce reliable but not outstanding performance. Since the 1970s it has been clear that this is not enough. Competitive advantage can be created out of high performance. High performance requires high levels of commitment which, if sustained, creates a mutually reinforcing virtuous circle.

In the commitment model, jobs are designed to be broader and teams, rather than individuals, are the units that are held accountable for performance. Performance expectations are set relatively high. Continuous improvement is expected and encouraged. The management structure tends to be flatter. People rely on shared goals for coordination; influence is based on expertise and information, not on position. In Table 2.1 we set out, in somewhat modified form, the control model

Table 2.1 Management models (from Walton, R.E. (1985) © Harvard Business School Publishing)

	Control model	*Transitional model*	*Commitment model*
1 Job design principles	Individual attention limited to peforming individual job	Scope of individual responsibility extended to upgrading system performance, via participative problem solving groups in QWL, 'right first time' and quality circle programmes	Individual responsibility extended to upgrading system performance
	Job design de-skills and fragments work and thinking	No change in traditional job design or accountability	Job design enhances content of work, emphasizes whole and separates doing and task, and combines doing and thinking
	Accountability focused on the individual		Frequent use of teams as the basic accountable unit
	Fixed job definition		Flexible definition of duties, contingent on changing conditions
2 Performance expectations	Measured standards define minimum performance. Stability seen as desirable		Emphasis placed on higher 'stretch objectives', which tend to be dynamic and orientated to the marketplace
3 Management organization: structure, systems and style	Structure tends to be layered with top-down controls	(No basic changes in approaches to structure, control or authority)	Flat organizational structure with mutual influence systems
	Coordination and control rely on rules and procedures		Coordination and control based more on shared goals, values and traditions
	More emphasis on prerogatives and positional authority		Management emphasis on problem solving and relevant information and expertise
	Status symbols distributed to reinforce hierarchy	Some change, e.g. existence of participation councils	Minimum status differentials to de-emphasize inherent hierarchy

→

	Control model	Transitional model	Commitment model
4 Reward policies	Variable pay where feasible to provide individual 'incentive'	Typically no basic changes in reward concepts	Performance-related rewards to create equity and to reinforce group achievements, e.g. profit sharing
	Individual pay geared to job evaluation		Individual pay linked to skills, performance
	In downturn, cuts concentrated on hourly payroll	'Equality of contribution' among employee groups	Equity of commitment and result
5 Employment assurances	Employees regarded as variable costs	Assurances that participation will not result in job loss. Extra effort to avoid redundancies	High commitment to avoid or assist in re-employment. Priority for training and retaining existing workforce
6 Open-door' policies	Employees views allowed on relatively narrow agenda. Employees see risks associated with stating views too openly. Methods include open-door policy, attitude surveys, grievance procedures and collective bargaining in some organizations	Addition of limited *ad hoc* consultation mechanisms. No change in corporate governance	Employee participation encouraged on wide range of issues. Attendant benefits emphasized. New concepts of corporate governance
	Business information distributed on strictly defined 'need to know' basis	Additional sharing of information	Business data shared widely
7 Employee-management relations	Adversarial employee relations; emphasis on interest conflict	Thawing of adversarial attitudes; joint sponsorship of QWL or emphasis on common objectives and purposes or change programme	Mutually in employee relations; joint planning and problem solving on expanded agenda. Unions, managements and and workers redefine their respective roles
8 Management acknowledge philosophy	Management's philosophy emphasizes management prerogatives and obligations to shareholders	*Ad hoc* shifts in stated priorities	Management's philosophy accepts multiple stakeholders– owners, employees, customers and public

and the commitment model, following Walton (1985). We also identify the transitional mechanisms needed to move from one model or organization to the other. Does this mean that all accountability in the commitment model is through teams? Walton (1985) does not make that clear. However, the view taken here is that modern thinking emphasizes a duality. The individual manager is accountable for the performance of his or her team, at all levels. However, in order to engage high-level performance the manager needs to develop strong team working. Only then will people's ideas, talents and commitment be harnessed.

Change versus stability

In a changing world the organization must change to survive and prosper. However, must everything change? Moreover, while we are changing we must still deploy people to produce goods and services as normal, even if we are demanding extra effort from them as they experience change. The final dilemma is that of balancing change with stability. In a real sense this book is about this final organizational dilemma. I thus propose merely to 'signal' the dilemma now. Throughout the book we shall deal with this dilemma.

Leadership and 'excellence'

O'er structures of government let fools contend.

Whate'er is best administered, is best.

Alexander Pope

These words, written long ago, direct our attention to the quality of leadership and to managerial performance. An appropriate organizational structure will not enable people to work effectively unless they are appropriately managed. Moreover, in many circumstances different organizational structures can be equally effective as long as management is practised to good effect. We often refer to the 'organizational choice' available to those concerned in the design of an organizational structure (see Trist *et al.*, 1963), by which we mean that the various technological, economic, social and political pressures on organizations do not require unique solutions. In reality, variations of the basic structure are not just possible but are often found in practice. In any event, the informal structure is much more important than the formal structure when trying to understand an organization. Moreover, the structure alone does not define an organization's solutions to the organizational dilemmas discussed above. Rather, corporate policies and management practice do so. Finally, therefore, understanding managerial performance is important if we are to assess whether or not an organization's structure is appropriate in practice.

This suggests that we must look at more than the organizational structure if we are to assess an organization properly. Much attention is now devoted to 'corporate culture'. A number of authors have attempted to define the corporate cultures they see as emerging in 'excellent' companies.

A number of books reviewing the characteristics of excellent companies have been published, notably *In Search of Excellence* by Peters and Waterman (1982) and, more recently, *A Passion for Excellence* by Peters and Austin (1985). Other books include Rosabeth Kanter's *The Change Masters* (1983). These books suggest that effectiveness is more likely to emerge from organizational cultures which encourage the following:

■ *Accountability*: this word is being used more and more when discussing management problems and practices. Where once we meant the fiduciary accountability of the board of directors to the shareholders, we now refer to something quite different. We now refer to direct and personal accountability for performance. The stress is on the individual manager and the performance of the unit or team. Clearer accountability and tighter central control of finance and strategy have gone hand in hand with decentralization of activities and resources to unit level. If the 1960s and 1970s were the eras of involvement in management books, the 1980s was the era of the individual. If we are now seeing the 'failure of collectivism' as both moral philosophy and organizing principle we are also experiencing the re-emergence of individualism. In the 1990s and beyond the issue is whether economic individualism can become transformed to moral or socially responsible individualism.

■ *Synergy*: this is the capacity to obtain cooperation and collaboration. People increasingly question instructions. Professionals expect to have a say in what they do. In consequence, effectiveness cannot be ensured by 'fiat'. Coercion may well generate compliance but will fail to produce effort or creativity. Thus it is that the task of management includes the skills of achieving cooperation and collaboration. Moreover, much work demands the efforts of people drawn from varying technical disciplines such as engineering, chemistry, metallurgy, marketing, accounting and so on. In practice getting things done usually involves gaining cooperation.

■ *Cross-cultural skills*: in all organizations we work with people from a diversity of backgrounds. Whether we are looking at a large public service organization in an urban environment or the various facilities of a multinational corporation, we deal with cultural diversity. Management development involves developing what managers do. Thus, building the cross-cultural skills for handling this diversity is important. We shall see that these skills emerge from developing the skill of empathy, but more of that later.

■ *Managing interfaces*: management involves the skills of coordinating the deployment of people, information, resources and technology in order that work can be carried out effectively. Managers in manufacturing, the public services, in charities and in schools are all exhorted to this end in books, journals, newspaper articles and television programmes. Yet managers spend most of their time engaged in fragmented and, often, problem-solving activities (see Stewart, 1982; Mintzberg, 1973). The nature of management work seems to comprise the resolution of problems arising from lack of coordination rather than the planned and systematic pursuit of coordination. Our knowledge of the circumstances of work is fragmented and incomplete. And thus interface problems are common – people concerned to carry out a task can find that the necessary resources, information or equipment are not available.

■ *Financial realism*: when I worked as an engineering designer I often made design choices on technical but not commercial or economic grounds. The cost implications of decisions were not considered during the design process. In an increasingly competitive world this approach has become recognized as outmoded. Finance is a crucial input to any organization – not the only one, or even the most important, but one which must be confronted in decision making. Effective or 'excellent' organizations appear to be characterized by managers taking financial issues properly into account alongside other issues such as technical or marketing factors.

If these are some of the characteristics of 'excellent' organizations, how can managers encourage them to emerge? To understand this it is necessary to understand how managers work.

■ Strategy and structure

Many argue that there is a definite link between strategy and structure. Chandler's (1962) classic study argued that to be successful organizational structure had to be consistent with strategy. It is certainly widely accepted that a number of factors will have an important impact on success, including the following:

1 The degree of uncertainty in the environment within which the organization operates.
2 The extent of diversity in products and markets, with larger firms in many markets often operating a divisional structure, based on products, or geographic regions, or even combinations of both.
3 Size – larger firms tend to adopt professional management approaches, more formalized procedures, etc. (but see below).
4 Technology – in the broad sense of both the physical infrastructure (machines, computers, factories, offices, etc.) and the 'software' (e.g. the organization of work, product knowledge, information flows, work flows, etc.).
5 Culture, in that there seem to be national differences in appropriate forms of work organization and management style; in some countries teamwork seems to be more strongly emphasized, in others managers rely less (or more) on formal authority. Quite a lot of research has been undertaken in this area since the landmark study by Hofstede (1968). Some argue that you can identify regional influences (e.g. 'European managers', 'Asia–Pacific' managers), while others suggest that either diversity within regions – even within countries – is too great for this to be meaningful, while others suggest that the advent of global corporations, information technology, integrated management training and development is creating some convergence. Be that as it may there are differences which, at the least, must be understood.

There are many research studies of the above (see below). A classic study on the growth of organizations (Greiner, 1972) suggests that they experience periods of evolution and revolution. Both size and age (of organizations) are important variables: the former can lead to problems of coordination and control, the latter to inflexibility as attitudes become fixed over time. The main message here is that as each period of revolutionary change creates a new form of organization, then new management styles, control systems, reward systems and structures are introduced.

Classic shifts in organizational structure include the emergence of the multi-divisional structure. Large corporations diversified into a variety of markets, often geographically widely dispersed. Problems of control and coordination, the need to achieve focus of management effort, allocation of R&D expenditure, etc. led firms to create divisions which then operated relatively autonomously (although in reality the true extent of the autonomy was often questionable and in many firms seemed to vary with the economic cycle – the centre tightening control in the downswing of the cycle).

Of course, there are many other factors to take into account. For example, divisionalized organizations may find it difficult to capitalize on efficiencies which may be derived from sharing certain resources (e.g. manufacturing capacity, R&D, sales and distribution outlets/resources, etc.). In addition many organizations face rapidly changing markets and customers wishing to buy changing configurations of products or services. Sometimes it is difficult to sell effectively where a client needs products from various divisions. Which division should 'own' the client is a key issue. In some cases (e.g. classic cases include computer companies such as Bull in France) some products compete. In any event the purchaser may wish to complete a single deal through a single point of contact. Divisionalized organizations can find this difficult to achieve. One solution to these problems was the strategic business unit concept (Barnett and Wilstead, 1988). Here the focus was on the product market, with a strategic business unit making sense where one could define a clear set of customers and a distinct set of competitors for which it was possible to create a separate functioning business with an identifiable strategy and in which financial performance could be measured.

In recent times, however, a rapidly changing market, technological and other pressures have led firms to create more adaptability and also to seek to focus on core competencies in which they are likely to achieve excellence. This has led to dramatic changes. Firms are 'delayering'. For example, at a recent conference I attended, a senior executive from the North American computer industry claimed that large organizations had removed between 1 and 1.5 layers of management *on average* in the last five years. In consequence there are, in those organizations, many fewer managers but they are carrying more responsibility and doing more demanding jobs than they used to. Information technology, through making access to data easier, is supporting team-based approaches to management. The need to respond quickly to market pressures is leading many organizations to push responsibility down the organization, whether under slogans such as 'empowerment' or through customer service or total quality programmes. For these and other reasons connected with shareholder value, many large businesses have 'demerged'. In many countries the public service is being reformed along similar lines. Public sector organizations which were once very hierarchical have been either privatized or taken out of the public service as independent agencies. We can see developments like this in North America, the UK, New Zealand and elsewhere. Healthcare reform in Thailand is proceeding apace on the basis of pushing responsibility down to providers (local hospitals and clinics) rather than managing them directly from the centre (in the capital city).

Over and above all of this, companies outsource, engage in joint ventures and strategic alliances in order that each element of the 'value chain' (see Porter, 1985) is delivered in a high value-added way. This development is having a powerful impact, creating what some call the 'networked' organization and others are now calling the 'virtual' organization.

Let us look at this trend in rather more detail (the discussion here derives from various sources, including Hastings (1993) and recent work by a colleague, Professor Bill Weinstein of Henley). Basically there has been a shift from a belief in the advantages of size to the advantages of adaptability. Thirty years ago many organizations set out to achieve integration from raw materials to final customer service, owning and controlling all functions in the value chain with only marginal subcontracting. That way one could control costs, create certainty of delivery, project innovation and limit transaction costs (here we refer to the avoidance of the costs associated with, for example, having to purchase supplies in the open market as opposed to simply ordering from one's own wholly owned supplier).

Increasingly some top managers are asking whether these larger groups are 'manageable'. The risks and problems of inertia are greater. Product development becomes a major problem. 'Time to market' grows with size. I well remember hearing an IBM Europe senior executive (in the late 1980s) complain that any new product proposal had to have seven different senior executives sign it off before it could proceed, including people located locally at the Paris headquarters and elsewhere. The possibility for delay is all too obvious. There is a growing literature on this time-to-market issue (see, for example, Clark and Fujimoto, 1991; Stalk and Hout, 1990) and no one is suggesting that size is the only problem, but the latter study shows that time to market can be reduced significantly by moving from a hierarchical to an 'entrepreneurial' structure, and even further if a 'time-based management' approach is adopted.

Thus we can see countless organizations focusing on their core competencies (Prahalad and Hamel, 1990), dealing with 'preferred' suppliers with whom they develop strong links, delayering, downsizing and focusing on 'invisible assets' like product market knowledge, competitor intelligence and the like as a source of added value (see Itami, 1987). The practical consequences of these trends are that organizations are now much more likely to be engaged in strategic alliances, joint ventures, outsourcing, networking, joint development projects and so on. This implies a new context for managers.

In the new organization the manager is much more concerned with managing across boundaries (often as well as across borders). There is more dependence on 'outsiders' and less reliance on 'insiders'. Any part of the organization can be 'outsourced'. In the public sector the process is 'market testing'. It creates new pressures. It also means that achieving added value is more a matter of external networking and possessing relevant knowledge about the outside world than it used to be. Increasingly managers find that rather than utilizing hierarchy and command and control they are managing exchange relations. Cooperation and negotiation are more relevant. Effective communication becomes vital, but this places greater emphasis on the need to develop internal managerial and technological skills. Without doing so the organization risks being excluded because it brings no added value.

All of this implies that empathy, the ability to seek gains for all partners, flexibility and learning all become vital skills in the new organization. As we shall see, they are also vital skills for those managing major change. Hastings (1993) writes about organizational networking in terms of the need to break down organizational boundaries, create successful partnerships, connect computers and connect people. This implies a new set of priorities for management in this new organization. New management roles that Hastings thinks may be emerging include those of mentor (long talked about, increasingly practised), broker (connecting people, ideas and resources) and what he calls the 'counterpart'. This he describes as a vital role for the success of joint ventures and strategic alliances, but it can be extended into project teams and other internal networks. The role is about providing explicit liaison between links (e.g. joint venture partners) over and above the informal linkages. Looking at cultural change at BP, he reported the company view of the old and the new culture (the latter being one intended to encourage networking) as in Figure 2.1.

Not least of the characteristics of effective people in the new culture is that of *personal impact* – influencing others through example and recognition of their needs. But to conclude, the new thinking about organizations emphasizes the need for new thinking about careers and career development as well as moves to develop what has been called 'the self-reliant' manager (Bones, 1994).

The other source of pressure for change to which we have briefly referred is that of internationalization. Doz and Prahalad (1991) identify characteristics of the diversified internationally operating company as follows:

■ Organizational solutions based simply on either centralization or decentralization will not meet the complexity of the modern environment.

■ Processes and structure need to allow differentiation to meet the needs of various products, functions and countries.

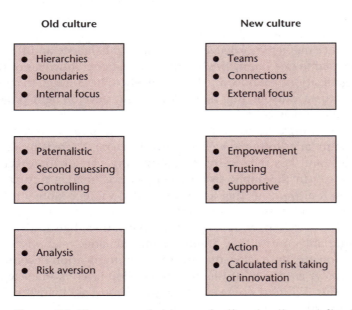

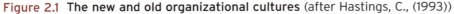

Figure 2.1 **The new and old organizational cultures** (after Hastings, C., (1993))

- Integrative processes are needed if diverse interests are to be balanced – that is, we must work at maintaining interfaces, networks, etc.
- Effective information flows throughout the business are a vital source of added value.
- Flexibility in structure and process and the capability of including external partners are important.
- There needs to be stability and consistency of purpose – a leadership task.

So once again the demands arising out of internationalization lead to the need to create and operate networks (see Bartlett and Ghoshal (1989) for an analysis of NV Philips as an international network).

It is important to realize that the issues we have referred to are not simply personal issues for which the solutions lie within the 'people skills' area; they are business issues demanding business skills – indeed the management skills required combine business and personal skills. Gould and Campbell (1987) articulate this idea through identifying three corporate styles which you can observe in large, diversified groups, as follows:

1 *Strategic planning style*: strong central management involvement in strategy development through an extensive planning review process and powerful initiatives to secure development of the business arising from the centre. Focus on creating shared vision leads to flexibility in performance targets, with performance being viewed in the context of longer-term objectives.

2 *Strategic control*: emphasis on planning at the business unit level, with the centre concerned primarily with the exercise of tight controls.

3 *Financial control*: the annual budget becomes the key control mechanism, focusing attention on short-term targets.

For Gould and Campbell, where the prime orientation of senior management is characterized by the belief in short-term results, the financial control style will emerge. Where the orientation is on longer-term competitive advantage seen as arising out of more than only financial success which can be developed, in whole or in part, from the centre, then one of the other two styles will predominate. In the former it is not necessarily the case that senior management do not accept that competitive advantage emerges out of factors other than financial performance, but rather they disbelieve the notion that centrally driven initiatives are the best source of competitive advantage.

They then link these styles to a number of factors including the shape, size and diversity of the product/service portfolio, stability in the environment, the personality of the chief executive, the financial condition of the business and so on. From all of this we can begin to see that over the last 20 or 30 years changes within the global economy have created new management problems demanding solutions both more complex and more demanding of management skills than traditional hierarchies. We now turn to what managers do.

ABB (Asea Brown Boveri), known as the European company the giants of Asia feared, is an interesting example of how these dilemmas of organization are faced, e.g. the global–local dilemma in particular. As a company it operates in 60 or more countries through over 1300 separate legal entities. It operates in a range of electrical and power engineering activities, often engaged in major capital schemes for governments in the developing world. Thus the local imperative is a strong one. How is the business held together globally? The CEO spends much of his time visiting subsidiaries articulating the group strategy and seeking to understand local needs. The group has a well-developed information system for financial and management control. Much attention is given to identifying and then developing the careers of a cadre of 'high fliers' seen as the future senior managers of the business. Thus considerable effort is devoted to integrating diversity. The approach is not simply about organizing for coordination and control. The group appears to organize around local needs and then wraps those local operations within arrangements designed to pursue integration across the world. Key technologies are managed by a senior executive with a global remit to maximize the leverage of that technology for the group.

Managerial performance

Managerial performance is a combination of knowledge and skill applied in practice. Management is about 'getting things done', about action. Managerial work is surrounded by circumstances which create problems including uncertainty, incomplete information, change in the environment or elsewhere in the organization and conflict. Mintzberg (1973) has developed a comprehensive empirical picture of the nature of managerial work through observing and recording what managers actually do. He describes the managerial job in terms of roles (see Table 2.2).

From his empirical work Mintzberg characterizes managerial jobs as follows:

■ They are remarkably similar and can be described in nine roles (see Table 2.2) and six sets of working characteristics (see below).

■ Much managerial work is challenging and non-routine, but every manager has some routine and regular ordinary duties.

■ A manager is both a generalist and a specialist.

■ Information is an important part of the manager's power.

■ The major pitfall for the manager is having to be superficial because the workload is too high.

■ Management science has little effect on how the manager works because when under work pressure he or she fragments activity and uses verbal communication, making it difficult for management scientists to help.

■ The management scientist can only break this 'vicious circle' with real understanding of the manager's job, and access to the manager's own views of the help he or she needs.

Table 2.2 **Managerial roles (after Mintzberg, 1973)**

Interpersonal roles	*Informational roles*	*Decisional roles*
Figurehead	Monitor	Entrepreneur disturbance
Leader	Disseminator	Handler resource
Liaison	Spokesperson	Allocator negotiator

The six working characteristics relate to the following:

1 The quantity and pace of the manager's work.

2 The patterns of the activities.

3 The relationship in work between action and reflection.

4 The use of different communications media.

5 The relationships with contacts.

6 The interaction between rights and duties.

Mintzberg (1973), Stewart (1977), Dubin and Spray (1964) and Horne and Lupton (1965) all confirm from empirical studies that managers' workloads are substantial. Managers work at an unrelenting pace. This is because the job is inherently open-ended and the manager never finishes his or her work.

Managerial work is characterized by brevity, variety and fragmentation. The manager is never able to concentrate on one aspect of the job alone or for any length of time. The trivial and the important are mixed so that mood and tone shift and change continually. Mintzberg found that half of the activities of five CEOs took nine minutes or less and only 10 per cent lasted more than an hour. The manager is seldom able or willing to spend much time on any one issue. He or she is constantly interrupted. Rosemary Stewart found only nine periods of half-an-hour without interruption in a four-week study of 160 managers.

The manager seems to stress the active element of work – activities that are current, specific, well defined and non-routine attract more attention: for example, processing most mail and reading written reports are low-priority jobs. The manager may be seen as the conductor of the orchestra and, conversely, as a puppet pulled by hundreds of strings. To find out the extent to which managers controlled themselves, Mintzberg analysed whether in each activity managers were active or passive and found only a small proportion of active work, with managers spending much time reacting. The initial construction of the manager's job may, however, have included decisions to allow these reactions and passive participation as a way of keeping up a flow of work and ensuring the involvement of others in the management process.

Conclusion

This chapter has examined how organizations are structured and managed. It has identified and described various management structures. But structures are not everything. Overlaid on the question of structure are at least six 'dilemmas' of organization. The reality of organizational life is that these 'dilemmas' are constantly presented to managers as the circumstances around them change. In practice, managers have discretion and choice in the work they do. The extent to which they will recognize and exploit this discretion will be related to the 'corporate culture' of the organization. This is a question to which we will turn in a later chapter of this book. For the moment I conclude by stating that defining an organizational structure is to define a 'moving target'. It only begins to establish the boundaries within which managers act or choose not to act, and within which they can obtain resources and information and be held accountable for what they do.

The above identification and analysis of managerial roles cannot describe the whole, but nor can a manager function who does not fulfil these roles to some degree. This is the real difficulty in team management which requires very careful reintegration and effective communication. Different managers spend different amounts of time on different roles.

To be effective a manager requires the following:

- Self-knowledge and insight.
- Understanding of the managerial job.
- Timely and controlled responses to the pressures and dilemmas which apply.

Managers must also find ways of dealing with the daily dilemmas and pressures of their working lives. Understanding organizations, then, involves understanding both what managers actually do and how it can be/should be structured.

In the next chapter I will develop the concept of a value-added organization taking forward the thinking established in Chapter 2 and building on the ideas set out above. I will seek to set out some of the tools and techniques which have been developed as managers have sought to devise and manage new forms of organization. We shall see that not least of the principles emerging in the value-added organization is the increased application of market mechanisms to induce change. We are in the midst of a shift in the mind-set. We need new means of managing changes, moving away from a reliance on planned changes towards an increased use of a mix of planned and market-induced change.

EXERCISES

1 How does your organization deal with the dilemmas we have identified?

2 To what extent is the commitment model one which encourages innovation and creativity? Can you think of any experience (in a company, at college, in a sports club) which represents a good example?

3 What management structure does your company (or department) have? Why? Is it likely to change? What are the main reasons for change?

3 The transformation perspective

Introduction

For 25 years I have engaged in teaching, writing, researching and consulting in the field of organizational change. Throughout that time I have taken the view that the implementation of change is difficult, time consuming and often requires 'mind-set', culture and value change. I have also believed that the route to such changes lies in behaviour: put people in new settings within which they have to behave differently and, if properly trained, supported and rewarded, their behaviour will change. If successful this will lead to mind-set change and ultimately will impact on the culture of the organization.

I have viewed the strategic change literature with a degree of scepticism in at least one respect. Much of the literature at least implies that the strategy bit is easy. This view holds that it is only when we get to implementation that the fun starts. This is natural enough. Corporate history is full of organizations which proved unable to implement strategy. Hamel (1996) convincingly argues that strategy is only easy when the process of strategy formulation limits the scope of discovery, the breadth of involvement and the intellectual effort expended. If the focus is on planning to convert market research into next year's budget then strategy is about programme, not about the future of the organization longer term. And yet many organizations are changing the 'rules of the game' within which they operate. The boundaries of industries are shifting. New entrants are revolutionizing industries. When computer companies enter education they bring an impetus towards revolutionary change. When retailers act as banks by offering cash at the checkout they do the same. When consumers can get a credit card from General Motors or where insurance is sold by telephone, we are looking at fundamental reconfigurations of industries. Thus it is that a book on how to change organizations must look at how organizations themselves have been and are being transformed. Part of the focus of this book is to examine the new forms of organization now emerging which are fundamentally different to the traditional hierarchical model. We seek to understand how and why they are emerging and how change can be handled within and through these new organizational models.

New 'rules for the organizational game'

To explore this theme let us turn to two case studies.

CASE STUDY
Ford and the Global Car

Under the label 'Ford 2000' the company seeks to transform itself into a global corporation deploying a new 'philosophy' of doing business (see Parry-Jones (1996) for more detail).

By 1993, despite being profitable, the world's second-largest automotive producer engaged on a major programme of development. Ford also recognized itself as part of a complex and intensively competitive sector, not least with issues of oversupply in various markets. The existing business philosophy emphasized the production of cars in the regions where they were to be sold. Yet Ford was engaged in separate development processes in different regions of the world for what were essentially similar products. Moreover, while Ford was well positioned in the USA and Europe it was less well placed in those areas where growth in demand is likely.

Moreover, customers are more sophisticated, more demanding and more aware of what is available around the world. The market is increasingly global. The company has merged its semi-autonomous regional operations into a single worldwide business. Product development will focus globally.

Change of this type had been attempted earlier in Ford's history. The Escort development had been shared by teams in Europe and North America but differentiation resulted. Amalgamations within Europe were achieved in the late 1960s. The Escort experience led Ford to realize that a world car development needed single leadership to achieve the needed integration – easy to say but not easy to achieve. The Mondeo development was a further stage in the process. Led from Europe, this work was facilitated by a communications infrastructure allowing the sharing and analysis of data and decision making across borders. The communications infrastructure supports a worldwide engineering release system, a worldwide purchasing system and a global conferencing facility. Are these infrastructure developments not as important as the concept of single leadership in enabling the company to overcome the problems of national pride and narrow perception that limited the past attempts?

In turn the Mondeo development led Ford to learn vital lessons, in particular 'simultaneous engineering'. Achieved via 'vertically integrated teams', it contrasts with the former sequential process with its attendant possibilities for conflict between those who design and those who manufacture the product. In early 1994 a 'study team' of 27 managers from a variety of functions and countries began a 10-week programme looking at how to learn the lessons of the past and achieve genuine globalization. It was decided to merge the existing operations in Europe and North America. Ford established five vehicle centres to take lifetime responsibility for the development of all vehicles of a given class produced and sold anywhere in the world. In addition Ford has created a single global unit for technology development. All employees with Automotive Operations have been deployed within this worldwide 'matrix'. The vehicle centre is responsible for developing and launching new vehicles and has lifetime responsibility for quality, serviceability, profitability and overall programme management. Formerly the development team's work ended at launch.

The focus therefore is on *horizontal integration*. Not least of the advantages is that decisions can be made closer to the action. With the introduction of an integrated global cycle plan for product launch, major product changes are planned to be achieved in half the time. The matrix combines vertical integration with horizontal integration and raises fundamental questions about the role of senior management in devising strategy, ensuring that the needed capabilities are in place and so on.

We point to two themes relevant to this book, as follows:

1 Ford has begun the process of rethinking itself as a business. Specifically it seeks to emphasize the horizontal process of creating value for customers, not least because doing so provides opportunities to exploit economies across the horizontal value stream.

2 Whether or not you deem Ford to be a 'learning organization', it is clear that Ford has learnt a number of lessons, each of which allowed it to create a new part of the 'platform' from which it now seeks to globalize.

As we shall see throughout this book, these two themes reoccur frequently when looking at leading-edge practice in strategic change.

Thus, from this and the following case study we see evidence of new thinking in three areas:

1 Rethinking the organization in terms of a horizontal stream of value-added activities focused on customers/clients.

2 The learning organization and how to achieve that state.

3 The vital role of partnerships.

It is clear, therefore, that the world of major change is no longer simply a world concerned with 'resistance to change'. Indeed I have often wondered why 'resistance to change' loomed so large in discussions about change. Many argue that people are motivated by challenging jobs, discretion, autonomy, etc. These same people also pointed to the prevalence of 'resistance to change' without posing the obvious question. Change seems likely to create the very conditions which people are supposed to find motivating. Why, then, are we so concerned about 'resistance to change'?

CASE STUDY *Changing Childbirth*

In 1993 the UK Department of Health published a report entitled *Changing Childbirth*. By the early 1980s evidence of dissatisfaction as a result of fragmented care and obstetrician-led services was apparent. Continuity of care was emerging alongside the perception that women desired choice of care and place of delivery and the right of control over their own bodies at all stages of pregnancy and birth.

While the research, evidence and analysis underpinning and providing the context for *Changing Childbirth* is complex and not short of controversy, for our purposes the focus of the report for maternity practice is best summarized by quoting the report's indicators of success (within 5 years, i.e. by 1998):

■ Every woman should know one midwife who ensures continuity of her midwifery care – the named midwife.

■ At least 30 per cent of women should have the midwife as their lead professional.

■ At least 75 per cent of women should know the person who cares for them during their delivery.

■ At least 30 per cent of women delivered in a maternity unit should be admitted under the management of the midwife.

Often measures designed to achieve these success indicators were being devised in the context of another development, integrated patient care (IPC).

IPC is an example of a general rethinking of patient care brought in from the USA in the early 1990s. It focuses on aspects of care such as continuity of care, improved documentation, physical redesign of buildings, locating facilities close to patients, staff role reviews, etc. Sometimes known as patient-focused care (PFC), this philosophy places the patient at the centre, seeks active involvement of the patient, continuity of care, decentralization, multi-skilling of care staff and streamlined documentation. Finally a further concept is the *pathway of care*, which in essence is the time sequence of events, tests, assessments, experiences and outcomes associated with the patient's care process. If the objective is to seek high-quality 'seamless' care for individual patients across the boundaries of department, directorate and discipline into which hospitals have been fashioned by history, then *horizontal focus* is a key issue.

At Brighton Health Care NHS Trust these concepts have been implemented along with team midwifery within the community. Three teams of six full-time equivalent midwives based in different geographical locations aimed to provide 24-hour care for 250–350 women. The service encompassed all aspects of midwifery care including home assessment of labour and care continuity. An early evaluation concluded that team midwifery enabled Brighton to provide a more patient-centred care service at the same high standard of care (avoiding a perceived risk of the team approach) with no evidence of decreased satisfaction for the women involved (there has been a very high reported satisfaction) or for midwives (again a concern which did not appear to materialize).

The early research (see Hart, 1997) indicates significant progress towards *Changing Childbirth* success indicators. While some evidence of tension emerged between team midwives and their labour-ward colleagues, it was also clear that there were many perceived advantages. Moreover, many of the negative points emerging appeared to be linked to other factors, i.e. workloads in general, problems of working conditions, problems over grading within the reward arrangements. Clearly continuity of care was seen as linked positively to job satisfaction. The general practitioners interviewed were satisfied both with the service overall and with team midwifery but this was not without perceived problems, some related to the adequacy of resourcing and GP involvement (which may lessen given continuity of team-based care).

Interestingly enough, recommendations for further development place much emphasis on developing relationships, partnerships and care protocols (which define the parameters within which care professionals practise). Care protocols are clearly intended as a means of ensuring clear definition of roles and thereby to create a platform for improved partnerships. Overall the case study powerfully reinforces the horizontal focus of strategic change, applied not principally to reduce costs but rather to create improved care. That said, we do not suggest that cost effectiveness is not a key driver behind innovations of this kind, albeit given the apparently infinite demand for healthcare this is probably more about securing a higher volume of activity within existing budgets, i.e. about reducing cost per case. The other crucial point here is the essential role of *partnership*. Partnership between professional groups both within the hospital and in the community is essential and represents a complex challenge in the healthcare environment for the latter part of the twentieth century.

Changing organizations

Many offered an easy answer. Change was being driven by new technology. New technology destroyed jobs and, some said, diminished many of the jobs which remained. At the time some commentators obviously felt that there was a finite amount of work to do. If technology destroyed jobs then either there would be fewer jobs around or working weeks would need to be reduced, the retirement age reduced and other innovations such as job shares would be needed.

Without suggesting that the economic problems of the modern world had been 'solved' and taking account of the point that the structure of employment had changed dramatically (e.g. more part-time work), even a cursory glance at employment statistics in the Western world suggests that much of this 'lump of work' or 'finite limits of work' argument is nonsense. Throughout the 1980s more people entered employment despite the fact that technology and other changes have increased productivity, often quite quickly. Again I recall being impressed by talk of 3–4 per cent p.a. improvements in productivity in the 1960s. Now 6–8 per cent p.a. can be commonplace, particularly when recession or competition stimulates corporate restructuring. Moreover, in many cases improvements of 50 per cent or more are not uncommon. Yet this is not the only change since 1971. The power of 'vested' interests is now by no means as strong. Whether you believe that this is due to 'Thatcherism' or to long-term social and economic changes is unimportant. It is nevertheless the case that collectivist ideas have given way to a focus on the individual. Indeed the moral challenge we now face is whether 'possessive' individualism is to be the order of the day (Macpherson, 1962).

Thus various changes have gone forward across much of the world. In particular, public sector organizations have been privatized, market mechanisms have been introduced, large organizations have been broken up and others have been 'flattened'. Decentralization has created corporate structures focused on 'strategic business units'. People talk about 'networked organizations', 'federal' organizations and empowerment.

It is obvious that all of this has placed greater demands on the capabilities of managers. But these changes have also transformed the nature of what some call the 'psychological contract between the employing organization and the employee'. If 'jobs for life' cannot be guaranteed then people have to apply for their 'own' jobs on reorganization; where flattened structures mean empowerment for some but redundancy for others you would expect that to happen. Where organizations use early retirement or voluntary retirement as an essential part of policy and where some organizations emphasize the benefits to organization and employee of subcontracting, maintaining a stable core of permanent employees and a periphery of subcontractors, they are reflecting a significant change.

Once upon a time managers and professionals and, for that matter, other employees, particularly skilled employees, expected to stay on one career path and in one organization throughout their careers. Now people expect careers to include periods in more than one organization and expect to have more than one career in a working life.

In general it seems not unreasonable to predict that managers are better educated, more creative, more ambitious, but less loyal. Indeed survey evidence suggests that this is true in various countries, even in Japan, although the relative position, particularly on loyalty, is different. I have discussed this view with hundreds of management audiences throughout Europe. All agree that the change is real. All suggest that this change is a consequence of various social, economic and technological changes. But all emphasize that loyalty is a two-way process and that organizations demonstrate less loyalty to their managers, mainly as a consequence of delayering and other major changes which have led to the 'redundant executive' capturing as much if not more of our attention than the redundant unskilled or semi-skilled worker.

All of this suggests that the statement so often articulated, 'the most important resource of this business is its people', is increasingly meaningful not merely as rhetoric but also in practice. If we depend more and more on fewer people and if the loyalty of those people, particularly managers, can no longer be assumed but rather must be earned and retained, then clearly we need to be concerned about how we utilize them, develop them and resource them and about the opportunities for rewards, promotion and success which we provide. If changes depend on the people who implement them then one must be concerned to ensure that those people possess the necessary skills. If those same people are motivated by challenge and opportunity then we must provide that as well. But if the latter will only follow if changes are successful then the introduction of changes which our people view as being credible, as likely to succeed, becomes a paramount issue.

Does this not then mean that the task of developing, implementing and managing major strategic changes becomes a key management challenge of the modern world? Some say that it must begin with the articulation of strategic vision. You need to be able to conceive of what the organization might become in three or five or more years' time. To do this managers must combine analysis and intuition, knowing and doing, thinking and feeling. Visualizing strategic change is not merely a matter of analysis, it requires the ability to think about, to conceptualize, the future, the willingness to experiment and learn, to see what might happen, to estimate how the organization might respond and much more.

But all of this relates to individual behaviour which will take place in teams, whether boards of directors, management teams, working parties or whatever. Thus we need a range of inputs into the discussion and debate on strategy if we are to understand the social, political, economic and technological trends with which we must deal, and so we need many inputs perhaps both from inside and outside the organization. However, if we are to bring these people together effectively then we must adopt managerial styles conducive to learning, to development, to creating and to articulating/communicating vision. In part it demands that we understand the processes of innovation, adaptation and change – what hinders change at individual, group, unit and corporate level and what can be done about these 'blockages'. Processes such as these are often referred to under the rubric 'culture change'.

Here we simply wish to make the point that successful strategic change seems to demand a combination of cognitive/analytical skills and knowledge alongside a range of behavioural or process skills and knowledge. Figure 3.1 sets out a 'map' of the cognitive/analytical components which appear to be needed. Here we suggest that successful strategic change requires knowledge and techniques for corporate diagnosis, in the culture change area and in putting together programmes of change. All of this is not enough, however, without the essential process skills needed to encourage learning and change.

Thus diagnostic surveys and competitive benchmarking techniques can provide data to formulate change plans. Moreover there are increasingly well established and codified techniques for business process engineering, total quality management and so on. But substantial change both demands and will lead to culture change. Thus doing it well requires process skills to advance overall integration in pursuit of progress. Progress for whom and on what terms is, of course, an issue.

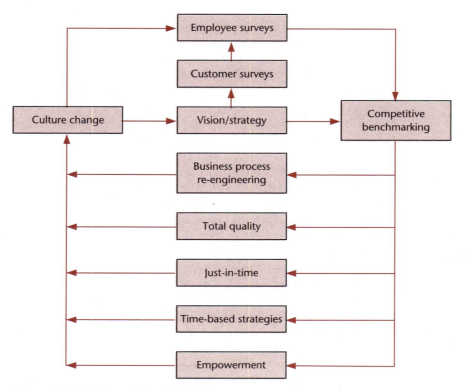

Figure 3.1 **Implementing strategy**

In a world in which the ability to change is a key 'engine of success' the shift from strategy into capability demands leadership, action planning, the ability to cope with pressure and uncertainty and a willingness to learn. More analysis helps us in that it aids our understanding of where we are and how we came to get there – however, analysis alone will not create the future.

From Figure 3.1 we see that strategic diagnosis is driven by and/or formed by ideas formulated about the future of the organization leading to a 'vision of the future'. There are techniques available for vision/strategy formulation, employee surveys, customer surveys and competitive benchmarking and so on, but it is important to focus initially on what we are doing in the diagnosis process. We are not merely attempting to collect symptomatic evidence but to understand what has happened. Thus falling sales or increasing costs are problems which demand some form of change, but it is impossible to say what without understanding why. So much is obvious enough but rarely do we really attempt to understand what has happened as part of a preparatory diagnosis of what and how to change an organization.

Miller (1990) provides us with an impressive treatment of the dynamics of corporate success, decline and renewal. This is important both because it extends the ideas of how the seeds of success and failure can be understood and because it provides us with a better understanding of the corporate dynamics within which we are enmeshed and attempt to transform and introduce changes. In turn this is vital simply because much treatment of change is too narrowly focused.

What does this mean? Basically most studies of change are narrowly focused on what is being changed and are treated in rather a static way. Thus we see that an organization is deemed to need improved quality and the discussion focuses on the implementation of a total quality management programme and the associated culture changes needed for it to be successful. Rarely is any attempt made to carry out a longitudinal study (there are a few rare exceptions to this) but even less often is there any real attempt to examine the dynamics which created the need for a total quality management programme in the first place. Thus it is that we often cannot judge whether or not the programme will succeed.

Why is it that people are often managed inappropriately in a period of change? There are two main reasons. Managers managing change are under pressure. This pressure undermines their own performance. Also, organizations often do not possess managers who are sufficiently skilful in handling change. Kotter (1988), for example, suggests one 'syndrome' associated with inadequate leadership, which we might similarly associate with inadequate change management. In summary, the argument is that successful organizations can carry the seeds of their own later decline unless managers learn to be both successful and adaptable. The syndrome is set out in Figure 3.2. The tensions created by declining performance create performance problems.

Thus the argument combines the success of a few key people, a period of early success and growing organizational complexity followed by declining performance creating pressures towards short-termism and an inward focus. All of this can lead to a lack of credibility among top management combined with a 'fear of failure' throughout the organization.

Particularly interesting is the point about 'fear of failure'; the pressures are dual in nature. On the one hand the short-term approach, combined with a

| **The opening** |
| Early in life cycle, low competition |
| Depends on leaders not systems |

| **Maturity: steady state** |
| Growth and complexity. Management professionalized and developed |
| The firm survives because of reputation and scale. Good people leave in search of better opportunities |

| **Decline** |
| Silo mentality plus divisional and function US corporate agendas creates tension and problems |

Figure 3.2 **Syndrome of ineffective leadership and change management (after Kotter, 1988)**

functional or departmental orientation, centralization and autocratic management styles, creates a powerful tendency to limit risk taking. On the other, managers moving rapidly through careers and not having to face up to their mistakes do not learn the interpersonal skills needed to do so. They find facing up to performance issues difficult. Therefore, when forced to do so by those same short-term pressures, they often do so inadequately and in a volatile, even primitive, fashion. This further reduces risk taking, over time creating an organization within which the 'fear of failure' is very high indeed. There is a powerful 'vicious circle' in place continually reinforcing any tendency to underperform.

Kotter (1988) identifies a number of the 'characteristics needed to provide effective leadership', overcoming the problems identified in the syndrome outlined above. To be effective, leaders need a range of knowledge of industry, business functions and the firm. Also needed are a broad range of contacts and good working relationships in the firm and the industry. Linked to this will be a good track record in a relatively broad set of activities. Kotter also refers to 'keen minds' (whatever that means), strong interpersonal skills, high integrity, seeing value in people and a strong desire to lead.

All of this points us towards the new strategy paradigm proposed by Hamel and Prahalad (1994). For them, competing for the future means lifting our sights. Re-engineering internal processes is not enough, we must regenerate strategies. Transforming the organization is essential but the winners (such as CNN) transform their industry. Having strategic plans focuses attention internally; what is needed is a new strategic architecture. The essential point is that it may be necessary to re-engineer our processes to reduce cost and improve service but that is insufficient to gain competitive advantage because our competitors can do the same. To be successful we must create new strategies aimed at transforming our industry whether it is food, medicine, education, entertainment or whatever. In the modern world renewal demands that we do more than identify how to do more, better and for less. We must also regenerate what we do.

Kay (1993) attempts to identify the origins of corporate success from distinctive structures of relationships between the corporation and employees, customers and suppliers. Continuity and stability in these relationships allow for a flexible and cooperative response to change. At the core of his analysis lies the concept of added value. This, he argues, derives from the architecture of the firm (basically the structure of relationships referred to above) and the application of distinctive capabilities in particular markets. Continuity and stability provide for the development of organizational knowledge (of its identity, vision, distinctive capabilities and invisible assets (Itami, 1987)), the free exchange of information and a readiness to respond quickly and flexibly to changes in the world.

In turn the distinctive capabilities which provide the basis of competitive advantage are architecture, innovation, reputation and strategic assets. Architecture is both internal (the corporate structure and management processes) and external (networks of relationships with suppliers and other organizations – joint ventures, strategic alliances, etc.). Strategic assets are the inherent advantages a corporation may possess (e.g. licences, access to scarce factors) which cannot easily be copied.

'Strategic benchmarking' has taken up a vital role in organizational diagnosis for change. This adds an important idea to the concept of diagnosis. The vital point is to compare your own organization with the world's best. Thus we identify where we are, the causes of our present situation and (through benchmarking) we identify the potential for improvement and ideas for change. Benchmarking as a technique has evolved (at least in principle and concept) from first-generation benchmarking in which the focus would be on benchmarking a particular product or system, through competitive benchmarking, process benchmarking and strategic benchmarking to 'global benchmarking'. Thus the ambitions of its proponents are nothing short of being world class.

Most importantly, benchmarking represents a learning technique. Essentially cognitive in orientation, it applies rational analysis based on comparisons to the process of diagnosis. It is also (like all diagnosis) an intervention in the system and must be understood as such.

Similarly, business process re-engineering has attracted wide attention and many adherents (and cynics). Admittedly more than a technique for diagnosing what needs to be changed, it nevertheless incorporates techniques for diagnosis. Most importantly, proponents of this approach conceive it as a technology for breakthrough or 'discontinuous leaps in performance'. The focus is on the 'business architecture' – locations, structure, technology and skills. Alongside the analysis of the business architecture conceived in terms of value added is risk assessment looking at change and organizational issues. Our contention is that in techniques such as benchmarking and business process re-engineering we see a combination of the soft organizational development approaches of the 1970s and the socio-technical systems school, but now operationalized because of the opportunities provided by new information infrastructures. Thus diagnosis has become more thorough and broader in scope.

Transforming the organization

Managing major changes successfully requires us to take an organization-wide approach. Change creates stress and strain both for those who support change (through overwork, the challenge of leading change in an uncertain world, the pressure of dealing with other, often anxious, people, the inherent uncertainties all are subject to in some degree and so on) and for those who are either indifferent, opposed or fearful of change.

Organizational learning is a vital component of effective change. Following the work of Quinn (see in particular Quinn, 1992) organizational restructuring and strategic change should be based on effective diagnosis and benchmarking, information and incentive systems. A key point, however, in achieving strategic change amidst organizational circumstances looking less and less like traditional hierarchical structures is that 'managed incrementalism' is a strategy for change implementation explicitly designed to manage risk. However, this does not need to imply that change is slow, random or gradual.

All of this assumes that change implementation requires the following:

- that we build an awareness of the need for change;
- that the case for change is made convincingly and credibly;
- that the process of change is a learning process – you don't get everything right initially;
- that dramatic change can feel chaotic and uncertain as people seek to come to terms with new skills etc.;
- that attention must be given to broadening and mobilizing support for change, whether through task forces and project teams, through the use of incentive systems and training, through pilot schemes and so on;
- crystallizing the vision and focus for the organization but not necessarily at the outset – indeed initially, the vision may be very broad, and much has to be learned before an emerging strategic vision can be articulated;
- that the focus is on people and on the process of change.

Alexander (1988) provides a review of the implementation literature. He supports the idea of Pressman and Wildavsky (1973) that 'policies are continuously transformed by implementation actions that simultaneously alter resources and objectives'. Thus strategy (or policy) and implementation interact and emerge. Alexander also notes that implementors are, or should be, concerned both with preventing failure (by avoiding the common implementation problems) and promoting success.

There are three learning modes which are of relevance to managers concerned by change:

1 *Learning by doing*: this is an internal process. We learn by experimentation, by trial and error, by pilot trials and so on.

2 *Learning by use*: this is essentially learning from the external world. We learn about how to improve our own products/services by gaining feedback from customers and by competitive benchmarking. Thus we gain from the customer's experience of using our products/services and through comparing ourselves with competitor organizations.

3 *Learning from failure*: which speaks for itself but which, to be available to us, demands that we accept that failure will happen from time to time.

Our argument is that concepts such as transformational leadership, entrepreneurship and the learning organization each embrace these ideas. Beyond this we recognize that major changes are typically implemented as major programmes organized around simple themes (e.g. 'right first time' for total quality programmes or 'next steps programme' for major programmes of culture change).

A good example is that of 'time-based competition'. The key idea is that the way we manage time – whether in production, in new product development, in sales and distribution – represents a powerful source of competitive advantage. This idea has spawned another, that of 'business process re-engineering'. At the core of both is a strategy for change utilizing analytical techniques to analyse the organization seeking continuous improvements to work and information flows and to the use of time. The emphasis is on the organization doing the work itself, utilizing its own people empowering people at all levels to achieve change. Benchmarking is a key analytical technique utilized in such programmes, as are techniques such as 'pilots' and 'breakthrough teams'. According to Stalk and Hout (1990) breakthrough teams should be given radical goals such as reducing time by half in order that assumptions will be challenged. Bottlenecks, breakdowns, failures and unmet customer needs all become opportunities to learn. All of this implies radically new ways of thinking about the organization.

Finally Argyris (1990) explains something of the constraints to achieving effective learning in organizations by pointing to the distinction between what he calls single-loop and double-loop learning. At the core of his explanation are two key points about professionals (managers and a growing proportion of employees are professionals or quasi-professionals of one sort or another):

1 Essentially the life experience of most professionals through schooling, university and early career is characterized by success, not failure. Because they have rarely failed they have never learned how to learn from failure. Thus when things go wrong for them they become defensive, screen out criticism and put the 'blame' on others. Ironically their ability to learn shuts down just as they need it most.

2 In common with our earlier remarks, Argyris takes the view that organizations assume that learning is a problem of motivation. Create the right structures of communication, rewards and authority and accountability – designed to create motivated and committed employees – and learning and development will follow. Sadly, Argyris tells us this is fatally flawed. People learn through how they think – through the cognitive rules or reasoning they use to design and implement their action.

For Argyris, organizations can learn how to encourage learning, how to resolve these learning dilemmas. At the root of his solution is to find ways of constructively questioning the rationale or reasoning behind someone's actions.

Let me give you an example from my own experience. Recently I was acting as chairman of the audit committee of the board of directors of an organization in which I am a non-executive director. The organization had, last year, subcontracted its internal audit work to an outside firm. We were discussing the report from the internal audit for the last year and considering the plan for the current financial year. We had noticed that the budget for last year had included 25 days for 'management and planning'. The out-turn had been 30 days and the budget for the current year was 32 days. In our view 25 days (which represented 10 per cent of the internal audit budget) was high. No explanation was given for the 30 days out-turn nor to justify a budget of 32 days this year. We raised a series of questions. What activities were included in 'management and planning'? What was the value of those days? We also noted that overruns on various audit projects undertaken by the firm during the last year had been due to problems of getting information – was this a sign of good planning? Or of the need for more planning? The director of the internal audit firm was defensive. He referred to industry norms of up to 20 per cent for planning audit work. We acknowledged that but pointed out that the audit needed for our organization was relatively straightforward. Eventually he said, 'Well I had hoped that we could develop a cooperative approach and engage in a free and frank discussion'. To which our reply was: 'That's what we are doing!' There is little doubt in my mind that the criticism had placed him on the defensive, automatically. While he recognized that he sought an open relationship he felt drawn to defend the number of days ascribed to 'management and planning'. More importantly he felt constrained from explaining that the reason for the high number of actual days was that there had been so many problems during the previous year (in which the organization, and therefore the finance function, had been founded) that he and other senior colleagues had been forced to spend time on site problem solving in order to get things done. To say so would be critical of the finance director – or at least apparently so.

Argyris (1990) argues that people can be taught to reason in ways which reduce and overcome organizational defences. For example:

> **they will discover that the kind of reasoning necessary to reduce and overcome organizational defenses is the same kind of 'tough reasoning' that underlies the effective use of ideas in strategy, finance, marketing, manufacturing and other management disciplines . . . it depends on collecting valid data, analyzing it carefully, and constantly testing inferences drawn from the data . . . Good strategists make sure that their conclusions can withstand all kinds of critical questioning.**

At its basics, then, 'productive reasoning'.

The value-added organization

I recall completing the review of an MBA dissertation draft. The author worked for a global telecommunications business. His company is concerned that they are not achieving the rate of change required of world-class companies in that sector. I was struck by part of his diagnosis:

> **Current change methodologies are employed within functional silos and the informal way in which strategy is cascaded through various differentiated groups and departments dilutes the value of the strategy . . . [which] should be focused on understanding how the business processes deliver overall enterprise value . . . needs to develop a process for implementing strategic improvement ideas in those value streams.**

This quote captures two or three 'big' ideas about change. First, that many change programmes fail because they are implemented within a part of the organization – there is an absence of an integrated approach as between divisions, departments and the like. Second, that successful change may best be achieved by focusing change efforts horizontally, i.e. along the customer value stream rather than vertically up or down the structure. This idea does not negate all the notions of bottom-up, top-down and cascading change programmes which you will have read about, experienced and/or managed, but it does provide a different perspective when thinking about change.

Another 'big' idea is that of organizational learning, whether in the context of strategy, management development, organizational development or major change. Many practitioners and consultants/researchers point to the vital role of organizational learning in a period of change. In so far as major change involves implementing new organizational arrangements to deal with new conditions (whether in external markets or internally within the organization) it is obvious that change requires and leads to learning. It requires learning if the need for change is to be accepted. It involves learning particularly because our initial attempt to resolve the change problem needs to be evolved with experience.

However, the circumstances within which we seek to engender change are now fundamentally different. We are each of us aware of the fundamental changes going on: globalization, deregulation of markets, new technology, privatization, fundamental rethinking about the nature and role of the state, and so on. Moreover, we are each of us dealing with the organizational consequences, including downsizing, flattening of structures, empowerment, outsourcing, strategic focus, the 'lean' organization, acquisitions and mergers, joint ventures and strategic alliances, multi-functional team working and much more. Many now conclude that the 'mind-set' through which senior managers view the world has changed in consequence.

Therefore, the characteristic model of the successful organization has changed. Once we sought economies of scale via horizontal and vertical integration. Eventually we discovered that these economies of scale were often illusory. Some of the 'costs' of scale were increasingly alienated and demotivated employees but, in particular, inflexible and inwardly focused organizations. Observers concerned with these problems noted two linked points:

1 What appeared to be a growing alienation of many within modern society co-alesced around attitudes to bureaucracy–whether public or private. Organizations which could give genuine priority to delivering value to customers would begin to break down the alienation many felt about these large bureaucracies.

2 Whatever else we could say about large, multi-level bureaucracies it is obvious that they are expensive, but much less obvious that they deliver value for money.

And so many began to seek means of encouraging flexibility and entrepreneurship. This led to a fundamental shift in our thinking about how to change organizations.

Traditionally, we have sought to change the organization within its existing boundary. We have not sought to ask whether or not the boundaries themselves should be changed. The one exception is a change strategy adopted throughout this century – that of acquisitions and mergers. It is not our purpose here to discuss this topic. Here we merely point out that such a change strategy involves rethinking the boundary of the organizations as pieces (companies, divisions, etc.) are added or subtracted.

This tendency to rethink the boundary of the organization has accelerated as part of the changing mind-set we refer to above – and indeed may have caused that change in the first place. Throughout most of the last century the large, integrated and centralized organization was excellent at coordination and control – and may have been good at settling conflict (although personally I doubt it, though it may have been good at reducing the level of manifest conflict). Conversely, in order to seek higher levels of innovation, organizations first decentralized via the multi-divisional form. But faced with the continued problems and the inability to develop every new technology/capability internally, organizations increasingly decentralized through joint ventures, alliances and ultimately 'the virtual company'.

Here, however, we note something which is becoming a standard of management practice when the focus is on the supply chain. First, a company needs to build strong ties with its suppliers in order to secure its ability to pursue innovation, improvement and enhanced value. Second, a company needs to develop critical technologies internally if it is to secure its position on the value chain. Here we see the argument that strategic networks can be very effective as a means of acquiring particular capabilities and of creating high-powered incentives towards improvement, change and enhanced value. Our concern here is not to evaluate the argument but merely to emphasize the new style of thinking involved in even raising the question.

Most importantly for our present purpose, we have seen a tendency to replace planned, organizational change with market-induced change. Sometimes the market mechanisms are internal, and there is a long history of the development of such mechanisms, e.g. performance-related pay schemes, the emergence of strategic business units, the development of competence-based models for performance management, share option schemes and so on. Increasingly we see the tendency to use market mechanisms to secure change. Strategic alliances, networks, outsourcing, deregulation are all attempts to introduce or encourage market-based incentives. The idea of purchasing being separated from provision has influenced companies and governments. In the UK and elsewhere in the world, government departments have been converted to free-standing agencies. The UK health service has been reorganized into large-scale purchasing authorities and self-governing trusts providing hospital and other services alongside general practitioners providing primary care. Similarly, a global business such as Glaxo has reconfigured itself from having regional sales operatives supplied by regional factories to a situation in which the sales business is free to source from the best available supplier. Here the certainties of allocated budgets are replaced by the pressures, disciplines and incentives of competition.

But is this sufficient? At the same time we all of us point to our present anxieties and uncertainties. Some argue that this is a consequence of downsizing and a consequential higher risk of unemployment. Others point to the growth in part-time employment. Critics of this kind of thinking point out that unemployment has not changed in the world's leading economies over the last 20 years, although the level fluctuates, inevitably. You can counter this by arguing the view that the big change is that for the first time it is middle-class employees experiencing job insecurity. They are more vocal and we are experiencing the consequences. Perhaps also the shift in organizational mind-set referred to above is relevant. Where the focus of activity is the horizontal value chain it may be that people who once understood to whom they report must now report to more than one individual and meet multiple, and sometimes even conflicting (certainly ambiguous), performance objectives.

One formulation of how to achieve economic success in the midst of these ambiguities relates to the concept of 'trust' or social capital. The most influential recent work is that of Fukuyama (1995). For him one solution to the problem of scale lies in the emergence of networks such as businesses held together by family ties, cross-ownership, long experience of joint work and so on. In particular, he points to the advantages of establishing long-term relationships between members of a network. All of this is now known to us as supply chain management. He argues that networks based on reciprocal obligation enable scale to be achieved without the problems of size and alienation referred to above. These networks appear to have emerged in societies with cultures which encourage high levels of trust (e.g. Japan, South Korea, Germany, northern Italy). In 'low-trust' societies stable networks can be created via cross-ownership but will certainly be more difficult to sustain.

Increasingly, major corporates begin to work on the briefing of 'social capital' via value-added strategies. Here the organization is defined as a horizontal value stream supported by other activities (e.g. marketing development, senior management, finance). Each part of the organization has performance parameters defined in terms of value to its customers. Organizations use competence models and assessment, 360° feedback techniques and the balanced scorecard as a means of putting this into effect. The objective is to identify what each activity contributes by way of value to its customers, measure that and feed that information openly to the people involved in the activity, their customers and senior management. Part of the role of management is to help each activity to drive its performance forward in terms of these parameters.

A longer-term task of senior management is to identify and access the capabilities needed for the future. There are few organizations which have developed a coherent system of the type outlined here but there are many examples (in telecommunications, financial services, healthcare, manufacturing and utilities) of organizations working on such approaches.

The implications of the above can be sketched out graphically by looking at how we depict organizations. Traditionally, we depict organizations as structures of hierarchical authority whether we describe an organization of structure which is either functional or divisional. Thus we typically construct the pyramid as shown in Figure 3.3.

Rarely were organizations as simple as that. Rarely would the above describe behaviour within organizations, which is why sociologists created the distinction between 'formal' and 'informal' organization, where the latter describes how people work with, through and around the formal organization in pursuit of various objectives, their own as well as the organization's.

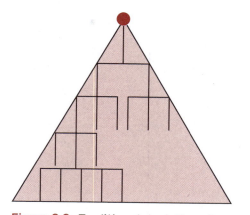

Figure 3.3 Traditional depiction of organization

Increasingly, managers recognized the problems referred to above, and, in particular, problems of change. This led many to complement 'top-down' models of change with 'bottom-up' models seen by some as particularly relevant in the field of implementation. But both are 'vertical' models, i.e. the focus is on how the organization arranges its internal affairs, how authority is used, how information is transmitted.

If the concern is to create change designed to ensure value added for customers and clients, the pyramid needs to be rethought because value added for customers flows horizontally (see Figure 3.4).

This led many to ask how it was that we could think through the management of change without thinking horizontally. From this some immediately reject the inverted pyramid shown in Figure 3.5 in favour of depictions such as those set out in Figure 3.6.

In both of these depictions the focus is on how or whether value is added either to internal or external 'customers'.

Many now conclude that we are in the midst of a paradigm or mind-set change regarding views on how to organize economic activity. New forms of organization are increasingly discussed and/or applied. Networks, virtual organizations

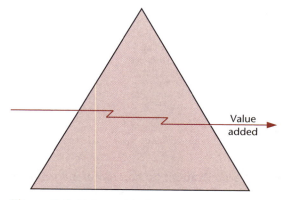

Figure 3.4 Value added

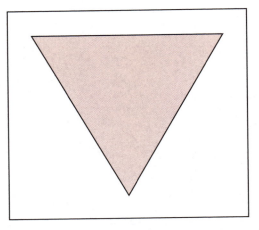

Figure 3.5 **Bottom-up change management**

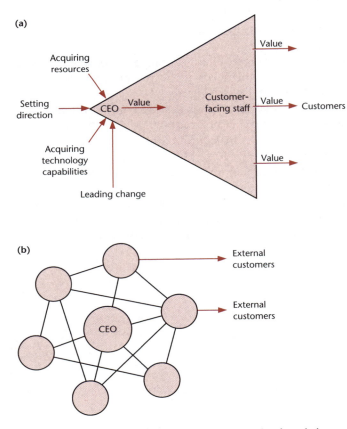

Figure 3.6 **Depictions of organization: (a) horizontal management; (b) cluster organization**

and homeworking are each variants which attract continuing attention. For our purposes there are two points to note:

1 Increasingly we see two approaches to change in use – a planned approach to change and a market-based approach. In the former we decide the direction, objectives, stages, milestones, change methods and so on. In the latter we seek to motivate people in pursuit of a particular direction, desired objectives, preferred patterns of behaviour, but we are less concerned about milestones etc. This is a topic to which we will return, but the basic argument is that too much attention to targets and milestones creates expectations which can lead to fewer results than were achievable. In the latter we establish market mechanisms as a means of motivating changed behaviour. So long as we also provide adequate resources, information and support this often leads to dramatic changes in behaviour.

2 It appears that innovations such as the virtual organization, networks, alliances or homeworking create the potential for isolation. Thus cohesion becomes a crucial issue. New forms or sources of cohesion are needed if the traditional sources of department and structure are no longer present. More generally, economists now argue that social capital is essential to success. Social capital can be seen as the extent of social cohesion and is firmly linked to a sense of social solidarity, shared values and common commitment. If these are high then we have a high level of social capital. In an increasingly fragmented organizational world, social capital becomes a crucial determinant of success.

Taking this second point further, the defining characteristics of the virtual organization are emerging as follows:

- They have a shared vision and goal and/or a common protocol of cooperation.
- They cluster activities around their core competencies.
- They work jointly in teams of core-competence groups to implement their activities throughout the value chain.
- They process and distribute information in real time throughout the value chain.
- They tend to delegate from the bottom up wherever economies of scale can be achieved or when new conditions arise.

These characteristics require and/or facilitate trust relations. This is social capital. It is interesting to note that these characteristics are also generally deemed valuable in other circumstances: mergers demand them and lean production requires them. In reality the changed focus of those concerned with organization from vertical concerns over control and coordination to a horizontal concern for value added creates the circumstances in which trust is essential to success. Fukuyama (1995) puts it thus:

> it is possible to argue that in the future the optimal form of industrial organisation will be neither small companies nor large ones but network structures that share the advantages of scale economies while avoiding the overhead and (other) costs of large, centralised organisations. If this will in fact be the case, then societies with a high degree of social trust will have a natural advantage.

> Networks can save on transaction costs substantially if their members follow an informal set of rules that require little or no overhead to negotiate, adjudicate, and enforce. The moment that trust breaks down among members of a business network, relations have to be spelled out in detail. [At this point the network resembles either a market or a hierarchical organization – author's note.]

In fact managing networks, managing professional practices, managing alliances and joint ventures, managing virtual organizations and managing lean production all share these characteristics.

Castells (1996) comes to a similar conclusion. For him 'the main shift can be characterized by the shift from vertical bureaucracies to the horizontal corporation'. This shift is characterized by seven main trends:

1 Organization around process, not task.

2 A flat hierarchy.

3 Team management.

4 Performance management based on customer satisfaction.

5 Rewards based on team performance.

6 Maximization of contacts with suppliers and customers.

7 Information, training and retraining of employees at all levels.

These developments derive from a recognition of the limits both of the original functional, hierarchical model and attempts to modify this model via the Toyota lean production model or later equivalents such as business process re-engineering.

Ernst (1994) identifies five types of networks,

1 Supplier networks.

2 Producer networks.

3 Customer networks.

4 Coalitions.

5 Technology cooperation networks.

The network does not replace multinational corporations but rather offers the means through which these organizations now operate. Indeed national companies, public sector organizations and even voluntary organizations operate within networks; hence the current interest in supply chain management and interagency working. Networks provide the means through which we deal with increased complexity and/or global scope.

In addition to the trends identified by Castells (1996), here are some other approaches to developing the future organization:

■ Activity-based costing combined with customer analysis. This latter approach identifies key processes in terms of importance and customer satisfaction (see Gouillart and Kelly, 1995). The focus is on internal and external customers.

■ Models of managerial competence.

■ The 360° appraisal, a process in which managers are appraised by boss, peers and subordinates thus focusing attention on the value they add.

■ Business process analysis.

British Petroleum Engineering

Quinn Mills (1991) suggests that a cluster organization makes the boxes and lines of a typical organization chart irrelevant. They are replaced by circles each representing a semi-autonomous cluster (Figure 3.7).

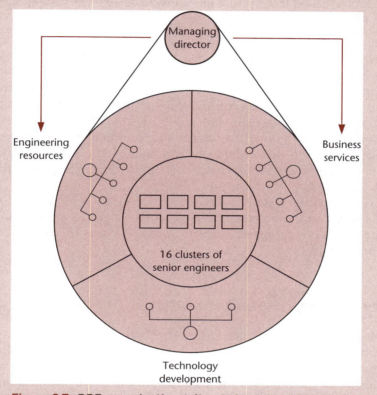

Figure 3.7 BPE organization (after Quinn Mills, 1991)

In essence, at the heart of the structure there are 16 clusters of engineers through which BPE meets client needs. The outer circle comprises three hierarchically organized activities – engineering resources, business services and technology development. These units work to ensure that BPE has the necessary engineering resources and technology and that it meets client needs. Thus, for example, business services seeks to fit client needs to the cluster's outputs, securing an agreed programme measuring performance as the programme unfolds. Business services therefore acts as an account manager. The managing director and the three general managers (of engineering resources, business services and technology development) form a core team. The hierarchical relationship is between that core team and the resources in the cluster. The focus of the organization is on how those resources can be configured to meet varying client needs, rather than on who is reporting to whom!

Another interesting point to note is that the role of the three 'departments' is configuring resources to meet either customer needs or development (i.e. acquiring the right profile of engineering resources and developing the right technologies). Does this focus represent a recognition of the need to develop learning (the learning organization), intellectual capital or invisible assets? It is now commonplace to argue that intellectual capital (i.e. the intangible assets of the organization) comprises renewal and development, customer knowledge and loyalty, and process knowledge. They argue that Skandia, one of Sweden's leading insurance and financial services organizations, defines intellectual capital that way. It is interesting to note the similarity of themes looking at the BPE situation.

Taken together these approaches represent an emerging value-added strategy to design and manage the new organization.

In the above I have tried to identify the nature of new thinking and practice which is leading managers to radically rethink organizations. I have looked at some of the consequences and implications of this work – although for a critique see Rifkin (1995) for projections regarding the end of work. Finally, in Chapter 7, when we look at value adding models for organizations, we identify some practical methodologies used by practitioners as they rethink and reconfigure their own organizations.

Clearly issues related to cohesion, sociability and mind-set are vitally important to an understanding of how to manage these new organizational forms. Thus corporate culture comes to centre-stage (see Goffee and Jones, 1996).

The network organization

A logical extension of the cluster organization model, the network model adds partnerships across the boundary raising the fundamental question of where the boundary of an organization lies. This can be depicted as shown in Figure 3.8, and one should note that the key aspect of a network organization is that it seeks to add the pursuit of flexible specialization to the advantages of the cluster organization (see Barnatt, 1995).

In principle a network can be a combination of a number of organizations, each of which can take any form. In Europe, Airbus Industrie comprises French, German, Spanish and British aerospace companies each of which is organized hierarchically, at least to some significant extent.

Lipniack and Stamps (1994) identify five organizing principles for networks:

1 *Unifying purpose*: the glue holding it together. Shared ideas, values and goals.

2 *Independence*: each member should be able to stand on its own while benefiting from being part of the network as a whole.

3 *Voluntary links*: characterized by multiple links as a means of attracting needed skills, resources, access to markets, etc.

4 *Multiple leaders*: networks comprise people, groups, companies, each of which has something unique to contribute.

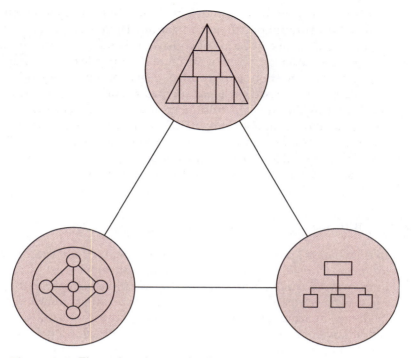

Figure 3.8 The network organization

5 *Integrated levels*: multi-level, not flat, because to survive networks need a tendency to action. Thus hierarchy remains a feature of this organizational form but not a documentary feature.

Clearly, therefore, the literature on strategic alliances has much to tell us about how these forms of organization can be sustained and we will return to that in a later chapter. For now suffice it to say that the key principle missing in the above is reciprocity.

Following Williamson (1975), the network is an organizational form through which resource allocation decisions are made, not simply through hierarchy but more extensively through market mechanisms. A network will only continue if each 'member' believes that the net result is of advantage and that all 'members' contribute positively. Increasingly the issue of relative contribution is crucial to the longer-term cohesion of our organizations.

In fact regardless of the use of hierarchical, matrix, cluster or network organization models, the concept of value added provides the psychological and organizational 'glue' from which to create cohesion. I will develop this view in a later chapter, but in essence here two sets of principles may operate. Organizationally the work of each of us is aided through understanding and seeking to maximize the value of work of others whose input is needed for our work. This supply chain management is based on a process view of organization. Ultimately cohesion arises out of a shared sense of purpose. This is achieved from the perception that each contributes to the achievement of those purposes, i.e. that we all will the ends and will the means. We know that this is real only by understanding the contribution of all – hence the focus on value added throughout the organization. There was the practical and psychological consequence in terms of consistent behaviour and cohesion.

If some are deemed not to contribute then this leads to disruption, a sense of 'unfairness' to tension and conflict. This implies evaluative criteria linking rewards to effort based on ideas such as reciprocity, contribution (or performance), capacity, need or the fulfilment of commitments. Often evaluative criteria will be based on a complex mix of such ideas. The important point here is to note that ultimately cohesion in an organization arises out of perceptions and I argue that a primary focus of perceptions of an organization relates to issues of value (see Carnall (1986) for a fuller treatment of these issues).

Conclusion

In this chapter I have suggested that various 'drivers' for change have created a critical mass of organizational change. This appears to have led to a fundamental shift in the way we configure and manage organizations. Moreover, the mechanisms we use to achieve change are also changing. Where once planned approaches held the field, now increasingly market mechanisms play a vital part. New forms of organization have emerged based on a horizontal and value-added metaphor (as compared with a vertical or command and control metaphor). These create new management concerns and challenges, not least that of how to achieve integration.

EXERCISES

1 Can you think of examples of market-induced change in your own organization? Have such changes under- or overperformed in terms of the achievement of objectives? Has their introduction been easy or has it raised new issues and anxieties for the people involved?

2 Is your organization beginning to think about horizontal value chains? Does this lead to a rethinking of the role of senior management? How?

3 Can you identify examples of cluster or network structures in your own or any other organization? How well do they work?

Part II

THEORIES OF ORGANIZATION CHANGE

4 Theories of change: traditional models

5 Theories of change: critical perspectives

6 Theories of change: strategic management models

4 Theories of change: traditional models

Introduction

Much of the change management literature positions leadership as the key source of 'energy for change'. From a pragmatic viewpoint this is a natural enough starting point but doing so does involve begging a number of questions. Which leaders, positioned where in the organization concerned, and doing what exactly in order that change be put in place? In any large, multi-sited organization (and note that even a hospital employing say 4000 people may operate over 10 or more sites) we can hardly propose that leadership for change only comes from the top. Clearly there is a need for leadership at various levels of the organization and for varying leadership 'roles' to be undertaken with regard to any significant change.

Before we explore these and other related questions more fully we should note that the purpose of arguing for any particular organizational change should be that its implementation will give rise to the achievement of certain desired outcomes. Of course we can immediately ask which outcomes, desired by which stakeholders, how defined and agreed, and not least, how measured? Leaving those questions to one side for the moment it is clear enough that this view of change comprises a nexus between 'knowing' and 'doing'. It is assumed that it is possible to identify ways and means of resolving problems in an organization, thereby enabling those involved to define changes which, if implemented successfully, will lead to improvement. Here we see a belief in the idea of continuous improvement and of the possibility of progress viewed as a linear process. Albeit, as we shall see, researchers and practitioners will readily accept that with any particular change there may be 'unintended consequences' arising out of the implementation of changes, viewed as emerging from the use of too narrow a model of the organization involved.

So at the outset it should be stated that there is a growing body of change theory which adopts a more pessimistic line. This theory tends to challenge the linearity of the traditional models, arguing either that real world change is either much more complex than traditional models allow for, or that there are fundamental differences relating to the nature, role, constitution and governance of organizations in modern society to the extent that the idea of 'progress' is altogether too problematic. We will review those perspectives in the next chapter. Suffice it to say here that while some of the theory reviewed in this chapter is linear, or at least based on pretty simple assumptions, that is not true for all, as we shall see. However, I have selected theory for inclusion in this chapter where it seemed to be based on the idea that change and improvement is both possible and desirable within the existing organizational arrangements (or paradigm).

The process of change can be summarized as comprising two elements, namely leaders and followers. Leaders give 'signals' that changes are needed, can be described, 'pathways' to change can be sketched out and plans, resources and support for implementation provided. But without 'followers' no change is possible because leaders cannot do everything. But not all 'followers' will embrace change. Neither will all 'followers' resist change. Borrowing an idea from innovation theory, we can identify a 'change vanguard' and 'early adopters'. These are the groups on whose support successful implementation is based. They carry forward the change ideas and practices within the organization. As we shall see, success in change management to some extent is based on identifying and supporting those people. But leaders must also provide resources, facilities, training, 'space' and 'organizational cover'. What does this mean? Well, early on in the process of implementation, plans will go wrong, not work and be misunderstood. Often indeed people implement plans incorrectly, sometimes just because they do not understand. In these circumstances the change vanguard and early adopters must necessarily experiment, problem solve and so on in order to get things on the right track. But there will be detractors around. Senior people need to provide those seeking to get things to work with the time and resources to do so. Often this is as much about keeping the detractors at bay.

All of this happens at both the individual and the organizational level. At the individual level leaders must articulate change ideas with 'frame resonance', to use an idea from research on 'social movements'(see next chapter) in which leaders seek to direct attention not at descriptions of new values, nor indeed at new behaviours, but rather at 'acceptable' ideas regarding the organization's desired 'direction of travel'. Thus they seek to use words and phrases which stakeholders and others see as meaningful in relation to the organization's purpose. Thus an environmental organization might focus attention on 'polluted streams' hoping that this will strike a chord with current and potential supporters, encouraging them to action just as the phrases 'save the planet' and 'feed the world' have had similar impact. Colt Telecom used to describe itself as 'building rings around cities' at once symbolizing to its customers that it sought to service companies in financial centres and that it offered certainty of access. This is similar to the idea of 'resonance' in Howard Gardner's book *Changing Minds* (2004). Leaders must also provide for 'quick wins' and 'demonstration projects'; showing that progress is being made and is therefore possible in the future.

In turn, this argument suggests that the ideas which underpin any particular change initiative need to be influential throughout the organization. We know that adults learn best from direct experience, even allowing for what we certainly know about the varying learning styles across the human population. Ideas are considered in relation to problems we seek to resolve. We test them in practice.

Thereby we learn how more effectively to resolve that problem. The positive feedback thus generated creates the learning which leads to changes being more fully established as people become more confident about the relevance of the ideas to their own situation. Here we can see the possibility of using 'social influence' or 'contagion models' as a basis for assessing progress from initial concept through early adoption to the achievement of critical mass support for change. This notion is drawn from both the innovation literature (Rogers, 1995) and work on 'social movements'. The latter is covered in more detail in the next chapter. Ideas such as the 'tipping point' then become relevant. Is there a point where the accumulating evidence from experience is such that change becomes irreversible?

Where 'social influence' models are used this raises the same question about leadership. Which leaders, positioned where in the organizational system, are likely to be most influential? As soon as you accept the notion that social factors play a part you must immediately question the idea that change is created on a straightforward top-down basis. Even where the organization is a relatively simple affair where change involves embracing new technology then we know that existing power bases become challenged. This is simply another way of accepting that in that context leadership may well come from different sources.

Kelman (2005) has published a study of changes to procurement policy and practice in the US government using innovation theory to examine how positive feedback can create a self-reinforcing process which consolidates change. For Kelman the 'change effort' can feed on itself. In effect his claim implies that a 'tipping point' can be reached beyond which change is irreversible. However, this idea is presented rather simplistically. For example, he argues as follows:

> **In this view simply launching the change effort and continuing it over time generates forces building support for change. Thus launching and persisting in a change effort itself increases the likelihood the effort will succeed. What is amazing about this is that it occurs automatically, with no further intervention on the part of change leaders other than to launch and persist with the effort.**

Many observers might add that given the positioning of his own office in the Clinton White House (he was appointed to lead this process of procurement reform) and the importance attached by the Clinton administration to the reform programme, doubtless of interest to the budget office and others in government and the Congress, means that this conclusion obscures as much as it reveals. So we may reasonably conclude that the support for these changes is rather more extensive than Kelman is suggesting, but we must nevertheless note that his core idea is worth remembering. Indeed it is based on the 'diffusion of innovation' work he relies on. There is likely to be a slow start but eventually the pace of change will grow and irreversible change will result.

However, Kelman is rather begging the question of what is meant by 'persist in the effort', even though we certainly acknowledge his contribution relating to the importance of 'positive feedback' as a source of reinforcement for change efforts. Note also that in Kelman's study while senior executive and middle management efforts in support of change had a positive impact on employees successful overall experience with change, 'most respected co-workers' also had a positive impact.

Indeed the impact of the latter was substantially more important. In practice this implies that one effective strategy for change implementation is as follows:

1 identify people in teams who are respected members of those teams;

2 convince them of the value of the intended changes;

3 train them in the new methods and in change facilitation;

4 encourage them to support other members of their own team through informal or on-the-job training;

5 invest some of your training effort in the sharing of best practice across the teams;

6 ensure that supervisors and others support and provide 'organizational cover' for the efforts of those 'most respected co-workers'; and finally

7 senior executives must secure the 'space' for this to take place, for example in relation to performance management processes.

Leaders then 'deepen' the impact of change by persisting in the changes, not moving on to other initiatives but rather constantly reinforcing existing efforts. Not least this is signalled by the way leaders categorize those efforts, the words they choose to describe change and by the profile they continue to maintain on what some will deem as 'yesterday's solution'! For example, is there a difference between 'better value' and 'best value'? Of course there is and early on leaders might call for the former and then, following early successes, change the message to the latter. At the very least leaders need to be cognizant of the impact of their words and behaviour as important 'signals' in the change process.

In effect leaders operate on a 'knowing–doing' axis. Putting ideas into action is the essence of the implementation of change. The models set out in this chapter seek to gain a better understanding of what leaders contribute to achieving change implementation. While we refer to one category of models to be considered as linear, all are linear in the sense that they tend to describe change as a series of steps and stages, and also because they tend to rely on relatively clear cut ideas about cause and effect. Note, however, that the last model we examine (that of emergent change) could be viewed as being rather more subtle in terms of underlying philosophy and therefore foreshadows the so called 'critical theory' models to be examined in the next chapter.

We will consider four approaches to theorizing about how major changes can be implemented. These are:

1 'Clinical' approaches.

2 Linear approaches.

3 'Systems' approaches.

4 Emergent change.

Interestingly enough, theorists following each approach appear to start from an assumption shared among them. This assumption is often stated early on in any writing about organization change. Change is depicted as difficult. People instinctively resist change and 'most change efforts fail'. As I argued earlier in this book this commonly held view hardly stands up to critical scrutiny. Which organization do you know that has not been changed dramatically over the last twenty years? Like it or not organizations around the world are changing. So how is it that most changes fail? More of that later. For the moment we summarize the four approaches.

The 'clinical' approach

Here the engagement of individuals and teams is seen as central to success or failure. Within this form of analysis themes such as resistance to change, team effectiveness and dynamics as effected by changing circumstances and the leadership dynamics of change are each important. The concept of a 'psychological contract' between employer and employee and the attitudes of those involved in change are also central. Some authors associate these approaches described under the rubric of 'organizational development' with planned change. Thus Burnes (2004) concludes that the planned approach to change is closely associated with the practice of organizational development (OD). He quotes what is perhaps the most widely known text in the area in his favour. French and Bell (1995) state that:

> Organization development is a unique organizational improvement strategy that emerged in the late 1950s and early 1960s . . . evolved into an integrated framework of theories and practices capable of solving or helping to solve most of the important problems confronting the human side of organizations. OD is about planned change, that is getting individuals, teams and organizations to function better.

They go on to argue that OD is based on 'valid knowledge' about organizational dynamics and how to change them. For French and Bell valid knowledge derives from the behavioural sciences such as psychology, social psychology, sociology, anthropology, systems theory and the practice of management. To say that OD and planned change are synonymous is to overstate the position however. Perhaps the best longitudinal study of OD in practice in a single organization is Pettigrew's study (1985) of strategic change in ICI the large British chemicals conglomerate, since it was demerged. Here various OD initiatives are described, some in pursuit of specific change programmes and objectives but some intended to enhance capacity and capability for the longer term. Clearly both such seek change but in reality the former are planned changes, the latter emergent change.

What is clear is that organizational development seeks to create a credible basis for intervening in the management of organizations, whether in pursuit of a specific planned change or in order to build capability in the organization. It seeks to do so on the basis of valid knowledge. This knowledge primarily relates to people and how they behave, perceive, feel and react to the organizational setting. Often the interventions are undertaken within a process known as 'action research'. OD specialists, sometimes depicted as change agents, lead these interventions. Change agents are assumed to be committed to the purpose of enhancing organizational effectiveness but this is not clear-cut. Within the OD philosophy, as most adherents describe it, organizations are considered to exist to meet human need. But whose needs and in what sort of balance is the question. OD practitioners in the 1960s and 1970s often assumed that their purpose incorporated a tendency towards the democratization of organizations through power equalization. The growing concern for customers and clients, along with the realization that much pension provision involves stock market investment, rather complicates that notion.

However, there is much real value in this approach for those seeking to better understand the dynamics of change settings. Most large organizations conduct (or have specialist survey organizations conduct) regular attitude surveys of their employees and of customers. Action research has found wide application. The concept was introduced by Lewin (1947). Simply put, he argued that we study problems in order to solve them and we do so most effectively if our analysis of the problem is based on full and valid data, that all possible solutions are considered and that the most appropriate solution is selected. This begs the questions of how it is selected and why, and also effectively makes the assumption that a solution is possible. Nevertheless, action research and action learning (originally formulated by Revans (1972) are widely practised today.

It is worth noting that 'resistance to change' is commonly seen as a problem which OD practitioners are particularly well positioned to resolve. Note here that this is not necessarily viewed solely as a matter of resistance to change among lower level employees. Often it is seen as driven by 'vested interests' and can encompass behaviour from professional groups such as senior managers, clinical staff in hospitals, senior officers in the armed forces and so on. Indeed, as I write these words, 'resistance to change' arguments are being advanced in the media to explain the reported controversy between Donald Rumsfield, former Secretary of Defense in the President Bush administration, and some senior officers, including some recently retired officers. It is clear that there is a range of individual, team and organizational antecedents to 'resistance to change'. Moreover, resistance to change takes various forms (see Carnall, 1986) from opposition to apathy or indifference. We do need a diagnostic framework and conceptual schema to allow us to understand how and why people react to change and the OD tradition and practice provides these tools and concepts.

It is worth noting here that the real value of the OD approach may lie in the ability of practitioners to reveal what is currently 'hidden' in terms of people and their views, ideas, perceptions, attitudes and so on. The idea of the psychological contract is that it is different from the more clearly specified economic contract in that the expectations which comprise the psychological contract are likely to be tacit, unstated and only partly understood. Add to this the well known 'Johari Window' idea, which is that individuals do not fully understand what feelings and emotions drive their own preferences and behaviour, and place it all in a period of change and uncertainty and the need to seek valid data on people is obvious enough. Finally, it should be noted that OD practitioners were among those who developed an interest in organizational culture (Schein, 1996). We will look at this in Chapter 17 because it deserves a fuller treatment.

Linear approaches

This might be labelled the 'managerial approach' because models tend to describe change as a series of steps from vision to implementation. Often of value because they at least specify the tasks which managers need to undertake, these models are also commonly criticized as too simple. The experience of managing a change of any magnitude is generally more complex with many stops and starts and much 'side-tracking' along the way. Stacey (1996) is clearly of this view, identifying three assumptions leading to that conclusion:

1 That managers are able to identify organizational adaptations ahead of environmental changes (note that this appears to be a rather purist view; why must it be *ahead* of those environmental changes?).

2 That change is a linear process.

3 That organizations are systems tending toward static equilibrium (i.e. a stable state within which the organization's position in its environment is 'stable').

Of these the first seems both purist and unnecessary. Why is the timing such an issue? The other two certainly appear to characterize many models of organizational change. The first might be reworked to say that models of change tend to view the process as operating within the existing organizational system, that is with senior executives starting and then dominating the process. Perhaps the most influential of these linear or managerial models is that proposed by Kotter (1988). He does at least consider the importance of external stakeholders and recognizes the need for constant adaptation and change.

Indeed, it is worth noting that changes can be categorized in terms of rate of change. It is common for observers to note that the rate of change in the environment is important (Lawrence and Dyer, 1983). Similarly Kanter *et al.* (1992), responding to the distinction between incremental and transformational change, notes that the latter may be achieved via a 'bold stroke' or revolutionary approach, or by a series of incremental changes leading to transformation over an extended period of time. To my mind the missing concept here is that of ambition. For whatever reason the bold stroke starts out with an ambitious challenge to the status quo which is articulated as such from the outset. The incremental approach to transformational change may seek the same ambition but may proceed along a trajectory of change which leaves options more open. All of this is similar to the Beer and Nohria (2000) distinction between theory E and theory O change. Theory E change pursues the maximization of shareholder value through financial incentives, downsizing and divestment. It is about tough choices driven by financial imperatives and financial performance. Theory O aims at incremental performance improvement through incremental interventions to the organizational culture, capability and the promotion of organizational learning. Could we argue that theory E states tough and challenging strategic objectives in stark financial terms while theory O obscures the tough choices in pursuit of organizational cohesion and long-term survival. That is to say both seek the same outcome but theory O seeks a trajectory to that outcome which will keep the organization in being. Theory E, once applied, may lead to rapid and disruptive change.

Can both operate together? Probably only in circumstances where competitive and other pressures allow. You can also argue that theory E may be the place to start if radical change involving job losses is needed. But then theory O may also be needed once those initial changes have been established in order that the organization which emerges can be transformed for the longer term. As I shall argue in Chapter 18, it becomes important to understand the level of ambition being adopted in any change programme before deciding how to approach the design and implementation issues.

Linear models tend to understate the role of external stakeholders such as government, shareholders, fund managers and so on. Where such groups are taken into account they tend to incorporate them within the organization's system. Only when we examine complexity theory in the next chapter will such an open systems approach be examined, and even then there is little real attempt to consider let alone research the impact of external stakeholders other than in the case of mergers and acquisitions and, to a lesser extent, turnarounds and strategic alliances. Note, however, that the main focus in these latter studies remains targeted on the internal changes rather than the orientation or intentions of external stakeholders.

The linear paradigm reflects the influence of Lewin's well-known three-stage model of change (Lewin, 1947), which encompasses the following:

1 *Unfreezing*, a stage within which those involved come to recognize that something must change.
2 *Moving*, during which stage new ideas are tested and new ways of working emerge.
3 Followed by *refreezing*, a stage within which new behaviours, skills and attitudes are stabilized and commitment to change is achieved.

This view of change has influenced many subsequent authors, notably Kotter (1988). But it is too easy to condemn these ideas as being unitary in focus (taking only the concerns of the most powerful into account) and linear in approach (viewing change as sequential). Most authors do not take a unitary approach as such although some argue that even where this is not explicit such an approach can be inferred. Be that as it may, there are obvious exceptions. For example, one proposed developmental model comprises four stages:

1 The conceptualizing process.
2 The motivation process.
3 The commitment process.
4 Implementation and evaluation (implementing new ideas and installing the means for performance monitoring and evaluation).

This approach is based on learning theory ideas and while it assumes that change is 'driven' by executives they are not conceived as being 'all-knowing'.

Similarly, Dawson (2003) adds context and the politics of change to the mix. His model comprises three stages, namely conception, transition (tasks, activities and decisions) and operation (of new organizational arrangements). But he views these stages as operating within a context (that is, markets for products and services and for labour and skills) and the politics of change. In some senses the most influential model of change to adopt the linear approach is Kotter (1996). He identifies eight stages:

1 Establishing a sense of urgency.
2 Creating the guiding coalition.

3 Developing a vision and strategy.

4 Communicating the 'change vision'.

5 Empowering employees for broad-based action.

6 Generating short-term wins.

7 Consolidating gains and producing more change.

8 Anchoring new changes in the culture.

Clearly no unitary view here. Creating a guiding coalition is clearly a 'political process' and 'anchoring change' clearly requires a recognition of the social context of particular changes.

Bullock and Balton (1985) offer a four-phase model embracing exploration, planning, action and integration with the latter phase being of relevance here because they define it as integrating changes within existing organizational arrangements and note the importance of increasingly not having to rely on consultants. They also make much of the processes for diffusing successful aspects of change throughout the organization, a concern shared by Kelman, see page 65. Cummings and Huse (1989) support this model but also build on the work of French and Bell (1995) in identifying the new organizational practice, known as organizational development (OD). Thus 'organizations are being reinvented . . . the rules of the game are being rewritten . . . the nature of organizations is changing' and so there is a need to broaden attempts to manage change beyond the level of individuals and groups.

Burnes (2004) notes that OD practitioners have developed their approaches along three main themes:

1 With the advent of the job design approach in Europe and the USA and the emergence of socio-technical systems theory (see below) OD practitioners came to see that they needed to adopt an organization-wide perspective. Although it ought to be added that other changes may have forced that issue. Thus the organization change focus of the literature may well have moved from a departmental/divisional focus, in the period 1950–1980, to an organization-wide or even sector-wide landscape since, just as the idea of the value chain has concentrated attention across organizations and therefore has demanded a cross-silo orientation.

2 This has lead to a focus on culture change programmes and on other organization-wide interventions, for example Total Quality Management, Kaizen, Six Sigma and others. Few, if any, large organizations and many smaller ones now fail to conduct attitude surveys of all employees on a regular basis and increasingly customer attitudes are also regularly surveyed. In turn this has lead to a growing concern for learning and knowledge management as organizations have sought better means of both capturing and making sense of data on performance issues.

3 In particular, OD practitioners have adopted the action research approach as a basis for achieving change in client organizations. It is worth noting that OD practitioners have been primarily concerned with issues of organizational effectiveness (see Argyris, 1990) and organizational health. They have typically

conceived of organizational change as requiring the active participation of those directly involved in and effected by intended changes. Lewin viewed change as a process of problem solving through social action, essentially dialogue. But while this may well work at the level of the individual and the group how can this be made to work where scale, including geography, is involved? In reality as the focus has moved to an organization-wide scope OD practitioners may have needed to become more directive. But this would need to be based on the assumption that all those involved are willing to see change introduced. This may ignore the reality of organizational politics (Wilson, 1992). But this may only present a problem for those who view OD practitioners as operating within a set of values in which participation of all is a precondition to effective change. Some mistakenly label these values as democratic ignoring the reality that, depending on the form of democracy, those who are governed often disapprove of at least some of the policies of the governing elite. Views differ. Policy choice and organizational choice rarely can be both successful and satisfy everyone involved.

OD certainly represents an enormously influential mode of thinking about and practice in the change management field. It has focused attention on the people and behavioural issues in change management and provided a wealth of techniques to help organizations do so in an evidence-based way. By doing so it has helped us take into account the possible consequences of implementing change and provided the means for at least considering and working with these consequences. The impact of OD on organizational practice should not be underestimated but we should note that the work of OD has typically been based on the assumption that the changes to be made cannot be modified too substantially, rather the task of OD was to find ways of helping people and organizations to implement change in a sensible way, given the human dimension involved. One exception ought to be noted here, that of systems theory.

Systems theory

Systems theory is claimed by its adherents to take the whole system into account as the basic unit of analysis, though rarely is this achieved in reality. The socio-technical systems theory school originally based at the Tavistock Institute of Human Relations in the UK was for many years the leading institutional base for research and thinking. Researchers such as Trist, Emery, Rice and others proposed to optimize jointly the social and technical subsystems in work settings. In effect the claim was that there exists a range of technological possibilities and options in any given setting. Thus 'organizational choice' exists. By going for a less than optimal technological design you might achieve, overall, a more effective design where the design chosen created more satisfying and meaningful work, thus avoiding other performance inhibiting behaviour like absenteeism. If you look at Emery and Trist (1963) you can see just how attractive this theoretical stance proved to be, but you can also see its limit.

Emery and Trist (1963) is a study of mechanized coal mining. By contrasting different levels of technology the researchers were able to show that some technology options made organizing work teams into 'semi-autonomous work groups' easier. The groups were also shown to be more likely to be associated with work seen by employees to be more meaningful, more satisfying and likely to be more effective in terms of indicators like absenteeism. Actually a careful reading of the book reveals that this idea of organizational choice was not activated within the period studied but rather that the research looked at two stages in the level of mechanization. That said, the idea evolved into the notion that you might take any given technology and seek to design or redesign the jobs involved to be more meaningful. Out of this emerged the 'job design' field and in the 1980s the managerial competence movement. Both were efforts to design roles around both the demands of the tasks to be performed and what we know about human attitudes, motivation and capabilities.

Other approaches within this body of work include 'open systems theory', see Checkland (1986) and the systems dynamic approach. The latter comprises work aimed at modelling social systems, made famous by the work of Meadows (1972) and recently applied to the field of organization change by Rieley (2001). Systems dynamics provides the analytical means of modelling social systems and can allow the study of various design options when rethinking an organization. The focus is largely on how to choose rather than on how to change but clearly the process of choice is part of change and the fuller evaluation of options helps us avoid 'unintended consequences'.

Emergent approaches to change

Finally, Collins (2001) has brought forward a model of organization and change which represents a significant step forward in the literature. It goes beyond most linear models without losing the step-by-step logic inherent in them. He distinguishes 'great' from 'good' companies, identifying as great those companies which have outperformed their sector peers and competitors on financial indicators, such as share price, over a period of 20 years and by an order of magnitude of between four and twentyfold. He was able to identify 11 such companies. In this 'Good to Great' model there are two stages, *build-up* and *breakthrough*.

The focus therefore is not on a particular change programme no matter how extensive or strategic, but rather on the characteristics and processes associated with achieving breakthrough change to sustained competitive advantage. This model therefore overcomes one of the fundamental problems associated with the change literature, that of viewing any specific change in isolation from other changes going on in the organization at the same time. Each stage comprises the resolution of three fundamental issues. These are presented in the model diagram as sequential steps but we prefer to take them as issues to be resolved, to a large extent in parallel.

1 *Build-up stage* – within which you need to appoint, nurture and encourage 'level 5 leaders'. These are leaders who combine leadership qualities alongside a willingness to acknowledge personal limitations. It represents a counterpoint to the notion of the charismatic leader but not a rejection of the idea. Thus 'level 5 leaders' may well have charisma. Ultimately the notion is that leaders

need to inspire and connect with people. Accepting your own limitations, bringing as it were 'human scale' to leadership, may be thought to help with the latter need. Organizations need also to get the right people into place in terms of knowledge, experience, skills and motivation. Finally, in the build-up stage Collins emphasizes the need to face reality rather than not face facts because people feel threatened or uncomfortable when doing so.

2 *Breakthrough* – during which the organization needs to build a passion for its business, its products/services/sector/capabilities/technology and people. Moreover, the organization must learn to think and act in both a disciplined and decisive manner. For Collins speed is important but so is discipline.

The essence of the approach is to say that organizations need to plan to provide certain defining characteristics of successful operation and ways of deciding, working and performing. If these are diffused throughout the organization success will emerge. However, the most important point to note here is that the model does not require that we specify specific goals around the changes but rather that we identify a direction of development along with a long-term goal of being a lead or 'defining' company within a particular sector, of out-performing competitors and so on. Incrementally you would plan such goals, not least as part of an annual budget process. So this is not a planned change model. Rather it is a planned process of emergent change.

Both research and practical experience have shown the limitations of linear models of organizational change. Such models appear to be such an over-simplification when looking at the decisions and choices senior executives must make during a period of change. This is not to argue them as being without value. The author is well aware that practising managers find the Lewin model, the Kotter model and OD as very meaningful when thinking about, planning and critiquing particular changes in terms of the effectiveness of change planning and implementation. However, they often prove to be inadequate in a wide range of circumstances. This is particularly relevant where organization change is involved and where any given change is one of a multiplicity of changes underway. Commonly organizations have hundreds of change initiatives underway. This is common even for quite small organizations. Yet most of the models do not include this as a category in the model. At best it is subsumed within the organization context or implied by reference to 'organization politics'. But this is viewed by some observers as leading to serious over-simplification.

The idea of emergent change and the linked idea of emergent strategy (Mintzberg, 1994) was developed to provide greater realism to discussions of strategy formulation and change. They do so either by relying on complexity theory or by requiring less to be specified in advance. We ought to note that logically open systems theory is at least a precursor to this line of thinking.

Emergent theories based on complexity theory (e.g. Wheatley, 1992, 1996) will be considered in the next chapter which reviews critical theory, postmodernist ideas and complexity theory. Here we will consider leadership models of emergent change (Higgs and Rowland, 2005) and market-induced change (Piercy, 2004).The former comprises a model of change leadership and change competencies in which leaders are viewed ideally as change enablers. The latter looks at the role of incentives and rewards combined with disincentives all utilized as a means of inducing change via competitive/collaborative behaviour in pursuit of economic goals. The Higgs and Rowland change leadership competence model has been tested initially through research at Shell.

<table>
<tr><td>CASE STUDY</td><td>Learning your way to improved performance: British Petroleum</td></tr>
</table>

BP Amoco is one of the world's largest and highest profile companies. This organization is global in its operations and impact, highly profitable and self-evidently a leading business in the energy sector. The company has gone through a series of changes since the early 1990s during the incumbency of three successive CEOs including Lord Browne, who has been in post since 1996 having worked with BP since leaving university (Browne is to be replaced by Tony Hayward as CEO in the summer 2007). Structural changes focused on cutting out layers of management, clarifying financial accountability at business unit level and improving performance in the 1990s were seen, in retrospect, as necessary to build a platform for a transformation of performance. Most tellingly under the then CEO, David Simon, capital expenditure was reduced leading to a need to be much more disciplined about focusing exploration spending (for example) on fewer, and therefore the better, prospects. There was a clear need for scale and for global reach. Thus there began a series of mergers and acquisitions positioning the emerging group to enable it to deliver improved returns and to expand capital spending, having already first worked on enhancing the effectiveness of capital spending.

All of these moves created a large and fragmented company by 2000. In fact from 1995 onwards the company sought to apply four organizational principles:

1 People work better in smaller units.

2 But larger organizations create proprietary knowledge and it makes sense to share that knowledge quickly.

3 Peer group dialogue and challenge around performance was very different to superior–subordinate discussion of performance and this difference could and should be leveraged.

4 Reputation is a crucial resource both externally and internally.

Applying these principles has lead the organization to recognize a fifth principle which it has sought to exploit to the fullest possible extent:

5 While formal or explicit knowledge is important, it is at least as important to share 'tacit' knowledge.

Tacit knowledge (see below) is neither effectively captured nor well shared through knowledge management systems. You need to bring people together.

This fifth principle has long been known. Indeed the original idea of the university and of scholarship which emphasized tutors and students working either one-to-one or in small groups was based on this idea. In any event BP sought to build sharing via a structured process, creating what Argyris calls 'productive reasoning' and what has also been called 'purposeful conversations' by establishing peer groups. The business units were organized into 15 'peer groups', each comprising units within a particular business stream. Business unit targets are set within a performance contract. These targets are set through a process of conversations within the business units, within the peer group and with top management. Within this process the peer group represents a powerful source of challenge across

75

the business units as peer groups seek to ensure that each carries its share of the growth in revenues, margins and so on needed to deliver longer-term strategic goals. Peer groups provide a mechanism for deciding resource allocation and for knowledge sharing.

Pivotal to this was the notion that high-performing business units in a peer group must assist under-performing units to improve. Indeed the expectation is that the top three performers will help the bottom three. The performance of the top three in doing so is measured each year and this is built into the bonus structure. Overall therefore these changes are backed up with both economic incentives and a high degree of transparency.

This is extended via a 'peer assist' process within which executives work to help particular business units work on issues or projects of various sorts. This often spanned peer group boundaries and regularly involved many executives committing significant amounts of time to the process. The belief is that everyone gains. The business unit draws on the experience throughout the organization. Those involved see it as a development opportunity. These peer processes emphasize horizontal/collaborative working and dialogue, building the capacity for learning and greater creativity.

In 2001 continued growth required further reorganization with a consolidation of business units, reducing the total number. As has been argued elsewhere, decentralization is a matter of balance. So is knowledge sharing. The BP approach has been to create purposeful conversations across the organization. But business units must also sustain 'business as usual' so balances must be struck over time. Of course, peer group members have a shared interest in seeing that these balances are maintained. Nevertheless one is looking at a continually evolving picture.

The peer processes help create value through the transfer of best practice, via peer advice, shared expertise and by creating a firmer basis for major business development/strategic moves. This is supported by organizational arrangements which promote but also discipline peer group behaviour. These include the use of incentives and the substantially enhanced economic transparency evolving through the peer group process. In addition BP's ongoing investment in the development of people creates an environment in which development is a legitimated activity for executives. This is balanced by making clear at all levels that disciplines are also needed.

In turn, the value of these processes has been reinforced by the definition of 'human portals'. Often not business unit leaders but rather experienced people who have a multiplicity of contacts throughout BP, they are people who have been identified as those to whom you can go if you seek expertise. Their role is to 'connect' you to that expertise wherever it may exist within BP. Again we have long known that these people are potentially an invaluable resource. Indeed in some ways when we distinguish between formal and informal organization this is part of the distinction being made. The point here is that the explicit organizational recognition gives legitimacy to the role, and therefore to these people. This has been called applying a 'behavioural net' onto a decentralized structure. The organization creates the conditions for cross-unit learning and collaboration without undermining the flexibility and accountability for performance at business unit level. At the same time the peer group process drives forward performance in what after all is a highly 'connected' organization. These are complex and evolving balances which need continually to be worked on and with.

These organizational changes seek to balance the obvious advantages of scale (e.g. by pooling purchasing volumes via centralized purchasing) with the benefits of decentralized and horizontal networking, in which contact between people, above all, provides for learning.

Sources: Rogan, 2002; Hansen and van Oetinger, 2001

Conclusion

Linear models possess the merit of simplicity. These models fall down in respect of 'unintended consequences' but the notion of emergent change does allow for the dynamics of real world change to be taken into account. Here, however, the key point to note is that linear models break down because reality is too complex. Nevertheless, the idea that organization change can be viewed as a linear process has been influential, representing at least a starting point for practitioners to think about change strategy and tactics.

EXERCISES

1 Consider the cases set out early in Chapter 3 (see pages 38–39 and 39–41), particularly Ford. Can you utilize linear models to describe the sequence of changes recorded? Would a systems model serve a better analytical purpose?

2 Can you think of changes where 'unintended consequences' arose? Why?

3 Review the BP case presented above. Does the emergent model usefully explain the series of changes and the change strategy adopted?

4 Does BP use a planned approach to some changes? If so which and why?

5 Does the recent BP experience (as reported extensively in the second half of 2006 and early in 2007) lead you to suppose that these changes to performance management and learning now need review?

5 Theories of change: critical perspectives

Introduction

One of the difficulties many observers have with the change management literature is that it is overly pragmatic. It lacks theoretical depth. The change process is depicted as a series of neat steps and stages. Yet in the real world organization change is not like that . . . it is altogether more complicated. Moreover, the change management literature can be read as suggesting that it is possible to set out a well articulated theory of how to achieve successful change. Yet most of the world's problems appear to be full of uncertainties and often the steps we take to resolve them are themselves the origins of 'unintended consequences' which give rise to either new problems or to pressures making the problems we sought to solve worse, not better.

Technology, demography, globalization and social change are all and each leading to external, environmental changes. None is new. But all have an impact now in a world where less organized activity is determined by hierarchical relationships of power and control, whether these be feudal or based on corporatist principles. To an increasing extent market solutions prevail. While the most developed version of this argument is deployed by Bobbitt (2002) in his formulation of the concept of 'the market state', it is clear from any application of Williamson's original approach (1975) that in both the private and the public sectors there has been an accelerating tendency to rely on market solutions to the problems of change. In essence the argument is that the rewards and punishments of the market create a dynamic arising from competitive pressure which is hard to achieve within an hierarchical organization unless crisis threatens. Thus the 'market decides' becomes a mantra for many seeking to lead change. That in turn means that outcomes are determined by the millions of choices people make. Thus is created the dynamism we referred to above which encourages innovation. But it also removes many of the certainties created by the checks and balances of former solutions to the problem of how to organize for agriculture, commerce or war. Now this is not to argue that the market dominates all aspects of human endeavour. However, market forces are increasingly relied on by politicians and business executives alike.

Thus the organization and its environment are both increasingly dynamic and uncertain. For Clark and Clegg (1998) this has lead to 'a transformation of management knowledge'. For these authors 'successful management in the future must be based on intelligence and creativity and the capacity to question and learn'. Moreover, there is a constant need to seek an appropriate balance between continually confronting uncertainty, paradox, trade-offs and contingencies and the need for balance, direction and motivation. More simply, executives must learn how to combine continual change with the ability to sustain 'business as usual'.

One organizational model designed for such a purpose is the 'virtual organization' (Nohria and Berkely, 1994). Project-based, this model emphasizes peer group working rather than 'command and control'. Behaviour is mediated through definitions of desired outcomes and the creation of the conditions for those engaged to accept of accountability rather than by rules, procedures and orders. The accountability question is likely to be answered largely via market solutions. Do virtual organizations exist? Well, where organizations work together over long periods of time the combination of those involved may take on some at least of the characteristics of virtual organizations. Certainly, where activity is based on the use of data in a digitized form structures are being created which possess some of these features (airline booking systems, Ebay?). Traditional organization designs derive from assumptions about behaviour and motivation which may no longer be relevant in a world of networked databases, e-mail, remote access and so on. Technology presents an 'enabling mechanism' allowing time and geography to be merged, facilitating the speeding up of information flows.

But what does this mean for the management of change? Of course, one assumption inherent in the change management idea is that someone knows the appropriate organizational arrangements to change to and why. While this point is often dissected by theorists into questions of strategy, organization design and human resources including reward, motivation and so on it is worth stating that the essence of this assumption relates to the questions of organization or business model. The central question facing people seeking to change an existing organization is one of identifying an appropriate model with which to offer products or services. This requires decisions of which products/services, to which customers, at what prices, through which delivery channels or systems, when and in what quantities (noting here that for some rationing is a key element of the model). Whatever the context, these questions need to be resolved effectively if stakeholders and/or customers are to be satisfied.

You can immediately add the question of in whose interests are these judgements to be made but it is at least possible that the switch from the corporatist to the market solution changes the nature of that question. Here we must note that this is a significant simplification. Economic categories such as feudalism, globalization, corporatism and so on do not provide a means of straightforward analysis. Historians argue over the problem of how to create meaningful datelines for their purposes. But that ought not to matter for our purpose here so long as we note that the emerging dominance of market solutions around the world may not be permanent, is certainly not emerging consistently around the world and still leaves many real questions open.

To return then to our theme. Can we assume that someone knows what to do next? On what basis would such a view be judged? Only on results? Surely this is not enough? Implementation will lead to costs being incurred. Thus the legitimacy of the decision process becomes part of the question. This is controversial both in practice and in the change management literature, for the following reasons:

1 Too often a unitary frame of reference is assumed, i.e. that the interests of all involved are shared and common, or at least can be reconciled, whether shareholder, manager or employee and irrespective of gender, ethnicity or religion.

2 The so called classical and human relations schools tended to see external factors such as economic or demographic change and technology as not manageable in practice.

3 Moreover, proponents of both viewpoints tended not to consider size of organization as being particularly important.

4 The contingency theorists (and those writing in the Peters and Waterman genre, popularized by the success of *In Search of Excellence* (1982)) and others concerned with corporate culture (from Schein onwards but perhaps not including some recent contributions), shared one particular assumption. These observers accept contingencies as given and largely immutable. But this is clearly not true, not least because organizations can choose where they work around the world. Thus in time and space given contingencies may indeed be immutable but organizations can and do choose to respond by reorganizing globally.

5 Some have attempted to work with these limitations. If a simplistically applied and objective science cannot resolve these issues then a more complex paradigm may be developed and here culture models such as that offered by Goffee and Jones (1998) and Trompenars (2001) and theories of organizational learning (e.g. Senge (1990)) are of relevance.

6 Clearly it is necessary to construct ideas about change which encompass the notions of power and politics (e.g. Pettigrew, 1973).

While all of this is of real interest to students of organization and change, and perhaps even to practising managers, each comprise ways of looking at organizational reality from a partial perspective, whether of scientific management, power and politics, technology, individual and group motivation and so on.

But the changes outlined at the start of this chapter have demanded an altogether more flexible response from organizations. The emergence of rapidly changing markets, and significant changes of consumer expectation and taste require ever more flexibility of response. Not least I refer to rapid changes to expectations regarding supply, access, delivery and price. While particularly predominant in the private sector it increasingly also applies to the public sector . . . healthcare being the obvious case, at least in those countries with public provision.

It is not difficult to find examples of once great companies which have failed this 'test' of expectation. Thus in an issue of *Fortune* magazine (February 2006) we see an analysis of the position of the US automobile giant General Motors. Having once been a defining organization for US-based global capitalism and having been the major force in the US market for new cars, with 45 per cent of that market in the 1980s, it now has only 27 per cent and falling. With an underperforming automobile business and other substantial liabilities the GM share price in December 2005 had fallen below $19, the lowest level since 1982. Is this a business challenged by customer expectations regarding design and price? When such dramatic examples are considered the partial approaches listed above seem unconvincing at best.

Emerging thinking about organizational change

Piore and Sable (1984) long ago argued that only decentralized firms have the necessary flexibility, skills and commitment to respond to sudden shifts. A number of theorists have developed ideas which are often labelled as 'postmodernism'. Modernism was the emergence of rational, objective science combined with an underlying belief in human progress. Historians refer to the 'enlightenment' which comprised the evolution of laws and knowledge conducive to human progress given rise to, but also given effect by, the application of science to the study of human problems.

Postmodernism self-evidently is thought to 'replace' modernism. Darwin, Johnson and McAuley (2002) make useful distinctions between critical theory, postmodernism and complexity theory. We now take each in turn noting that each seeks different ends while emerging out of a very similar critique of traditional theory in this field.

Critical theory

This body of theory relates not to the notion of criticism (of prior theory) but rather to a social constructivist critique of positivism. The idea that management is a neutral, technocratic discipline is rejected (Willmott, 1984). Relying on the work of Habermas (1974) critical theory seeks to understand how knowledge is derived, identifying two knowledge domains, one of which arises out of our human practices of interpersonal life, and a third knowledge domain emerging out of our capacity for reflection.

Now it is clear enough that most thinking about strategy is based on a commitment to positivist thinking. This holds true whether we examine Kay (1993), Mintzberg (1994), Whittington (2001) or Mansfield (1986) even though these authors start from very different positions in terms of discipline and perspective. Alternatively Darwinist style formulations examining forms of adaptation are presented (Porter, 1985), or more specifically Hannan and Freeman (1983), looking at the population ecologist idea of selection via 'survival of the fittest'. More recently, of course, Hamel and Prahalad (1994) have examined organizations achieving rapid strategic change in terms of 'strategic fit' or of the evolution of new 'strategic competencies'. In essence, albeit perhaps to differing degrees, these approaches are based on the assumption of an objective reality which, once understood, can be exploited by organizations.

Critical theorists view strategy writing as having been dominated by a positivist logic (see Stacey,1996; Alvesson and Willmott, 1992). It seems obvious that knowledge is socially constructed. Therefore 'strategy talk', if dominated by owners or by senior executives, is socially constructed by them and will not necessarily reflect wider interests nor deal with questions and concerns others might seek to impose on them.

This is a challenge to legitimacy. Sure enough there are ways of responding. Stakeholder theory is one such response. In this theory the modern organization must respond to the concerns of the various stakeholders to which it relates and, in any event, must operate within the legal framework established by the modern state. Thus it is that these so called broader concerns can and are responded to. In the context of the emerging 'market state', assuming for the moment that we accept that idea, the view of Milton Friedman (1972) would still hold true. In such a context the modern business organisation, in pursuit of profit maximization and operating within the law, would act in ways which would be effective both to owners and the society of which it is a part. Nevertheless, the current interest in ethical management, sustainability and social responsibility suggests a tendency to reject at least the extreme form of that argument.

In any event it is not obvious that all thinking and writing about strategy and organization is powerless to take account of the concerns raised by critical theory. There is no monopoly on the ability to see that the existing organizational paradigm does not always work effectively. For example, Argyris and Schon (1978) clearly do so by distinguishing between 'espoused theory' and 'theory in use'. Or at least they show that decision making in organizations is not as simple nor as deterministic as the critique of positivism supposes. In a similar vein Senge (1990) argues that reflexivity and dialogue enable people in organizations to explore issues and assumptions more freely. Why would that be needed in a positivist world? Why would senior executives spend time and money on training managers in such approaches? As a smoke screen? No, that will not do as an argument. There is too much evidence that in learning settings executives can and do pursue a fuller exploration of thought and experience. This brings forward the possibility of transcending current views and ideas.

Fraher (2004) has presented an even tougher challenge to critical theory (which is not to say that this was her intention). She has written a history of group study and the psychodynamic organization through a study of the origins and development of the Tavistock Institute of Human Relations and the A.K. Rice Institute. Utilizing the ideas of Freud, Jung, Melanie Klein and Wilfred Bion these organizations developed approaches to the study of groups and of organizations. The initial impetus was the problem of rapidly expanding the UK armed forces in the early Second World War, giving rise to the need to establish an effective officer selection board process. The emerging ideas and practice were subsequently applied to conferences of practitioners interested in issues of authority and leadership in groups and in organizations. Viewing both organizations as 'idea organizations', Fraher shows that each achieved transformation through reflection, the willingness to experiment, and to openness to new ideas and groups, but neither disregarded the past thoughtlessly. To achieve transformation organizations 'must find ways to acknowledge and then mitigate intergroup rivalry that inevitably arises when competing ideas are engaged' (Fraher, 2004).

To what extent does this study provide a challenge to critical theory? The idea that the construction of knowledge and 'strategy talk' may disadvantage those without power needs serious consideration even though in practice it may be an inevitable consequence of various stages of the development of society and not least of a 'meritocratic' society. The whole apparatus of organization development as described by French and Bell (1995), Kotter (1996) and Kanter (1983) may be a process based on collusion with power-holders, at best, or 'brainwashing' at worst. However, it appears difficult to conclude that such a simplistic critique can convince during a period of rapid change or throughout a population of organizations as diverse as the Tavistock Institute of Human Relations, public bodies of varying kinds, professional organizations, hospitals, colleges and many more.

In summary, then, critical theory raises real and important questions. This body of work seeks to replace so called positivist thinking. This is right as far as it goes. What is less clear is the extent to which critical theory raises questions not already posed within the existing paradigm. In one sense critical theory brings forward the important idea that all of human history is not best judged as a process of continued progress, based on the view there just may not always be a solution to a dilemma we face. There may be no way forward. But it is not clear that critical thinkers writing within the management field take such a view.

Postmodernism

Postmodernism places language and discourse at the centre of analysis. It is otherwise very similar to critical theory. For the postmodernist 'multiple truths' are always possible. As a body of thought it draws on the work of Foucault (1970, 1972, 1977, 1980, 1986). Knights and Morgan (1991) note the tendency of much strategy literature to be based on a supposition that it provides certain knowledge of practical relevance to organizations. This seems to be rather an extreme claim, not in any way consistent with Mintzberg's rejection of much of the strategic management literature and theory. He argues the case for 'emergent strategy'. The idea of emergent strategy is that strategic thinking and practice are linked but not the same. While Knights and Morgan rightly see strategy as a series of discourses this is exactly the situation Fraher describes. In reality most writing about strategy seems to me at least to be based on the supposition that it is by engaging with carefully argued models and by contrasting models with real experience that readers and practitioners learn how more effectively to understand their own situation. This seems hardly different to the Fraher observation that the process of transformation requires that contending ideas be understood and considered.

Emergent models of strategy formulation typically include the idea of differing discourses being engaged but take account also of the changing circumstances most likely to give rise to these discourses, not least strategies which are seen not to be working effectively by key stakeholders. Nevertheless, postmodernist thinking has led to work seeking to codify and understand discourse about strategy and to look at the idea of 'strategic credibility'. Here the strategist needs to deploy narrative devices both to ensure credibility and to create a sense of novelty when presenting strategy. This is a particularly helpful contribution not least because these authors link discourse to strategic 'genres', identifying ten such genres in Mintzberg's seminal survey of the strategy literature (Mintzberg, 1994).

Naturally enough, postmodernist thinking on strategy is subject to the very criticism its proponents level at others. If they seek to deconstruct discourses used by others (e.g. managers) they do so using discourse. In turn their own discourse can be (should be) deconstructed. We need not concern ourselves with the criticism relating to the danger of double standards, which is obvious enough, and at least the postmodernist is directing our attention to that very line of criticism. Rather we are interested in the idea that a postmodernist stance might help with the design of interventions in organizations (Barry, 1997). If we can break the power of the 'expert' by a thorough analysis of client ideas, narratives, descriptions and the like we may move towards a position of being able to base such interventions on a more reflective dialogue and thereby an improved understanding of problems and issues facing the 'client system'. Is this not the basis of much of the work of Argyris (1990, 2004)?

■ Complexity theory

Darwin, Johnson and McAuley (2002) provide a convincing survey of the emergence of complexity theory within the organization behaviour literature. They note that the fundamental idea underlying the application of this body of theory is that of the complex adaptive system, defined as follows:

1 It is a network of 'agents' acting in parallel, often interconnected, ways but without any 'command and control' framework.
2 These agents are 'adaptively intelligent'; constantly seeking and making sense of patterns, testing ideas, evolving and learning.
3 Change is achieved through learning, evolution and adaptation.
4 Control of the system is dispersed throughout the system.
5 Coherence within the system arises out of competition and cooperation among the agents as they see advantage in alliances and other arrangements for mutual support.

In effect this thinking is based on the idea of 'self-organization'. Harré (1984) and Wheatley (1996) consider how ideas and practices can emerge from groups which transcend the ideas of the individual members of the group. As people act in the world new issues arise (including as a result of 'unintended consequences') and often new possibilities arise, for example the discovery of penicillin. A reductionist approach emphasizes the analysis of individual elements of a situation or issue and may not bring out a broader perspective on important emergent themes.

Capra (1996) traces the emergence of the concept of self-organization from the early years of 'cybernetics'. Darwin, Johnson and McAuley (2002) also note that the interest in complexity theory within management studies has derived from the attempt to understand problems relating to planning systems which appear not to be able to predict the future. I might add here that we all of us experience systems which seem unable to predict the future when we look at weather forecasts, for example, certainly those beyond 48 hours duration. More seriously we are each of us to some degree engaged with the often confusing attempts to predict the longer-term causes and impacts of 'global warming'. The question of how to agree public policy or corporate strategy in the midst of high levels of uncertainty is not new but increasingly it looms large as our global political–legal–economic activities become both more complex and more interconnected.

Fraher (2004) and Pascale (1990) both seek to show how organizations adapt not by valuing consensus above all but rather by stimulating innovation through processes emphasizing tension, contention and conflict and debate. Emery (2004) goes well beyond this position in presenting an analysis of open systems theory-based action research as an enabler of learning and change.

Emery's starting point is that learning is essential to sustainable change. Second she argues that to achieve sustainable change practitioners (here she means the organizational development practitioner) must work with people at all levels of the organization involved; from senior executives to customer-facing staff. Moreover all levels and functional areas must be involved in some sort of process within which they can engage with this learning (not an identical process please note). This creates problems for some practitioners who may, for example, be members of an 'elite' with their own 'language', frameworks and meaning systems. In reality it can be hard work to operate collaboratively, at least in the perception of the often thousands of employees involved and impacted by a set of intended changes, whatever the intentions of those involved.

For sustainable change to be achieved every step of the process must lead to learning which engages and energizes action (see Strebel (2000) and Collins (2001)). But people learn at different rates and through different learning styles. Also, and inevitably, people positioned differently in any large organization have very different learning opportunities depending on many factors, for example the nature of their roles, variable access to information and experience and so on. Thus the crews of the early space missions organized by NASA developed knowledge and experience others could not access in the same way. The early transplant surgeons similarly. Clearly in both cases they were supported by teams and operated within an evidence-based system designed to capture and codify the data such that it could be shared. This is important but nevertheless it is hard not to conclude that, in the midst of complexity and uncertainty, when we think about engaging people in learning and change processes and activities we are going to do so in varying ways and at differing stages of the process because knowledge and experience is variably distributed. None of this is to argue that we should not engage with people at all levels during a period of change. Rather it is to note that saying so begs a range of questions to do with who, why, when and in which ways, through which mechanisms and so on.

For Emery, however, the key idea is 'diffusive learning'. Diffusive learning is that form of learning which motivates the learner to recreate the learning environment for others. This is particularly interesting because it links powerfully to a study by Kelman (2005). He uses the diffusion of innovation literature and in particular the seminal work of Rogers (1995) noting that this literature takes differences of opinions about innovation seriously. Rather than label people as 'resistant to change' Rogers views people as ranging from enthusiasts to critics. Some are 'early adopters' and Kelman refers to them as the 'change vanguard'. This is very important in practice when he combines this notion along with the identification of people as 'opinion leaders' within organizations.

Rogers (1995) had noted that the 'early adopters' were not likely to be 'opinion leaders' in an organization. More oriented to external ideas (i.e. external to their own social group) they were more likely to be viewed as 'deviant' and perceived as having 'low credibility'. In his study (of procurement reform in the US government) he found that the 'early adopters' were likely to be opinion leaders. What explains this difference? In truth Kelman does not really explain this adequately. The most likely explanation is that senior managers, working through their own line managers, have identified 'opinion leaders' at local level. Kelman refers to them as 'most respected co-workers'. Significant efforts are then made to engage them in the change process including training them in the relevant skills and knowledge and involving them in working groups, task forces and so on. By going through this learning and the change-related activity these people become knowledgeable and skilled in the new procurement systems and ways of working. No doubt these people derive satisfaction and even status from this engagement but it is interesting to note the process involved. To follow Kelman these 'most respected co-workers' are being provided with a 'psychologically safe environment' within which to learn. Senior executives both argue the case for change and then create this 'learning space'. In effect this creates 'organizational cover' for this learning. Sponsorship from the senior team creates legitimacy for the activity. Traditionally in the organization behaviour literature this is known as 'organizational slack'. Burns and Stalker (1961) in an early study of innovation within organizations note that innovation requires that there be some slack or unused resource in an organization to provide for experimentation with new ideas. Of course, this is a task for leaders. Providing the 'learning space', creating sufficient slack, sponsoring particular individuals may be seen as part of what the idea of the 'leader as coach' is all about. Note that this idea is increasingly brought forward as essential by organizational theorists and is certainly beginning to be influential within at least the human resources community in large organizations.

But then the change process observed by Kelman relies on the same process cascading down the structure. But now the 'most respected co-worker' appeared to play a pivotal role. Kelman refers to a process of 'behavioural facilitation' which he describes as a process of influence which includes the creation of a psychological safe environment within which to innovate. We would rework this as the creation of the conditions for learning, and therefore of change at the individual level. It is interesting to note that from Kelman's data, while supervisors and local office managers were shown as playing such a positive role, in fact the 'most respected co-workers' who were also pro reform were shown as having a substantially greater impact within teams. So much so that Kelman concludes that the 'most respected co-worker' may well be seen as the best source of change-related training.

In practical terms this is of real interest. Often the investment in change-related training is seen as too inadequate (CIPD survey, 2003). What this data implies is that organizations should invest in pro reform 'most respected co-workers', both in providing training and in engaging them in the change process and then rely substantially on 'on the job' training led by those same people. On this basis training investment, once change implementation is underway, might focus more extensively on sharing best practice. This may be particularly relevant in situations where lots of local adaptation is needed for successful implementation, a condition most likely to arise in large, dispersed and complex systems. We will return to this point in Chapter 18.

Kelman's data also showed that social influence is of central importance to the achievement of sustainable change. The proportion of any group who were members of the change vanguard had a positive impact on change attitude as one would expect. But the 'most respected co-workers' attitude also had a positive impact. Lesser than the impact of the proportion of the group being within the change vanguard but very significantly more than the impact of the local leader attitudes. Thus ideally the group embraces change. However, if not, it is more important what the 'most respected co-worker' does on this evidence. This is certainly consistent with Emery's idea of 'diffusive learning' and we should note that for Kelman these processes are about consolidation of change. The arguments for change, the articulation of those arguments at local level and early success create a mutually reinforcing set of processes through which change efforts can accelerate. Again we will return to this idea in Chapter 18.

Now Emery is very clear on the point that organizations do not learn because organizations do not have a nervous system. For her the best definition of a 'learning organization' is an organization structured in ways which encourage learning continuously. She also questions the idea of 'organizational memory' because in periods of rapid turnover organizations often find that the memory leaves with the people. While these doubts are worth raising it is also possible to observe organization so codifying learning in new working and business models that patterned and permanent changes are achieved. Taking her own work on its own terms such a view must be accepted otherwise action research would become an expensive luxury, whereas the body of work within which Emery appears to ground her own contribution is based on the idea of action research as the basis for learning and change within organizations and involves identifying and working within design principles for doing so effectively.

Boonstra (2004) notes that organizations often must deal with complexity in the processes of production, innovation and creation. As we have observed this leads to greater flexibility and the emergence of network solutions, combining the skills, resources and market access of the partners involved. In turn this can lead to pressures for decentralization and self-management at the local level. Scholars working on this issue have deployed a dynamic systems theory approach (see, for example, Checkland and Howell, 1998; Stacey, 2003).This approach views organization as being permanently situated between equilibrium and disequilibrium. In fluid dynamics this is called 'dynamic homeostasis' – a condition of movement at the atomic level with an inbuilt tendency to seek equilibrium. So it seems to be in organizations, so long as those involved can comprehend the dynamics of the situation in which they are located and are able to intervene within that situation, even where those interventions involve working with others. Central to creating the conditions where this is so appears to be creating the conditions within which people can learn. Most important here may be the ability to express feelings and assumptions which challenge the status quo, and the social space within which to do so. The links between the practice proposed here and the argument presented above are self-evident.

In consequence, change and learning requires that those involved can share and exchange views on the organization and its context and on how effectively it is operating. Consistent with the ideas of critical theory in particular we also note the relevance of the work of Weick (1979, 1995) on dialogue and conversations about strategic change (see Chapter 10) and also of the Argyris concept of double-loop learning which may well be essential to the achievement of sustainable change, at least in some circumstances (Argyris, 2004). Specifically the circumstances where this conclusion applies may be where the leadership of an organization has become dysfunctional for the achievement of its purposes and leadership behaviour becomes characterized by the 'organizational defensive routines' identified in Chapter 10 of this book.

Boonstra (2004) refers to interactive learning which he argues involves the following:

1 Viewing the process of organizing as involving feedback, positive and negative.
2 Creating 'space' for self-organization.
3 Creating transparency of process and relationships in a period of change.
4 Legitimating multiple constructs of reality, problems, issues.
5 Legitimating the expression of feelings, ambitions, knowledge, experience and insight.
6 The pursuit of shared views, ideas and ways of understanding events and perceptions.
7 Allowing time for interaction, reflection and learning.

All in all, a process like that proposed by Kolb (1984) in his analysis of experiential learning.

Does this imply the need for 'equilibrium' in order that learning can be facilitated by the provision of support and space (and/or organization cover)? Dynamic balance or Stacey's (1996) 'dynamic instability' may not be conducive to learning. Lack of balance can be a basis for learning and change (de Caluwe and Vermaak, 2004). His argument is that lack of balance or 'bounded instability' requires organizations to choose between competing goals, practices, structures, technologies and so on. It is lack of choice, the unwillingness to decide and the absence of ambition that leads to disruptive levels of performance, chaos and the possibility of failure. These authors quote Fritz (1996), as follows:

> **Every time we go through some major organizational change, our executive managers find 'tools' or methods to help. ABCM, re-engineering, different process consultants bring in other methods. We implement them, then we find half way through the process the organization isn't taking them on. So then we abandon them, but later new tools are brought in. People are really up in the air about it all. . . .**

> Fritz, 1996, quoting a manager at BC Telecom

Is this not the very conditions for the antithesis of the learning organization? We shall see in Chapter 14 that this situation is all too common. Change initiatives cascade in ever-increasing numbers. Few are properly explained, codified, described or understood. Thus the conditions for interactive and diffusive learning are not satisfied. All too often that is the reality of change management. Thus instability can follow. Indeed one central and practical conclusion of all of this thinking is that the best and most effective strategy for strategic change is to make a few changes and to ensure that they are sustained by investing in learning in order to consolidate them throughout the organization.

Experience-based design

Certainly in the public service but also increasingly in large multinational organizations there is a growing recognition that current change management models are no longer adequate or 'fit for purpose'. These models do not help us deliver the pace and scale of change required. Experience-based design is one solution. It is part of a tendency in the field of innovation in service delivery variously labelled 'co-design', 'participative' or 'interactive' design. The traditional view of the service user as a passive recipient gives way to a view of users as co-designers and as integral to the improvement and innovation process.

Experience-based design is a user-focused design process with the goal of making user experiences accessible to designers in order that design focuses on the experiences created rather than the service to be delivered. Following Bate, Bevan and Robert (2004) this requires a focus on 'delivery systems', pathways and processes. We need to identify where users come into contact with the service and where their subjective experience is shaped. Thus 'experience mapping' is different from 'process mapping'. These authors discuss the application of this design methodology to healthcare where it seems likely to have important application. The key weakness of their approach is that to the extent that the effective delivery of healthcare involves expertise (clinicians for example) which is based on long experience, the paper is silent on how you would seek to create a proper balance between clinicians and users where that would prove needed. By definition this is most likely in situations where it is hardest to achieve.

But clearly it is necessary to seek a balance between the professional who delivers service and users whose needs are being addressed. Just because it is difficult cannot be a reason for not trying. In fire services, police departments, the armed services and in education we cannot be constantly using experience-based design. If consumer preferences and expectations change then constant adaptation will be needed. If we are not careful we are designing systems for the patients, consumers and clients of yesterday, not tomorrow. However, this cannot be a sound basis for rejecting the experience-based perspective. Clearly it has some value. The question is one of balance.

Social movements and large-scale change

We have already observed that the organization change literature has not really embraced the literature on innovation until quite recently. Similarly it has not sought to build on the 'social movements' literature. This is interesting because 'social movements' are about achieving large-scale change. Whether we are looking at civil rights, the ban the bomb campaign, the anti-smoking campaign or the campaign (in the UK) to ban fox hunting (with hounds) it is clear that social movements may have something to tell us about how to engage people in large-scale change. Lack of ambition is not something one would associate with campaigns of this sort.

Bate, Bevan and Robert (2004) offer the following contrast between a project or programme approach to achieving change and a social movements approach. Mainly the difference is about engaging people at a 'deep' or even emotional level. Change is essentially self-directing and follows an absolute, some might say messianic, commitment to the cause. Ultimately 'social movements' are voluntary.

Of course we have already argued that the change management literature is richer than this contrast allows for. You have only to look at Collins (2001) to realize that this comparison just will not do. Moreover, can we really argue that 'social movements' have no leader? Martin Luther King? Nelson Mandella? Nevertheless, while the comparison may not stand up to detailed scrutiny there is something to be said for it. While Martin Luther King was a civil rights leader who captured world attention how much progress would he have made without someone like Rosa Parkes? Certainly change models do not always work on crude 'what is in it for me' assumptions about people (see the Collins (2001) 'Good to Great' model as an example). Nevertheless, it is right to note that social movements often inspire courageous choices where cost or danger or hardship may be, and sometimes is, involved for those making choices.

While it may be reasonable to characterize traditional organizational models as emphasizing questions like 'What is this programme seeking to achieve and what evidence is there that it will have the desired effect?' it is simplistic to contrast that with a social movements emphasis on 'Who supports the programme, how were they mobilized and how much influence can they deploy?' Following Kelman (2005) it is clear that such questions could and would be asked by the organization practitioner and theorist. However, it may be reasonable to argue that within the context of 'social movements' change is released, liberated, channelled and enabled. Elites seek to mobilize processes rather than engender specific programmes of change. Clearly the organization change literature provides for this through the idea of emergent change and concepts such as 'whistle-blowing' have some of the characteristics of social movements.

To summarize, social movements can lead to transformational change, albeit the achievement of many social movements may be more modest. Traditional approaches to organization change and the social movement notion share some characteristics, particularly if one is contrasting the idea of emergent change with social movements ideas. The latter involve collective action by people who have voluntarily come together around a common cause, typically, although not always, they involve radical action and protest and have spontaneous beginnings. Interestingly enough organization changes often have less spontaneous beginnings and are more typically a process of learning, systematically carried out. Conversely social movements are informal networks, based on shared beliefs and mobilized around conflicting and often very controversial issues through the frequent use of protest.

The evolution of theory about organization change

In the United Kingdom the evolution of organizational change theory happened at roughly the same time as another theoretical explanation was being set out and became influential for some of those seeking to explain the inability of the UK economy to compete successfully in the post-Second World War era. In essence the idea was that the UK economy was in long-term decline. Wiener (1981) and Barnett (2002) offered historical explanations relating to the behaviour of elites. Barnett concluded that behind the decline lay an assumed disdain on the part of British elites for business, a preference for the arts and classics over science and engineering, and the dominance of these beliefs and educational preferences in the UK civil service and in government. The lower status of engineers and business people in the UK contrasted with other countries, notably the USA, Germany and Japan. In part Barnett, but not Wiener, was arguing that underinvestment in defence (with spin-off benefits for industry) was part of the explanation. Clearly this was a difficult case to argue, at least when comparing the UK to either Germany and Japan between 1945 and, say, 1980. However, it was possible to argue that the British were neither investing in defence spending, as compared with the USA, nor, with the acceleration of welfare state provision since 1945, prioritizing social programmes and pensions as compared to defence investment in the crucial period 1945–1960. Note also that over that period the UK carried the costs but perhaps few benefits of imperial 'over-stretch' and yet had not experienced the devastation of the bombing campaigns fought in 1943–45. Clearly the decline was not terminal! The so called 'Thatcher era' of the 1980s saw the UK economy change significantly but the interesting point to note here is that the idea that organizational change is inherently difficult and often fails in its purposes was certainly well established in the 1960s. This was despite the clear evidence of output growth under the stimulus of war during the 1939–1945 conflict. It was also despite the experience of many organizations achieving substantial changes over the last 30 years. Of course, critics can question whether these changes are creating desirable outcomes and they can point to unintended consequences. Moreover, doing so is important. We should challenge the longer-term consequences of the many changes going on around us. But we cannot use that to say that change is not being achieved. So while we can ask questions about who benefits and who pays we can hardly argue that changes fail in and of themselves.

As far as the USA is concerned perhaps the most interesting point here is to note the pessimism regarding organization change of much of the literature on the topic published in the last 40 years. While some authors (e.g. Kanter and Kotter) strike a more positive note the surprise is that so many researchers take a more pessimistic line. After all the USA has seen very significant output and productivity growth over the last 20 years. However, we should not ignore the point that many of the iconic US companies have experienced major problems with changed market conditions over those same 20 years (e.g. IBM, GM and Hewlett Packard), although there are many very successful companies (e.g. Microsoft). Are the concerns about organization change exclusively a European concern? Clearly not. But is the incidence of these concerns to be explained simply by notions such as 'resistance to change' or other explanations limited to the organizational level of analysis? Just as clearly the answer to that question is also no. Suffice it to say that the theories reviewed in this chapter include those which really require us to ask questions related to the economic performance in particular sectors and to questions related to social, cultural and elite formation in particular societies and the consequences of this for organizations.

Conclusion

The perspectives and theories considered in this chapter start from the premise that there is much to question in the organizational change field. Traditional models are considered to be too simplistic. In particular, organizational change raises questions about the broader social, cultural and economic context if we are to really understand what is going on when senior executives seek change. It must also be noted that public service reforms raise a new set of questions about change and how it is to be achieved. In truth most of these theories raise more questions than answers. Nevertheless, for any student of organizational change these perspectives encourage a critical view. The first step to understanding and resolving a problem is to acknowledge that it might exist. These models will certainly achieve that end for those who take them seriously.

EXERCISES

1 Consider a 'disaster' such as the crash of the US space shuttle 'Challenger'. Does complexity theory help us understand how that happened?

2 Would it be fair to say that traditional theories are at least capable of providing practical help to people engaged in change while critical theory only raises doubts, questions and challenges?

3 Critically consider the organizational development model of change. On what assumptions is it based? Would it work in all situations and in all cultures?

6 Theories of change: strategic management models

Introduction

Are markets autonomous or does the availability of a product and service influence demand? Where does the balance lie and/or does this balance shift? Was there a demand to fly between London and New York before the aeroplane was invented? Clearly people wished to travel between these places, and just as clearly the availability of the aeroplane led to them doing so by air, and the development of mass transport by air had an impact on patterns of travel, leisure and so on. This leads to a resource-based view of strategy as being of importance. From this point of view resources and capabilities drive strategic change.

Strategic management: the resource-based view

The resource-based view of strategy derives from the observation that business success cannot be explained wholly by market factors. If this were possible then in the long run all companies operating in a given industry or sector would tend to converge in terms of profit performance. This is clearly not the case. Why? Answering this question does not preclude the need to be concerned about sources of sustainable competitive advantage or to identify customer needs. Rather it requires us to look at how each company goes about doing so. In effect it is based on the notion that the way a company is configured to do so will vary according to a range of circumstances including its history.

Lynch (2000) identifies the six main elements which appear worthy of examination when seeking to look at how companies may variously be positioned:

1 Prior to acquired resources.

2 Innovative capability.

3 Competitiveness.

4 Substitutability.

5 Appropriability.

6 Imitability.

Following Kay (1993) we can note that the above list, while of use, begs a further question. This relates to the extent to which a company has *distinctive capability* which relates to its *architecture*, *reputation* and to *innovation*, and these ideas also relate to the widely adopted idea of *core competence* (Hamel and Prahalad, 1994). These are delivery technologies and capabilities which allow a firm to provide benefits to customers.

Clearly this view makes good sense. How can we understand the success of the Walt Disney Company without recognizing that much of it relies on the way it manages its assets, tangible and intangible; the film library, the brand name, the Disney Channel and so on. Using its in-house film-making capabilities, it produced major box office hits such as *Beauty and the Beast* and *Aladdin*, which it exploits vigorously. At least in part this success arises out of strategies designed to exploit existing resource bases.

This is particularly relevant to this book for two reasons. First, the focus on exploiting resources drives forward the importance of value added as a strategic management concept – and the linked concept of synergy. Second, as we shall see, I will be seeking to show that much of the success in change management situations is derived from leverage and connectivity. Where changes seek to leverage existing resources and capabilities and where there is a higher degree of connectivity between existing resources and processes – and these are put in place to manage change – there is a higher likelihood of success in strategic change.

These ideas are depicted in Figure 6.1 which seeks to map out some initial ideas linking strategic management and change management. Thus if strategic management comprises means of identifying vision, strategy, business model and strategic implementation, change management deals with behaviour, structures and configurations, delivery and so on. Both are conceptually underpinned by ideas such as creativity, adaptability and innovation; albeit the nexus of strategic management is to look at environmental uncertainty regarding markets, competitors, technology and the like, while the nexus of change management is in the field of measurement, efficiency and effectiveness.

Strategic management thinking seeks to help us decide what we should do; change management thinking starts by taking such decisions as inputs and looks at how we can put them into effect. But, and this is crucial, the two 'fields interconnect'. We need to ensure we can learn from our attempts to put new strategies into effect. The experience of doing so on the ground, with customers, suppliers and employees, needs to be fed back into the strategy process. Thus success requires a high degree of connectivity between strategic thinking and change architecture.

But effective change management is hard. The more you can base the change architecture, processes and thinking on existing resources and capabilities, the more you will build in stakeholder buy-in, and the more likely you are to be successful. Thus it is that strategies, no matter how innovative, should seek to leverage existing resources, thinking capabilities and so on. We shall see that leverage and *connectivity* are two important dimensions for success in change management.

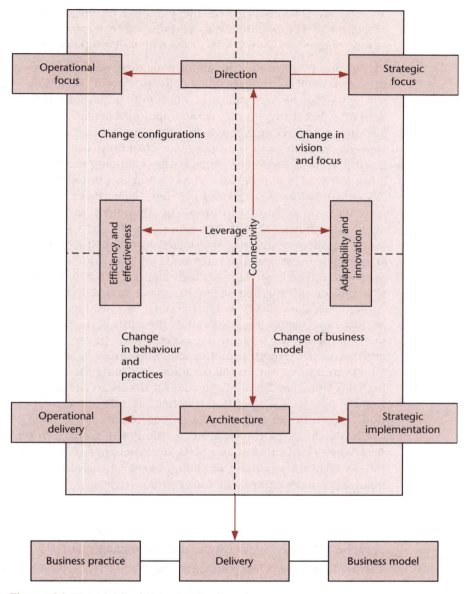

Figure 6.1 The strategic change map

The level of ambition

Let us turn then to the question of ambition. Why is this important? Markides (2000) puts it rather well:

> There is no question that (corporate) success stems from the exploitation of a unique strategic position. Unfortunately, no position can remain unique or

attractive forever. The firm lucky enough to be in one will be imitated by aggressive competitors, and, perhaps more important, supplanted by even more aggressive competitors, those which develop new positions in the market.

By position he means clarity about which customers are served with what products and services through what delivery system (including channels, product configurations, service offerings, etc.). But the important words are *unique* and *aggressive*. What this implies is the impulse to be *different* as a means of securing advantage. This requires tough choices. Thus it is that success demands ambition. Indeed companies which become successful do so not by trying to beat the dominant players at their own game, but by changing the rules of the game, by creating innovative approaches. Thus Canon in photocopiers, Dell in computers, CNN in broadcasting, easyJet in airlines, First Direct in banking, Direct Line in insurance, Komatsu in earth-moving equipment and Starbucks in coffee have achieved prominence in their business.

But daring to be different is to take risk because it requires you to pose and then answer new questions. You must both improve your ability to offer your current proposition (not least via re-engineering, restructuring and so on) as well as identify new or unexploited segments, needs and delivery methods. Interestingly enough Markides (2000) is clear about how you identify a distinctive strategic position – it is about breaking out of the existing mental model, about creating a questioning culture, organizing diverse inputs in the strategic planning process, and it requires experimentation and learning. It is also about working on the 'blocks to innovation' in the organization. Being successful requires implementing with sufficient flexibility to adapt if things go wrong. Implicitly this suggests that the new strategic position is either too little or too great in the level of ambition. So how do we judge this level of ambition?

Clearly this is partly a matter of risk. But it is also partly a question of how ready the organization is as a platform for change. We deal with this in a structured way in the readiness for change checklist and also via the idea of an implementation index comprising four components:

1 Is there a critical mass of support from key stakeholders?
2 Is there a sufficient problem orientation within the change process?
3 Is there sufficiently robust programme management?
4 Is there sufficient focus on clear goals?

In effect we propose that our ability to conceive of and deliver ambitious change programmes is about the ability of the change architecture we deploy to deliver various forms of infrastructure quickly enough. Is the stress experienced within radical change programmes largely a reaction to the fact of change (i.e. resistance to change) or at least partly a consequence of inadequate change architectures? These may not be delivering needed infrastructure quickly enough given the rate of change, which may be largely externally imposed (via competitive pressure or government action in the public sector). There we seek not to take this issue as a given.

Moss Kanter (2001) provides some clues in discussing 'inspiring visions'. In her opinion, inspiring visions include a dream of what our world will look like when we achieve our goal, but she also believes that success will follow only where the passion of 'the change leaders' matches their aspiration as judged by how strongly they feel about that aspiration, how convinced they are of its accomplishment, how excited they are, what sacrifices they are prepared to make and so on. But the advocate might be wrong. So another dimension is: can the advocate enlist backers and supporters, and, ultimately, the sanity check of gaining support from key stakeholders?

But these remain indicators of acceptability as much as of ambition; that is at least likely to be the case. Can we more unambiguously address the question of how to estimate the level of ambition in any set of proposals for strategic change? Carnall (2004) presents a readiness for change index and McGrath and MacMillan (2000) set out profiles for technical uncertainty, competitive insulation (basically means of defending your competitive advantage expected in a new venture) and the assumption-to-knowledge ratio (in essence the proportion of the knowledge needed for a new venture based on assumption rather than hard evidence). Clearly therefore we have thought it right to include the idea of the level of ambition involved in any set of changes (effectively the extent to which changes are radical as opposed to incremental) in our readiness for change index. What issues need to be considered in doing so? Before looking at that we need first to think about *unintended consequences*.

I recall reading a short piece in *The Times*. It went as follows:

> **Schools in London implementing government healthy eating policies have limited the number of days on which French fries are served at lunch to twice per week. The police are horrified at a dramatic increase in truancy rates.**

And how are these statements connected? The truancy was largely post lunch. Seeing no French fries on the menu, the attractions of McDonald's were just too good, and once they left the school grounds . . .

We need to add a further idea, that of *vicious circles*. Masuch (1983) bases his analysis on the simple thought that actions lead to consequences, not always intended, still less always desirable. Using ideas from cybernetics and control theory he notes that from the consequences of action comes feedback. Positive feedback tends to amplify any consequence in future. Thus if a manager chooses to ignore the poor performance of a subordinate, this will both undermine future performance of the subordinate and have a negative impact on colleagues (e.g. they may need to work harder in consequence and may become demotivated in consequence).

Radical or transformational change

Jack Welch, former head of General Electric, is the business leader most frequently identified with ambitious, transformational strategy. Tichy and Sherman (1995):

> **The self-confidence that had characterized the company's managers began to erode. Left to pursue its course for another decade or so, this apparently healthy company might have been another Chrysler. Instead of waiting for trouble, the CEO pushed for radical change . . .**

And, quoting Welch directly:

> **Changing the culture starts with an attitude. I hope you won't think I'm being melodramatic if I say that the institution ought to stretch itself, ought to reach to the point where it almost becomes unglued.**

Adopting the Schumpeterian notion of 'creative destruction', breakthrough change demands new rules, quantum leaps and a radical approach to the balance between control and autonomy – emphasizing relative autonomy within a 'business engine' which demands performance.

The well-known overarching rule Welch adopted sets the tone. Be number 1 or number 2 player in your sector or a business would not remain a part of GE. The revenues and margins which flow from having either the number 1 or number 2 position in market share is sufficient for strategic choice. But the challenge that this demand for market leadership poses is clear enough. The detail behind this is interesting.

Behind the market leadership rule lay objectives:

1 Well above-average real returns on investments.

2 Distinct competitive advantage.

3 Leverage from strengths.

So analysis underpinned the strategy. But one example illustrates the ambition.

'Work-out' was a programme of employee involvement and continuous improvement introduced in the late 1980s but the ambition lay in the scale of this activity. Tichy and Sherman (1995) again:

> **By mid-1992, over 200,000 GEers – well over two-thirds of the workforce – had experienced work-out. On any given day, perhaps 20,000 are participating in a related program.**

Instead of pursuing pragmatic goals the company focused on operations, process and continuous improvement, customer satisfaction and partnerships. As these authors put it, refocus from hardware to software; from seeing people and organizational development as needing to move from developing awareness of new possibilities via the development of new skills toward the development of new 'rules of the game', new ways of thinking about the business model. The interventions become emergent (from within) rather than applied (to the organization (by outsiders)). They become intensive, high risk and time consuming. They move from working only on the cognitive level to working not simply on behaviour (a naïve misunderstanding) but on new modes of discourse, new ways of thinking about the business model. If a domestic appliances business can cut the cycle time between receipt of order to delivery by 75 per cent, guaranteeing *next day* delivery to the customer, then new ways of thinking are evident. But GE went on to build on the success of 'work-out', developing a change management programme so that all GE middle managers would become 'change agents'. The one became a platform for a fundamental development focused on accelerating change.

However, we still are not clear about how to assess the degree of ambition. Is there not a risk of over-ambition? Clearly executives sometimes develop overly ambitious market plans. Just as clearly we may seek to handle too much change in any given situation. And yet, as we have seen, you can mobilize large-scale endeavour in pursuit of continuous improvement if you get the balance of control and autonomy right. Part of the answer may be revealed in Hampden-Turner (1996).

He argues that value creation involves a configuration of values. Products have two sorts of values, unit value or market price and integral value, the value of the product to other products present or future. Here we see the GE idea of leverage. Put another way, any change idea which is *scaleable* cannot be overly ambitious – probably an overstatement but the essential point is that scaleable changes create an *accelerator* effect, thus cascading enhanced value around the organization. Thus, again, the GE work-out was scaleable in its own right but it, in turn, became a platform to accelerate change in the subsequent change management programme. And the accelerator effect includes learning, explicitly in the GE case and elsewhere (see below).

Rieley (2001) writes about these issues using cybernetic theory as his source of language and thinking. But the essence of his argument is equivalent to that of Argyris' view of simple versus double-loop thinking. Faced by evidence of a gap between desired and actual effectiveness, organizations too often seek to deal with symptom rather than underlying cause and thereby often make matters worse. He calls this 'gaming the system'. Thus a company faced by high procurement costs incentivizes purchasing staff to reduce costs. This leads to pressure on suppliers, which in turn leads to quality and delivery issues, which mean that total cost is increased, not reduced.

Of course this is the very problem which management techniques such as the balanced scorecard are intended to reveal (see Chapter 7) but in essence Rieley argues that managers can be locked into a 'mind-set' which equates reorganizing to deal with immediate symptoms as the way forward. Repeated reorganization increases complexity and reduces alignment. This lack of alignment reduces effectiveness and sustainability. More importantly:

> **The addiction to change will decrease the ability to see and understand the long-term vision for the organization.**

And this is rather like Miller's concept of the Icarus Paradox. Built into earlier success can be an unwillingness to focus on new causes of lack of current success, leading to a tendency to incremental rather than fundamental change. He proposes the use of a vision deployment matrix as an analytical tool to help people focus on the impact of change. This requires managers in an organization to articulate vision, mental models (beliefs and assumptions aligned to the vision), systemic structures (consistent with the mental models and vision), patterns (of behaviour) and events (indicative of the vision having been achieved) alongside definitions of current reality, desired reality, gaps, action steps and measures of progress. As a pro forma this may well be helpful. But for us the key point is that openness and alignment are argued as means toward fundamental change – and therefore ambitious change?

McGrath and MacMillan (2000) write about the need for an 'entrepreneurial mindset' for dealing with uncertainty. For them:

> **Uncertainty was seen as essential to the capture of profits from creating new combinations of productive resources, because profit came from perceiving an opportunity not obvious to others and then investing to capitalise on it.**

They go on to observe that this generally involves the Schumpeterian idea of 'creative destruction' as new business models replace old ones. The strategists' task, they claim, was that of 'melding the best of what the older models have to tell us with the ability to rapidly sense, act and mobilize, even under highly uncertain conditions'.

Any methodology for doing so will clearly help us with analysing the degree of ambition inherent in a given strategic change programme. What tools do they propose?

1 They identify 'deftness in the "project" team' as a key indicator for success – looking at the level of interpersonal confidence, confidence of the team in the capability of others, information flows (i.e. the extent to which people have the information they need, when they need it) and the quality of feedback.

2 Emerging competence – in terms of budgets, deadlines, costs, standards, service objectives, client satisfaction, etc.

3 The potential for 'distinctive value' being delivered by the project.

4 The potential for 'distinctive operational efficiency' being delivered.

5 Reworking their terminology we would insert leverage – the extent to which the 'project' will enable leverage of existing resources or capabilities.

6 Emergence of durable competitive advantage (a combination of two of their indices).

7 While they do not present such an index, in effect they argue for, and therefore I include, the disproportionate allocation of resources and/or talent.

Clearly the last point is a dilemma but, just as clearly, the more ambitious the 'project' the more you could justify the disproportionate allocation of resource and talent. Some of the above (in particular 3, 4, 5 and 6) appear strongly influenced by the thinking underpinning GE's market leadership rule, and these authors tell us that one of them spent four years working with the GE work-out programme.

Martin (1995) distinguishes between processes of continuous improvement (such as *kaizen* or total quality management (TQM)) and what he variously calls value stream reinvention or 'enterprise engineering'. He argues that the latter strives for 10 times, not 10 per cent, improvement. As one example, he refers to a bank which had taken 17 days to process a mortgage request which it reduced to two days while it moved from handling 33,000 to 200,000 loan requests each year – and reduced error rates. But there are many examples of how technology application combined with other changes has led to 'breakthrough changes' in organizations as diverse as Ford, GE, Canon, Wal-Mart, CitiCorp, IBM, DuPont and many others.

Ultimately, Martin concludes that breakthrough change can best be achieved where organizations adopt the concept of the 'learning laboratory'. He does not really define this formally but the essence of his concept is that of an enterprise in which there is 'total integration' of four knowledge sets:

1 Knowledge from TQM, *kaizen* and other problem-solving activities.

2 Knowledge from pilots, research, experiments and innovation.

3 Integrated external knowledge.

4 Integrated internal knowledge.

But he also argues that radical change can be achieved by a more effective understanding of economic activities as whole systems. He argues that organizations within a supply chain are within a complex web of activities and often consequences within such webs are counterintuitive. Take the following example I heard from the chief executive officer of a global logistics business. He was managing a port for his business at which they landed goods from a ship from the USA daily. The cost of doing so each day was £1 million. He noted that the 'dwell time' (of the landed goods remaining in port) was five days. By focusing on dwell time he was able to reduce the frequency of shipping to once every two days, thus making substantial savings. When he first proposed the idea there was major opposition on the grounds that this reduced customer service. By reducing 'dwell time' he enhanced customer service directly and was able to invest some of the savings in customer service enhancement.

Arguably, what we are discussing is the ability to recognize and harness discontinuities externally and internally. Gilbert and Strebel (1989) refer to the idea of 'outpacing', which they define as 'the explicit capability of a company to gain product leadership and cost leadership simultaneously'. In effect they argue that those seeking radical change cannot afford to adopt traditional one-paced strategies. Success in radical changes comes to those who can integrate approaches which traditionally have been seen as incompatible. This is likely to result in a change which outpaces competitors – changing the 'rules of the game' in the industry or sector. Their observation of 100 companies identified common capabilities for successful organizations:

- the ability to innovate;
- the ability to configure and deliver a competitive offering;
- the ability to do so at a competitive price;
- the ability to perform these moves simultaneously.

They illustrate this with the case of Nintendo. Through the ability to develop and deliver hand-held electronic games, Nintendo became the largest toy manufacturer globally in 1988, having not been in the top 10 in 1983. They explain this in terms of the ability to simultaneously develop hand-held games – attractive to young people thanks to high-quality images – to drive down costs via supply arrangements and to price competitively. Similar conclusions might also be offered to explain the success of Benetton and Ikea!

The vital argument here is that to be successful radical change demands balance, integration and simultaneous actions. Ansoff and McDonnell (1990) contrast American and Japanese models of decision-making, noting that Japanese managers operate parallel activities, i.e. they begin to launch implementation activities before decisions are finalized. At that time American managers would not do so, thus putting more pressure on the decision process, often leading to less commitment to the decision and less effective implementation. This resonates with the conclusions of Clark (1995). For him, organizations where knowledge is a premium, which operate in uncertain and complex environments, cannot be managed by planning and command and control. Rather like Rubinstein and Furstenberg (1999) they see too much planning as a real weakness. For Clark the answer is 'simultaneous, cheap explorations of multiple options' and trying not to try too hard – evolve options ground-up rather than impose them via grand strategy. For Rubinstein and Furstenberg, more effort devoted to problem-finding leads to less effort problem-solving later on, and more changes earlier mean fewer changes later on in a development cycle. Again these ideas appear to overlap, each with the other. But perhaps the key difference to note is the Gilbert and Strebel focus on simultaneous change in the various competence areas relevant to a business.

All of this leads one to think of time-based competition and concurrent engineering. This of course was the very stuff of a wide-ranging critique of Western manufacturing businesses during the final 20 years or so of the last millennium; see, for example, Clark and Fujimoto (1991) and note the themes they conclude as important for all sectors of the economy:

1 The need to achieve superior performance in product development in terms of time, productivity and quality:
   ■ lead times a driver;
   ■ productivity a key differentiator;
   ■ total product quality and integrity – i.e. in terms of the whole system on which it sits and over its whole life.

2 Integration in the development process in terms of:
   ■ communication;
   ■ organization;
   ■ multi-disciplinary working.

3 Integrating the customer and the product:
   ■ credible product management;
   ■ customer access and orientation;
   ■ leadership by concept.

4 Manufacturing for design, i.e. world-class delivering performance.

What is this, but the out-pacing referred to above with the word integration internally and externally the key?

But can you take this too far? Can you seek to move too fast, too radically? Are there circumstances in which you need to spend more time in planning, designing and analysing before you act? Handfield (1995) raises this question in what he refers to as 'the dark side of concurrent engineering'. We might widen that to question whether some organization changes require incremental rather than breakthrough change. For Handfield the key issue relates to the technology. If it is new technology, he argues that an incremental approach is superior. Indeed, he also suggests that his evidence points to breakthrough methodologies more often being attempted where the product development involves an incremental change with an existing technology, i.e. where the technology is well defined.

But he goes on to imply that increasingly it is possible to use simulation, piloting and prototyping methods which allow for breakthrough approaches even where the technology is novel. We see this, for example, in the BBC case study (see Chapter 14). Whatever else may be said of it, 'Producer Choice' was a new paradigm for the BBC.

For what it's worth, this seems helpful but we should beware seeking to be too precise. Overall it seems possible to argue that a balanced approach may be more likely to deliver significant changes, which in turn deliver competitive advantage by 'changing the rules of the game'. This implies integration as a key determinant of success in breakthrough change. That, in turn, implies a degree of concurrent engineering in what we call 'the change architecture' – see Chapter 14. However, that does not always mean radical change in any particular field. In principle the notion of integrated change could be taken to be the pursuit of advantage by the simultaneous adoption of incremental changes to product, organization quality, service, etc. However, within that any particular element may be subject to break-through change, made easier if the change architecture allows for prototyping, simulations and so on and also if the technology and other capabilities needed for that breakthrough are readily available.

This is not very different from the ideas D'Aveni (1994) offers for the hyper-competitive firm which requires multiple moves to escalate the cost/challenge to imitators. But crucially he argues that in a more volatile environment it is crucial to seize the competitive high ground in a series of small steps – small steps, mul-tiple moves, simultaneous change, integration. The conceptual territory exam-ined clearly overlaps.

Conclusion

This chapter dealt with breakthrough or radical change by looking at the overlap between strategic management thinkers, in particular those who follow the resource-based view of strategy and the field of change management. This enabled us to offer two important dimensions for successful change programmes, connec-tivity and leverage.

We examined what we mean by radical or ambitious change programme and identified various characteristics of radical change. Clearly mental models, new rules of the game and the implementation index are important here. But per-haps also the GE market leadership rule provides a helpful guide to those seek-ing to go for radical change alongside ideas such as scaleability, the accelerator effect and the notions of deftness in project teams, distinctive value and effi-ciency and the disproportionate allocation of resources. These, to some extent, may be necessary features for success in radical change rather than simply a means of judging the degree of ambition, but they do at least give us some ideas for judging and working with the level of ambition in any given change programme.

We looked at the idea of integration as a component of successful break through or radical change, which led us to note that a key component may be the ability to adopt incremental or radical changes in each element of a business. Success goes to those who can create advantage not least by 'raising their own game' and disrupt-ing their opponents by doing so. Integration in radical change becomes the ability to put these simultaneous changes together. Thus the question about ambition and change becomes quite complex. It is not an absolute – in effect we refer to ambition as compared to our competitors.

Also, we dealt with the extent to which intended changes are based on the following:

1 Leverage of existing resources and other platforms.
2 A high degree of connectivity between the strategic thinking driving a change programme and the change architecture deployed to achieve it.
3 Scaleability.
4 Integration of simultaneous conceived and delivered changes.

EXERCISES

1 Review changes of which you have knowledge. How ambitious were they?

2 Are there any obvious differences in the way you would go about implementing radical as compared to incremental changes?

Part III

THEMES AND ISSUES IN ORGANIZATION CHANGE

7 Organizations in the twenty-first century: the value-added organization

8 Sustaining organizational effectiveness

9 Leadership in practice

10 The learning organization

11 Strategies for change

7 Organizations in the twenty-first century: the value-added organization

Introduction

In this chapter I seek to present a set of practical tools to assist you in rethinking your own organization along the lines set out in Chapter 3. Throughout I combine some explanatory text with a sequence of exercises and instructions. It is intended to help you to think through and apply the ideas set out in the book. You may wish to return to this chapter as you work through the book. The workbook has been designed on the assumption that you are seriously engaged in a process of organizing around the flow of value to customers and intend to adopt 'cluster' structures. However, the techniques can be applied even if you do not propose to apply those specific ideas.

The global business environment is changing faster than ever. We are living in an era where businesses constantly need to reshape their ideas merely to survive. But to achieve sustained success it is not sufficient merely to manage existing operations better: businesses need to do things radically differently to secure an advantage over their competitors. Thus, in the future, we shall need to focus not on re-engineering processes but on re-engineering markets, not on restructuring the organization but on transforming it.

If you recognize one of more of the following pressures increasingly impacting on your organization, then the need for radical transformation could be just around the corner:

- The transition from growth to maturity in developed economies, leading to overcapacity, more competition and fewer larger players.
- The need to compete against global leaders, even in once secure local markets.
- The challenge of managing a shift from a wide competence/local market focus to a narrow competence/international market focus.
- The entry of small, aggressive competitors into niche segments, using these as a springboard to challenge the leaders.
- The shift from integration (ownership or control of all elements of the value chain) to specialization (leveraging capability in one key element of the value chain).

- The shift in power or added value from one player to another in the value chain (from manufacturers to distributors or suppliers, or vice versa).
- The need to cope with and exploit the increasing speed of business processes, in particular time to market for innovative new products and services.

These are critical issues for competitive organizations. Business transformation is a philosophy which challenges established practices and boundaries in a fundamental way. It involves challenging 'the rules of the game'.

Changing the rules of the game

'We've restructured, we've delayered, we've got close to our customers, we've achieved zero fault manufacturing and service capability. Now what do we do for an encore?' Questions like this indicate that 'business as usual plus' is no longer an adequate means of achieving sustained competitive success. In future, this will go increasingly to organizations which are able to achieve radical change either internally or externally, or, more probably, both. *This is the central idea of the business transformation philosophy.* This approach to competitive strategy is based on five key propositions:

1 Discontinuity in the market is more likely to result from *radical* rather than *incremental* change, and this is likely to be driven as much by companies themselves as by social and economic factors.

2 Coping with strategic change needs to move from an emphasis on forecasting to creating an organization which can *respond to change fast.*

3 Approaches to gaining and sustaining competitive advantage need to shift from *erecting barriers* (vertical integration, proprietary technology, piling up fixed costs to create scale, etc.) to *overcoming* or *ignoring barriers* (through outsourcing, building strategic alliances and the aggressive elimination of fixed costs).

4 The basis of strategic thinking, therefore, needs to shift from a current perspective of market attractiveness and competitive capability to *changing the rules of the game,* thus destabilizing entrenched players.

5 The role of leadership in this context is to affirm that '*it's achievable*' (provider of a business vision), rather than '*it's impossible*' (controller/naysayer).

By changing the rules of the game, a business may be able to wrong-foot competitors to such an extent that they may never recover; this can be achieved by driving radical changes internally or externally. Thus the competitive breakthroughs of the future are likely to go to businesses which can transform either their market or their organization, or both. This will involve radical rather than incremental change and needs vision and leadership to bring it about. But before business transformation can realistically be contemplated, a sound strategic basis must be formulated on which subsequent actions can be built. Strategic thinking must be the foundation of any intention or attempt to change the rules of the game, and the programme will commence with a searching review of this essential management skill.

Techniques for a value-added organization

These are as follows:

- Assessing the value added.
- Process redesign – mapping the value flow to enhance value added.
- The balanced scorecard.
- Activity-based costing and customer satisfaction analysis.
- The 360° appraisal.
- Competence models.

Figure 7.1 provides an overall structure for this activity. In essence any organization represents a flow of value-adding activities. We can seek to assess the value added

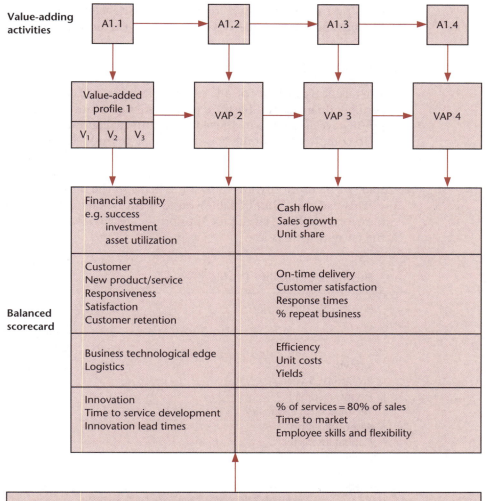

Figure 7.1 Business performance metric

of each activity (value-added profile), build a balanced scorecard and assess overall business performance. Each represents a successively higher level of analysis.

The workbook is designed to focus on the application of the first four steps of stage A1 in the organization design process. The combination of these techniques is shown in Figure 7.1.

The main *stages* in the organization design process are:

A Assess the strengths, weaknesses and development priorities of the business (A1: business performance metric) and the value added from the existing business (A2: value-added metric).

B Assess the process design by identifying the value-adding activities in the business, identifying cost drivers and seeking new business process configurations both to manage cost effectively and to enhance the performance and value-added metrics.

C Using the business performance metric development priorities as a starting point, develop a balanced scorecard for the unit, business, etc. (see below).

■ Stage A1: Business capability profile

The business capability profile below seeks to assess a company's managerial, competitive, financial and business process strengths and weaknesses. The completed profile reveals 'gaps' which need to be corrected and strengths on which to build.

To complete the profile you should first go through each item scoring it 1 to 7 for the current situation (actual). Thus, is your company growth rate currently low–high, scored 1–7? Having completed that you should then identify no more than 24 high-priority items from the items in the profile.

This exercise should enable you to identify strengths, weaknesses and development priorities. Development priorities are those where the priority is high but the current score is low.

Business Capability Profile

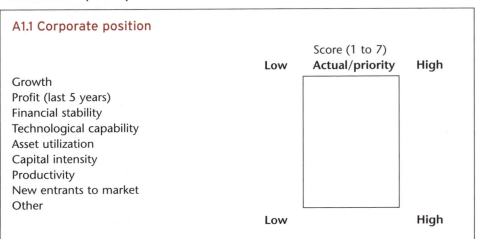

110

A1.2 Organizational factors

Score (1 to 7)

Low	**Actual/priority**	High

Integration across the business
Brand image
Flexibility
Performance focus
Ability to attract and retain
Creative people
Ability to change
Investment in new product development
Access to information
Team-based problem-solving
Other

Low   **High**

A1.3 Competitive position

Score (1 to 7)

Low	**Actual/priority**	High

Market share
Product quality
Product differentiation
Product life cycle
Selling/distribution costs
Time to market
'Tender' success (bid 'hit rate')
Customer loyalty
Capacity utilization in the industry
Technological capability
Other

Low   **High**

A1.4 Financial strength

Score (1 to 7)

Low	**Actual/priority**	High

ROI
Liquidity
Availability of capital
Stability of costs
Order book
Cash flow
Ease of exit
Risk in industry
Other

Low   **High**

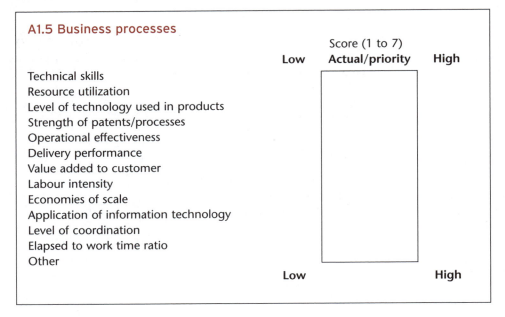

A1.5 Business processes

	Score (1 to 7)	
	Low Actual/priority High	

Technical skills
Resource utilization
Level of technology used in products
Strength of patents/processes
Operational effectiveness
Delivery performance
Value added to customer
Labour intensity
Economies of scale
Application of information technology
Level of coordination
Elapsed to work time ratio
Other

Low   High

■ Stage A2: Value-added metric

If the goal of your company is to create value for all stakeholders, this metric, presented below, can help you assess how well prepared it is to achieve that goal.

Value-added metric

1 Does the company seek to solve problems so that all stakeholders benefit (customers, employees, shareholders, the local community) or does it consistently favour one or more stakeholder groups?

Focused on one stakeholder	Often makes trade-offs between two stakeholder groups	Seeks mutual benefits
1 2 3	4 5 6 7	8 9 10

2 Is there an integrated performance measurement framework which links individual level to corporate level performance covering employee, customer and shareholder issues and concerns?

No framework	Fragmented framework	Integrated framework
1 2 3	4 5 6 7	8 9 10

3 Do we have a good understanding of the value drivers of our business?

No clear understanding	We focus on everything	We focus on the key value drivers
1 2 3	4 5 6 7	8 9 10

4 Does the company approach market and employee performance measurement as rigorously as financial measurement?

Financial measures only	Some of each, but biased to one area	Balanced
1 2 3	4 5 6 7	8 9 10

5 Do we make decisions using a rational approach based on 'the figures' or do we seek to combine factual analysis and intuition in our judgement?

No analysis at all	Rational analysis	Combine 'facts' with intuition
1 2 3	4 5 6 7	8 9 10

6 Is reward based on tenure or value?

'Equitable' tenure-based rewards	Performance pay	Rewards linked to creation of value
1 2 3	4 5 6 7	8 9 10

7 Is the value created by all parts of the company (from the CEO down) clearly defined and understood?

Not defined	Defined only within store operations	Defined throughout the business
1 2 3	4 5 6 7	8 9 10

8 Does the information, work flow and reward infrastructure support flexible responses or do investigations and studies drive change in the business?

Nothing changes without a major study	Lots of data, poor insight	Flexibility
1 2 3	4 5 6 7	8 9 10

9 Is the organization of work designed around the needs of the customer?

Defined by the corporate hierarchy	Designed around teams	Designed around the customer
1 2 3	4 5 6 7	8 9 10

10 How does the company compare with others inside and outside the industry in value created for shareholders, customers and employees?

Below average	Average	Excellent value creator
1 2 3	4 5 6 7	8 9 10

■ Stage B: Process design – mapping the value flow

It is normal to define the value flow (or chain) of activities for customers, distinguishing primary and support activities. Once the value flow is identified you need to decide how to organize these activities, e.g. on functional, product–service or geographical bases and either 'command and control' or into value-added clusters.

1 Value-added design

1.1 Map value flows.

1.2 Identify important transactions with customers.

1.3 Assess level of input needed from other functions for each activity.

1.4 Estimate/assess customer perceptions of:
  – cost (high, medium, low; stable, changing)
  – importance (high, medium, low)
  – satisfaction (high, medium, low).

1.5 Estimate elapsed to work time ratio.

1.6 Assess whether to 'cluster': proceed to steps 2 and 3.

2 Estimate value-added problems of 'command and control' mode

2.1 Value flows across functions.

2.2 Narrowly defined tasks.

2.3 Multiple handovers (and queries).

2.4 No 'owner' for the customer.

2.5 High elapsed to work time ratios.

3 Value-added clusters

3.1 A cluster of end-to-end activities which create value for a customer.

3.2 End-to-end activities contain most or all tasks from start to delivery of outputs (note: but shared service clusters may need to be involved).

3.3 *Value* on customer-critical issues such as speed, cost, quality, service, delivery.

3.4 *Customer* – internal or external.

3.5 *Size* – no final answer but in professional businesses 30–40 people the norm.

4 Value-added contributions

Once steps B.1, B.2 and B.3 are complete we can define the value-added contribution each 'cluster' brings to the total business process. For example, a management team might deliver the following:

Strategy

■ decide and recommend new directions;

■ guide and drive strategy;

- develop plans in support of strategies;
- manage the asset portfolio.

Performance management

- monitor and appraise performance;
- manage external image and brand.

Resourcing

- allocate resources;
- agree service levels;
- acquire new technologies, capabilities and people.

A *primary cluster*, however, would seek to achieve a flexible, delayered and business-oriented approach delivering the following:

- customer satisfaction;
- competitive prices;
- team work;
- high-quality, integrated solutions;
- ability to learn and to change;
- provision of product/service with better functionality and value.

If the business operates internationally and for that *purpose is organized regionally into operating units, then there may be a need for business interface managers* who link the clusters to those operating units via 'service agreements' or contracts. These managers would deliver the following:

- act as account manager for the operating unit;
- ensure that the operating unit's needs are responded to in plans and programmes;
- agree contract variations within agreed authority limits;
- work with clusters to ensure 'deliverables';
- leverage common technology interests of operating units to ensure maximum benefits to company;
- leverage best practice;
- spend significant time in the operating units.

A *support cluster* such as an IT group might be tasked to deliver:

- computing infrastructure;
- data management and QA;
- IT integration projects;
- software integration platforms.

The important point is to identify the necessary organizational components *including* clusters *and* to identify how each contributes value added to its customers (internal or external). This facilitates the development of balanced scorecards.

■ Stage C: The 'balanced scorecard'

This is a technique to measure business unit performance which can also be used at departmental or 'cluster' level developed by Kaplan and Norton (1996). The scorecard uses various perspectives to give a balanced picture of current performance and the drivers of future performance. Typically the four perspectives are financial, customer, business processes and innovation. Many argue that managers cannot operate with multiple measures and therefore argue priority for aggregate financial measures (such as operating income, return on investments, economic value added). These are widely used and provide a basis for unambiguous and objective goals.

The counter-view is that on the whole financial measures focus on past performance, saying little about the drivers of future performance. Moreover, experience with the technique shows that managers can make effective use of the balanced scorecard as a performance management and improvement tool so long as each is limited to around 20 measures. In practice the alternative is to have financial measures plus a bewildering variety of other measures, often not understood, not reported consistently and not widely or effectively disseminated.

In addition, in a 'value-added' organization the balanced scorecard is a means of making the organization more transparent. It enables the organization to focus on how activities interconnect to provide customer service. It shows the contribution each makes to the total. It provides a better basis for cohesion and integration of activities. The balanced scorecard can be depicted as in Figure 7.2.

The measures selected within each perspective need to be based on a particular view about the business:

1 What do *customers* value?
   – response times
   – accuracy
   – implementable solutions
   – price.

2 *Business process*: at what do we need to excel?
   – order processing
   – delivery to customer
   – flexibility
   – integrated service packages.

3 *Innovation*: how can the organization improve?
   – transfer of best practice

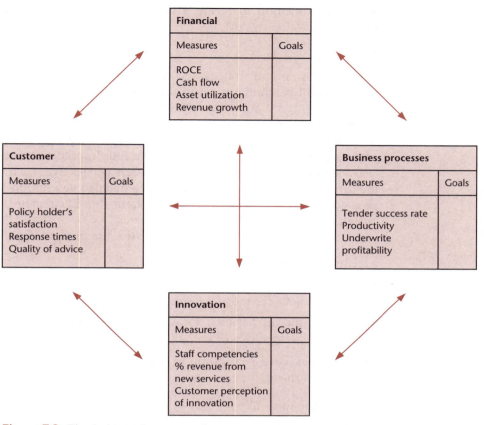

Figure 7.2 **The balanced scorecard**

 – training

 – development of new services

 – delivery of integrated solutions.

4 *Financial perspective*: is the organization creating value?

Typically, creating and implementing a balanced scorecard is part of an overall performance management system in which strategic vision links through unit level balanced scorecards to personal objectives and rewards, plans and budgets and performance review. Building a balanced scorecard is usually undertaken through a programme including senior management with the following objectives:

■ to guide the construction and measures for the scorecard;

■ to gain commitment;

■ to clarify the framework for the implementation and management processes needed to use the scorecard effectively.

A typical workshop to create a balanced scorecard comprises the following stages.

The workshop activity

Agree the vision and strategy and make any decisions necessary to define how resources will be configured into units, groups, clusters, etc., in pursuit of that vision.

Agree the four perspectives to be included and brainstorm possible measures. Discuss each on its merits and not on comparison with the others. Once all measures have been considered, select three to four 'candidates', voting if necessary.

Divide into four subgroups, one for each perspective. Each subgroup should identify three to four measures, provide a detailed description for each and propose goals for each (*Round 1*). The facilitator should circulate a summary of the output.

At the next meeting the subgroups review the measures/goals:

- refine the wording;
- identify the detail for the measure;
- identify sources of information and how to access it;
- identify linkages between measures within the perspective and with other scorecard perspectives (*Round 2*).

Arrange an executive workshop to sign off the balanced scorecards (*Round 3*) as part of the implementation plan.

Selecting the measures

Measures relevant to the activity are essential, but the following often appear:

- *Finance*: ROI, profit, revenue growth/mix, cost reduction/productivity.
- *Customer*: market share, customer acquisition, customer retention, customer satisfaction, customer profitability.
- *Innovation*: flexibility, percentage of sales from new products/services, time to market.
- *Business process*: resource utilization.

Creating an implementation plan

Define a detailed implementation plan including training, roll-out of measures and a further executive workshop to sign off the scorecards.

Conclusion

In this chapter I have presented various tools to help you think about the level of value added by your own organization or department. This is an important part of identifying what could be changed and for providing a coherent justification for proposals for change.

EXERCISES

1 Can you depict your own organization as horizontal management of value added?

2 To what extent does your company seek to develop its 'social capital'?

3 Assess your own unit, department, division or company using the business capability profile. What are its strengths and weaknesses?

8 Sustaining organizational effectiveness

Introduction

Change creates challenges for us all. It brings stress and anxiety as well as opportunities and the possibility for optimism. We have already seen that effective organizational structures are more conducive to change. It is easier to implement change in a more, rather than less, effective setting. Moreover, organizational culture and management style have an important effect by creating a climate supportive of change. In this chapter we turn to three related issues. First, we examine the blockages to effective change. These operate at individual, group and organizational levels. Second, we develop the notion that effective change demands learning. Moreover, effective learning through change requires specific situational conditions (to minimize or avoid the blockages) and a personal and managerial style appropriate to learning and encouraging others to learn. Finally, we examine some ideas on the characteristics of effective organizational structures and designs.

Blocks to problem solving and change

Systematic models of the change process abound. But the issue in planning change is about how to generate creative solutions to what are generally novel problems. We argue that, generally speaking, there is no shortage of ideas about how to reorganize, deal with problems, create new markets and so on. What is usually missing is the framework and support appropriate for encouraging the emergence of creative solutions. I will now deal with a range of 'blocks' to creative problem solving as a means of looking at practical ways of organizing and sustaining the process of planning change.

It is easy enough to say that management support is a key to innovation. We now take this a stage further to consider some of the blocks to problem solving in order that we can better understand how to manage this process. The ideas listed below are from Adams (1987).

■ Perceptual blocks

1 *Stereotyping*: we see what we expected to see. Over recent years we have become increasingly aware of stereotyping. Women only come to work for 'pin money' – therefore there is no point in reviewing jobs to see if they can be improved. This is an obvious example. There are many, many more.

2 *Difficulty in isolating the problems*: a friend of mine gave a classic example of this. He was a member of a team of consultant designers given the brief to design an apple-picking machine. All sorts of solutions were put forward. None seemed feasible – in general all the machines were too big and too unwieldy. It was a month before a team member said: 'Our problem is that we are focusing on the wrong problem – we should look at the design of the tree.' Eventually, a new strain of apple trees only a few feet high was created. The problems of designing the machine then disappeared. The height and spread of apple trees had been the essential difficulty, not the design of apple picking as such.

3 *Tendency to delimit the problem area too closely*: all too often we define problems very narrowly. In the CAC Consultants case study (see page 133) each group of partners defines the problem narrowly; thus neither faces the real problem – their own motivation.

4 *Inability to see the problems from various viewpoints*: increasingly we talk of 'trained incapacity'. As we train and develop professionals (doctors, lawyers, accountants, engineers) we run the risk that people see problems only in terms of their own discipline. Seeing problems from different viewpoints helps to conceptualize the problems. It also helps when we come to attract support for solutions.

5 *Saturation*: data may come in large measures, or in large measures only occasionally, or in the presence of distracting data. It can be difficult to distinguish the relevant information from all the available data.

6 *Failure to use all sensory inputs*: we need all the data we can get, but do we utilize everything that is available to us? Thus when trying to decide on a new organizational structure for a new venture we should try to find other organizations facing similar problems. How have they solved them?

■ Emotional blocks

1 *Fear of taking a risk*: the fear of making a mistake, to be seen to fail, is a common block. If managers 'punish' failure, then this fear is at least realistic. But often the worst that can happen is pretty minimal. Excessive importance is attached to the risk of failure.

2 *Incapacity to tolerate ambiguity*: the solution of a complex problem is a messy process. The data will be misleading, incomplete, full of opinions, values and so on. While creating solutions, plans, etc. requires that we eventually establish order, too early an attempt to do so may mean that we miss promising ideas.

3 *Preference for judging rather than generating ideas*: judging ideas too early can lead to early rejection. The onus of proof is all too easily placed on the person with

the idea. Yet if the idea is novel it may be ill thought out and may not present a good 'fit' with the hazy and incomplete data. Thus rejection is easy. We should recognize that finding reasons to say 'no' is easier than finding reasons to say 'yes' – particularly if we are poor risk takers who are intolerant of ambiguity!

4 *Inability to incubate*: an unwillingness to 'sleep on the problem' often because there seem to be pressures for solutions: 'We must have a new pricing policy because the sales department is pressing for one'. In planning the process of managing change we should plan enough time for ideas to incubate.

■ Cultural blocks

1 *Taboos*: issues which cannot be discussed and therefore cannot be faced are taboo. For example, at International Engineering (see page 142) it was impossible to question whether or not the admitted technical excellence of the company was relevant for its new markets.

2 *Focus rather than fantasy*: Adams forcefully makes the point that psychologists have concluded that children are more creative than adults. This might be explained by adults being more aware of practical constraints. However, as he says, 'another explanation, which I believe, is that our culture trains mental playfulness, fantasy and reflectiveness out of people by placing more stress on the value of channelled mental activities'. Worth thinking about!

3 *Problem solving is a serious business*: linked to item 2 above is the notion that humour has no place in problem solving. And yet humour is often based on the process of associating apparently unrelated ideas. Creativity is the same in that it often involves the association of unrelated ideas or structures. Adams argues, therefore, that humour is one essential ingredient for effective problem solving.

4 *Reason and intuition*: we often seem to believe that reason, logic and numbers are good and that feelings, intuition and pleasure are bad. Adams suggests that this is based on our (west European?) puritan heritage and our technology-based culture (which raises the question of how this point applies in cultures without a puritan heritage). This has been complicated by the tendency to assign these characteristics to sex roles, namely, that men are logical, physical, tough and pragmatic while women are sensitive, emotional and intuitive. Creativity demands a balance of these characteristics.

5 *Tradition and change*: traditions are hard to overcome, particularly when people do not reflect on their traditions and their present problems/dilemmas together. We need tradition – it is on our traditions that much of our personal commitment and motivation is based. We need to respect tradition and we also need to recognize the need for change. Adams distinguishes primary and secondary creativity: primary creativity generates the structures and concepts which allow the solution of a family of problems; secondary creativity deploys these structures and concepts to develop and improve particular solutions. He argues that primary creativity demands more intuition, humour, feeling and emotion; secondary creativity seems more likely to be associated with logic and reason – as the structures already established are deployed systematically to solve specific problems within a now well-understood field. Secondary

creativity involves applying rules; primary creativity requires that existing rules be ignored, so that new rules can be generated (precisely what Newton did!).

Environmental blocks

1 *Lack of support*: we have already seen that a non-supportive environment is not conducive to innovation, nor to creative problem solving. Change is often seen as threatening and new ideas are easily stopped by ignoring them, by laughing at them or by over-analysing them too early.

2 *Not accepting and incorporating criticism*: but those with good ideas can create blocks too, by not being willing to accept criticism. The ability to accept criticism builds an atmosphere of trust and support and leads to improvements in what will necessarily have been an imperfect idea.

3 *Bosses who know the answer*: many managers are successful because they have ideas and can push them through. But only if such a manager will listen to subordinates will he or she be able to utilize their creativity.

Cognitive blocks

1 *Using the incorrect language*: whether mathematical or professional (e.g. accounting, marketing, etc.) or visual. Using an inappropriate language can hinder creativity in problem solving.

2 *Inflexible use of strategies*: there are many strategies available. We often use them unconsciously, but not necessarily to best effect in problem solving, perhaps because of the various blocks we have already discussed.

3 *Lack of the correct information*: clearly a limiting factor. But again balance is needed. Information makes you an expert, which can mean that you think down the lines of that expertise – closing you off from creative solutions?

Working through the blocks

Or, to follow Adams, 'block busting'. Various techniques are available. Here we need to do no more than list one or two very briefly. More details can be found by referring to Adams' own account. Identifying them in the first place helps enormously. A questioning attitude can take us further. Various thinking aids can also be applied, including attribute listing, 'checklists' and list making. Being able to suspend judgement as an individual or in a group can enhance creativity. Another useful technique is 'synectics' (Gordon, 1961).

The following actions seem to encourage creativity in problem solving:

- Stay loose or fluid in your thinking until rigour is needed.
- Protect new ideas from criticism.
- Acknowledge good ideas, listen, show approval.
- Eliminate status or rank.
- Be optimistic.
- Support confusion and uncertainty.

- Value learning from mistakes.
- Focus on the good aspects of an idea.
- Share the risks.
- Suspend disbelief.
- Build on ideas.
- Do not evaluate too early.

The following actions seem to discourage creativity:

- Interrupt, criticize.
- Be competitive.
- Mock people.
- Be dominant.
- Disagree, argue, challenge.
- Be pessimistic.
- Point out flaws.
- Inattention, do not listen, use silence against people.
- React negatively.
- Insist on 'the facts'.
- Give no feedback, act in a non-committal fashion.
- Pull rank.
- Become angry.
- Be distant.

■ Limits to problem solving

Still more limits or 'blocks' can be listed. At the individual level people may engage in 'satisficing' or 'incrementalism', accepting satisfactory solutions and/or making only incremental or limited changes to previous policies. At the group level we have 'group think' and 'risky shift'. 'Group think' is characterized by complacency and lack of critical evaluation of ideas (Janis, 1972). 'Risky shift' is a condition observed in experimental groups, where groups seem likely to take more risky decisions than the individuals involved might have gone for (diffusion of responsibility perhaps) but still without critical examination. At the organizational level various typical limits can be identified. Some we have already seen. People seem to 'distance' themselves from problems. Where organizations are highly centralized, responsible managers may be 'out of touch'. There can exist an 'illusion of reliability' in existing techniques or people (the Greeks had a word for this, *hubris*, which means overbearing arrogance). Highly specialized organizations can lead to parochialism, the tendency to conceal dissent or disagreement and to problems of communication (Wilensky, 1967). Solutions to all these limits involve opening up the problem-solving process, being willing to change and allowing the 'block busters' to operate. Our assumption is that the ideas are there, among the people – the challenge is to encourage them, to help them find expression, then to evaluate realistically, to apply them and learn from our experience and then to change.

Thus a simple model drawn from the work of Argyris is as set out in Figure 8.1. In essence the various counterproductive norms focus decision-makers' attention on the simple issues, often the things we can measure quantitatively rather than the crucial issues – frequently the blockages to change and improvement. This reinforces a risk-averse culture leading to people 'covering up' mistakes etc. Can this be conducive to change? Not if you conclude that the model of planned change provided in Figure 8.2 has any relevance. This illustrates what some would call the 'virtuous circle' of change, i.e. successful experience of change reduces anxiety, lessens resistance and encourages measured risk taking and leads to more change. So far so good, but clearly we will need to examine how to avoid the one and encourage the other.

Janis (1989, pages 235–64) presents a range of ways in which these counterproductive dynamics can be avoided. His advice includes ways of maintaining scepticism about the 'obvious' solution as well as of limiting criticism of 'wild' suggestions. In particular he argues for a willingness to make 'temporary' arrangements with other groups in order to buy time (admittedly his focus, and therefore his examples, deal with national policy but one can readily see equivalents

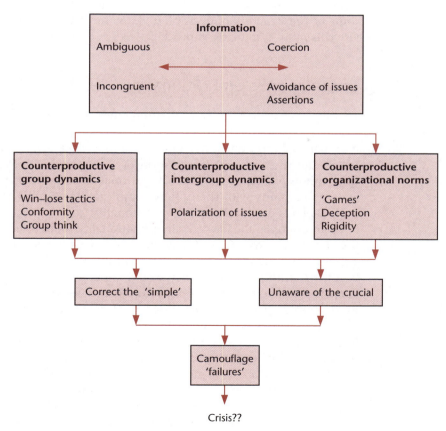

Figure 8.1 **Organized 'irrationality'**

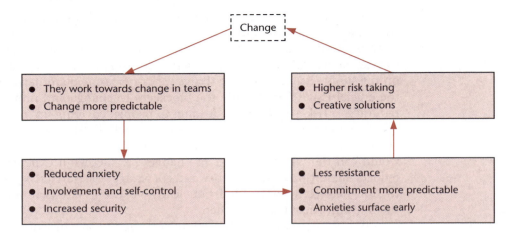

Figure 8.2 Planned change: effects on people

in the organizational area – for instance, in the context of mergers and acquisitions, where joint ventures are involved, in difficult technological change situations and so on). Basically the approach he favours is to take any and all measures likely to lead to a more systematic approach to planning, decision making and implementation. Some of his recommendations relate to leadership style and some to the structure of decision making, but all are designed to create or facilitate this more systematic approach.

Organizations and rationality

All the above must lead us to question whether what happens within an organization is rational. Moreover, do we believe that effective organizations are 'rational' organizations? Are organizations designed and managed on rational lines? Can the thorough application of a systematic approach to change planning and implementation lead to a 'rational', perhaps 'optimal', result? Not if we equate rationality with the notion of optima drawn from the scientific method. It all depends on our definition of rationality.

As an example, the idea of 'clinical' rationality is often seen as dominant within healthcare systems. The decisions of doctors govern the pattern of care provided and the use of resources. This does not mean that all doctors have the same views, beliefs or attitudes, or that they would argue for the same vision of healthcare. People are not automata, without autonomy or freedom of action. At the outset we must make clear that our definition of rationality owes nothing to the 'scientific method'. There is no simple dichotomy between rationality and irrationality, the former based on 'science', the latter on emotion, feelings and so on. On this view we suggest that when subject to changed circumstances in their environment (which might be a budget cut or the advent of a new 'bit' of medical technology) people will reflect on the courses and consequences of the change, developing responses and decisions based on reason. People use reason based on knowledge and experience. In turn these emerge through the processes of thought, emotion, action and decision making in the 'practical world'. We argue that there are various 'sources of rationality' which lead to men and women constructing different arguments about, and drawing different conclusions in respect of, the changes which affect them.

Any definition of rationality must allow for the doubts which beset us all, and for the uncertainties, vested interests and ignorance of the world in which we live. Weick (1979, page 87) summarizes the position succinctly, as follows:

> **rationality is best understood in the eye of the beholder. It is his aims and how consciously he sets out to accomplish them that constitute the clearest, most easily specified component of rationality.**

He goes on to argue that people in large organizations are unlikely to employ the same rationality; rather, 'organizations will have several different and contradictory rationalities'. Herein lies the reason why many of us find that discussion about the problems an organization faces (whether about the one in which we participate, or when we listen to others) is often confused and confusing.

The literature abounds with theories of decision making ('garbage-can model', March and Olsen (1976); 'satisficing', Simon (1957); and 'incrementalism', Lindblom (1959)) which reflect this problem (although we note that they are also attempts to deal with different 'problems', including the peculiar difficulties of choice under conditions of uncertainty).

Bryman (1983) suggests that there has been a 'retreat from rationality' as a consequence of attacks on the rational systems model of organization. He identifies two ways of arguing for some form of rational systems model of organization. The first, exemplified by Weber's writing on bureaucracy and by the classical school (see March and Simon, 1958), has been under attack for many years. In recent years a second wave has emerged: namely, the development of the 'contingency' approach. Proponents of both views see organizations as goal-seeking, functional systems: the first adopt a closed-system perspective; the latter adopt an open-system view (Scott, 1981) which has been subjected to critical scrutiny from at least four directions: the 'garbage-can' model, institutional, political and Marxist approaches. Bryman (1983) concludes that scholars in the fields of management theory and economics are now uneasy about their 'rationalist infrastructures'. Here he refers to a rationality placing particular emphasis on notions such as utility and profit maximization, taken from economics.

He notes that this is an extreme form of rationality and goes on to discuss 'soft' rationality, incorporating ideas such as Simon's notion of 'satisficing' and Watkin's (1970) discussion of 'imperfect rationality'. He concludes this discussion by noting the methodological and conceptual weaknesses of the alternative views of rationality, and of alternative models such as the political or Marxist approach. When he discusses one empirical study of the capital investment process, which found the economists' version of rationality to be of little empirical use (Bowers, 1970), he concludes that purposiveness had greater usefulness. Here lie reasons for hope, he seems to suggest.

Landes (1967, page 204) provides us with a clear definition, based on the idea of purposiveness, as follows:

> **Rationality may be defined as the adaption of means to ends. It is the antithesis of superstition and magic. For this history, the relevant ends are the production**

and acquisition of material wealth. It goes without saying that these are not man's highest ends; and that rationality is not confined to the economic sphere.

Rationality is a way of doing things: the application of the principles of rationalism to action, rationalism being defined as the doctrine that the universe of perception and experience can be understood in terms of thought or reason, as against emotion, intuition or extrasensory modes of apprehension.

We accept the means–end definition of rationality; however, we depart from Landes' equation of rationality and the doctrine of rationalism. We need to recognize the limitations of the individual. We cannot pretend that men and women do not use intuition as well as empiricism. Some may use one or the other to a lesser or greater extent – but not at all? We doubt that. We tend towards Weick's position on this point.

The notion that political models of organization represent an attack on rational models needs careful analysis. Close examination of alternative modes of decision making proposed by Pfeffer (1981) makes this point clear. He compares rational, bureaucratic, decision process/organized anarchy and political power models. For *rational* decision making the ideology is seen as 'efficiency and effectiveness'; for *political power* the ideology is 'struggle, conflict, winners and losers'. Decisions from the former flow from 'value maximizing choice', from the latter from the result of 'bargaining and interplay among interests', but this is hardly a satisfactory distinction. We must ask what it is that the 'interests' bargain over. Definitions of appropriate action, policies, means–ends sequences and strategies will form the calculus of any answer to this question. By saying that the political power model demands the analysis of interests we immediately adopt a rational model – at the level of the interests themselves. Thus this model differs from the rational model only in that the proponents of the rational model are seen to model choice in essentially unproblematical terms. But Bryman (1983) makes it entirely clear that only proponents of the 'hard' version of rationality could be accused of that. Thus the apparent difference collapses in all but the most extreme of juxtapositions. We conclude that the extreme or 'hard' definition has never had much application for those concerned with the management of organizations. (In parenthesis, it is worth noting the growing number of studies examining the work of F.W. Taylor which cast doubt on whether or not Taylor, for one, ever believed in such a straightforward view – see Rose (1975) and Merkle (1980).) However, by distinguishing 'hard' and 'soft' rationalities Bryman seems tacitly to admit that the latter is not properly 'rational'. Here he appears to be following Landes, equating rationality with rationalism. To do so is to adopt too limited a view of rationality. The concept of multiple rationalities does not imply a 'softer or weaker' view. Ill-understood it may be, but we believe it is possible to establish, empirically, rationalities in use.

If we accept that people attempt to make sense of the confusion of the world as they experience it and that they do so by employing a particular rationality, then to understand their attempts so to do we must understand the rationality in use. Moreover, if we are to understand the confusing talk we often hear when problems are under discussion we need to understand the different rationalities and the nature of the contradictions between them.

Finally, when examining a particular institution over a period of time we should be concerned to identify, and then understand, periods during which the dominating rationality, ordering decisions and action in the institution are changed. Such change would represent a watershed in the 'life' of the institution concerned. Here would be a significant period in which to study the institution and its relations to a wider society.

If all this is accepted how do we proceed? In essence we must search for the frames of reference which make intelligible the choices and decisions of people within a given institution. A particular 'rationality' comprises 'rules of action' that are deemed suitable for given circumstances. Thus our approaches require us to observe the choices that people make, and the reasons they give for making them over long periods of time, examining many of them in order to discern the 'rules of action' and 'frames of reference' in use.

Important consequences flow from the existence of alternative sources of rationality which people use to establish and maintain order as circumstances change. Each apparently rational strategy for 'getting things done', for maintaining order, for ensuring that employees work hard, are loyal and committed, obey instructions, and so on, has counter-rational consequences associated with it – that is to say, counter-rational viewed from the perspective of the particular rationality in use.

An example: organization and counter-rational behaviour

Argyris (1982) provides us with a good example of this situation. A group of senior university administrators attending an executive course were examining a case study on a particular college which included a set of recommendations for the future of that college, produced by a working group of senior academics and administrators from the college. The working group had been asked for 'concrete recommendations'. The course members were asked to evaluate these recommendations. Criticizing the recommendations, course members expressed the view that the recommendations were vague and cliché ridden, the typical output of a committee which had not been well briefed. Such an evaluation of working groups, working parties or committees is not uncommon. Argyris suggests that it was based on several assumptions about organization and management.

The first is that giving people specific goals will lead them to actions which are more relevant and specific (in this case produce more specific recommendations). The second is that goals will motivate people or, if not, will at least make it easier to confront them on the quality of their performance. Finally, it is assumed that effective control of performance requires objective monitoring of performance. Underlying these assumptions is the fear that people will *not* obey, follow the rules, perform their tasks. Many managers see rules, regulations, systematic procedures, objective performance monitoring and control as the basis for order.

So far so good! But implicit in this is the belief that rules, systems, monitoring and control cannot in themselves bring about consequences that are counterproductive to order, that obstruct progress, that make it harder to 'get things done'. Yet we all know this to be false. When we think of bureaucracy, we tend also to think of 'red tape'.

Here we refer to what R.K. Merton (1940) has called the 'dysfunctional' consequences of bureaucracy and what March and Simon (1958) refer to as the 'unintended consequences'. For Merton, a bureaucratic structure exerts constant demands on officials to be methodical and disciplined. To operate successfully there must be reliability, conformity and discipline. However, adherence to the rules, originally conceived as a means, becomes transformed into an end:

> **Discipline, readily interpreted as conformance with regulations, whatever the situation, is seen not as a measure designed for specific purposes but becomes an immediate value in the life-organisation of the bureaucrat. This emphasis, resulting from the displacement of the original goals, develops into rigidities and an inability to adjust readily. Formalism, even ritualism, ensues with an unchallenged insistence upon punctilious adherence to formalised procedures.**
>
> Merton, 1940, page 16

This may be taken to the extent that conformity to the rules obstructs the purposes of the organization, known to us, familiarly, as 'red tape'.

To return to our example, how did Argyris explain the apparent paradox? Remember that the original diagnosis was that the working-party recommendations were vague and unusable, and that more specific goals and directions combined with methods of monitoring and controlling performance would overcome this difficulty. However, should such a strategy be implemented, the members of the working party may feel mistrusted and constrained. In any event, Argyris points out that faculty members and administrators within a college are likely to pursue different ends and will not work together on critical issues. There is a need for integration between the two groups, the members of which are trained in different ways, work to different rules, with different methods and styles, and are likely to emphasize different views of the college. There might well be advantages in keeping goals vague. Specific goals might be interpreted as limiting and not allowing the freedom to think creatively. They may result in emotional reactions which inhibit performance. Thus actions which appear rational (setting specific goals) may lead people to produce counter-rational consequences (judged in the light of the rationality of those specific goals).

Argyris suggests that these counter-rational consequences can emerge in three ways. First, individuals may distance themselves from the tasks in hand and the responsibilities involved. Not feeling any personal responsibility for producing the problem, they do not see it as their responsibility to solve it. Second, tacit acceptance may develop that the 'counter-rational' behaviour is 'undiscussable'. Where motivation is falling, where people feel mistrusted and where behaviour appears to be disloyal there seems to be a tendency for people to find these issues difficult to talk about openly. So difficult, according to Argyris, that all agree that the issue is 'taboo', in principle undiscussable. Finally, people may prefer counterproductive advice: that is to say advice which reinforces the counter-rational behaviour. Thus, on the course we have been discussing, members suggested that the college president should play a game of deception in order to save face for himself and the faculty and in order to keep his options open. They proposed that he accept the report, thank the working party and at the same time arrange for a new committee, or implement specific action. Such behaviour would, of course, reinforce the undiscussability of any problem and the distancing of the working-party members from the issues at stake. It is clearly a form of collusion aimed at avoiding making the issues, or the working party's difficulties, explicit.

It is important for us to recognize that by counter-rational we do not mean irrational or emotional. Counter-rational behaviour may be highly rational from the viewpoint of the individuals concerned, given their situation, the power and resources under their command and so on. By counter-rational we simply mean based on different sources of rationality.

Forrester (1969) discusses this problem when he refers to the 'counterintuitive' behaviour of complex systems (such as urban systems or large corporations). He tells us that we have been 'conditioned almost exclusively by experience with first-order, negative-feedback loops [which] are goal-seeking and contain a single important variable'. This form of experience suggests that cause and effect are closely related in space and time. He argues that complex systems appear to be the same, i.e. they appear to present cause and effect close in time and space. However, causes of a problem may be complex, may actually lie in some remote part of the system or may lie in the distant past. What appears to be cause and effect may actually be 'coincidental' symptoms.

Action to dispel symptoms in a complex system will often leave the underlying causes untouched. Forrester claims that intuitive solutions to the problems of complex systems will be wrong most of the time. He also suggests that change programmes will often have an effect that is less than originally anticipated because they tend to displace existing internal processes. Pressman and Wildavsky (1973) quote one example of an 'underemployed-training programme' training 19,100 people per year which led to only 11,300 people becoming employed, this being a consequence of declining job starts occurring naturally. Based as it was on simulations, this is not an entirely convincing example.

However, Pressman and Wildavsky (1973) describe a programme aimed at developing employment opportunities for ethnic minority groups in Oakland, California. The federal government, through the project, committed $28 million during a four-year period with little result as far as the aims of the project were concerned. Their evidence suggested that the majority of the benefits derived from the programme went to people other than members of the ethnic minority groups. We do not need to interpret this as failure; we merely offer it as an example of counterintuitive behaviour.

People in organizations, whether representing themselves or their groups, tend to advocate views and positions with a degree of certainty which discourages further enquiry. Moreover, they tend to act in ways which inhibit the expression of negative feelings. We often talk of the need to 'sweeten the pill' or not to overdo criticism in case people are 'upset' by it. Sometimes we offer presentations in such a way as to emphasize that there is nothing new or radical in a set of proposals. People appear to design their behaviour to appear rational. Thus they focus on what they argue to be necessary and attainable goals, realistic means and clear objectives. All this is to suppress issues that might upset other people. Moreover, people tend to control meetings to maximize winning, minimize losing, minimize the expression of negative feelings and to keep others rational. Following Argyris (1982, 1985), I summarize these ideas in Table 8.1.

Table 8.1 Ineffectiveness–effectiveness patterns

	Behaviour	Response	Outcome
Ineffectiveness	Not defining goals Maximize 'winning' and minimize losing Minimizing the expressing of feeling Appearing always to be 'rational'	People become defensive Inconsistent, feel vulnerable, act in manipulative ways, mistrust, lack risk taking or take very high risks, withhold information, adopt power-centred behaviour	Limited testing Issues not discussable 'Distance' themselves from issues
Effectiveness	Depend on people	Builds confidence, 'self-esteem'	Effective testing
	Allow tasks to be jointly controlled	Creates learning and trust	Informed choice
	Make the protection of feelings a joint responsibility	Leads to less defensive relationship and group dynamics	Internal commitment
	Discuss issues, performance and problems, not people	Open confrontation of issues	

All this can have important consequences. People attempt to 'distance' themselves, to treat key issues and events or norms as 'undiscussable' and to offer advice which, while ostensibly aimed at increasing rationality, actually inhibits it. All this tends to hinder the production of valid information for diagnosis and decision making. Yet these behaviours are most prevalent just when valid information is needed – when people are dealing with difficult and threatening problems. Argyris (1985) suggests that we are dealing with a powerful set of individual, group, organizational and cultural forces which are mutually reinforcing. These forces create contradictions. Yet success can, and does, occur. But this will be based on routine performance, on stability, which can mean that people do not feel it necessary to pay attention to the deeper issues until the impact of these contradictions becomes so powerful that the stability is itself under threat. Now the organization is seen to be in a crisis. Drastic action is possible; 'turnaround' becomes the objective. These factors will all influence the process diagnosing the need for change. In essence, therefore, we need to deal with the 'blockages' before we can identify, let alone make progress towards, the organizational changes we need.

Sadly, as Argyris makes clear, people can become highly skilled at maintaining these patterns of ineffectiveness. He calls this 'skilled incompetence' (see Argyris, 1990). He demonstrates the relevance of this to major programmes of change by reference to a study of six large US corporations which had invested heavily in change programmes that had not worked, in which the authors found evidence of the following:

Inflexible rules and procedures.

Managers not understanding customer needs.

Managers not committed to, or skilled in, handling change.

Inter-group problems.

Poor communication.

Lack of strategic thinking.

Top managers evidently believing that declining revenue was only temporary.

Low levels of trust.

Beer *et al.*, 1988

Here we have the 'blockages' to change all over again.

Argyris goes on to argue that characteristic solutions to these problems seem purposely to avoid the problem. Thus a structural solution will not deal with the real issues, nor will a solution which emphasizes clearer definition of roles and 'better' communication, because neither deals with the causes but rather attempts to deal with symptoms. His main idea to deal with these problems is to get participants to 'map' how decisions are actually made as a means of recognizing their own 'skilled incompetence'. He refers to work by Putnam and Thomas (1988) on a performance-related pay system which was ineffective because too many people received high ratings.

CASE STUDY

CAC Consultants

The 'problem'

CAC Consultants is in the business of marketing highly sophisticated knowledge and professional skills, particularly in the field of project management. The key to the firm's success lies in the professionals and the skills they develop and deploy. Attracting and keeping first-rate professionals is a key issue, and senior partners hold strong opinions on it. The company comprises a chairman and six senior partners (each responsible for a major area of business activity) and 14 junior partners, each reporting directly to either the chairman or a senior partner. In addition some 40 professional staff and 60 support staff are employed, all organized into teams within the major areas of activity.

Some senior partners believed that career development was needed to attract high-quality young professionals. Another group had serious doubts about this, believing that the firm could attract people of the right level of skill. In any event, these people believed that it was impossible to appoint additional senior partners because of the impact of that on the income of the current partners. Finally, it was felt that career development would retain only the less able professionals; others would 'naturally move on'.

Both groups of senior partners recognized problems, however. For some the problem was how to attract and retain able young professionals. For others it was how to motivate effort and commitment from them in order to increase company income.

The former saw the solution as lying in that of career development, the latter in the field of recruitment procedures. It was decided to hold a one-day meeting of senior partners to discuss the problem. Prior to the meeting there had been much discussion with individuals, often attributing various views or motives to others. People were seen as unfair, emotional, 'empire building', overreacting or overprotective. At least one senior partner had been attributed as using career development as a means of rewarding a junior partner working for him.

The 'meeting'

At the meeting one senior partner proposed that regular reviews of individuals be carried out and that the senior partners should agree a policy regarding career development and promotion, to both junior and senior partner level. It was argued that this was not a panacea but would allow for modest improvement in present practice. It would not undermine existing practices or lead to a fall in the technical competence of staff. Moreover, it was proposed that the process be largely informal and be designed so as not to threaten anyone. One response to these ideas was: 'I'm glad to hear that we intend to move slowly and build on present practices. The most important thing is to ensure that we recruit the right people and ensure that they perform well.' All agreed on the need to build up the firm's position. One pointed out that some of the junior partners were overcommitting themselves in order to ensure promotion. Others felt that this would not matter 'if kept within reasonable limits'.

One partner passionately put the point that the firm's growth and reputation would be harmed unless they could develop new services to allow them to meet rapidly changing needs. It was essential to attract people with ideas. Others responded: 'We don't seem to have any problems attracting people, and in any event we are highly profitable now. What's the problem?'

When the meeting convened, several partners proposed that part of it be used to review the performance of the practice. Moreover, other commitments that people mentioned meant that it had to end at noon, rather than go on to late afternoon. The review of performance lasted until 11.20 a.m., allowing only a short discussion of the career development issue. There were constant interruptions as various senior partners were 'called to the telephone'. At the end the chairman summed up. Nothing would be done that was costly in terms of time and money. He proposed that a subcommittee of the partners be formed to develop ideas and a policy. One senior partner asked that the subcommittee's representation should include the range of views. This was agreed. The meeting ended with much comment about the progress made.

Background to the meeting

Interviews afterwards identified the following points:

■ The senior partners concerned to see significant progress on the career development front felt they had to avoid anything which made other partners defensive. No mention would be made of the need to develop new ideas, services and business.

■ They also wished to avoid overstating their case because this would lead to the issue becoming personalized.

■ Overall it was felt important to keep the discussion on 'rational lines'.

■ Others clearly felt that the best approach to the meeting was to give those who wished to see career development 'their head': 'Let them talk so they cannot accuse us of having our heads in the sand'.

■ Thus it was that everyone appeared to rule out discussion of the validity of the views being put: 'If people are upset they become emotional and you cannot test their views'. 'After all, we must be rational.'

Putnam and Thomas (1988) sketch out an organizational action map which shows that in various circumstances (e.g. low economic growth), cultural norms such as that of attempting to give all employees equal treatment and the wish not to upset people combine with management behaviour (covering up conflict) to create consequences such as resentment by good performers of poor performers, protection of mediocre performance and so on. Any attempt (e.g. by good performers) to refer the situation to the grievance procedure would simply lead to mistrust, polarized attitudes, less coaching of them by managers whose performance reviews were being criticized and, even worse, the acceptance of mediocre performance. To escape these patterns of behaviour, managers map their situation. By making the behaviour and its consequences explicit there emerges a better understanding of the situation, a fuller diagnosis and a greater willingness to engage in what Argyris calls 'productive reasoning'. At the core of this as a successful strategy is the need for all involved to see learning as an essential characteristic of 'productive reasoning', a thought we shall return to as an essential ingredient of effective change.

In the CAC Consultants case study it is not difficult to see that the key issue is the future of the practice itself. There are two questions to be faced – What new markets and services can/should be developed? To what extent should the practice grow? Some senior partners are tempted to maintain the status quo. They have built it and it does provide good profits, and therefore good incomes, at the moment. Growth and change will be uncomfortable. But will competition mean that the status quo is not a viable option? This point needs careful discussion and analysis.

The question of attracting and retaining new staff is very much a matter of means. A status quo and a growth/development strategy will require different approaches. Therefore, to make progress the senior partners need to discuss the overall strategy and their own motivations. These are the forces relevant to the choice that needs to be made. To make progress there is a need for senior partners to discuss these issues more openly. We will return later to how such progress may be made. For the moment I will merely state that it requires effective leadership and good team working among the senior partners.

The 'block-busting' ideas of Adams (1987) are relevant, as are the practical recommendations to be made in chapters following. In general we suggest greater openness, but two points should be made. First, openness and honesty are not the ultimate purposes of learning; rather they facilitate learning in the circumstances that we are considering. Second, it is important to enable people to control this process (a point made by Argyris). Only then are we likely to minimize the sources of ineffectiveness that we have discussed. Handy (1983) identifies the following blocks to learning:

- *We don't see the questions*: we do not critically examine our success and failure. We do not habitually question events. Yet to learn we must constantly experiment, trying out new ideas and skills.

- *We see the question but seem unable to come to any answers*: answers do not come automatically. We need to search for them, compare a problem situation from the past, talk to friends and colleagues.

- *We are sometimes unable to see how to put an answer into action in order to see if it works*: here the issue is one of turning ideas into practical action in such a way as to allow for monitoring, feedback and learning. It is important to identify people who can help, provide support, counsel and encourage. This also demands internal motivation and energy. If we can get so far, we are learning how to learn.

Contingency, choice and organizational environments

So far in this chapter we have seen that various blockages can impede decision making and choice. We have also seen that deeply held assumptions about people and about the need for so-called rational behaviour can limit effectiveness. Assuming for the moment that we can find ways of handling these difficulties, can we define the characteristics of effective organizational structures and design? This seems to depend largely on the 'fit' between the organization's structure and its environment.

The design of organizational structures to suit the needs of the particular business enterprise or organization, which provides for the coordination of the diverse activities carried out within the enterprise or organization but also provides for adaptability to respond to changing circumstances, presents a challenge to management which cannot be overstated in its importance. The structure of an organization allows the pursuit of objectives and the *implementation of plans*. People and resources are allocated to the tasks which must be performed, and coordination is provided. Working methods, rules and procedures define the ways in which tasks are to be performed and/or establish criteria for task performance, output or quality. These are typically all related to reward systems, planning and scheduling systems and monitoring systems. The structure of an organization is directly linked to the *information system*.

The structure of the organization provides a *decision-support system*. Arrangements are made for the collection and processing of information relevant to the decisions taken by managers. Specialist posts are often created to provide for such arrangements. Accountants and organization and methods personnel will, for example, collect and process information on various aspects of the performance of the organization. This information will be evaluated and presented to decision makers, either regularly (to a senior management meeting) or in response to particular circumstances (e.g. when a major project is under consideration). The tasks of the organization create decisions to be made. In practice decision makers decide, from the range of tasks which could be undertaken, those tasks to be pursued and for which a market exists and those to be dropped. For a decision system to be effective, provision for monitoring trends in the market is essential. Changes in technology, in resource markets for capital or labour and in the product market will affect the performance of any organization and will thus require adaptation.

Following Child (1984), the main dimensions of an organization's structure are as follows:

■ The allocation of tasks and responsibilities, providing appropriate discretion over methods and use of resources.

■ The designation of formal reporting relationships, determining spans of control of managers and supervisors.

■ The grouping of individuals into sections and departments, and the grouping of departments into divisions or other major units.

■ The delegation of authority with associated procedures for performance monitoring and evaluation, which may either be regular or operate by exception.

- The design of communication and coordinating systems, to provide information and participation in decision making.
- The provision of reward systems to motivate individuals.
- The establishment of decision-support systems such as regular management meetings, project teams and specialist posts or departments.

Where the structure of an organization is inappropriate or deficient we would expect to see a number of possible problems emerging, including the following:

1 Low motivation and low morale of employees.

2 Delayed or poor decisions.

3 Conflict between departments.

4 Rising costs.

5 A tendency to stick to the rules and regulations, whether or not appropriate action will follow.

6 Lack of the capacity to adapt to changing circumstances.

If we observe problems such as those listed here (and this is not meant to be an inclusive list) then we have reason to conclude that the structure of the organization is deficient in some way. It is important to recognize that the dimensions of an organizational structure can be designed in different ways and that they vary considerably in practice.

The organizational form with which we are all most familiar is bureaucracy. Bureaucratic structures are characterized by a high degree of job specialization, by reliance on formal procedures and paperwork, by hierarchy, by clear and significant status differentials and by an emphasis on control. Bureaucratic structures are intended to provide for equal treatment for all employees; a reliance on the expertise, skills and experience relevant to the job; specific standards of work and output; the maintenance of records and files dealing with work and output; the setting up and enforcement of rules and regulations that serve the interests of the organization; and a recognition that rules and regulations are binding on managers as well as on other employees.

In environments which are changing rapidly, however, rules, regulations and working procedures can quickly become out of date and irrelevant. Moreover, rules and regulations can become barriers behind which individual managers hide or which they use to justify incorrect decisions. Inflexible systems or procedures can create demotivating conditions for employees and can reduce the ability of managers or employees to innovate. From this we could conclude that a bureaucratic structure might be suitable for an organization dealing with a stable and simple environment. Conversely, an altogether more flexible and innovative structure would be suitable for a changing, complex environment.

Contingency theory is a label applied to a body of research based on the assumption that there is 'no one best way' to design an organizational structure but, rather, that the effectiveness of the design of a particular organization is contingent on various factors. These factors are normally stated to include the technology, the environment, the history of the organization, norms and expectations of employees and/or customers or clients, and the size of the organization. Lawrence and Lorsch (1970) were the first to use the term 'contingency theory' as a convenient way of describing this empirical view of organizational structures and processes; however, the earlier work of Burns and Stalker (1961) and Woodward (1965) are important applications of the approach.

Exponents of contingency theories have advocated a shift in the approach of organization designers from prescription to the creation of the organizational choice. Rather than propose one strategy as being of universal application within organizations, contingency theorists have suggested that design, management and control strategies should be developed to meet the situation within which they are to be applied. The theory suggests that organizational performance depends on the extent to which the organization secures a good match between situation and structure. Child (1984) summarizes it as follows:

> Contingency theory regards the design of an effective organization as necessarily having to be adapted to cope with the 'contingencies' which derive from the circumstances of environment, technology, scale, resources and other factors in the situation in which the organization is operating.

The components of organizational structure (e.g. the degree of formalization of procedures, centralization of decision making, number of levels in hierarchies and the spans of control of managers) can take different forms. Lorsch (1970) suggests that the 'structure of an organization is not an immutable given, but rather a set of complex variables about which managers can exercise considerable choice'.

The contingency theory approach to organization design attempts to take account of all four factors, uses the organization as the unit of analysis and tends to accept a managerial framework, particularly in respect of organizational purposes. By stating that the components of an organization can be changed they introduce the idea of choice, called 'strategic choice' by Galbraith (1977). For Galbraith, organization design involves attempts to make the goals of organization, the means applied and the people 'coherent'. The phrase 'strategic choice' is used to emphasize the available choice of goals, means and processes for integrating individuals into the organization and also the choice as to whether some or all of these goals, means and processes should be changed to meet changes in the environment.

■ Organization design, resources and complexity

From what we have said so far it is plain that organization design is not a precise science. Yet there does seem to be evidence to suggest that issues such as control, resources and the complexity of the environment are important issues in organization design. Lawrence and Dyer (1983) have examined these points in an interesting way. Their argument is that appropriate organization designs are related to the complexity of the environment and the scarcity of resources for the organization. Figure 8.3 summarizes this idea.

In effect Lawrence and Dyer (1983) identify what they feel are the most appropriate organizational forms for each combination of information complexity

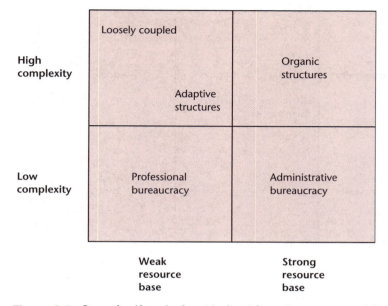

Figure 8.3 **Organization design** (derived from Lawrence and Dyer, 1983)

and resource scarcity (which might mean high levels of competition for sales in a private sector example or government restrictions on expenditure for a public sector organization). Information complexity refers to the diversity of (uncertainty about) the technologies and opportunities (and threats) in the organization's environment. For example, where the organization is dealing with a complex and changing environment with high levels of competition then a fluid and responsive organizational structure is essential. A trading company is a typical case. Conversely, professional bureaucracy is an appropriate structure where the organization deals with low levels of competition and well-established technology. However, such organizations experience significant tensions if the environment changes suddenly and dramatically. A typical case would be universities – compare the typical university in the 1960s with the changes that took place in the 1980s.

Figure 8.4 reproduces Figure 8.3 with typical functions substituted for each organizational form. For example, where markets are tight and the environment complex, the emphasis may well be on sales (to generate income) rather than on marketing (which costs money, takes time and may rapidly become outdated). This is a controversial view. Many marketing people will argue the contrary position, yet the situation we describe is that of the trading company – which tends to do little formal marketing. In practice organizations attempt to control their environments to some degree. Is there a tendency to operate at medium levels? In any event, perhaps most organizations find themselves operating in environments where adaptation and general management are both crucial.

What specific changes are needed to move an organization towards the adaptive structure? These are summarized in Figure 8.5 (again following Lawrence and Dyer, 1983), from which it is clear that these comprise either means of achieving more focus and business-orientated effort (or at least efforts that are more

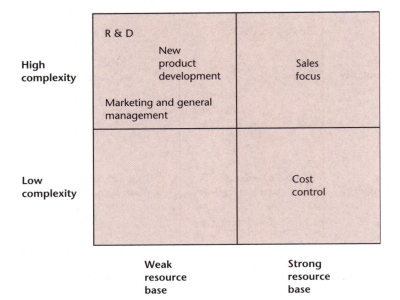

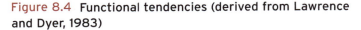

Figure 8.4 Functional tendencies (derived from Lawrence and Dyer, 1983)

attuned to corporate objectives) or ways of developing people and groups to improve the emphasis on innovation.

Criticisms of the contingency approach

Various criticisms have been made of the contingency approach:

■ In reality the design of organizations is subject to 'political' and ideological factors as different interest groups come into conflict when defending their own interests (e.g. nurses and managers in healthcare or, more accurately, different groupings of both 'nurses' and 'managers'). Hence structures are often the result of bargaining and compromise.

■ The environment itself is problematic and cannot be taken as a given determinant of the organization. Instead it requires interpretation and is likely to generate differences within the enterprise. In any event the structure of an R&D department is very likely to be very different to the structure of a production department – note, however, that contingency theory could account for this difference.

■ Within given situations it appears that a significant degree of choice exists for managers as to how they structure their organizations, without serious diseconomies being incurred.

■ At worst, contingency theory may become a trivial exercise for managers in encouraging a sort of 'checklist' approach which ignores how the variables themselves may interact, often in a complex way.

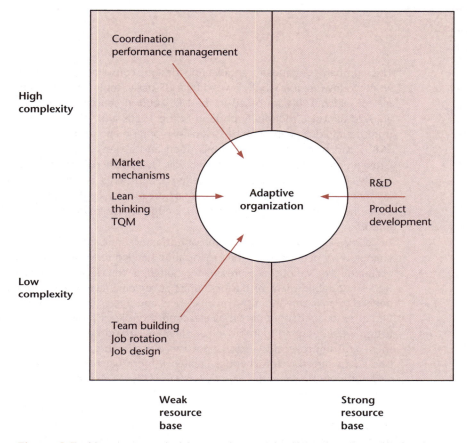

High
complexity

Low
complexity

Coordination
performance management

Market
mechanisms

Lean
thinking
TQM

Adaptive
organization

R&D

Product
development

Team building
Job rotation
Job design

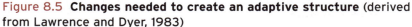

Weak
resource
base

Strong
resource
base

Figure 8.5 **Changes needed to create an adaptive structure** (derived from Lawrence and Dyer, 1983)

- Finally, it is worth noting a renewed belief in universal principles of organizational structure. These have been broadly enunciated through a research method which has focused on 'successful' or high-performing companies and asked whether they have any common organizational characteristics. Peters and Waterman's *In Search of Excellence* (1982) is the best known of this type of work. Some care has to be taken to avoid reading these books uncritically, however; by not concentrating on unsuccessful companies we cannot assert with certainty that a culture of 'success' is due to certain structural forms. It might even be that there is no relationship.

Similarly, some writers, such as Ouchi (1981), have argued that Japanese forms of organization represent a superior model which could be imitated. To some extent Japanese practices such as 'right-first-time' production, flexibility in tasks among operators and participative styles through such mechanisms as quality circles have been tried by many large firms and notably those suffering most from Japanese competition, such as the automobile producers. However, again, care has to be taken in assuming that it is easy to create new attitudes or an improved company culture. Such changes require long-term effort.

International Engineering

This company engages in engineering design, consultancy and project management work worldwide. It is wholly owned by a US-based multinational. It employs 2000 people, of which 1500 are based in the UK, 1000 in central London. This company had enjoyed almost a monopoly position in the 1950s and 1960s and then had benefited from the rapid growth of North Sea oil exploration engineering work in the 1970s. The 1980s had brought growing competition and a declining market in the North Sea. Growing markets required new technology. Overall the company was structured in a relatively *ad hoc* way. Within the engineering departments, and within specific projects, the company was structured as a professional bureaucracy. By the early 1990s the board was concerned that it was losing competitive edge and therefore being unsuccessful in any important bids for new business.

To develop a more adaptive organization, various main threads of organizational change were needed. First, the organization needed to be structured to achieve clearer accountability. Various measures were required, as can be seen from Figures 8.6, 8.7 and 8.8. The establishment of business units at regional level was designed to strengthen general management, improve efficiency and focus effort to meet market needs. Organizational changes aimed at elevating the role of projects, engineering and marketing were designed to improve coordination, strengthen operations/project management and improve efficiency. Under the old structure, too much depended on the operations director. The changes created a more balanced allocation of responsibility and authority between the various functions. The business unit approach involved the adoption of market mechanisms. For accountability, each general manager was to be responsible for profit, and was to be left to be relatively autonomous, as long as profit and market objectives were attained. It was intended that business units buy in services from both group and other business units, or from elsewhere, thus strengthening the market approach.

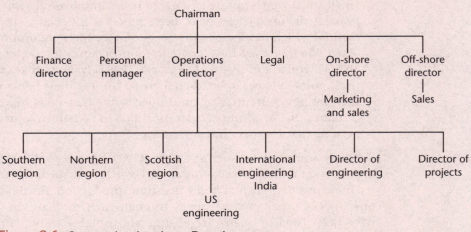

Figure 8.6 **Corporate structure, Pre-change**

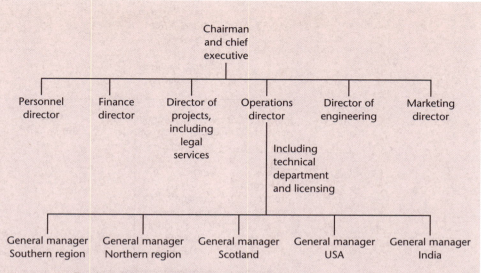

Figure 8.7 **Regional decentralization, Post-change**

Developing an organizational structure and an appropriate management style demands attention to a range of issues, including technology. For example, typical 'success' criteria for an organization such as International Engineering are listed as follows:

■ Control of factors critical to the successful penetration of existing and new markets, including technology.

■ Clear sales accountability.

■ Quality control in clearly branded products and services.

■ First-class systems support.

■ Developing and retaining effective people.

■ Management development.

■ Effective market development.

These success criteria were developed for the company by the top management team. I set out the existing structure and two new structures, one for the new regional structure and one for the new corporate structure. The new structures make technology easier to develop, partly because it is now to have board-level representation by having the director of engineering no longer reporting to the overburdened operations director, and partly through regional decentralization, which will allow a more effective marketing approach at regional level. More effective market intelligence from the marketplace, combined with higher-level attention to the development of technology, will provide for a more coordinated approach in this field. Moreover, decentralization will provide for and encourage a more open management style, thus encouraging more initiative throughout the organization.

All these changes require the development of new management styles and skills at various levels and, indeed, many of the managers and engineers will need to develop

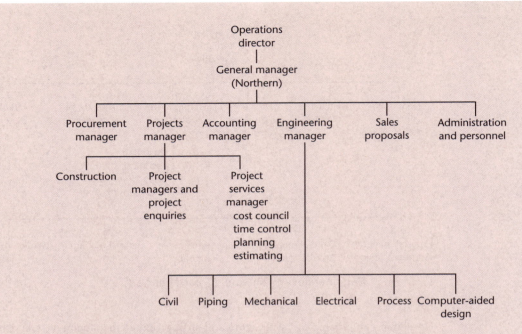

Figure 8.8 **Regional decentralization: regional structure**

new skills. Performance appraisal is needed to support these changes. New technological disciplines will be needed. We can readily see from Figure 8.6 how all these changes are intended to move International Engineering to a more adaptive structure. We will be returning to this case study in later chapters to discuss various aspects of these changes and their implementation.

The innovative organization

To what extent does effectiveness include innovation? A number of management books dealing with innovation have been published since the early 1980s. Peters and Waterman (1982) attracted particular attention. They identify the following eight characteristics of an innovative organization:

1 Bias to action.
2 Proximity to the customer/client.
3 Autonomy.
4 Productivity through people.
5 'Hands-on' management.
6 Concentration on strengths.
7 Simple structures.
8 Centralization of core issues and decentralization of actions/implementation and day-to-day control.

In essence the emphasis is on getting things done, allowing autonomy as far as is possible to middle-level managers. Linked to this is a concern for individual accountability.

In much the same way it has been argued that 'excellent' or 'high-performing' companies emphasize the following nine characteristics:

1 Concern for the future.
2 A concern to develop human resources.
3 A focus on the product/service being provided.
4 An orientation to the technologies in use.
5 A concern for quality, excellence, service and competence.
6 An orientation to 'outsiders', clients, customers, the community and shareholders.
7 Constant adaptation of reward systems and corporate values.
8 A focus on the basis of 'making and selling'.
9 Open to new ideas.

Here the same concern is shown for the basics of the organization's business, whatever this may be, and the same concern to balance internal and external issues is in evidence. For many organizations the concern expressed for the external environment, combined with quality, involves a new emphasis on service and on marketing as a means of achieving competitive advantage or more effective utilization of resources and public support (notably, but not exclusively, for public sector organizations).

It is interesting to contrast these ideas with the following view of what makes for an effective organization which emerges from the organizational development (OD) literature (see Strauss (1976) for an excellent and critical review):

- Lack of status differentials.
- Innovation.
- Sharing of responsibility.
- Expression of feelings and needs.
- Collaboration.
- Open, constructive conflict.
- Feedback.
- Flexible leadership.
- Involvement.
- Trust.

This makes important additions to the first two sets of ideas. Open and constructive conflict is important, as is the recognition of individual needs. Interestingly enough the concerns are essentially, if not necessarily, internal concerns. The OD literature appears to give primacy to the staff and rarely mentions clients or customers. Nevertheless, organizations which can create an 'organizational climate' which encourages those latter characteristics and achieves the balance of internal and external concerns referred to above seem likely to establish effectiveness.

If innovation is a central element for improving effectiveness, then we need to understand why some circumstances seem to be more innovative than others. Rickards (1985) has identified the following key issues to be faced when deciding on a strategy for innovation:

- *Innovation is systematic*: all the factors involved (social, economic, political, technological, cultural, commercial) are interrelated.

- *Innovation is non-linear*: it experiences stops and starts and is often characterized by 'accidents' (e.g. penicillin).

- *Innovation is creative problem solving, requiring imagination and flexibility*: managers need to learn how to support people and to facilitate team work and problem solving.

- *Innovation is situational*: there is no one best way. Success will be dependent on such factors as top management support, sensitivity to market needs, effective communication and technological expertise.

- *Innovation requires appropriate structures*: traditional hierarchies are too rigid. Project teams and task cultures are effective structures.

- *Innovation can be stimulated*: this requires major effort, however, and involves significant learning.

- *Innovation requires various communities of interest*: customers and clients can and should play a part.

- *Innovation is mission orientated*: thus it creates impetus, high viability and 'success'.

- *Innovation involves negotiation and participation*: it will involve conflict which must be resolved through negotiation or participation.

- *Innovation is itself innovation*: it will never go the way of past innovations.

- *Innovation and information are closely linked.*

- *Innovation is personal and global*: it involves and affects individuals and communities.

Conclusion

In this chapter, we have considered a number of approaches to effectiveness. We have seen how blockages to effectiveness and change can be created and how they can be handled. We have also examined the link between organizational structures, the environment and effectiveness. Most importantly, we have seen how organizational ineffectiveness can hinder progress. We turn now to our treatment of how change can be managed to create and sustain effectiveness. As we shall see, this depends on our ability to generate greater understanding of the issues to be faced, the willingness to face these issues and the ability to learn from the process of more informed choice, from changing and experimenting with new ideas and from the experience which follows.

EXERCISES

1 Can you explain the problems being experienced at CAC Consultants?

2 How can CAC Consultants resolve their problems?

3 In what ways is International Engineering seeding to encourage adaptability?

Leadership in practice

Introduction

Can we identify the key elements of effective leadership? Can we assess individuals on those elements, looking at their skills and performances? Can we help individuals to become more effective leaders? Are leaders born or made? Or both? This chapter answers these questions. Leadership is a key to managing organizations in periods of change and crisis and is thus important to all of us working within organizations.

Hersey and Blanchard (1988) write that leadership occurs when one attempts to influence the behaviour of an individual or group. They go on to state that there are three general skills (or competencies):

1 *Diagnosing*: being able to understand the situation as it is now and knowing what can reasonably be expected in the future. The gap between these two – sometimes known as the 'performance gap' – is the problem to be solved. This is what the effective leader will attempt to change. Diagnosing is a *cognitive* skill.

2 *Adapting*: involves adapting one's behaviour and other resources in ways that help to close the 'performance gap', a *behavioural* skill.

3 *Communicating*: even if one knows what needs to be done and is able to adapt oneself to meet the new needs, this will fail unless one can communicate all this to others in ways that they can understand and accept, a *process* skill.

Warren Bennis (1984) has completed an interesting study of 90 outstanding leaders. Based on this he identifies the following four areas of competence shared by all 90 leaders:

1 *Management of attention*: the ability to communicate clear objectives and direction to others.

2 *Management of meaning*: the ability to create and communicate meaning clearly, achieving understanding and awareness.

3 *Management of trust*: the ability to be consistent in often complex circumstances fraught with dilemmas (so often the potential trap for the unwary) so that people can depend on them.

4 *Management of self*: the ability to know oneself and to work with strengths and weaknesses.

Leaders empower their organizations to create an environment where people feel significant, where learning and competence matter, where there is team spirit, flexibility and excitement. Also where quality and excellence matter and are something to strive for.

All things to all men!

Kotter (1996) notes 'management is about coping with complexity. Leadership . . . is about coping with change'. Goleman, Boyatzis and McKee (2001) describe 'primal leadership', noting the role of emotional intelligence in leadership.

In a period of great uncertainty and change, and amid the outward evidence of the rewards available to both the individuals and organizations who seize 'opportunities', it is not surprising that there has been a resurgence of interest in leadership. The study of 'great leaders' seems to provide little evidence on how to select, develop or encourage potential leaders. Self-evidently, perhaps, 'leaders' need not be 'selected' or 'trained'. Nevertheless, if we are to understand the role of leadership then we must understand why only some succeed and how they emerge as successful.

The notion of 'transformational leadership' is both appealing and uninspiring. If 'managers are people who do things right and leaders are people who do the right thing' (Bennis and Nanus, 1985, page 21), it hardly helps us to understand what corporate leaders do to achieve these transformations. That said, it is clear that individual corporate leaders can and do play roles in periods of change which enable dramatic transformations to take place.

It is commonplace to mention outstanding corporate leaders such as John Egan of Jaguar, Richard Branson at Virgin or Sir John Harvey-Jones of ICI (see Pettigrew, 1985) as examples. But any careful study sees the corporate leader firmly in context. This is described plainly in Stewart and Chadwick (1987), an excellent study of change in the Scottish railway network. For these authors, large organizations experience 'systems crisis' through overspecialization, bureaucracy and low risk taking. Organizations capable of overcoming this crisis seem to share the following characteristics:

- Decentralization.
- Combined with decentralization, evolution of roles for head office as consultant, power-broker and financier rather than direct controller.
- Positive attempts to encourage the entrepreneurial spirit and risk taking.
- Breaking down of interfunctional barriers.
- More emphasis on leadership, and on people.
- An evolving client or customer focus.
- Established informal links at all levels.
- A move from controlling to enabling approaches. Systems control the minimum necessary, rather than controlling each and every activity.

Trust turns out to be central. If leaders seek new ways of dealing with clients, deploying services and products, and of negotiating change, then people must trust them.

Thus it is that Burns (1978), in his seminal work, was concerned with 'follow-ership' as the other side of the coin to 'leadership'. How do leaders establish the conditions under which people will follow? Writers often mention vision. Successful corporate leaders are capable of articulating a clear vision of the future. Capable of engaging support to that vision, they work with the values and ide-ology of the business or organizations. But what does this mean? Itami (1987) adds the key concept of 'invisible assets': technology, consumer loyalty, brand image, control of distribution, corporate culture and management skill are all invisible assets. Physical, financial and human assets are essential for business to be transacted but the invisible assets of knowledge, values and skill are needed for competitive success.

Itami tells us that invisible assets are the key to adaptability and competitive advantage for three reasons: they are hard to accumulate, are capable of multiple uses and grow through further use. Developing brand image or technical skills is time consuming and costly. Money cannot buy a change of corporate culture. Thus a firm can differentiate itself from the competition by developing its invis-ible asset. A firm's reputation with customers will impact on its business across a range of products and sectors.

People are important assets of the firm, largely because they develop knowl-edge and experience; they are the accumulators of invisible assets.

Leadership, vision and strategy

Following both Stewart and Chadwick, and Itami, the corporate leader enables people to contribute, solve problems, learn from and by experience and to accumulate invisible assets. The leader must do so both by making strategy explicit (vision) and by using the process of strategy formulation to mobilize the organization.

The need for explicit strategy is clear enough: it allows for coordination of activity; it provides direction to people; it can boost morale and sustain self-esteem; it can provide a shield against anxiety in a period of change. Explicit strategy also fosters better planning. Rather than merely reacting, people can plan change. Thus explicit strategy allows people to plan, create change and then learn from the experience. Explicit strategy allows for the development of invis-ible assets.

Corporate leaders must make strategy explicit and ensure its diffusion through-out the organization. Words and actions are important. Repeated attempts to inform and persuade must be supported by appropriate actions. Selecting people with strong reputations to lead new projects can help. Visits to departments with key roles display the importance of the new strategy with powerful symbolism. Reward systems designed to recognize excellent performance are important (see Stewart and Chadwick, 1987), just as are slogans. IBM's 'right-first-time' campaign articulated the company's concern for service with a powerfully simple slogan.

Finally, charisma or personality features in both Stewart and Chadwick's and Itami's views. It may be dangerous for organizations to become overexposed to, or too dependent on, charismatic leaders. Nevertheless, we live in what seem to be times in which individual values have gained growing recognition. People will respond to personality. Can system, order and consensus not feel dehumanized?

If the strategy is made explicit how may its content mobilize the organization? From Itami we see that this operates at three levels:

1 By providing a unifying focus.

2 By creating momentum.

3 By sustaining creative tension.

The strategy should be simple and clear, based on an identifiable core concept, priorities should be clear, resources should be clearly allocated, continuous adaptation and improvement should be stressed and it should match the corporate culture. To create momentum leaders must sell the core concept, ensure and reward early success, involve people in clear tasks and pay attention to timing. Accumulating resources and people can create the invisible assets so crucial to the launch of a major new activity. To avoid complacency the leader will put continuing pressure on the organization. Constantly seeking new methods and procedures, improvements, new products and services is an excellent means of sustaining creative tension. Strategy formulation should seek the limits of the organization's consensus and explore beyond it. Generally, consensus is agreement that the policies successful in the past will continue to be so in the future. This consensus needs careful but continual pressure and questioning. Finally, placing people in conditions where the resources are inadequate can encourage a creative effort to resolve the problems so created, usually a very uncomfortable working situation. This can encourage the development of the invisible assets needed as people seek their own ways out of the impasse thus created.

Leaders and situations

From this sketchy analysis it seems that the effective corporate leader uses skills, knowledge, charisma and much else besides. These are deployed to encourage the development of the invisible assets so central to competitive advantage. In turn, this development flows from involving people in change, enabling them to act, allowing them to learn and develop, sustaining them with confidence and with vision.

Can we identify corporate leaders as individuals? Cooper and Hingley (1985) studied 17 'change-makers' in the UK. From this study the following pattern emerged:

■ *Early childhood experience*: early feelings of insecurity and loss led to a subsequent drive and need to control their own future.

■ *Later childhood experiences* also developed self-reliance.

■ *Motivation and drive*: a recurring element was strong motivation and drive.

■ *Value system*: each had a well-developed value system and clear vision and purpose.

■ *Early responsibility*: development of executive careers had been facilitated by early high-level responsibility.

■ *Charismatic leadership*: leadership style and charisma were unimportant for the individuals studied.

■ *Communicator*: the ability to communicate was a powerful element that all change-makers possessed, particularly the ability to be open and honest about feelings and attitudes.

Another survey (Norburn, 1988) focused on 108 chief executives and 30 executive directors from the FTSE 500 companies. From this study key features which distinguished chief executives from other members of the top management team were as follows:

■ The length of tenure within their organization.

■ The early stage at which their grooming for senior management responsibility began.

■ The variety of managerial functions they experienced.

■ The rapidity of promotion to a general management position.

■ Their exposure to overseas cultures and business.

Both studies point to early responsibility as a key feature. Perhaps the ability to communicate and having clear vision flow from breadth of experience. There seems little doubt that the successful leader brings wide experience and varied knowledge to the tasks of leadership. Perhaps, then, the individualism to which we respond is the credibility flowing from wide experience?

But if we know little enough about the individuals who are successful, what do we know of the circumstances within which success is more likely? Are some circumstances better than others? Also, how? During the last 50 years the focus of leadership studies shifted first from studying the traits of successful leaders to looking at leadership style and finally to focusing on the idea of contingency.

Figure 9.1 outlines the contingency approach. In essence the approach argues that the effectiveness of any given leadership style or behaviour will be contingent on the situation. Various models exist. Fiedler (1967) offers one which looks at

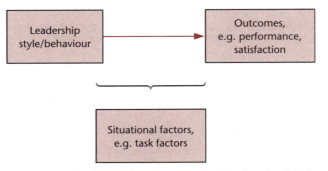

Figure 9.1 **The contingency approach to leadership in outline**

leader–member relations (quality of personal and effective relations between leader and group members), task structure (structured vs unstructured) and position power, as situational variables. Vroom and Yetton (1973) offer a contingency model of leader decision making. The focus is a positive one. The model offers a framework by which leaders might improve both the quality and the acceptability of decisions. Hersey and Blanchard (1988) offer an outwardly practical approach to Situational Leadership®. Little researched, it has become very popular among practitioners (see Bryman, 1987). These authors identify the 'readiness' of followers as a key factor in deciding on an appropriate leadership style. They believe that the leader's task behaviour (providing guidance and direction) and relationship behaviour (team building, providing socio-emotional support) should accord with the readiness of followers. They define readiness as the willingness and ability of people to take responsibility for defining and directing their own task behaviour. The theory is set out in Figure 9.2. Four leadership styles are defined: delegating, participating, selling and telling. Each style represents a different combination of task and relationship behaviour by the leader. The diagram proposes a particular combination of leadership style and readiness of followers. A 'telling' style is proposed for those of 'low readiness', namely for people who are

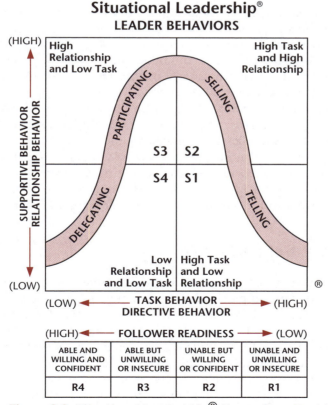

Figure 9.2 Situational Leadership® theory from Paul Hersey et al, 2000

unable and unwilling or insecure to take responsibility. A 'selling' style is recommended for those who, though willing to take responsibility, are unable to do so. By 'selling', Hersey and Blanchard seem to mean providing direction combined with explanation, support and feedback to maintain motivation. A 'participating' style, described as appropriate for those with 'high readiness', they suggest is appropriate for able people whose motivation and commitment might be increased by involvement in decision making. Finally, a 'delegating' style leaves 'high-readiness' followers to take responsibility for what needs to be done.

The approach has powerful intuitive appeal. It is a development of various situational models but still lacks credible research support. Yet the author is aware of a number of major international companies which use this approach within internal management development programmes to good effect, at least as far as the reactions of the managers of the programmes are concerned. However, the model considers only the situation 'below' the manager, relating it to leader behaviour and effectiveness. What of the context *within* which the manager operates? At whatever level of management, managers are often concerned about crises, problems and opportunities in other units, divisions and organizations. Thus the divisional manager is concerned about what happens at group level; the managing director is concerned about what happens in client companies or in government. For example, I spoke recently to a senior manager of a major manufacturer of precision machinery. This company had never sold equipment to a major potential user in its own country. It had always bid but had always been beaten by competitors. In the preceding year it had decided to change this position. It 'targeted' key managers within the company concerned and other key 'players' in government and consulting firms used by that company. It identified major upcoming projects and analyzed its own strengths and weakness *vis-à-vis* those projects and its own competitors. Thus it attempted to deal with the problem of not having worked for a major potential purchaser by creating and working with networks of people and organizations. This it followed by managing the uncertainty through competitive analysis to identify the most appropriate targets to bid for – and while bidding for all projects across the board the bid effect was more effectively targeted and coordinated to be successful in target projects. Managers operate within real constraints, which they work with to create new business, organization change, and so on.

The context of leadership

The real context of leaders thus involves much more than their 'followers'. Leaders find themselves in complex and often changing networks of people, institutions, opportunities and problems. Thus if we are to understand or even assess top managers as leaders we need to view their actions in context. What can they do? What can they not do, at least immediately, or even in a longer-term perspective?

We have examined this question in some detail. If the context within which leaders work is pretty unsuitable in the short term, what actions can they take? The following five sets of actions appear to be open to them:

1 Set values.
2 Support problem solving and risk.

3 Design systems to support action.

4 Focus on the manageable.

5 Develop skills in people.

By setting the overall 'values' of the organization they provide ideas to people about the issues that are important and the priorities to pursue. I spent some considerable time working with the top management team of a large, international process engineering group (International Engineering). The work focused on the development and implementations of new corporate strategies. One of the key values that the chief executive emphasized throughout is that of 'delivered service'. The company delivers a high-quality engineering service in a range of industries and in a variety of forms. All too many senior staff saw the company as producing engineering structures. The chief executive was doing two things here: first, he was opening up the definition of 'the business we are in'; second, he was setting new values. Value of technically optimal design was replaced by the value of high-quality engineering service. One leads us to develop sophisticated engineering solutions, the other to combine technical with commercial factors in delivering a service on time, to cost and appropriate to the client's needs.

Top managers support problem solving and risk because it is from these that innovation is born. Innovation requires risk taking, but most fundamentally it is driven by commercially defined needs. The innovator is the manager who can translate the creative idea into commercial or organizational reality. Possessing perhaps some of the attributes of the 'dreamer', first and foremost the individual is the 'mandarin' (Kingston, 1977). Such people solve problems, obtain resources and support, achieve action. They get things done.

Top managers can design systems to support action. Reward and appraisal systems can focus on and support action. Corporate strategy formulation can be designed to encourage and achieve action. I once spent a day with the project manager of a large offshore development (installed value £800 million) only to observe that this manager spent two hours 'signing off' expense claims. On asking about this I discovered that he 'approved' all expense claims, roughly 700 each day. Was this system designed to support action?

We can focus on the manageable. We cannot change everything overnight. So let us focus on the issues we can deal with, which give us some scope for improvement. A company facing losses this year and next will probably be best advised to focus on rationalization, the use of resources, cost, cash flow and the like. The development of costly technology centres might attract rather less attention *in the short term*. Of course, this is not to say that the latter are not needed but, rather, that in the circumstances the survival of the company seems to demand a different approach.

Finally, we come to development of skills in people. Ultimately, in all companies people are a limiting resource. Development, improvement, performance, managerial succession all depend on people: development of people to engage in problem solving, to be willing to take measured risks (i.e. to assess the risks and take them consciously), and to achieve action, focused on improvement. All this combined with appraisal and feedback can contribute to the effectiveness of the business.

Other things that managers can do include focusing attention and support on key people and projects. Partly, this involves simply paying attention to them, and being seen to do so. Key values can be articulated through simple phrases; 'right first time' is a simple and memorable phrase which various companies (e.g. IBM, Rolls-Royce) have used as the title for quality improvement programmes.

But perhaps most fundamental of all, top management can pay attention to timing. New programmes, new product launches, organizational changes, new strategies should, where possible, be planned with timing in mind. Where is the likely opposition? Can it be isolated? What other 'events' are likely? Will they be relevant? Do they provide opportunities as far as the current project is concerned? Behind all the argument, presentation of the case and 'selling' of the programme, how much analysis has been undertaken? What pattern and profile of resources are required? What is available or capable of being obtained? Which are the limiting resources? Shorter implementation periods can create confidence and lead people to feel that top management really support the change. But longer periods may be needed if more experience is needed, or if the resources are not available.

Thus pilot programmes may form part of the process, along with fuller involvement and clear communications. Have accountabilities been made clear? By identifying the leadership of the project or programme we clarify its implementations. Attention to these issues can aid top managers in finding the means to achieve action, even in complex circumstances. The timing of announcements is a crucial issue. Whether we want more or less immediate attention to be paid to our announcement will influence both how we market it and how we time it.

Managers and leadership

In looking at the leadership aspect of managerial jobs we have focused on the context within which managers work. We turn now to the whole job. How do management and leadership 'fit' together? Managerial performance is a combination of knowledge and skill applied in practice. Management is about getting things done, about action.

Managerial work is surrounded by circumstances which create problems, including uncertainty, incomplete information, change in the environment or elsewhere in the organization and conflict. Mintzberg (1973) has developed a comprehensive, empirical picture of the nature of managerial work through observing and recording what managers actually do (see Chapter 2).

Managers seem to stress the active element of their work – activities that are current, specific, well defined and non-routine attract more of their attention: for example, processing most mail and reading written reports are low-priority items. The manager may be seen as the conductor of the orchestra and, conversely, as a puppet pulled by hundreds of strings. To find the extent to which managers controlled themselves, Mintzberg analysed whether in each activity managers were active or passive; he found only a small proportion of active work and that managers spent much time reacting. However, the initial construction of the manager's job may have included decisions to allow these reactions and passive participation as a way of keeping up a flow of work and ensuring the involvement of others in the management process.

The effective leader may well be the 'mandarin', i.e. politically shrewd (in the ways of his or her own organization). Ready to respond to the needs of others, such leaders control enough of their time to give the lead, to sustain effort, to maintain momentum, to motivate others, to articulate vision and so on. The effective leader may well be the person capable of meeting the varying demands made on him or her while undertaking a workable balance of the various roles, workable for the given organization at a particular point in time. It has to be said that we do not know. Many of the biographies produced by well-regarded corporate leaders might be read along these lines but we are woefully short of clear evidence. What I have attempted to do in this chapter is piece together the various ideas and some relevant evidence to illustrate what we do know about corporate leaders as people and about the situations within which they work. If the picture turns out to be rather complex, at least we have the outline of the emphases that effective corporate leaders might provide for their organizations and their own people. In later chapters I will develop this into guidelines on how to analyse situations, recognize the management and leadership options available and assess the likely advantages and disadvantages of each.

However, what seems clear is that Deal and Kennedy (1982, page 8) may well be right when they suggest that 'Business certainly needs managers to make the trains run on time; it more desperately needs *heroes* to get the engine going.' They go on to say that heroes do the following:

- Symbolize the company to the outside world.
- Preserve what makes a company special.
- Set a standard of performance.
- Motivate employees.
- Provide role models.
- Make success attainable and human.

Perhaps this last point is the key. The effective corporate leaders bring human scale to risk, change, success, challenge and crisis. They translate the pressures that can confuse or paralyse so many into acceptable levels. They are not afraid to fail. Nor are they afraid to question, to ask why. Their approach to leadership is both skilled and thoughtful (following Mant, 1983). Thus it is that they become credible and successful.

Ben & Jerry's is a company which created a new vogue in ice cream. It was created by two friends, Ben Cohen and Jerry Greenfield and grew quickly to rival Haagen-Daz in the premium market. In 1995 they appointed a new CEO. The appointee famously produced a poem called 'Time, values and ice cream' as part of his submission for the appointment. It seems clear that in seeking a new CEO they looked for operational experience and a commitment to the values which had driven Ben & Jerry's, which sees prosperity emerging out of commitment to the product, to a social mission in the community and to an economic mission. How can a new leader expect to provide the necessary unifying focus without similar beliefs? But that is not enough. Also needed is the operational credibility to create momentum for change and to bring to bear new ideas to achieve improved performance. But a belief in the product was also essential – hence the poem. Was the most convincing aspect of the new CEO's contribution that he brought human scale to the process of leadership?

Leadership and 'human scale'

What do we mean when we say that effective leaders are those who bring human scale to risk, challenge, success and crisis? Tennyson captures part of our thought in the line:

Pray God our greatness may not fail, thro' craven fears of being great.

Tennyson, 1885

We argue that the effective leader is not afraid to fail. The fear of failure can be as paralysing as the fear of freedom (Fromm, 1944).

Summarizing Fromm's powerful argument very briefly, modern industrial capitalism (he makes no distinction between state and corporate capitalism) has freed us from traditional bonds of nature, caste and religion. It contributed tremendously to the increase of positive freedom, to the growth of an active, critical, responsible self. However, it also made the individual more alone and isolated, creating in the individual a sense of insignificance and powerlessness. Isolated and powerless, many individuals are afraid to depend on themselves; rather, they attempt to submerge the self. Taking risks, trying out new ideas and experimenting bring attention to oneself. This is difficult for many and, as we have already seen, much of the way in which we structure and manage organizations serves to reinforce this already powerful tendency. What then can the leader do? Fromm suggests that 'progress . . . lies in enhancing the actual freedom, initiative and spontaneity of the individual . . . above all in the activity fundamental to every man's existence, his work'.

In my view the leader who can bring human scale to organizational problems can do two things: first, cope with the pressure on the self, the leader's fear of failure, the stress and pressure of the circumstances to be handled; second, find ways of helping others to cope with the pressures on them. In practical terms this means facing the issues addressed in previous chapters. Fromm identifies three escape mechanisms which are directly relevant to our argument.

People experiencing the fear of freedom will also experience the fear of failure because they must take risks in order to build their own selves. Those incapable of doing so rely on three principal escape mechanisms: authoritarianism, dull conformity and destructiveness. How many times have you come across managers, at all levels, who become more autocratic as the pressure on them builds? ABF Ltd is an example of both the situation and its consequences, a vicious circle leading to decline (see Chapter 11). How many times have you noticed that employees subjected to changes respond with apathetic conformity? One has the changes 'bolted in' but does one have commitment? How many times have you seen opposition to new ideas before they have been given a chance? These are the three mechanisms to which Fromm refers – emerging out of the pressures and uncertainties of a changing world.

Conclusion

Bringing human scale to the problems of organization and change is about pragmatism. It is about resolving today's problems today. One needs to give people a vision of the future, but one also needs to help them to see the stepping-stones along the way. The leader needs to cope with change, so do followers. It seems to me that this is the ultimate defining characteristic of effective corporate leaders. They can energize and sustain people to act, to try things out, to get on with the job in hand. They can energize people to try. Thus to conclude this chapter I argue that the practical side of leadership depends not on grand theories but, rather, on the ability to encourage others into action. This depends on the management of attention, measuring trust and self, as Bennis (1984) makes clear. But it also depends on credibility. The leader's vision needs to be credible. People need to perceive the credible actions that they can take and that they feel they can control. Thus we bring 'human scale' to leadership and change.

Few would argue that risk aversion has not been a common characteristic of organizations, particularly larger organizations. Many may think that this is changing. One fairly recent survey suggests that the problem lives on. A survey of the role of IT (Birchall, 1993) examined 'barriers to change'. A sample of respondents from large and medium-sized companies was asked to list barriers to IT implementation. Items such as 'staff prefer structured organization' (60 per cent of respondents), management control of homeworkers (50 per cent), organization risk averse (38 per cent), rigid organization hierarchy (15 per cent) all may well be linked to risk aversion. The leadership challenge is all too clear given also the other barriers linked to perceived lack of IT capability. Clear vision and leadership will evidently be needed where risk aversion is combined with perceived lack of capability. As we shall see, success here includes the leader's cognitive style which here we suggest may relate to the ability to create 'human scale'.

EXERCISES

1 From your reading of the business press available to you, can you identify a key corporate leader? How does this leader display the competencies we have listed?

2 How important is the situational model of leadership as a training and development tool?

3 What do you think are the behaviours required of successful leaders in a period of change?

10 The learning organization

Ideas and concepts such as 'organizational learning' and 'the learning organization' are widely used by human resources management practitioners. Senior managers express the wish to create 'learning organizations'. At various points throughout this book we argue the view that effective change necessarily involves learning. What does this mean? Can we claim that organizations learn? Does it matter? It is clear that managers may learn as part of the process of change either about themselves or about the company, its environment and so on. This much is illustrated by the previous chapter. But can an organization learn?

Not least of the reasons for interest in the question is the observation that business techniques appear suddenly, rather like fashion. Moreover, the use of such techniques ebbs and flows, waxes and wanes. Often one can also readily conceive today's latest technique as comprising old ideas recycled, repackaged and projected as novel to gain attention, or so it seems. In reality it appears that organizations adopt fashionable techniques but are unable to incorporate them as a sustained way of doing business.

At one level, organizational learning clearly is of interest. If only individuals learn then when people leave an organization the learning they have achieved goes with them. This happens a great deal in practice. On the other hand, learning is often reflected in changing procedures, patterns of behaviour, evolving cultures and so on. Some would argue that these do change and that therefore learning is 'captured'. In that sense organizations learn.

The central point is whether or not we can observe systematic changes in behaviour and culture over time. If we can there is clearly a basis for arguing that while the process of learning may be individual, the consequences may be more wide reaching.

Thus if the individual processes lead to enduring changes in behaviour and culture (in teams and throughout an organization) then the learning is 'captured' at the broader level. So we might refer to 'organization' as opposed to individual learning, and organizations which seek to encourage the 'capture' of learning could be said to be 'learning organizations'. However, there is no accepted model of organizational learning and, moreover, not everyone agrees about whether an organization can learn.

There are two main points here:

1 The debate may be largely irrelevant to those concerned with developing organizational practice.

2 Many ideas about organization and 'organizational learning' are incomplete.

We would accept the following:

> **Scholars of organisations have developed theories that not only don't work for them but won't work for others.**
>
> Weick, 1991

In any event, the focus of this chapter is on how an organization can be designed, systems created and a climate developed to encourage learning and effectiveness.

Changing perceptions of organization

We have already seen (in Chapter 2) that our perception or mind-set related to how organizations are described, designed and experienced is changing. This is due to technological, market and competitive changes and challenges. However, part of the change is associated with the impact of rapid, often discontinuous, change and attempts by those involved to find ways of dealing with this increased pace and complexity. In addition, issues such as managing diversity, cross-cultural influences, gender and the environment are creating new challenges to rethink the organization. Finally, the challenge of the long-term switch from a 'career for life' model for at least some employees to a more individually centred concept of career perhaps adds a new impetus to 'learn how to learn'.

In consequence, new ways of describing organizations are now beginning to replace more orthodox approaches. Peter Senge maintains that it is now necessary to think more carefully about what is meant by learning and organization. His work challenges practising managers to recognize that 'mind-set' is a crucial aspect of learning.

> **The most accurate word in Western culture to describe what happens in a learning organisation is one that hasn't had much currency for the past several hundred years. The word is 'metanoia' and it means a shift of mind. To grasp the meaning . . . is to grasp the deeper meaning of learning.**
>
> Senge, 1990

Looking back at the Ford case study given in Chapter 3 (see page 38), whether or not you conclude that Ford was (or is now) a 'learning organization' it is clear that over a period of time the company believes it has learned lessons and/or developed systems (e.g. the worldwide engineering release system) which provide an important platform for the global developments now underway.

Van der Erve (1994) argues that evolution is the engine of corporate success. He argues that evolution requires that we both understand the changes impacting on us and know how to ride those changes. Evolution involves a succession of differentiated 'life forms'. Clearly organizational change involves differentiation whether of product features, or target markets or internal capabilities, employee attitudes or customer loyalty or whatever. A chairman of Nestlé offered the following prescription for successful change and growth:

Be first, be daring, and be different.

But you cannot expect to be so by accident (by random mutation as it were). On this view corporate success demands a high order of cognitive capability or, to follow Argyris and Schon (1974), the capacity for 'double-loop learning', the capacity to break the mould, to challenge the established norms, policies, objectives, resource configurations and corporate architecture.

All of this argues for the notion of paradigm shift as an important element. Capra (1986) defines a social paradigm as 'a constellation of concepts, values, perceptions and practices shared by a community which forms a particular vision of reality that is the basis of the way the community organises itself'. He goes on to argue that the social paradigm which drives 'the modern world' is evolving from a mechanistic and essentially fragmented view into a new paradigm through shifts on various dimensions, as follows:

- from a focus on the part to the whole;
- from a concern with structure to process;
- from revolutionary to evolutionary change;
- from objective science to an understanding of how we learn;
- from hierarchy to network as the metaphor for knowledge;
- from truth to approximate descriptions;
- from domination and control of nature to cooperative approaches.

The reader should note that I have modified and thereby simplified the Capra text essentially because I seek to summarize these ideas for a particular purpose. It seems to me that we are in the midst of a shift in the mind-set (or paradigm) related to economic activity towards one which emphasizes networks as learning and collaborative resources, which emphasizes proximate to optimal solutions, which emphasizes process and learning through evolution above all and which depends less on a need for certainty to precede action and more on the use of action as a means of achieving certainty.

Van der Erve (1994) describes this paradigm shift thus:

- from quantification and certainty to differentiation and uncertainty;
- from parts to wholes;
- from organization to enable tasks to 'self-organization' to enable creation;
- from single-loop to double-loop learning.

My view is that this shift in the paradigm has been associated with changes in the language of business which, in turn, has provided the possibilities for new solutions. Where once we talked of organization, tasks, systems, products, technology and customers, we increasingly talk about competencies, capabilities, added value, performance management, process design, information flow. In turn this has happened in consequence of the increased competitiveness of the world post 1970. Increasingly, when faced with tough competition the successful organization is the one which changes the rules of the game. Hamel and Prahalad (1994) conclude:

> **Market research and segmentation analyses are unlikely to reveal such opportunities. Deep insight into the needs, lifestyles and aspirations of today's and tomorrow's customers will.**

As far as major change is concerned, this paradigm shift has moved our thinking about how to achieve change. Where once the concern was with 'top-down' or 'bottom-up' change with most of our discussion being about why change programmes fail and how to use involvement programmes as a means of buy-in and success, we now seek the following, often via cascade communication programmes, change workshops, performance management programmes and the use of market mechanisms:

- Providing people with a new frame of reference about the company, its performance, its markets, etc.
- Uncovering hidden or 'tacit' knowledge (see below).
- Learning by scoping perceptions.
- Circumventing destructive politics.
- Seeking rapid change via differentiation.

In summary then, achieving mind-set shift is first and foremost a cognitive task undertaken within a social context. While communication, involvement and empowerment will form a part of the process, *unless* we are prepared to engage with the cognitive challenge we are unlikely to succeed. In turn this implies or requires certain skills to be deployed and particular organization characteristics to be in place.

Another interesting theme emerging in the strategic change literature is the focus on 'conversations'. In essence the argument runs as follows. Change is introduced, managed and experienced by people. This is given its most obvious expression by conversation. Central here in research terms would be conversations which are undertaken as part of a change effort, whether organized formally to do so or not. Researchers seek to understand how these 'conversations' both lead to and develop commitment to change being made. For example, Beckhard and Pritchard (1992) describe a 'vision-driven change effort' at Statoil in Norway. A key stage of the process developed as follows:

> **The top managers have set up a series of meetings to develop and review jointly the corporate values and principles for managing and acting. The meetings include the top management team and other senior managers as participants. The top leaders believe that, as with the vision, it is crucial for these values and principles to be 'owned' by the entire senior management. They hope the outcome of these meetings will be the commitment by the organization's leaders to use these principles and values as the guide to their behaviour.**

Clearly then conversation serves various purposes.

Ellinore and Gerrard (1998) show how the use of dialogue can help people talk through issues in ways conducive to achieving change. They define two forms of dialogue:

1 *Convergent* conversation, which narrows discussion down toward a single perspective, opinion or answer.

2 *Divergent* conversation, which expands discussion by allowing for a multiplicity of perspectives.

The crux of this is to engage in each at the appropriate time and the latter early on in discussions about change. Emery and Purser (1996), Bunker and Alban (1996) and Jacobs (1994) look at how best to gain a critical mass of people involved in change discussion in order to evolve a sense of inclusion, commitment and so on. Following Jacob in particular, it is clear that the period of divergent dialogue about change needs to be significant before attempts are made to close down and move to a more convergent dialogue, even though many people engaged may seek closure more quickly. Bryman (2006) has analysed conversations as a means of progressing strategic change. He identifies four types of conversation from a functional perspective:

1 Conversations for 'making sense' of the issues change need address.

2 Conversations for making choices.

3 Conversations for reaching commitments about change.

4 Conversations over revisions to change plans.

These he describes as a learning cycle. He goes on to observe that the 'sense-making' conversations have the profoundest impact on the content of any emerging set of change proposals. He notes the importance of divergent and convergent conversation but also notes that we may observe conversations which are either about innovation or replication. That is that at some stage the changes under discussion are genuinely innovative. Sooner or later the changes are replication, as the organization seeks to roll out change. For him, where the talk is innovative you need both divergent conversation, because this facilitates the widest search for ideas, but also finally more convergent talk for this allows for focus on the innovations to be put into place. Conversely, where replication is involved convergent conversation can create a sense of community and commitment. Clearly managing discussion, whether informal or structured as part of change events, workshops conferences and so on, requires attention to these categories and ideas.

Disciplines for the learning organization

Senge (1990) indicates how such an approach can be generated and identifies what he calls *five disciplines* as the key characteristics which everyone must develop if they wish to create a learning culture which produces an organization capable of facing the challenge of making sense of emerging complexity.

The five skills or characteristics are:

1 *Systems thinking*: everyone must learn how to view things as a whole and that one set of events impacts on others.

2 *Personal mastery*: for Senge this is 'the discipline of continually clarifying and deepening . . . personal vision, of focusing . . . energies, of developing patience,

and of seeing reality objectively. As such, it is an essential cornerstone of the learning organisation – the learning organisation's spiritual foundation.'

3 *Mental models*: these are about 'learning to unearth . . . internal pictures of the world, to bring them to the surface and hold them rigorously to scrutiny'.

4 *Build a shared vision*: this is about everyone holding a shared vision for the future. Leadership is the key to creating and communicating the vision. However, Senge sees leadership being about creating structures and activities which relate to a person's total life activity. The leader creates vision but is prepared to have it reshaped by others.

5 *Team learning*: teams, not single individuals, are the key to successful organizations of the future and individuals have to learn how to learn in the context of the team.

The key observation here is that when an organization faces increased complexity in its environment (caused perhaps by competitive and technological change) there is a need to rethink. This implies a 'mind-set' shift such as that referred to above.

How can this mind-set shift happen? Hurst (1995) argues that, faced with complexity, a performance organization needs to become a learning organization if change is to be achieved. To this end an emphasis on recognition, networks and teams replaces tightly defined tasks, control systems and rigid structures. One of the necessary conditions, Hurst argues, is crisis, i.e. a clear failure of the status quo which cannot be rationalized away, hidden or denied. He argues that all organizations go through an ecocycle comprising eight stages:

1 Strategic management.
2 Consolidation.
3 Crisis.
4 Confusion.
5 Charismatic leadership.
6 Creative network.
7 Choice.
8 Innovation.

Without needing to deny that some organizations will fail, what Hurst's model implies is a renewal process through which an organization recreates itself – more specifically in which people rethink what they seek to achieve, with whom and how, and thereby recreate the organization. Whatever else this may be, it is certainly a learning process.

How does this ecocycle model relate to the coping cycle model discussed in Chapter 13 (see page 241)? In effect the coping cycle model deals with the process associated with a single change whereas the ecocycle model presents the same ideas (i.e. initial shock, denial and confusion followed by adaptation and change) in a circular fashion in order to add the dimension of renewal.

Thus we can see that over the medium term change can be part of an overall renewal process. Moreover, we have seen that for this to happen organization processes may need to be rethought. But at the heart of this learning process are people who are either stimulated, helped or hindered by the circumstances which prevail. What do we need to think about as far as the 'fit' between individuals and the organization is concerned if we wish to engender learning and renewal?

One of the often mentioned but little analysed issues in strategic change is that of 'timing'. It is often claimed that timing is vital. One sees it in the Ford case (Chapter 3). Hurst's (1995) view of the organizational ecocycle provides one way of viewing the question of timing. By way of introducing this model I first list Hurst's own summary of its key features:

1 Change is continuous.

2 The pace of change varies, sometimes smooth and linear, sometimes rapid and non-linear.

3 Renewal requires destruction. In a resource-limited world the only way to create new structures, opportunities, possibilities is to dismantle structures which are currently claiming the resources.

4 Emerging structures and processes are a product of a multiplicity of factors including constraints imposed by the environment.

5 However, the organization's people are self-conscious 'actors' capable of rational action.

While the reader may refer to Hurst for a full treatment, here suffice it to say that the essence of the ecocycle model is to argue that organizations go through crisis and renewal through three phases:

1 Emergent action.

2 Rational action.

3 Constrained action.

The model starts with the recognition of a market opportunity which turns out to be repeatable. Hurst gives the example of Nike, a company initially established in high-performance track and field shoes, which was able quickly to expand as it moved from basketball to tennis, American football, soccer and many more activities. Also an early mover in the use of endorsements by top athletes, the company exploited a huge, untapped market. By contrast the 1980s saw increased specialization as between sports, new materials and designs combined with flexible manufacturing. Nike were then attacked by competitors such as Reebok (in the aerobics market).

In effect, therefore, Hurst argues that behaviour (action) is rational at the outset (as we seek to enter a given market), constrained as we proceed up the product life cycle (by competition not least) and then emergent as the need for renewal emerges, often because crisis has occurred or has to be precipitated before significant change can be achieved. By rational we take Hurst to mean the broader rationality we refer to in Chapter 3 rather than narrowly, scientifically rational.

The similarity between the Hurst and the Van der Erve views is obvious enough. Both are evolutionary models. In effect both argue that 'nothing fails like success', i.e. that given a successful formula which then begins to underperform, it is very difficult to get an organization to do more than seek incremental improvements which fail. Clear differentiation is what is needed. For Hurst the cycle is a learning cycle. What he does not analyse is how the learning is captured such that the organization could be said to have learned, but what he does clearly do is show business development and corporate change as a social process within which learning is embedded.

Convergence and the learning organization

Putting these ideas together a number of points appear to emerge. The most important is that if an organization is to achieve long-term benefit from the learning which is undoubtedly achieved through change then appropriate processes are needed. In fact we need *convergent systems* designed to capture and create knowledge. We need to secure a convergence of the IT infrastructure's capacity to capture knowledge, the management structure and systems design focused on the encouragement of learning, and corporate development processes aimed at achieving learning and applying it in new circumstances. All of this needs to be 'energized' by appropriate leadership, vision, rewards and 'mental maps'.

Thus we need a process which facilitates 'productive reasoning'. At root that is hard cognitive work to do with identifying and challenging assumptions, collecting and analysing data, challenging the status quo, opening up tacit knowledge and converting it to explicit knowledge, bringing in new knowledge and thinking through the unintended consequences of systems, decisions, the status quo, new ideas and so on. New techniques in the field of cognitive modelling can help in training these cognitive capabilities but at root the issue is about overcoming the organizational defences against 'productive reasoning' (see Chapter 13 for more detail).

CASE STUDY Oticon

Oticon is a Danish manufacturer of hearing aids. Having established a dominant position in its sector through the 1950s and 1960s, its performance declined in the 1980s. It was caught out by the advent of in-the-ear aids which it was slow to develop, but its decline was masked by the steady strengthening of the Danish krone in the 1980s.

This meant that when finally the need for change was accepted, action needed to be more immediate and wide ranging. Under a new chief executive a turnaround was put in place, focused initially on survival but eventually on innovation and change (from 1990 onwards).

In summary, the organization has sought to 'think the unthinkable'. In manufacturing it had a flexible manufacturing approach based on cellular approaches. In head office a 'spaghetti organization' has been created. In essence the organization is an 'internal market'. People are expected to carry out their normal jobs and be involved in projects. *Everyone* is expected to be involved in projects. There is no paper!

→

But an organization depending heavily on projects may be less effective in professional and technological development, and in particular not good at leveraging technology to maximum effect. Valuable gains in knowledge may be lost or not shared around the business. Thus it was that the role of 'guardian' was created. Guardians, often past functional managers, oversee the development of a specific professional skill (e.g. marketing, finance, technology). They are expected to ensure that Oticon's competencies meet the developing strategic requirements of the business.

Of course, we need the IT infrastructure to capture learning, e.g. to create a database of customer profile and customer complaints as a resource for product development. But best practice increasingly seeks to provide by electronic means building blocks of management knowledge, examples of best practice, best practice protocols, performance measures, diagnostic tools, etc. But new roles are also implied (see above).

But then following Nonaka and Takeuchi (1995) we can conceive of organizational learning as those processes we utilize to capture and convert tacit knowledge into new explicit knowledge and/or to obtain new explicit knowledge. Tacit knowledge is important because when organizations are faced with problems and challenges they rarely emerge overnight. Normally people within the organization have begun to recognize the problems and conceive solutions. Usually these are incomplete solutions and not thought through. They represent tacit knowledge. We need a process to 'collect' that emerging knowledge. The solutions we adopt may need new knowledge as well – say of a new technology. Thus we would seek new explicit knowledge.

Doing so, i.e. capturing and converting tacit and explicit knowledge to integrate it into our business system (into our strategy, structure procedures, product portfolios, etc.), helps the process of shifting mind-sets by adding new possibilities. Here the thought is that mind-set change is unlikely to result from directly challenging people's ideas. Rather it follows by adding new ideas, and therefore new possibilities.

Such a view has something in common with Orgland's (1997) concept of 'vision influencing'. He describes his lack of clarity of the role middle and junior managers had played in a major process redesign change undertaken by a consumer goods manufacturer. He notes that when asked to contribute to a process redesign project driven by consultants, 760 employees submitted nearly 1000 ideas. While we cannot judge the extent to which the 'bottom-up' dimension was substantial, it may well be that, by adding new ideas and concepts, the process redesign methodology created new possibilities for these managers thus helping with mind-set change.

Therefore, the ability to capture and work with knowledge is a pivotal capability creating a:

1 Knowledge base – *capture* and *convert* tacit knowledge to explicit knowledge and create *accessibility* to this knowledge.

2 Knowledge base often *organized* to achieve:
   (a) open *access* to all;
   (b) effective *sharing* of information – conferences, meetings, etc.;

(c) focus on *technology*;

(d) *integration* across corporation;

(e) systematic capture, analysis and retrieval of *customer* information.

For example, Kao Japlin's leading household and chemical products business handles 250 customer calls a day and now has 350,000 customer questions/complaints stored in the system, which can be analysed and recalled using 8000 keywords by customer name, product, division, date or geographical area.

Competence development in handling change

I set out a model widely used in the training literature which looks at the stages of competence development. In any change setting we move from unconscious incompetence to unconscious competence via conscious incompetence and then conscious competence (Figure 10.1).

The typical analogy to draw is that of learning to drive: the process of moving from unconscious incompetence (in which we are not aware of lack of competence or what it means) to a state of conscious incompetence when we first sit behind the driving wheel. In a state of heightened awareness we become immediately aware of lack of competence. This initial process is one of awareness raising. In a change setting, this may come via communication processes, visits and so on, but will often come from facing new demands from customers or sources of competition which cannot readily be met. The latter are generally brought out through diagnostic studies, internal reviews, etc., undertaken by consultants (external or internal), task forces, etc.

The next process is that of skill building as we move from conscious incompetence to conscious competence. Here we have the first stage of implementation.

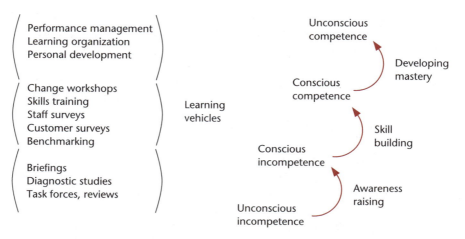

Figure 10.1 Competence development in change

Skills in new systems, procedures, etc are developed and practised. The learning vehicles include change workshops, staff training, surveys, etc. Here awareness of the process is high and the level of personal risk taking at its highest. Management support for risk taking is vital, as is an understanding that the most important process here may well be experimentation. Early attempts to use a new approach enable us to identify the modifications usually needed to make it work effectively. This is the process within which individual learning is at its highest and is therefore the time during which organizational learning should be maximized. Yet how often do we seek to capture the lessons from early change trials and change workshops in order to transfer systematically the emerging best practice?

The final process is that of developing excellence through long practice. Here the learning vehicle is performance management systems and includes attention to personal development and organizational learning. Now the competence becomes so practised that we no longer think about it. It becomes embedded in the organization, part of the background. Thus it is that further learning demands the specific attention that performance management systems (use of a balanced scorecard, value-added approaches, performance appraisal, etc.) can provide. Here, as excellence in performance is achieved, the rate of learning declines.

Overall then there is an obvious dilemma. Compare this model with the coping cycle model. In the middle of the change process, just as learning is at its fastest, self-esteem is at its lowest. Thus it is that people need encouragement, support, role models (the superuser concept) and the security which comes from being able to go through the learning process in clear and incremental steps and at their own pace. *Do things fast by moving slowly* becomes the watchword!

Conclusion

Some argue that we learn too little from history. A.J.P. Taylor, the famous historian, argued that we learn too much – always seeking to adapt structures which earned us past success rather than adapt to changes. The dilemma is that customer service requires consistency, reliability, efficiency and stability while change and learning is necessarily a volatile, questioning process. Thus we seek means of combining certainty and stability with adaptability and the ability to 'flex' to changing needs.

While many argue that the key to developing a learning culture is concern for people, this seems not to be obviously true – even though this does not make concern for people undesirable nor vitiate the notion that you may need it for other reasons. As has been argued, learning appears not to be an issue of motivation as such. Rather it may be one of removing constraint in order that a natural tendency to development and learning can be harnessed by the organization. Does this leave us with the thought that learning, both a cognitive experiential and social process, is nevertheless a process largely the preserve of a cognitive elite?

EXERCISES

1 Is your own organization a learning organization? Explain.

2 Can you identify an example of tacit knowledge – about product, processes or customers – in your own situation?

3 How does your company seek to 'capture' knowledge?

11 Strategies for change

Introduction

Our problem, in essence, is a simple one. We never have enough time to do anything, but we always find time to do it twice.

President, French Pharmaceutical Company

In a changing world the only constant is change. So why write a book about managing change in an organizational world which is already changing at a dramatic rate? I run workshops on managing change for management audiences around the world. Over the last 10 years or so managers have gained more experience with, and more confidence in, the management of change. The reality is that the stability which seemed to characterize the corporate world in the 1950s and 1960s has given way to increased and global competition, technological innovation and change, limited resources, deregulation, privatization of public sector organizations and change in much more besides. But with that growing confidence there is a growing interest in learning how to manage change more effectively.

What does all this mean to us, as employees and as managers? How can we seize advantage from the process of change? How can we help ourselves and others cope with the often stressful experience of change? How can we ensure that we manage changes well? How can we create more effective organizations? Is it possible to do so and still encourage people to learn, develop and fulfil themselves? Can we do all this and make money as well? By gaining a better understanding of why certain approaches to management seem to work we can pursue each of these objectives more fully.

In today's world, managers face complex and challenging pressures and opportunities. They must ensure the efficient use of resources and, at the same time, find ways of guaranteeing the long-term effectiveness of the organizations for which they work. Effectiveness includes the ability to identify the right things to do in the future (the right products and services to offer, the appropriate technologies to exploit, the best procedures and structures to introduce, to find, recruit and retain people with appropriate skills). Effectiveness also requires the ability to adapt so that we can achieve these new tasks. It therefore comprises the ability to adapt to changing circumstances.

Planning, implementing and coping with change has been, and seems likely to remain, one of the main challenges facing managers, in both the private and public sectors, today. In manufacturing, banking, education and healthcare change is the norm. The merger and acquisition boom of recent times brings change on its trail throughout industry and commerce. Frequently, for many, these changes must be undertaken in testing circumstances. Sales and profitability may be falling rapidly. A merger bid may lead managers to review performance and strategic plans. All this might form part of a defence against the merger. In any event, whether or not the merger or takeover succeeds, change seems likely. Many organizations face deregulation. Banking is a good example of this but not the only one. Transport deregulation has had a dramatic impact in some European countries (e.g. the Republic of Ireland). Central government spending decisions can create powerful pressures on expenditure within public service organizations, often with dramatic effects on the attitudes of staff and clients.

BMW bought Rover from British Aerospace because (among other reasons) it believed that Rover had manufacturing facilities which operated more flexibly and at lower cost than much of its own plant in Germany. Japanese companies source units in Taiwan and Malaysia for much the same reasons. An international consultancy firm identifies its Singapore operation as a centre of excellence in software design. It project-manages design projects but utilizes the services of designers in the USA and Europe, all linked by electronic means. Thus the Singapore centre manages a design process which is going on 24 hours a day. No one can dispute that the world of work and working is seeing dramatic changes. Still less would anyone argue that the challenge of managing in a changing environment is getting any easier.

Growing competition, privatization and deregulation across many parts of industry, commerce and the public sector have led many organizations to try to develop in their staff more commercial awareness and more concern for quality. Managers are concerned with value for money, the development, launch and marketing of new products and services, greater flexibility of design, manufacture or service, and in less definable issues such as corporate image and identity. Customers and clients are ever more vocal and critical. The main focus of management is switching from largely internal concerns to a more balanced focus on internal and external concerns. This chapter is concerned with understanding how managers can create more effective organization in a world of change. It examines why and how approaches to management have been changing and sets out practical guidelines for management action in today's world.

For instance, when five long-established corps of the British Army were merged to form a single Royal Logistics Corps, this presented substantial change issues. As members of each corps struggled to position themselves in the new corps, a number of important issues were faced. Not least important was what badges and uniforms were to be used? How best to make such decisions? It was decided to establish a working group of senior non-commissioned officers to resolve these issues, partly because they were seen as less likely to fight 'turf' wars over the issue but also because the army culture places senior non-commissioned officers as a source of continuity within the regimental system. Thus the approach was seen as even handed between the five corps about to be merged and defused what might have been quite disruptive conflict over these highly symbolic and, in a uniformed service, very contentious issues.

However, the objectives of this part of the book are pragmatic. The intention is not to develop a grand theory of how organizations should be structured and arranged in any 'ideal' sense. Here the reader will find no elaborate propositions, hypotheses or theories. Rather, we have attempted to synthesize what we take to be the most useful approaches to the problems of managing changing organizations. Through that synthesis we intend to achieve a rather better understanding of what can and cannot be achieved and to point the way towards improved managerial practice and performance.

In Figure 11.1 an 'outline map' of the organizational change area is proposed. It sets out the key influences on the nature of any organizational change. This relates to the scope, scale and complexity of change, these being important determinants of many of the issues which arise for those managing major changes. For example, the greater the complexity of change the more likely we are to adopt a radical approach to change. The more concerned we will be to develop a clear programme of change with accountabilities, project plans, milestones, task force inputs, etc., the more likely we will be concerned to achieve change quickly. All

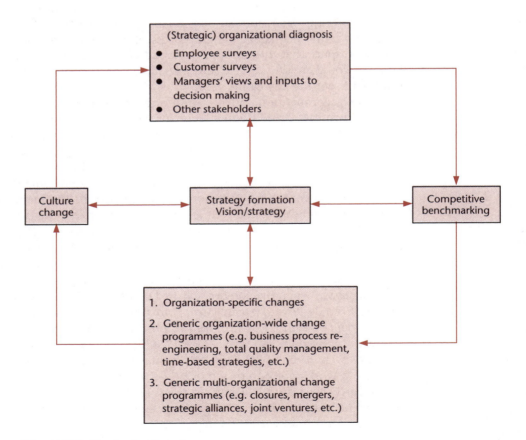

Figure 11.1 **Strategic change**

of this will be explored later; at this stage I identify some of the issues the book will address.

At the core of any major change programme is the process of strategy formation. Some say strategic choice or strategy formulation, but that implies a conscious as well as rational process of choice, whereas in many organizations that would be an incomplete view of how strategy 'emerges'. Here I follow the widely accepted view expressed in Mintzberg (1994). This sees strategy as emerging without necessarily being wholly or even partly the outcome of explicit strategic planning activities. This does not mean that it is necessarily irrational, nor that processes of choice may not be involved. Strategy may emerge from a succession of 'choices', some explicit some implicit (i.e. in people's behaviour) and therefore directly a consequence of the corporate culture (see below).

In a period of major change there is more likely to be an explicit process of strategy formation. The argument here is that such a process will be more effective if careful diagnosis is involved. Here we argue that the 'acid test' of strategy is implementation. Preparation for implementation will obviously be more effective if we have identified the 'stakeholders' involved in the changes, assessed the impact of change on them and involved them in diagnosis and planning where possible and appropriate (not always possible, see below). Moreover, careful diagnosis provides a partial assessment of the capability of the organization for change and improvement.

Furthermore, diagnosis of the capability for change is enhanced if we also carry out competitive 'benchmarking'. Measuring your own organization on dimensions such as marketing capability, logistics, operations people and organizational issues can and will lead to the generation of ideas about strengths and weaknesses and how performance can be improved. But will it mean that we can readily identify the maximum potential? One way of doing so is through the technique of competitive benchmarking. Two definitions offered are:

The continuous process of measuring products, services and practices against the toughest competitors or those companies recognised as industry leaders.

An ongoing process of measuring and improving products, services and practices against the best that can be identified worldwide.

Milborrow, 1993

Benchmarking therefore involves a comparative audit of your own and one or more organizations. For example, a US white-goods manufacturer was concerned about high distribution cost. It compared the design of its North American distribution facilities and the fact that all return journeys were empty with the performance of freight forwarding companies. This has led the manufacturer to introduce changes which have achieved dramatic reductions in distribution costs, not least by utilizing route planning to ensure that many of the 'empty' return journeys are 'filled' through contracting to carry goods inward to its own plants.

A Coopers and Lybrand survey of 105 board members drawn from *The Times* Top 1000 companies draws the following conclusions:

- 67 per cent of the companies used benchmarking;
- 82 per cent of such programmes were seen as successful;

- 88 per cent of companies using benchmarking do so regularly;
- 66 per cent of benchmark users started within the last five years.

The main areas regularly benchmarked were the following:

Human resources	60%
Customer service	72%
Manufacturing	68%
Information services	35%

Similarly the senior vice-president of a major teaching hospital in Chicago responsible for total quality management regularly benchmarks on management costs, treatment costs and quality/service.

At best, benchmarking allows us to assess the organization's performance. This becomes an integral part of the diagnostic phase of performance improvement and change. Comparison with direct competitors (if feasible) and/or with the 'best in the world' in a particular field (e.g. distribution) is a worthwhile part of this process. It promotes organizational learning. It can motivate people to tougher yet realistic goals and it can provide early warning of competitive disadvantage. There are, therefore, many good reasons to include benchmarking in the change process (see Watson, 1993).

While this may lead to the introduction of a number of *organization-specific* changes (e.g. a new information system, a new product, a new factory, etc.) it may also lead to the development of a more *generic organization-wide change programme*. Examples of such programmes include business process re-engineering programmes, total quality programmes, just-in-time manufacturing programmes, time-based strategies for product development, empowerment (including 'delayering') strategies and culture change programmes. These are particularly important because success in implementation typically involves, and has impact throughout, the organization. Changes to the corporate culture are necessary for each of them, which is why I have separated culture change from the others in the 'map'.

Finally it is worth noting that closure programmes and merger/integration programmes are major changes in their own right, as are the adoption of strategic alliances and joint ventures. These are present problems of strategic change and ones which I will touch on in this book but of which time and space do not allow full treatment. However, I will suggest some additional reading. We refer to these issues as *generic multi-organizational change programmes* because more than one organization will be directly involved. This may be true for a generic organization-wide change programme – for example, a consulting firm may be utilized, a trade union may be involved – but in the multi-organizational case such involvement is unlikely to have as important an influence on the outcomes as in the single-organization case. Note, however, that a closure programme (clearly a single-organization case) is on the borderline in that while a union may be involved it may have little practical impact. However, closure programmes often attract significant and often 'political' attention, regionally and even nationally, with the consequence that other 'organizations' become involved (e.g. government nationally or locally, other organizations seeking to purchase the activity due to be closed, management buy-outs, etc.). For example, the closure of a naval base in

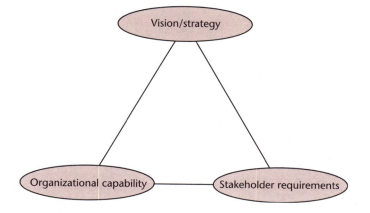

Figure 11.2 **The learning loop**

the USA attracts immediate attention and is never straightforward (indeed some would certainly argue that this is quite right on public policy grounds). Achieving strategic change can thus be described as a 'learning loop' (see Figure 11.2) comprising organizational vision and strategy and understanding of 'stakeholders' and of the organization's capability.

To be successful I suggest that strategic changes need to be managed in such a way that three necessary conditions for effective change are in place:

1 *Awareness*: stakeholders understand and believe in the vision, the strategy and the implementation plans, etc.

2 *Capability*: stakeholders involved believe they can develop the necessary skills and can therefore both cope with and take advantage of these changes.

3 *Inclusion*: stakeholders involved feel that they value the new jobs, opportunities, etc., and *choose* to behave in the new ways (new attitudes, skills and ways of working).

Much of the remainder of this book will deal with how to create the conditions for effective change. To conclude this section, however, consider one vital element: namely, the importance of achieving an effective 'fit' between corporate and 'functional' strategies if effective change is to be achieved. At root most major changes fail in implementation and often because we have not considered the impact of the new strategy on the different functions and activities (strategic business units, divisions, etc.), nor indeed have we thought about the interaction between functional (or divisional) strategy and overall strategy.

We turn now to an illustration, that of ABF Ltd. This case presents a company wherein changes in organization, manufacturing methods and management and reward systems could only be made if tensions with the management team could be resolved. It demonstrates that the idea that change *will only* be possible with support from top management is a serious oversimplification. This is true enough as far as it goes but it begs the question of whether or not top management need to change themselves as part of the process of change.

ABF Ltd

ABF Ltd designs, manufactures and markets hydraulic filters. It comprises two product groups (industrial and process control). It is a relatively autonomous subsidiary of a larger group. The company employs 350 people. Its turnover in 1994 was £22 million, with a profit of 8 per cent of turnover. The managing director of ABF Ltd reports to the group board and is held accountable against a set of targets of profit sales volume, capital spend, market share and growth. In the late 1980s profit had been slowly declining, both absolutely and as a proportion of turnover (since 1984), and this despite reasonable growth in turnover.

At the time of the study the current managing director had worked with the company for 21 years, 10 as managing director. All his senior colleagues were long-service employees. During late 1985 the group chief executive had begun to devote increasing attention to ABF, visiting on several occasions and asking for more detailed performance figures. Following discussions between the group chief executive and the managing director it was decided to bring in a team of management consultants to review procedures throughout the company. There was growing concern about both direct and indirect costs. The consultants were asked to look at the following five areas:

1 Planned maintenance policies.

2 Quality levels and quality assurance.

3 Utilization of machine setters and technicians.

4 Information and control systems.

5 Manufacturing organization.

As this review proceeded a number of significant changes were introduced, particularly to tighten up quality control procedures and to provide improved information. The finance director (who was also responsible for personnel and administration) was the prime mover behind many of these changes.

The management team also experienced a range of what we often refer to as 'human relations problems'. Confrontation between managers was a regular occurrence. Often, managers would adopt an aggressive approach in discussions, taking entrenched and always 'departmental' positions. Conflict between the production director and staff in the sales department was particularly prevalent. On the face of it there was little understanding (or attempt to understand) by each department of the objectives and problems of the other.

Communication was also very poor. Rarely were the production departments notified of priority orders in good time. Little attempt was made to coordinate sales plans with production plans. There had been several instances of large orders agreed, with short delivery schedules, without any consultation between the two departments. This often led to disrupted schedules within production departments. Machine utilization was poor, ranging from as low as 11 per cent to rarely more than 45 per cent.

Managers tended to treat subordinates autocratically, issuing orders but allowing no discussion. Ideas were either suppressed or ignored, particularly if they came from younger employees. People were expected to conform to 'the way we have always done things around here'. Managers appeared to feel that change was both a threat and an implied criticism of their own personal performance.

Managers seemed obsessed with objectives set years ago. For example, in production, the main concern was with the sales value of output and with efficiencies. The disrupted schedules made both harder to achieve. Little concern was directed at quality of output. In fact deliveries were often late and there was a high level of returned goods. Attempts to start discussion of these latter problems led to intensely defensive reactions by production management. However, much patient work by the finance director, with the production director, created some movement here. A review of quality control procedures led them to agree to appoint more quality inspectors who were to be located at the problem areas in the production sequence. One of the concerns was that quality problems were being discovered late, subsequent to further work having been carried out on the already defective items.

The company had originally experienced strong growth between 1978 and 1986, but since 1986 profits had stagnated, and even begun to decline. The morale of the company appeared to be low. Delegation to middle and junior management was very limited. No management training ever took place. Promotion was entirely from within. The managing director expressed the view that someone who had been promoted would 'know what to do or else we should not have promoted them'. Discouraged in taking the initiative or in promoting ideas, and thus lacking in self-confidence, many junior or middle managers tended to leave decisions to the directors. In consequence the directors were often vocal in their criticisms of the managers, and felt that the managers were unable to make effective decisions.

As can be readily seen, there is something of a 'vicious circle' at work here. Given the management style in use it seems quite likely that the growth between 1978 and 1986 placed senior managers, directors and the company's various systems under pressure leading to declining performance. This appears to have led to a redoubling of the directive management style in an effort to regain control. However, instead of gaining control, this merely made matters worse. More staffing in key areas would help and the recently agreed increases in the number of inspectors was the first such increase. In fact, the declining performance meant that the managing director had always opposed increased indirect staffing. Ultimately, of course, more staffing was not the answer. An approach to improving style and managerial effectiveness and performance needed to be developed.

The finance director often suggested that management performance needed improvement. He thought that management training was worth investigating. The managing director tended not to listen to other people's views; thus there was very little exchange of ideas. People tended not to approach the managing director to discuss problems, the only exception being the finance director who had worked with him as a senior colleague for 16 years. The managing director and others found discussing attitudes and feelings difficult and they thus avoided doing so. This was often explained as a means of protecting other people's sensitivities: 'We don't want to press the point for fear of upsetting X, who is under a lot of work pressure.' There was very little open statement and testing of views. The finance director's early attempts to discuss quality were hindered by the managing director claiming that quality was a production responsibility and refusing to talk about the problems with anyone other than the production director so as not to undermine him. However, if an important customer complained about the level of returns the managing director would often criticize production bitterly, aggressively and openly. Eventually, the finance director's attempts to discuss quality problems were welcomed by the production director with a great sense of relief. Someone was interested. Someone was listening.

Appraisals of senior staff were not carried out. Indeed, recording performance reviews on paper was seen to be counterproductive. However, the managing director had, and

179

was known to have, strong views about individuals and often discussed them at length with other senior colleagues: it seemed that he liked to get general confirmation of the views that he felt unable to confirm with the individual. Consequently, he formed views of people which he did not share with them. In conversation with these people he gave the impression that he did not trust them; they then felt unable to approach him to discuss this because he always avoided such discussion.

All this became very clear to the finance director. It must also be said that the managing director had a wealth of contacts and experience in the industry and had generated, mostly by his own efforts, much of the business growth from the late 1970s. He was widely respected in the industry. The consultants were making it clear to him that changes were needed within the production department. They were reporting very low productivity, rising costs and poor motivation of employees. They were now proposing a package of changes to deal with these problems. However, the consultants had indicated that their greatest concern was the views of shop-floor and clerical employees. There was a general rejection that the problems were anything to do with them. If problems existed this was entirely a consequence of poor management. They felt that any change of programme would have to be managed participatively. While management performance needed improving, many of the changes that the consultants wished to introduce would have a direct bearing on shop-floor employees. Their acceptance was going to be important if change was to be implemented quickly.

The 'vicious circle' was now complete. Unless management style could be changed no one could possibly expect other changes to be handled participatively. The company needed to work on management style, managerial effectiveness, management team working, management systems and structures and changes to manufacturing organization. The finance director and the managing director were beginning to realize that some fundamental changes were needed.

As a first stage it was agreed that the finance director would develop a system of performance appraisal for senior managers, working with his other board-level colleagues. He and the production director were beginning at last to make inroads into the quality problems. Return rates and rework costs were falling and improvements in information were providing production managers with better control over production schedules and progress. By working together improvements were being delivered, as a result of which the self-confidence of production managers began to improve. A more open and systematic approach to performance appraisal seemed to be leading to some more honest discussion of performance and problems. Slowly but surely a less defensive approach was being adopted.

Once improvements began the finance director was able to convince the managing director that he and the production director, supported by the consultants, should now carry out changes within manufacturing. A key and highly contentious problem was the bonus system; it was outdated. Direct employees were paid a productivity bonus representing, on average, 60 per cent of gross pay. The link between productivity improvement and bonus payment was unclear. Moreover, the bonus in the industrial product group had risen more slowly than that in the process section.

A strategy for change

As a first stage the finance and production directors met with union representatives to discuss these problems. The representatives firmly rejected the idea that the bonus system itself needed changing, although they did hope that the disparities in bonus could be resolved. The directors provided very detailed information showing productivity, cost, pay, quality and other relevant data. They gave guarantees that no cut in pay or redundancy would result from a review of the bonus system and that employees would be involved in any effort to resolve the problems. However, they made it clear that they were determined to improve both productivity and quality, and that, in the long term, factory numbers would depend on performance. The position of the company was becoming increasingly uncompetitive. Something needed to change.

It was agreed to bring in the consultants to work to the following brief, agreed between these two directors and the union representatives:

1 To undertake a survey of attitudes in the production departments.

2 To provide an independent check on the problems of productivity and rising costs.

3 To design a wage system acceptable to management and employees *and* equitable as between the process and industrial product groups.

4 To indicate any further areas where significant improvements to industrial relations might be achieved.

For the first time for some years a more open management style was in use. This appeared to be creating some 'movement' by both managers and employees.

The attitude survey revealed some surprises. Employees seemed to prefer higher basic pay and lower, but still significant, bonuses. They felt that much of the low productivity stemmed from inadequate control by supervisors and managers. There clearly was some truth in this (see above). It was agreed to establish joint working parties to devise a means of achieving the following amendments over a six-month period:

1 New working practices and improved quality.

2 A bonus system using the 'added value' concept to link company performance to bonuses.

3 Revised standards based on methods study.

4 The introduction of new technology.

Now followed a period in which many of the initiatives were moving forward together. In practice, there were many problems along the way. In general, however, a more open approach by senior management and more effective team work involving various functions and departments were leading to dramatic improvements. Increasingly, the various initiatives were becoming mutually sustaining. The early success of the first quality changes and more effective information and control meant that production schedules were less disrupted, and manufacturing therefore somewhat more orderly. This meant that production managers were under less constant pressure. That being so, they were less autocratic, partly also because of the changing examples coming from the finance director and the production director. The managing director, by recognizing that change was needed and by trusting the finance director, was also changing his style.

Over a period of four years (to 1993) productivity increased by 60 per cent. Costs were first curtailed and then reduced. New machinery and new staffing could now more readily be justified. Self-confidence began to build sustained by positive feedback, both informally and through the performance appraisal system. The case raises a number of issues which typically must be addressed when significant organizational change is needed.

Management performance and learning

One thing is clear from this case. Senior managers needed to *learn* that preceding systems and styles were no longer working. A narrow focus on outdated objectives was one problem, the autocratic management style another. Until they learned that change was needed their approach was simply more of the same, only making things worse. Where fundamental changes are needed we must first look at how managers see the problems. What feedback systems are used? How do they monitor performance? What do they monitor? What strategies and approaches are they using to effect improvements? How do they monitor and review these strategies? Do they modify their approach in the light of feedback? Are new ideas encouraged? Are they examined carefully? Are the needed resources available? Do the existing systems of performance appraisal, promotion, product development, pay and benefits training, corporate culture and management style encourage or inhibit either the achievement of corporate objectives or improved performance? First and foremost, therefore, we need to review managerial performance.

■ Effective team work

I well remember hearing a senior manager from an international oil company state that 'the problem of managing change is, in essence, a multi-functional problem'. We have worked hard in our organizations to develop highly competent and professional functions, but as the functions have changed, developed and improved so we have more and more problems in obtaining collaboration between them. Integration becomes a key task. Thus we must add to managerial performance and learning the need to gain more effective collaboration across functional boundaries.

Partly, this is a matter of attitudes and understanding. Partly, it is a matter of effective information and control. In ABF Ltd it was vital to integrate the work of sales and production. Partly, it is a matter of jargon. The oil company manager gave the management of information technology projects as an example. He argued that it was increasingly recognized that the key to success in such projects was to gain effective user and specialist collaboration. This is often made the more difficult given the specialist jargon that both information technology and user departments may use. Going a stage further, he noted that his company, in common with many others, now always allocated responsibility for managing IT projects to user department managers.

■ Effective organizational structures and systems

Next an effective structure and systems need to be in place either to sustain existing strategies or to implement new ones. There must be appropriate accountabilities, reporting systems, information and authority, and resource allocation. Revised systems, performance appraisal, promotion and so on need to be defined in order to sustain or improve performance against the organization's objectives. Without effectiveness here, other changes (say new products or new technology) cannot be properly deployed or exploited.

■ Organizational change

All the above may, of course, give rise to the need for change. However, without effectiveness in the above three areas other changes will be more difficult to implement, such as new strategies, new products/services, new markets or client groups and new technologies. It will be more difficult to measure where we are, to decide what we wish to achieve, or monitor progress and problems unless these three core areas of management and organization are on the right lines. It will be difficult to generate effective new strategies, let alone achieve acceptance of the need for change, unless the above is right. We introduce changes either to improve effectiveness or to adapt to external changes. The present level of effectiveness of our organization provides the context within which we wish to introduce change. The more effective the present organization the readier employees will be to accept change. Thus we are concerned with both effectiveness and change.

■ Learning from changing

The effective organization is the one which encourages and supports learning from change. This means that an open management style, encouraging initiative and risk, is needed. However, the ability to measure and monitor progress and problems is also required. What did the managers of ABF Ltd learn from the changes they introduced? Below are set out the main conclusions of the finance director:

- There must be a clear set of objectives, linked to pressing problems which people do actually recognize.
- Planning and participation must focus on specific issues and problems.
- Employees will respond to a sustained initiative from senior management.
- It is essential to make improvements in managerial performance at an early stage.
- Creating success early on, supported by positive feedback, enables the building up of self-confidence.
- Managing change is often a slow and difficult process.
- Managers must be seen to act on solutions/ideas derived from employees.
- Monitoring and evaluation are important means of following through with change seeking further improvement.
- Managing change is a learning process for all concerned.

Looking at the ABF Ltd case study in retrospect it is clear that the company represents a good example of our 'map' of change. There was a systematic diagnosis which did lead to an organization-wide change programme. Culture change was very much to the forefront of this case. It is perhaps not surprising that benchmarking does not feature in the case – it was not a feature of change programmes in the early 1980s. What the case study does provide (both here and in Chapter 16) is an excellent example of the dynamics of change and managers' role in major change. The lessons are as relevant today as they were in 1993. But looking back, it is probably true that a company dealing with these problems today would have included benchmarking in the diagnosis, would have been more explicit about the need for culture change and would have 'sold' the changes as a single and integrated programme of change with clear accountabilities, more extensive communications planning and so on. Some argue that by doing so you can attract more attention, more resources and more commitment to change and therefore proceed more quickly. I will return to the question of how to design successful change programmes later on in the book. For the moment let us merely observe the comparison and move on.

CASE STUDY   ## SmithKline Beecham

The early 1990s saw dramatic shifts in buying behaviour regarding healthcare costs in general and pharmaceuticals in particular, whether through government action (in countries such as the UK, Germany and New Zealand) or through the actions of insurance companies (e.g. the USA). Spiralling expenditure has led to significant attempts to control costs. Since the creation of SmithKline Beecham from the merger of SmithKline and Beecham, a major change programme focused on enhancing SmithKline Beecham's ability to change and to achieve change faster than its competitors has taken place. Known as 'the simply better way', it comprises a clear change architecture within which *core concepts* such as process thinking, quality improvement, evidence-based management, continuous improvement and waste elimination are articulated via local level *improvement processes* developed within a three-year strategy. In turn the three-year strategy spells out *strategic initiatives*, *breakthrough programmes* and *improvement themes*. Longer term there is a 10-year statement of strategic intent focused on achieving sustainable competitive advantage in terms of customer satisfaction, innovation, integrity, people satisfaction and performance.

Thus there is a long-term vision linked to carefully integrated moves – three-year strategic changes, one-year process improvement projects and daily improvement actions. Clearly the intention is to make sure that everyone understands how it fits together. Within this architecture much of the improvement momentum arises from the 'daily improvement system' through which continuous improvement is sought. Here methods and techniques, team activities, measurement and recognition/reward are combined to activate improvement efforts.

All of the above has been 'rolled out' according to a 'road map' over the period 1990 to date. The road map specifies key elements as the focus of successive years and indicates the processes of conferences, communications, education, training, support and change roll-out over time. The clear purpose of the road map is to show how the architecture is being put in place over time.

Conclusion

Following Woodward and Buchholz (1987), we conclude this chapter with a final pragmatic thought. Let us pretend that there is a scale of the extent to which we manage a changing organization (in a changing world) effectively. At one end of the scale is ideal, well-planned, sensitively handled, carefully timed, sufficiently resourced change; at the other end of the scale is 'bolt on, rah rah management'. Here the idea is that the new system, procedure or structure, or whatever, can be 'bolted on' to the existing system from a technical and logistic point of view. Once that is arranged we need to sell the new system, and this is what 'rah rah' management is all about: 'You'll like this system'; 'It'll solve all your problems'; 'Don't worry, you won't lose out' are some of the things managers may say. The idea is to 'fire up' the enthusiasm of staff and to press on, regardless of problems: 'It's a great success' and 'It'll be all right on the night'. Selling *is* a part of change management, yet to be effective it must be sensitive to problems and to people's needs. Only then can the real problems, uncertainties and anxieties of change not merely be handled but, rather, be harnessed in support of the change itself. This book attempts to demonstrate how this can be done *but* we start from a pragmatic position. The 'ideal' state will not be achieved. Our view is that through better understanding we can do a *little better*, no more. To return to our opening quote, by being a little more careful about how we handle change, doing it a little more effectively, we can ensure earlier and more effective implementation, creating the capacity to manage change more effectively in future.

EXERCISES

1 What do you think are the key features of ABF's change strategy?

2 How important is benchmarking as a component of change strategy?

3 What management styles might promote more effective change in the case of ABF Ltd?

Part IV

CHANGE MANAGEMENT TECHNIQUES

12 Diagnosing change

13 Managing major changes

14 Change architecture

15 A strategy for organizational effectiveness

12 Diagnosing change

Introduction

To achieve change we must first recognize that change is desirable and feasible. We must get people to recognize that changes are needed: 'We've always done it this way', they say when you ask why a particular procedure is used. But is the fact that we have always done it this way good enough reason either to continue to do 'it' (whatever 'it' may be) or to continue to do 'it *that way*'? There is a famous story in a company I know. It is known as 'The chairman's rice puddings'. This story will help to identify the key issue here.

A senior manager had been given the task of leading a review of head-office systems and procedures. As he and his team proceeded with the review, all manner of good ideas were identified and implemented. Then, one day, the team examined the chairman's kitchen. They found that every day two rice puddings were made at 12.15 p.m. The same two rice puddings were thrown away at 2.45 p.m. When asked about this the chef said that they had always made two rice puddings. No one had ever eaten one to his knowledge. This had been happening since he joined the company eight years before. They never included the rice puddings on the menu! Further investigation revealed that 17 years before, the then chairman had chosen, on a whim, to visit the kitchen. In conversation with the chef of the day he had said that his favourite sweet was rice pudding. When he left the chef gave instructions that two were to be made each day but not included on the menu. The head waiter could then offer the chairman a rice pudding. Being a shrewd character the chef asked for two, thinking that if the chairman did ask for one then so would someone else. Four years later that chairman had retired, five years further on the next chairman died. But eight years later on the chef still made two rice puddings every day.

The point is that people become 'locked' into patterns of behaviour, systems and procedures. Once entirely sound and effective, in a changing world they may become much less so. Yet recognizing that something is no longer effective involves the willingness to consider evidence of ineffectiveness and then to question *why*, how and what might be done instead. All organizations have 'rice puddings'. What we need are systematic and workable means of monitoring performance, measuring effectiveness, measuring potential for improvement, monitoring the environment for new products, markets, distribution channels, technologies, etc. We shall see that making change is not simply a rational process. Yet diagnosing change involves and requires systematic effort, even if the diagnosis itself may need 'selling' if we are to gain acceptance for it. Having the right diagnosis is of no use if we can do nothing about it. The diagnosis must not only be right, it also needs to gain acceptance enough to make implementation feasible.

Monitoring performance, measuring effectiveness

What do we mean by effective? How do we assess whether or not our organization is doing well? What do we mean by 'doing well'? Are we concerned with profit? Or sales value? Or market share? Or service levels? If so, what level is satisfactory? The same as last year? Last year plus 5 per cent? Profit expressed as a percentage of turnover? Rate of growth of sales volume or of profit? Satisfactory for whom? Shareholders, managers, employees, clients, customers? What about comparing our performance with that of competing, or at least similar, organizations? A manufacturing company would compare itself with other companies in its own industry and sectors. A hospital would be compared with other hospitals of a similar size and case load and mix. We can readily see that the question of how well we are doing becomes quite complex.

We need to assess effectiveness for two reasons: first, identifying sources of ineffectiveness might lead us to restructure or reorganize in order to improve; second, because ineffective organizations present a tougher context in which to implement technological, product or service changes. We are often involved in both. We need to introduce new technology and discover that progress will be impeded by lack of in-house expertise and by poor attitudes to change. Part of our preparation for the new technology involves bringing in the expertise (whether by forming a new department, through secondments or transfers or by hiring consultants). Also involved may be a training programme designed to introduce people to the new technology carefully, partly to allay any fears they may have about the impact of change.

Dealing with sources of ineffectiveness as part of the implementation of change provides us with two advantages: first, it will allow us to implement change more effectively, and more speedily; second, it will make future changes easier to implement because the organization will have become more adaptable. In essence, this will be because the people involved will have learned through the process of change, learned about themselves, about the new technology and about how to prepare people to cope with change. A positive experience of change, properly exploited by all those involved, leaves people more capable of handling future change. Following Itami (1987), this means that the organization has developed its 'invisible assets'. Invisible assets are the knowledge base from which all employees operate. To quote Itami:

> **Invisible assets are the real source of competitive power and the key factor in corporate adaptability for three reasons: they are hard to accumulate, they are capable of simultaneous multiple uses, and they are both inputs and outputs of business activities.**

Developing the knowledge base from which people operate takes time and energy. Once accumulated, a knowledge base has multiple uses. If a retail company develops an excellent reputation for merchandising high-quality goods then it can use this reputation to promote products in new sectors, e.g. financial services. The reputation will attach to new stores, and this may help the company attract high-quality staff. Invisible assets are both inputs and outputs.

Having attracted high-quality staff to aid its development of a new market, these staff bring in new ideas to the company. This enables the company further to improve its operations and therefore enhance its reputation; thus being more effective as an organization is both an input to and an output of organizational change. More effective firms are more capable of handling change. Handling change effectively helps to sustain and create effectiveness in the future.

Efficiency and effectiveness

Most people distinguish between efficiency and effectiveness. Efficiency comprises achieving existing objectives with acceptable use of resources. Effectiveness means efficiency plus adaptability. The effective organization is both efficient and able to modify its goals as circumstances change. It can solve one of the dilemmas of organization: 'When we are doing well, why change?' 'Why break a winning streak?' 'Why upset a winning team?' These are everyday expressions which capture the dilemma. If we are doing well people will find it hard to justify change with all its potential costs and disruption. Yet in a changing world we must continue to adapt, and when better than while we are doing well? Doing well provides us with the resources, the time and the confidence to accept change.

Consider a company manufacturing electromechanical weighing equipment in Europe in 1970. To be efficient it needed to manufacture its products at economical costs. It needed to market its products with competitive pricing and service support. Above all, it needed to achieve 'acceptable' profits (although we must define what we mean by 'acceptable'). To be effective that company would also need to be developing electronic technology. In the 1970s electromechanical weighing machines were replaced by electronic designs which were more accurate, more reliable and smaller in size. To be effective in its market sector the company needed to be looking to electronic designs in 1970, indeed before then. It needed to be training people in the design, manufacture, sales and servicing of such equipment. The technology was available and would be applied to secure specific product improvements. Thus competitive advantage would be secured through this technology. Effectiveness implies the ability to recognize and respond to changing market or other environmental circumstances.

In looking at effectiveness, Argyris (1962) focuses on the following three core activities relevant to any organization:

1 Achieving objectives.
2 Maintaining the internal system.
3 Adapting to the external environment.

Achieving objectives is the accomplishment of the objectives specified by managers in budgets, targets or corporate plans. These include profit, turnover, market share, quality, delivery and many more. However, we need to add resource utilization here. Merely achieving objectives, at any cost, is a recipe for ineffectiveness, in the long run certainly and usually very much in the short run in competitive markets or where costs are under close scrutiny (say a police force in a city in which budgetary pressures are severe and creating impetus for 'cuts').

Maintaining the internal system includes activities and systems such as performance appraisal, management development, training and reward systems. The ability to attract and retain high-quality staff at all levels is crucial and forms a useful indicator of effectiveness.

Adapting to the external environment includes marketing, product/service development and public and community relations. How adaptable is the organization? What external reputation or image does it create? The ability to adapt springs from generating income and confidence (through achieving objectives), and developing invisible assets or learning, and through the attention devoted to the internal system. Therefore, these factors interact. In monitoring effectiveness we need to take account of all four factors: *achieving objectives, resource utilization, maintaining the internal system* and *adaptability*. But what should we monitor? There are a number of quantitative and qualitative measures available. In general, quantitative measures help us assess *the past*, although we can establish trends over time which may help us look at the future. Most importantly, quantitative measures may have a tempting but rather illusory certainty about them. The quality of a set of figures on, say, costs is only as good as the data input and the assumptions (regarding, for example, overhead allocation) involved in the cost calculations. Yet they can appear to be 'hard' data.

However, that is not the key point. All data have their limitations. The most important thing is to avoid narrow, or even single, measures of effectiveness. A famous retail store was reputed to assess the effectiveness of its store managers on 'shrinkage' (the loss of stock from stock rooms and shelves). Taken to the ultimate, the best way of minimizing shrinkage is to lock the stock room, even to lock the store. There are no sales but also no shrinkage! There is a famous story of a Soviet nail-making factory which for many years exceeded its annual target in successive five-year plans. The factory director was assessed on the weight of nails produced. He had discovered that with the machinery available to the factory, output would be maximized by producing nails one foot long. He did so – millions and millions of them.

Recently I was working in a famous furniture manufacturing company, a household name worldwide. The company had quality problems with a high rate of rejection. Most rejection took place predespatch, but after the whole manufacturing process was complete; 35 per cent of faults occurred in the first stage of an 11-stage production cycle. Considerable value added was being built into this furniture, wastefully. Yet departmental managers were achieving their targets. They were assessed on volume, not volume *and* quality!

Narrow approaches can be misleading. What is needed is a broad approach to assessment. If we are making profit are we making as much profit as we can? How are our competitors doing? Where can we improve? Is there any evidence of ineffectiveness? Also, we need to avoid the tendency to concentrate only on that which we can readily monitor, such as the weight of nails produced. In a rapidly changing world we must work harder than that. Quantitative measures are important and measuring quantitatively creates an analytical discipline. But experience and intuition are also important. Thus we need to make qualitative judgements of employee satisfaction and attitudes, of management style, of adaptability and of management development. We need to monitor a balanced set of indicators over all four quadrants of the effectiveness matrix (see Figure 12.1).

Looking at the matrix allows us to consider an appropriate set of factors with which to assess organizational effectiveness. We need to monitor a balanced set of factors for the reasons stated above. Yet we must recognize that assessment itself costs money. We cannot assess everything. What we choose to assess will vary from organization to organization. The most important point is to recognize that to monitor effectiveness we must look at factors in all four quadrants in a systematic way, and that we must look at both objectives and resources. The use

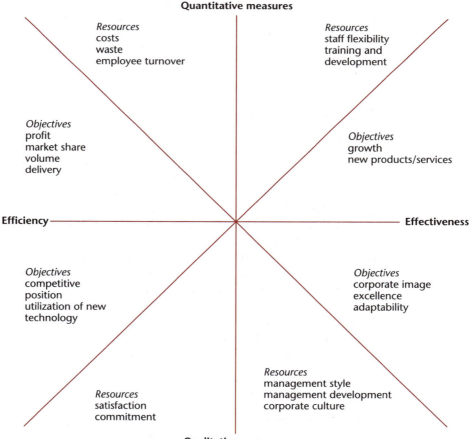

Figure 12.1 The effectiveness matrix

and development of resources (maintaining the internal system or building invisible assets) is the main impulse to effectiveness. Identifying the right strategy is not enough if we lack the people and the commitment for its implementation. As Will Rogers once said: 'You can be on the right track but you'll get run over if you just sit there.'

Many organizations are pretty good at the top left-hand quadrant. Information systems have been developed to provide managers with quantitative information on various aspects of performance, both objectives and resources. That said, I often make this point to audiences of managers and then ask: 'How well is your organization doing?' 'Not well enough' is one way of summarizing their response! Few organizations systematically monitor factors in the other quadrants. However, organizations are increasingly moving in this direction. Some monitor the extent and scope of training and development. For example, at least one European bank monitors staff development regularly because it recognizes the challenges that the bank, and therefore its staff, must meet on the IT front. Training and development form a central feature of this bank's strategy in this area.

An international computer company assesses attitudes and satisfaction of staff to various aspects of the company, the policies, the work setting and so on every two years (bottom left-hand quadrant) and instructs all employees to appraise the performance of their own manager every year. This latter, combined with performance appraisal carried out by managers with superiors, provides a regular input to the bottom right-hand quadrant.

Techniques for assessment

The problems we face are changing and complex. If you cannot measure them you cannot manage them. This is why we need to develop a balanced set of measures.

We turn now to techniques for monitoring effectiveness. These comprise a checklist for completing a functional analysis of the organization and a diagnostic questionnaire. The data to be collected are often expressed quantitatively. However, these techniques are really focusing on factors within the qualitative end of the matrix; not all the data obtained are quantitative – at least some qualitative comment is generally either asked for or received when techniques like these are used; moreover, the limitations of these kinds of data mean that interpretation is always and ultimately a matter of judgement and experience.

In the next section we present an exercise for assessing organizational effectiveness with typical data drawn from International Engineering, a large engineering design and project management company discussed previously (see pages 142–4). These data were collected by myself as part of a consultancy assignment.

Assessing organizational effectiveness: exercise

This exercise presents an internal analysis of the organization in order to identify its strengths and weaknesses. In presenting the techniques, I have included data from International Engineering which we will analyse later in this chapter. I include the average score on each question derived from 92 managers who completed the exercise. This will allow us to identify the organization's capabilities and resources, and how well it is exploiting them. It will also help us to understand how effectively the organization is adapting to changing environmental circumstances. The exercise is divided into two parts: functional analysis and organizational diagnosis.

Part 1: Functional analysis

The functional analysis questionnaire in Table 12.1(a), below, has five sections that deal with five key elements within the organization – namely people, finance, marketing, operations/service and corporate/business development. Each section comprises a checklist of questions to consider and assess how well each supports the company's corporate objectives. Responses can be recorded as ticks or in note form. Score responses as follows:

5 Fully supports corporate objectives.

4 Adequately supports corporate objectives.

3 Does not support corporate objectives.

2 Makes achieving corporate objectives difficult.

1 Makes achieving corporate objectives very difficult.

Table 12.1 **Pro forma for assessing organizational effectiveness (a) Functional analysis**

	Fully supports corporate objectives (score 5)	Adequately supports corporate objectives (score 4)	Does not support corporate objectives (score 3)	Makes achieving corporate objectives difficult (score 2)	Makes achieving corporate objectives very difficult (score 1)
1 People					

1.1 The relationship between individuals and the enterprise regarding
 	
    Pay
    Promotion
    Training and development
    Performance improvement					

1.2 The skills, training and experience of personnel					
1.3 The organization's policy in respect of selection and placement of employees					
1.4 The organization's relationship with trade unions represented within the enterprise					
1.5 The extent to which human resources are considered strategically when formulating and implementing strategic decisions					

→

2 Finance

2.1 The process of budget preparation

2.2 The level of involvement of key staff in budget preparation

2.3 The extent of consistency between divisional (unit) budgets and overall organizational budgets

2.4 The extent to which financial budgets and strategic plans are compatible

2.5 The effectiveness of management control information in terms of accuracy, relevance and timeliness

2.6 The attitude of managers to management control information

2.7 The extent to which managers take corrective action to remedy problems of ineffective control

2.8 The extent to which feedback from the management information system is used to motivate improved performance

3 Marketing

3.1 The contribution of each product/service group (division, unit) to sales and profit. (Note: You may wish to tackle the question for each group, division or unit)

3.2 The market position of each product or service group (market share, growth, maturity)

3.3 The extent to which this organization competes in

       Price
       Quality/service
       Delivery

3.4 The quality and extent of our knowledge of competitors

3.5 The use made of market research and its impact on product development

4 Operations/service

4.1 The level of cooperation between marketing and operations/service

4.2 The extent to which the information received from marketing and finance is useful for managing this function

4.3 Management understanding of long-run trends in costs and performances

4.4 The extent to which management are able to control costs

4.5 The level of inventory in relation to output and sales (and the relationship between raw material,work in progress and finished goods, stocks)				
4.6 The adequacy, age and state of repair of plant and equipment				
4.7 The flexibility of use of plant, equipment and facilities				
4.8 The level of investment compared with the average for the industry				
5 Corporate/business development				
5.1 The organization's investment in development				
5.2 The ability of the organization to respond quickly to market or competitive pressures				
5.3 The organization's ability to exploit new products				
5.4 The extent to which the organization pursues opportunities for product/service improvement				
5.5 The integration of development with market, operations, finance, design, etc.				
5.6 The extent to which the organization is able to exploit outside sources for development purposes (e.g. joint ventures,consultants)				

Following the blank questionnaire above, is one showing average scores and comments relevant to International Engineering (see Table 12.1(b) below). Before examining these results you may wish to complete the functional analysis for your own organization.

Table 12.1 (b) Results: International Engineering

	Average score	*Comment*
1 People		
1.1 The relationship between individuals and the enterprise regarding		The company pays at or below the normal rate for engineers and is experiencing 15–20 per cent staff turnover per year. It promotes almost entirely from within. It has excellent technical training but limited management training. Performance appraisal is in use but is not very effective
Pay	2.24	
Promotion	2.68	
Training and development	2.56	
Performance improvement	2.10	
1.2 The skills, training and experience of personnel	3.28	The company has loyal, committed and experienced staff, is technically excellent and is perceived as such in the marketplace
1.3 The organization's policy in respect of selection and placement of employees	3.10	Problems of recruitment and rotation of staff have meant that the use of 'agency' staff has

→

		increased to approximately 40 per cent of the requirement for engineers
1.4 The organization's relationship with trade unions represented within the enterprise		Not relevant
1.5 The extent to which human resources are considered strategically when formulating and implementing strategic decisions	1.42	Not at all
2 Finance		
2.1 The process of budget preparation	3.48	The company has a well-developed budget system
2.2 The level of involvement of key staff in budget preparation	2.91	Often key staff have only limited involvement partly because of time pressures
2.3 The extent of consistency between divisional (unit) budgets and overall organizational budgets	3.88	The budgets are consistent (on paper)
2.4 The extent to which financial budgets and strategic plans are compatible	3.04	On paper, yes
2.5 The effectiveness of management control information in terms of accuracy, relevance and timeliness	2.87	While a large amount of data is available, their usefulness is limited
2.6 The attitude of managers to management control information	1.96	There is a widespread lack of a commercial approach. The company has been making losses in recent years. It is engaged in a considerable amount of work at prices which are not profitable
2.7 The extent to which managers take corrective action to remedy problems of ineffective control	2.72	
2.8 The extent to which feedback from the management information system is used to promote improved performance	1.84	
3 Marketing		
3.1 The contribution of each product/service group (division, unit) to sales and profit. (Note: You may wish to tackle the question for each group, division or unit)	2.71	
3.2 The market position of each product or service group (market share, growth, maturity)		
3.3 The extent to which this organization competes in		
Price	3.98	
Quality/Service	4.08	
Delivery	3.68	
3.4 The quality and extent of our knowledge of competitors	1.62	
3.5 The use made of market research and its impact on product development	1.44	

4	Operations/service		
4.1	The level of cooperation between marketing and operations/service	1.82	There is a strong feeling that contracts are agreed at prices and staff-hour rates which are not economic, and which do not provide
4.2	The extent to which the information received from marketing and finance is useful for managing this function	2.17	sufficient profit margin. Schedules, which bear little relationship to what is achieved. This means that project managers take on agency staff at high costs and also accept some disruption in consequence. There is limited incentive to improve cost performance
4.3	Management understanding of long-run trends in costs and performances	2.04	
4.4	The extent to which management are able to control costs	2.92	
4.5	The level of inventory in relation to output and sales (and the relationship between raw material, work in progress and finished goods, stocks)		Not relevant
4.6	The adequacy, age and stage of repair of plant equipment	3.42	The company has 'state-of-the-art' computer-aided design facilities
4.7	The flexibility of use of plant, equipment and facilities	3.47	
4.8	The level of investment compared with the average for the industry	2.91	
5	Corporate/business development		
5.1	The organization's investment in development	2.11	The company has lagged behind in technology and is therefore less able to enter
5.2	The ability of the organization to respond quickly to market or competitive pressures	2.76	or be credible in key new markets (nuclear energy, pharmaceutical applications, etc.). Little effort is devoted to innovation and improvement. Products/service development
5.3	The organization's ability to exploit new products	1.91	is inadequate. Little attention is paid to feedback from the marketplace through
5.4	The extent to which the organization pursues opportunities for product/service improvement	2.07	marketing department, operations department, etc.
5.5	The integration of development with market, operations, finance, design, etc.	2.01	
5.6	The extent to which the organization is able to exploit outside sources for development purposes (e.g. joint ventures, consultants)	2.71	

Closer examination of the functional analysis reveals a number of key organizational weaknesses. The pay, training, promotion and performance of staff are relatively low. This particularly applies to pay, where the company pays at or below current market rates. Its technical training is excellent, but management training is widely felt to be inadequate. These points are problematic on two counts. First, the company essentially exists to sell the services of its engineers. They specify, design and detail process plants and/or provide project management, maintenance management and, increasingly, operational management services. Second, the company increasingly provides the latter three management services. More and more, the company sells technical and managerial expertise. One estimate has it that halving the rate of staff turnover could return as much as £1.5 million each year into the profit and loss account, taking into account the costs of recruitment, lost time, induction and training against the costs of pay and other changes to reward systems.

A second area of weakness lies in that of management control information. The company has elaborate information systems but does not yet have systems on which managers can and do rely. Therefore, managers tend not to utilize information very effectively. This also impacts on performance. Little attempt is made to use feedback from the management information system to motivate higher levels of effort, or even as a basis for solving problems.

Marketing and marketing information is a further weakness. The company has only limited competitor information. More fundamentally, it does not seem to make good use of the information it does have available. Principally, the weakness lies within the bidding process. Bid teams appear to be put together in an *ad hoc* manner. There is no guarantee that a bid team will have a high-level input from engineering, project management, estimating, commercial or marketing functions. The organization keeps estimating and commercial functions apart and currently has neither a commercial nor marketing director. The chief executive, the technical director and the engineering director lead the bid process, although they may not lead the bid team. There seems to be scope to improve this process as a means of beginning to grapple with the company's core commercial weakness. It is unable to obtain high-value projects. It has obtained a record level of work but at relatively low staff-hour rates for its engineering personnel. The implication of this is that the company could combine record levels of activity with record losses.

All this links back to performance yet again. Engineers often feel that the contracts obtained have ridiculously low staff-hour rates, tight delivery dates and project milestones. Many of the contracts specify staff-hours and staff-hour rates. Yet engineers and managers feel no incentive to seek improvements in engineering work structures and systems: 'It's impossible to make profit from this project' is the response. Yet if we could find ways of achieving the same milestones with fewer staff-hours the company would, first, reduce its losses and, second, improve its market standing. The latter could help it gain more profitable contracts, and these exist. Other companies in the group are attracting profitable, high-value work. International Engineering's competitors are not all in the same situation. Many are very profitable.

The analysis of operations/service supports this conclusion. The main point is that there is a clear lack of integration between project management, engineering and marketing. This seems partly to be a problem of systems. The appropriate information is not available to various departments as people make decisions which have an effect across departments. More fundamentally, the *ad hoc* nature of the bidding process vitiates such integration as is often achieved on an informal basis.

Finally, the company has lagged behind in key technologies and is therefore less credible in certain areas of work such as nuclear engineering and pharmaceuticals. The company is seen as capable of responding to competitive pressures but this applies mainly to the markets in which it has been well established. These include the oil industry, a market which is relatively mature. Contract prices have been under downward pressure, partly as a result of the oil price situation with all its consequences.

Part 2: Organizational diagnosis

This exercise is provided to assist readers in making a structured analysis of their own company's internal system, processes and their effectiveness. Readers are asked to complete the questionnaire. The average scores are for the 92 managers from International Engineering referred to in the discussion above.

Organizational diagnosis questionnaire

In the following questionnaire, eight areas are assessed, each with five statements as shown on the checksheet that follows the questionnaire.

This questionnaire is designed to help you determine how well your own organization works in a number of related areas.

Assess how far you agree or disagree with the following statements as they apply to you within your own department or section, using this seven-point scale and circling the appropriate number:

1	2	3	4	5	6	7
Agree strongly	Agree	Agree slightly	Neutral	Disagree slightly	Disagree	Disagree strongly

In answering the statements, try to be as honest as you can. This is not a test and there are no right or wrong answers. The only correct answer is what you decide yourself. *The average score shown in the right-hand column below is from International Engineering.*

Statement		Average score
1 I understand the objectives of this organization.	1 2 3 4 5 6 7	4.62
2 The organization of work here is effective.	1 2 3 4 5 6 7	4.21
3 Managers will always listen to ideas.	1 2 3 4 5 6 7	2.11

→

Statement									Average score
4	I am encouraged to develop my full potential.	1	2	3	4	5	6	7	2.84
5	My immediate boss has ideas that are helpful to me and my work group.	1	2	3	4	5	6	7	2.91
6	My immediate boss is supportive and helps me in my work.	1	2	3	4	5	6	7	3.78
7	This organization keeps its policies and procedures relevant and up to date.	1	2	3	4	5	6	7	2.82
8	We regularly achieve our objectives.	1	2	3	4	5	6	7	2.94
9	The goals and objectives of this organization are clearly stated.	1	2	3	4	5	6	7	3.61
10	Jobs and lines of authority are flexible.	1	2	3	4	5	6	7	4.12
11	I can always talk to someone at work if I have a work-related problem.	1	2	3	4	5	6	7	3.72
12	The salary that I receive is commensurate with the job that I perform.	1	2	3	4	5	6	7	2.04
13	I have all the information and resources I need to do a good job	1	2	3	4	5	6	7	2.98
14	The management style adopted by senior management is helpful and effective.	1	2	3	4	5	6	7	3.17
15	We constantly review our methods and introduce improvements.	1	2	3	4	5	6	7	2.61
16	Results are attained because people are committed to them.	1	2	3	4	5	6	7	3.82
17	I feel motivated by the work I do.	1	2	3	4	5	6	7	4.24
18	The way in which work tasks are divided is sensible and clear.	1	2	3	4	5	6	7	3.61

Statement		Average score
19 My relationships with other members of my work group are good.	1 2 3 4 5 6 7	4.17
20 There are opportunities for promotion and increased responsibility in this organization.	1 2 3 4 5 6 7	2.71
21 This organization sets realistic plans.	1 2 3 4 5 6 7	2.56
22 Performance is regularly reviewed by my boss.	1 2 3 4 5 6 7	4.21
23 There are occasions when I would like to be free to make changes in my job.	1 2 3 4 5 6 7	2.08
24 People are cost conscious and seek to make the best use of resources.	1 2 3 4 5 6 7	2.92
25 The priorities of this organization are understood by its employees.	1 2 3 4 5 6 7	3.71
26 There is a constant search for ways of improving the way we work.	1 2 3 4 5 6 7	4.62
27 We cooperate effectively in order to get the work done.	1 2 3 4 5 6 7	3.50
28 Encouragement and recognition is given for all jobs and tasks in this organization.	1 2 3 4 5 6 7	2.51
29 Departments work well together to achieve good performance.	1 2 3 4 5 6 7	2.46
30 This organization's management team provides effective and inspiring leadership.	1 2 3 4 5 6 7	4.28
31 This organization has the capacity to change.	1 2 3 4 5 6 7	3.78
32 The work we do is always necessary and effective.	1 2 3 4 5 6 7	3.42

→

Statement									Average score
33 In my own work area objectives are clearly stated and each person's work role is clearly identified.	1	2	3	4	5	6	7		4.01
34 The way the work structure in this organization is arranged produces general satisfaction.	1	2	3	4	5	6	7		3.95
35 Conflicts of view are resolved by solutions which are understood and accepted.	1	2	3	4	5	6	7		3.07
36 All individual work performance is reviewed against agreed standards.	1	2	3	4	5	6	7		3.61
37 Other departments are helpful to my own department whenever necessary.	1	2	3	4	5	6	7		2.82
38 My boss's management style helps me in the performance of my own work.	1	2	3	4	5	6	7		4.58
39 Creativity and initiative are encouraged.	1	2	3	4	5	6	7		2.71
40 People are always concerned to do a good job.	1	2	3	4	5	6	7		2.93

Checksheet

1 For each numbered statement, enter the score recorded on the questionnaire.

2 Work out the total for the five statements in each area.

3 Divide by 5 to find the average score in each area.

I Key tasks	II Structure	III People relationships	IV Motivation
1	2	3	4
9	10	11	12
17	18	19	20
25	26	27	28
33	34	35	36
Total			
Average			

V Support	VI Management leadership	VII Attitude towards change	VIII Performance
5	6	7	8
13	14	15	16
21	22	23	24
29	30	31	32
37	38	39	40
Total			
Average			

For a sample of n people, first add together all the scores for a particular statement, divide the total by n, and proceed as above.

The results of the diagnostic survey were analysed by groups of managers from International Engineering. From this analysis it appears that the definition of key tasks, organizational structure and management leadership are all seen as areas of weakness. People do not understand overall objectives or how their jobs fit into the whole company picture. They do not feel motivated by the work they do, partly, it appears, because of this latter problem.

The organization is not seen as being very effective, for reasons covered under the functional analysis. Most important, jobs and lines of authority are seen as inflexible and little attempt is made to achieve improvements. The organizational structure is seen as inappropriate.

Management style is not seen as helpful to individual performance and, overall, people perceive relatively weak leadership. Conversely, there is a relatively positive attitude to change. Indeed, it might be argued that the perceived lack of leadership is felt to be particularly frustrating to employees who felt strong commitment to the company and a positive attitude towards change.

Increased competition led to declining economic performance. Greater attention to cost control and internal conflict within the organization meant that corporate policy reflected increasingly short-term pressures. Declining performance, short-term perspectives and limited investment in management development all contribute to the growing difficulty of improving the quality of management in the organization.

The functional analysis checklist and questionnaire results can then be subjected to more detailed analysis. For example, in the engineering consultancy firm 92 managers and engineers completed the assessment exercise. The data were reviewed by the executive committee in a senior management workshop. They concluded that a number of priority issues needed to be addressed, as follows:

1 *Commercial focus and accountability*
   (a) focus commercially both in defining accountabilities and in the management of the business;
   (b) decentralize responsibilities, clarify individual accountability.

2 *Performance appraisals*
   (a) to ensure more rigorous enforcement of appraisals;
   (b) to develop more commercially orientated targets;
   (c) to ensure that remuneration is linked to performance.

3 *Effective systems and information*
   (a) to ensure relevance to individuals;
   (b) to be user-friendly;
   (c) to provide a commercial focus.

4 *Effective communication*
   (a) of strategies;
   (b) of responsibilities;
   (c) of commercial requirements.

Understanding the 'human' dimension of change

Diagnosis for change is partly a matter of analysis and partly a matter of understanding the human dimension of the organization. While it is important that any diagnosis gives full weighting to the commercial and organizational issues, this is not enough. Attention must also be given to the people involved. Can they work more effectively? Could they be managed more appropriately? Can we engage their commitment to change? These questions turn on whether or not we believe that there is potential for improvement within our people. If the expectations that managers have about their people are relatively low then the response elicited will be low. Achieving higher levels of performance involves believing in the potential of the people involved, equipping them appropriately, training them where necessary and much more besides. Therefore the assumptions that managers make about people are very important. The wrong assumptions may tend to lower managers' expectations and thus lower performance. The wrong assumptions may also lead to the use of management styles not conducive to commitment and change.

The jobs that people actually perform are the fundamental 'building blocks' of any organization. Moreover, they form a key aspect of the experience of working. The extent to which valued skills are used, the discretion available to the individual, the degree of specialization and the extent to which the individual produces a 'worthwhile' product are all important. At the same time, however, individuals appear to differ in the extent to which they would wish these various attributes to be present in their job. There appears to be no simple link between the type of job that an individual does and his or her satisfaction with that job. Similarly, there is no simple link between job satisfaction and productivity. Other factors are also important. Nevertheless, many people find the jobs they do repetitive and boring, or at least will tell an interviewer that this is the case. In the 1960s and 1970s there was much concern over the design of jobs. Today the introduction of new technology provides organizations with the opportunity to review jobs, and perhaps improve them.

Both managers and employees have expectations about each other, and in particular about what motivates them to work. Schein (1965) has identified four sets of managerial assumptions about employees and the implications of them for management and job design strategies. These assumptions and the implications are set out as follows.

■ 'Rational–economic man'

The rational–economic model is clearly associated with the principles of 'scientific management' and, historically, its approach is founded in the early decades of the twentieth century. The model assumes that people evaluate the outcomes of different courses of action and select the one which maximizes the benefit they receive, i.e. they exercise rational judgement based on economic criteria. This general assumption can be broken down into the following eight specific assumptions about employees:

1 Employees are primarily motivated by economic incentives and will pursue those activities which result in the greatest economic benefit.
2 Employees are passive and can be manipulated, motivated and controlled by management, since management control economic incentives.
3 Feelings are essentially irrational and must be prevented from interfering with the rational calculation of self-interest.
4 Organizations should be designed so that people's feelings, and hence their unpredictability, are controlled and neutralized.
5 People are inherently lazy and must be motivated by external incentives.
6 People's own goals run counter to those of the organization and external forces are needed to channel efforts towards organizational goals.
7 People are incapable of self-control and self-discipline because of irrational feelings.
8 People can be divided into two groups: those who fit these assumptions, and those who are self-motivated, self-controlled and less dominated by their feelings. This second group must assume responsibility for managing the others.

The main thrust of these assumptions is that emotions have no place in management–employee relationships and must be prevented from interfering in the work situation. This implies a management strategy of financial and economic rewards for the employee's contribution and a system of authority, controls and punishment to protect the organization and the employee from irrational feelings (the 'control' model described earlier).

In the field of work design the main emphasis is on efficient task performance, since this leads to the greatest economic benefit. Rules and procedures must be established, and methods of improvement sought, so as to achieve maximum efficiency and it must be possible to identify shortcomings so that incentives or punishments can be used to correct the situation. Provided that the method of working is specified, and employees conform to it, adequate motivation and output will be ensured by manipulating rewards and punishments, and using adequate supervision.

■ 'Social man'

These assumptions may be listed as follows:

1 People are basically motivated by social needs and achieve a sense of identity through relationships with others.

2 The rationalization of work processes has removed the meaning from work and meaning must thus be sought from social relationships while doing the job.

3 The peer group, with its social pressures, elicits more response from the employee than the incentives and controls of management.

4 For people to respond to management the supervisor must meet the individual's social needs and needs for acceptance.

In the work design area this set of assumptions leads to a major change in approach. The manager should not direct attention solely to task efficiency but should consider employees' social needs. The manager should accept social interaction as a means of improving motivation, rather than as something which interferes with efficient performance, and should regard work groups as being an essential and contributory factor to employee motivation rather than as being a disruptive influence.

The assumptions about 'social man' lead to two related, though rather different, emphases. The first of these is an emphasis on human relations. The manager, instead of being a controller and creator of work, becomes a sympathetic supporter of the employee and enables him or her to do the job rather than ensuring that it is done by direct means. This leads to the need to adopt less autocratic/directive and more supportive management styles. The second is the socio-technical systems approach. Here a deliberate effort is made to integrate the social needs of the employees and the technical needs of the job, usually by designing work for groups of employees rather than individuals, and often by using group rather than individual incentives.

■ 'Self-actualizing man'

These assumptions about people can be summarized as follows:

1 People are not inherently lazy or resistant to organizational goals.

2 People seek to be, and are capable of being, mature on the job exercising a certain amount of autonomy, independence and responsibility, and developing skills and adaptability.

3 People are primarily self-motivated and self-controlled and do not need external incentives and controls to make them work.

4 There is no inherent conflict between self-actualization and effective organizational performance. Given the opportunity, people will voluntarily integrate their own goals with those of the organization, achieving the former through working towards the latter.

The implications of these assumptions for management are fundamentally different from the earlier two. Both rational–economic and social assumptions lead to a strategy which requires the provision of extrinsic motivation to elicit performance, while self-actualizing assumptions lead to a strategy which requires the provision of opportunities for the employee's existing motivation to be used. The former needs extrinsic rewards (economic or social) to be exchanged for performance; the latter needs the exchange of opportunities to gain intrinsic rewards (the satisfaction of higher-order needs within the work situation) for performance. In addition, the performance criteria used would differ. In the former, the emphasis is on compliance with desired behaviour patterns but in the latter emphasis is placed on quality and creativity.

The implications for work design are also radically different. Instead of telling people how to do the job, managers using this approach explain what is to be achieved and allow the employee to exercise his or her own discretion. Emphasis is placed on making the work itself more challenging and meaningful and management relinquish much of the direct control of work to the employee.

■ 'Complex man'

There is a certain amount of evidence to support all the assumptions outlined so far. In many cases the models can be used to explain and predict some behaviour, but there is also considerable contradictory evidence. People not only are more complex than the models suggest but also differ.

Schein (1965) outlines the following five assumptions on which this model of 'complex man' is based:

1 People are complex and variable. They have many needs, arranged in a hierarchy of personal importance but the hierarchy varies over time and according to the situation. In addition, their motives interact and form complex motivational patterns.

2 People can adopt new motives as a result of their experiences and hence the individual's pattern of motivation and relationship with the organization results from a complex interaction between individual needs and organizational experiences.

3 People's motives may vary in different organizational situations. If they cannot satisfy their needs within the formal organization they may do so in the informal organization or in other activities. If the job itself is complex, different parts of it may engage different motives.

4 People's work involvement may stem from a variety of motives and the outcome in terms of their performance and satisfaction is only partly dependent on their motivation. The nature of the task to be performed, relations with others, abilities and experience all interact to produce particular outcomes. For example, a highly skilled, poorly motivated worker may be as effective and satisfied as an unskilled, highly motivated worker.

5 People will respond to different management strategies in ways dependent on their own motives and abilities and the nature of the task. Therefore, no single correct managerial strategy exists.

The overall lesson of these assumptions is not that the earlier models are wrong, but that each is right with particular people in particular circumstances. Hence the implication for management is not that there is a single strategy to adopt but that management must be flexible in adapting to a variety of abilities and motives. This in turn means that management must be sensitive in diagnosing the differences, and must have the ability to vary managerial style and behaviour. This sensitivity is an important part of the interpretation of data collected from the organizational assessment techniques described.

Let us return to International Engineering for a moment. The management style had been autocratic and directive. Yet it is clear enough from the data presented here that the company was not organized to be fully effective. Part of the answer lies in restructuring. Partly, it lies in developing a 'sharper' performance and commercially orientated culture. Thus, in part, it is about placing increased demands on people. Any attempt to interpret these data through assumptions of either 'rational–economic man' or 'self-actualizing man', or a combination of these, may not help.

It seems likely that management have adopted some combination of these assumptions in the past. They may have believed that the engineers wish to pursue technical excellence alone. In any event the technical training was admittedly excellent: 'Let the engineers get on with the technical work and all will be well' seems to have been the view of many managers. In an increasingly competitive world this has proved to be inadequate. It is risky to believe that these engineers cannot be trusted beyond the technical contribution they offer. There needs to be a recognition that the situation is more complex, that many engineers can and will respond to performance and commercial orientation. Creating change at International Engineering involves the adoption of new organization structures and management styles compatible with the implications of the assessment data.

The change equation

But we can only go one step at a time. We must first create recognition that something is wrong. Moreover, change creates risks, uncertainties and costs, both economic and psychological. To engage commitment to change we need to generate a shared vision of how the situation can be improved and shared aims for the future. We also need to generate a clear understanding of the first practical steps forward. If I recognize that what I am doing is ineffective I need to be able to visualize a better way *and* see some steps that I can take to make progress towards that vision. Many people believe that generating the commitment to, and energy for, change depends on all these factors.

The change equation provides a useful way of dealing with questions such as 'Should I attempt to make change?' and 'What more can I do to improve the chances of introducing change effectively?' It can be expressed as follows:

$$EC = A \times B \times D$$

where EC is the energy for change, A is the felt dissatisfaction with the present situation, B the level of knowledge of the practical steps forward and D the shared vision.

Dissatisfaction with the present will only lead to high energy for change if there are high levels of shared aims and knowledge of what to do next. Without these shared aims and knowledge, dissatisfaction will lead to demotivation, despondency and apathy. There is another equation, however. For change to occur:

$$EC > Z$$

where Z is the perceived cost of making change.

The energy for change must be greater than the perceived costs of making the change, both economic and psychological. In fact, if we have no shared aims and no knowledge of what to do next there will be so much uncertainty that people will expect the 'costs' of change to be high. We shall see in later chapters that it is all important when designing and managing change to ensure that both the means of introducing change and the impact of change are designed to build the energy for change. This chapter aims to demonstrate a way of approaching organizational diagnosis and assessment and the importance of ensuring that any attempt to diagnose the need for change is carried out with the recognition that the appropriate end-point is acceptance of change and energy for changing.

To return to International Engineering, one of its main problems was that many of the engineers who developed management and leadership potential were believed to have resigned from the company frustrated by ineffectiveness. This left the company less able to create the energy for much needed changes. It had lost many of the people who might have been involved in developing new business, new technology and the like. The ability to attract, motivate and retain people is an important aspect of the effective organization.

Now we turn to the use of a survey to assess the ability to attract, develop, retain and motivate leadership talent. Kotter (1988) has developed a very useful questionnaire for use with senior managers.

The first part of the questionnaire deals with the managers' assessment of how well the systems and practices within the organization supported the objective of attracting, retaining and motivating a sufficient number of people with the leadership potential to fill senior management positions. Table 12.2 shows the results obtained from International Engineering. Listed on the left are the factors that the managers were asked to assess. The right-hand column shows the percentage of managers who felt that the factor was *less than adequate* to support the objective.

The questionnaire also reveals the managers' assessment of how well the organization's systems and practices contributed to its ability to develop leadership talent. Table 12.3 shows the percentage of managers who felt that, on the factors listed, the company was *less than adequate* in spotting high-potential people and identifying and meeting their developmental needs. When interviewed about the ineffective systems and processes reported in the questionnaire responses, senior managers often referred to short-term pressures by way of explanation. Management development was seen by some to have no immediate payoff and was therefore not used. Rotation was not practised because managers did not wish to lose good performers or people with potential. Ineffective and inadequate

Table 12.2 Attracting, retaining and motivating leadership potential

	Factors assessed	Less than adequate (%)
1	The quality of career-planning discussions with superiors	87
2	Availability of jobs with development opportunities	78
3	The information available to managers on job vacancies in the company	77
4	Management development offered to individuals with identified high potential	70
5	Outside training opportunities	66
6	The strategic/business and human resource planning processes which help clarify what kind of company will exist in 5–10 years, and thus how many and what kind of important management positions will need to be staffed	66
7	In-house training opportunities	61
8	The ability of managers to identify and select people with high potential	60
9	The promotion opportunities offered to people with high potential	56
10	The firm's performance-related pay scheme	52

feedback was common. Senior managers would *not* face poor performance and development needs directly. Recruitment was carried out on the basis of technical competence, *not* management potential. Hard-pressed managers needed to meet their targets! Middle management were sometimes seen as ineffective. Promotion and reward practices did not encourage high levels of performance.

Table 12.3 Identifying and meeting developmental needs

Factors assessed	Less than adequate (%)
1 The way managers are rewarded for developing subordinates	94
2 The advice given to people on how to manage their own career for long-term development	90
3 The use of lateral transfers made for development purposes across divisions	88
4 Assessment schemes aimed at identifying the development needs of managers	82
5 The mentoring and coaching provided to managers	79
6 The amount of carefully planned time and effort the company expends in trying tomanage the whole process of developing people	79
7 The way special jobs are used to develop people with high potential	77

8 The way feedback is given to subordinates regarding their progress	76
9 The capacity of the firm's managers to identify the development needs of people with high potential	71
10 The way responsibilities are added to a manager's job for development purposes	69
11 Formal succession planning reviews	67
12 The firm's participation in outside management training programmes	66
13 The opportunities offered to people to give them exposure to higher levels of management	64
14 The capacity of the firm's senior managers to identify people with potential	59
15 The firm's use of in-company management training programmes	52

Managers wanted obedience, not the threat of excellent performance (see Kotter, 1988, pages 72–3).

Yet these same managers were concerned about the ineffectiveness they had reported. They recognized the changes in technology, competition, expectations and so on: 'To continue to succeed we must become more effective in these areas' was a powerful message coming through these interviews.

In using the change equation idea we must be careful to consider the impact on it of changes already underway. We must avoid trying to view change in isolation. We are not dealing with discrete events; rather, we are dealing with organizations experiencing many changes, each at different stages. As we said at the outset, we must establish whether change is desirable and feasible. People will not readily see change as desirable. We are often all too ready to ignore the question of what is feasible in a given time. Circumstances sometimes demand that changes be made dramatically and quickly. If so, we should be aware of the tensions so caused, recognize them explicitly and seek to manage them. If you do not measure them you cannot manage them.

CASE STUDY   London Underground

This organization operates an underground or 'metro service' in a major European city. It was a public sector organization but in the 1990s it changed. Senior management reorganized to achieve a more commercial approach to its management. The organization had been dominated by engineers. Top management had followed a primarily technical approach. Much of its support work (e.g. track maintenance,

→

capital projects) was being put out to tender with no guarantee that internal departments would get the work if they were to bid. Now, for the first time in their careers, technical managers needed to understand costing and pricing. These were dramatic changes.

Part-way through this process, the board and senior management (approximately 100 people) completed an organizational diagnosis and assessment as a means of taking stock and looking to the future. All those involved completed the diagnostic questionnaire, described earlier in this chapter, in preparation for discussion of how to achieve further change in the future. In Table 12.4 I summarize the strengths and weaknesses of the organization as defined by these managers from the questionnaire results. They identified key tasks, people and attitude to change as strengths. People understood their own and the organization's objectives, felt motivated by their own work and understood priorities and their own work role. Relationships between individuals and within teams were good.

Table 12.4 **Strengths and weaknesses of the organization**

Strengths	Weaknesses
Key tasks	
People	
Attitude to change	
Structure	
Performance	
	Communication
	Support
	Motivation
	Leadership

There was a strong commitment to the organization and the need for change among employees. Technological change had been a regular feature of the organization's history. It had an international reputation in its own field.

Structure and performance were identified as neither strengths nor weaknesses. The managers generally felt that the management structure had changed dramatically and that these changes had yet to stabilize. Performance had declined somewhat because of the energy absorbed in making the changes that were already underway.

Communication, support, motivation and leadership were all rated as weaknesses. Managers felt under considerable pressure in consequence of the changes being made. Moreover, the changes had included staffing reviews which had led to staff reductions in many areas.

This combination of staff losses and pressure of work led to many managers reporting support as a weakness. One consequence of these problems was that many departments took an increasingly departmental focus, doing only those things that they needed, giving work for other departments (e.g. providing information) a lower priority.

CASE
STUDY

Health Service Trust (HST)

This case study sets out extracts from documents drawn from an organizational review of a National Health Service (NHS) Trust in the UK. Since recent reforms, health service 'providers' are organized as trusts which are managed by a board but remain part of the UK NHS.

Brief

1 This diagnostic study was undertaken to provide an input to the trust board. The objective was to present a summary of views of managers and professional staff about the effectiveness of the existing corporate structure and management arrangements of HST. The purpose of the review was to aid the board in ensuring that HST has in place a structure and management which aid the achievement of the objectives of the trust. Specifically, the terms of reference were as follows:

(a) Review the management arrangements of HST and make recommendations for change aimed at increasing the efficiency and effectiveness of HST.

(b) The review should consider and take into account the recommendations and suggestions made in a number of recent reports, including:
   – Hospital Manager–Consultant–Nurse Study Report, June 1992 (completed by a consultant).
   – Audit Commission's Nurse Management Review, August 1992.
   – King's Fund Organizational Audit Visit, September 1992 (both national organizations concerned with public service management and health service management).

(c) The study will be wide ranging and cover all aspects of HST's management.

(d) Any recommendations must fully support HST's philosophy of clinical management and devolving authority and responsibility as near to the point of delivery of care as possible.

(e) The review should aim to streamline channels of authority and accountability at all levels in the organization.

(f) The review should encompass management support.

(g) The proposed structures must not increase, and preferably should reduce, management costs of HST.

Approach to the study

2 A working group of managers was established who would work with the consultant in carrying out this diagnosis. This allowed a large number of interviews to be carried out quickly and ensured the relevance of the review. The consultant and the working group designed the interview schedule and identified the target group to be interviewed. A total of 121 interviews were carried out across HST from board level down to ward sisters. (Three people refused to be interviewed.) The consultant and the working group have been involved in summarizing the results and in drafting this report. In addition a number of individuals wrote to the consultant expressing views relevant to the management review.

→

3 The following information is included as appendices:
Appendix 1: the interview schedule.
Appendix 2: a list of specific comments drawn from the interview notes.
(Neither is included here.)

Arrangement review of HST

4 A number of points were held in common by the majority of those interviewed. HST was seen as a well-regarded organization comprising many capable people. It was seen as innovative and as having many specialties which were known nationally for various developments. Almost all respondents thought that the team of which they were a member was effective, cohesive and friendly. Individuals and teams were seen to possess the necessary technical, professional and other skills and were seen to work together well.

5 Communication was seen to need improvement but recent improvements were also acknowledged. Nevertheless an examination of Appendix 2 will quickly reveal many expressed concerns in this area. Linked to this, people expressed concern about management style and change. There has been a lot of change recently. Many feel that changes have been neither handled sensitively nor communicated effectively. Some suggest that there is too little cooperation and too defensive an approach; others feel that there are too many committees and working parties and that it is difficult to identify a decision-making forum. The UMT (Unit Management Team) is seen as too large and too diverse (regarding the interests represented on it) to be a source of effective decisions.

6 Many of those interviewed put the case for greater devolvement. Some called for devolvement of finance and for personnel to directorates, some called for greater devolvement *within* directorates, some called for devolvement of hotel services, some called for devolvement of other services. Linked to this, some referred to the importance of service agreements between directorates and directorates providing services.

7 Many of those interviewed held strong views about the impact of split sites on effectiveness; however, varying views are held. Some felt that certain smaller units are effective because they can be managed as small cohesive units and would not wish to lose this advantage; however, most recognized that split-site working brings duplication, higher costs, frustration and problems of communications, management and control. The infrastructure generally was seen as a source of constraint and all would prefer major new capital development while recognizing that this is an issue outside this management review.

8 There is a widely recognized lack of accountability of a range of issues. Beds are not managed as a whole – some of those interviewed indicated that HST needs to get to grips with this soon. Linked to this, admissions and discharge policies were seen as ill-defined by some. Purchasing and stock control were seen as in need of further improvement. The whole business-getting process was seen as needing organizing. As more and more of the workload comes from GP fund-holders, people-health purchasing is carried out by health authorities and GP fund-holders – general practitioners to whom budget has been devolved are questioning how to find the time to obtain this business, manage the expectations of fund-holders, engage in service development and relate to other purchasers. The role of clinicians was perceived to be central *but* no one could see how they were to find time to play it effectively. Most, if not all, clinicians involved in management

were already devoting all of their available management time. How more was to be made available was perceived to be an important dilemma.

9   Linked to this, there is a widely held view that while the principle of clinical directorates and the involvement of clinicians in management is sound, the individual clinician often finds that the demands of managing the directorate cannot be met within the existing sessional allowance. Conversely the need to, and their own preference to, maintain their clinical work makes providing more time not a valid option. This is clearly recognized as a big dilemma. Many clinicians also felt they had received little or no relevant training in management – some pointing out, however, that clinical and other demands had meant that they had been unable to attend what was provided.

10 There is complete agreement that much more needs to be achieved on information and on budgeting. Too many people either are unclear about budgets, costs and related matters (e.g. what budget is available, what things cost) or believe the available information (whether budget reports or other information) is too global, does not provide the right information, *or is wrong*. It is widely recognized that much improvement is already underway but there is a wide measure of cynicism about the present situation. All recognize this as a key constraint to further devolvement and to a flatter corporate structure.

11 It is important to recognize the strong feelings expressed regarding the need for a flatter structure and for a greater clarity of structure, accountability and of roles, job descriptions and so on. Some say HST is overmanaged. Some say it is impossible to find out who to go to in the event of problems affecting patient care. Widely held is the view that people have insufficient resources to deliver patient care. More consultants, more junior doctors and more space were constant comments from many, but this is not the whole of it. Many wish to see quicker decisions, more decisive management, more visible management and more access to top management. All of this is seen as requiring a flatter structure, greater clarity of accountabilities, much improved budgeting and information, improved communication, job descriptions and the like. In particular, decision making and professional representation needed review. The UMT was not an effective decision-making body and other medical consultative arrangements would need to be reconstituted. Many recognized that the roles of business development managers and nurse managers were not clearly distinguished in practice, and also varied across the clinical directorates. This created unnecessary confusion for some and needed to be resolved. Linked to this are a number of career issues, not least for nursing staff.

12 Turning to corporate structure and management, there was both a measure of agreement and significant controversy. These varying views are therefore set out more fully as follows:

(a) Of the 118 people interviewed, 67 made specific comments regarding the corporate structure. Of the 51 who did not so comment, all had indicated that other changes would lead to improvements at HST, and more than 90 per cent of them were clear that *management changes* were needed, most commonly to clarify roles and accountabilities, to improve communication and to devolve authority throughout the organization.

(b) Of the 67 who made clear comments on the structure, 45 argued that the number of *clinical directorates should be rationalized*, most commonly to between four and six. These views we expected alongside other views. Each of the 45 wished to see at least one of the following:

- greater clarity of roles and job descriptions starting at board level and throughout the organization;
- improved decision making, particularly at the UMT;
- improved professional representation;
- more authority to business improvement of support to directorates;
- managers and/or specialty managers.

Many were clearly concerned, however, that fewer, larger directorates implied changes in the workload of the clinical director which they, as individuals, would not welcome. Some made the point that they did not know whether clinicians would wish to take on the larger management roles implied by a rationalized structure.

(c) The remaining 22 interviewees wished to see *no change to the existing clinical directorate structure*; however, all of these people wished also to see one or more of the changes listed under (b) above. In addition, two stated explicitly that they felt there were too many directorates. Clearly, therefore, while there is controversy over whether or not to rationalize the clinical directorate structure there is a strong measure of agreement that significant management and other changes are necessary. It is difficult, therefore, to accept at face value the views expressed by a number of people that a period of stability is needed after so much change, and that this is a reason not to rationalize the clinical directorate structure because the people saying this are calling for other changes in any event. It is important, however, to take note of this desire for a period of stability (see below). One commented that he believed in smaller directorates but he noted that the existing directorates were not all working effectively and that there was a need to build up the role of specialty managers. Another indicated that the real constraint to a rationalized directorate structure was split-site working.

(d) Fifty-one of 67, commenting on the structure, proposed that the roles of clinical managers, business managers and nurse managers should be defined and/or standardized across the structure.

(e) Fifteen of those commenting on structure argued that *professional representation should be strengthened*. Most commonly this point was made in relation to medical representation; however, some made it with respect to nurses.

(f) Many interviewees argued either that support services should be devolved or that greater continuity be achieved (e.g. by nominating finance staff to take responsibility for particular directorates) and/or that service agreements be established.

Conclusions and recommendations

13 The first point to make is that the expressed need for a period of stability is accepted. This will allow consolidation of achievements to date and concentration on the development of the trust and its services/businesses. It follows that to be credible any recommendations must be seen to deal with the relevant issues. Moreover, it must be clear that any changes are fundamental enough to deliver significant improvements along the lines of the management review. Finally, any changes should be consistent with, and preferably supportive of, the patient-centred care initiative currently being planned.

14 Second, it is clear that any changes should deliver both a clearer, simpler and flatter organizational structure and one which creates career possibilities for employees. In addition it should engage clinicians in the priority work of management in ways which are consistent with the limited time they have available *and* which make the best use of their management time. The two priorities which this review points to are the development of service so as to grow the business over time *and* the achievement of the business plan in any particular year.

15 There seemed to be a clear view that any changes include attention to arrangements for professional representation. It is self-evident that not all professionals can be involved in management and that there are many and often complex professional issues to be dealt with in HST. Professional representation with inputs at board level and operational management level were therefore needed.

16 There was clear agreement that quality assurance and effective information provision were essential whatever changes to management arrangements were to be made. Much progress has been made and is in hand. Any changes need to be carefully and thoroughly planned alongside the planning of change in these two key areas.

17 Overall it is recommended that HST consider, in detail, a rationalized clinical directorate structure which does the following:

   (a) Organizes clinical care around four clinical areas, each with a clinical chair and an experienced general manager.

   (b) Devolves budget responsibility to specialty level.

   (c) It is essential that responsibilities be so organized that clinical chairs along with specialty managers can devote sufficient time to managing budgets and developing the business of specialties and the clinical area (requiring attention to clinical/service development and working with clients/potential clients such as GP fund-holders).

   (d) As part of this the positioning of diagnostic services, theatres and ITU should be considered carefully. Basically these departments provide services to the various specialties. To manage and resource them properly it is essential that the specialties be properly charged for the use of these services.

   (e) Any proposal for change needs to be integrated with plans to develop quality assurance and information systems. Responsibilities for operational management quality assurance, information and business management must be clarified at board level. In particular there seems to be a powerful case for a well-defined bed management procedure.

   (f) Finally, professional materials management should be considered. Moreover, wage payment arrangements should be integrated within the personnel department to avoid duplication of information. The key here from experience elsewhere is to ensure that the payroll is managed by an experienced and capable payroll manager.

18 The purpose of this report is to present the views of managers and professionals. These are to be worked up into specific proposals to be presented to the board in a separate document. This work is now underway by the executive members of the board supported by the author of this report. The objective is to complete this work by 3 February for presentation to the trust board on 10 February.

Options for change

These options for change were considered by the trust board in the light of the above and in order to achieve the following:

■ Support a move toward a more devolved patient-focused care organization.

■ Involve clinicians in priority management tasks.

■ Simplify the reporting arrangements and structure.

■ Create effective cost centres.

The five options were as follows:

1 No change.
2 Fine tuning.
3 Create an internal market.
4 Create a facilities directorate.
5 Reduce the functional directorates.

Option 3 was the most radical change involving reducing clinical directorates from eleven to four and requires the clinical chairs to contract with an operational services directorate for services (staff, facilities, beds, etc.) allowing them to focus on clinical outputs. However, this required extensive and sophisticated information systems not yet available and assumed a degree of attitude change and contracting skills not likely to be widely available.

Under option 4 the clinical chairs retain control over service inputs, except beds which would be controlled by the director of facilities. Under option 5 functional directorates are reduced by merging operational services under the director of operation services, clinical directorates are reduced to five, the fifth being clinical support services. Briefly, a version of option 4 was selected as the basis for change on the grounds that the capabilities for option 3 were not available and could not readily be obtained, whereas options 1, 2 and 5 brought insignificant operational benefits and made no progress toward a more devolved approach to patient-focused care.

Conclusions

There are three main conclusions to draw here:

1 The case deals with changes to a professional service organization in which issues of professional autonomy, public service and managerial/operational effectiveness must be balanced.

2 Given that point, the systematic approach to diagnosis created learning because attitudes were clearly changing as a consequence of the impetus created by the review; thus people who had opposed the streamlining of clinical directorates now came to accept the arguments for such a change, and the inevitability of it. Conversely the board was seen as being prepared to listen to contrary views.

3 Risk analysis always represents a key issue in change decisions. The two key issues in risk analysis are impact and capabilities. What impact will be created where and on whom (which groups) and how will they respond? What capabilities are required either immediately or as a consequence of the impact, and can they be acquired? Is the change feasible, and over what time scale?

Authenticity in diagnosis

It is important to recognize that diagnosis is not simply a question of data collection and analysis. Because any data will be partial, it is important that we engage all stakeholders in the diagnosis process and that we organize around the idea that diagnosis is a process of 'sense making', following Senge (1990) among others. Meaning and interpretation are important. We see a good set of figures for performance but what does that mean? Better than last year, but what does that mean? The best performance in the world for your, sector. And so on.

Following the work of Argyris (1990) and Argyris and Schon (1978), we are interested in *informed choice*. In a real sense we seek *authenticity* in diagnosis. Smale (1998) argues along similar lines, identifying three important patterns of behaviour relevant to any discussion of diagnosis:

- self-fulfilling prophecies;
- self-defeating strategies;
- mutually defeating interactions.

Regarding the first, he notes the example of a bank trading normally which is then hit by a rumour of failure. So all depositors rush to withdraw, creating a run on the bank. He also refers to studies of the impact of teacher expectations of performance on pupil performance. Obvious enough in truth. But what of the second pattern?

Where change requires significant alternatives to patterns of behaviour which are habitual, we can often observe self-defeating strategies at work. Clearly this is a challenging intervention. Often little attempt is made to follow up initial training with coaching. And yet the people involved may be behaving in ways which are so habitual that they do not really think about it, i.e. their understanding is at the tacit level.

Moreover, they may still be subject to performance management systems which reinforce old ways of doing things. Such systems will have more impact if early attempts at new ways of working appear to fail. Approaching such a situation with a 'resistance to change' model will be self-defeating.

Conflict is a natural part of change. In the setting just described, the clash of expectations will certainly lead to a level of conflict. For on the one hand my manager expects me to adopt a new working. On the other hand, as I begin to do so my performance is less effective – initially. But at the same time and faced by that lower performance, my manager places pressure on me to deliver – and it is easier to do so using the former way of working. Dissonance will often arise here. Moreover, if it is not possible to raise concerns over the impact of the existing performance management system and the lack of coaching during the diagnosis, then the change attempted is likely to fail.

But what of the third pattern? Smale (1998), looking at social work, notes:

Understanding how self-fulfilling prophecies, self-defeating strategies and mutually defeating interactions operate can lead to a clear analysis of the unintended outcomes of change agent activity, particularly where our attempts to help people further entrench them in their role as 'problem people': where our intervention to include them confirms them as socially excluded people.

Thus, social workers label families as pathological in order to get them into funded programmes of family support. Family members accept the label and behave in ways confirming the label. Managers assume that behaviour illustrates 'resistance to change' but they may have misread its cause. The anger they observe may be evidence of people really trying to embrace a new way of working. Coaching is what they need, not coercing.

Smale argues that these patterns can be more effectively handled if change diagnosis and management (my summary, not his) is characterized by *other centredness* and *sociability*. The former depends on active listening, empathy and the urge to see others' points of view. The second is about collaboration and links to the Goffee and Jones (1998) model of culture. Just as change is a process, so is change diagnosis. And for diagnosis to be effective it must be credible. In turn, then, we need to provide processes to challenge ideas, challenge the data and listen.

Creating authenticity in diagnosis requires:

- continuous and transparent process in diagnosis;
- bringing out the 'undiscussable';
- the management of contention and conflict;
- building trust and respect;
- creating a sense of urgency;
- engagement and alignment;
- learning to deal with 'breakdowns' or critical incidents.

Ultimately, then, effective diagnosis depends on meaningful dialogue rather than the management of 'impressions' and the acceptance of counterproductive behaviour.

At a greater level of detail the following might be taken as a summary of some of the practical ideas we have developed here and used as a checklist.

Insightful organizational diagnosis

- Authentic data.
- Shared meaning.
- Informed choice.

Effective change architecture

- Governance.
- Leverage.
- Connectivity.
- Scaleability.
- Management of expectations.
- Communication.

Adaptive culture

- Challenge.
- Allowing people to feel pressure.
- Resisting pressure to define new roles quickly.
- Exposing conflict.
- Challenging unproductive norms.

These, put in place with a willingness to move toward integration within the existing brand, can be powerful elements of the transformational change process.

Conclusion

In this chapter we have examined a number of checklists and questionnaires which readers may well find of use in assessing their own organizations. One thing is certain: no single measure of effectiveness is available. We need to adopt a broad-based approach. Readers may also find that they need to add some more specific questions to the various checklists provided here before using them. The next step is to try.

EXERCISES

1 To what extent could International Engineering be said to be efficient?

2 What are the three or four most important issues which International Engineering must focus on if it is to increase its effectiveness?

3 Critically evaluate the five options presented to Health Service Trust.

4 How authentic do you think the diagnosis of Health Service Trust and of ABF Ltd would be?

Managing major changes

Introduction

So far we have examined how to assess organizational performance and how to design organizations that are structured and managed effectively. We have considered individual, group and organizational issues and problems, and also ways and means of responding to these issues/problems. Various skills have been examined. In this chapter we consider how to manage the process of changing an organization. Here we will find that this demands that we consider the impact of changes on the people affected by them in order to understand how people (managers and employees at all levels!) cope with changes. Moreover, it will be clear that major changes create highly complex 'managing' problems, particularly if the people involved are to learn from the process. Achieving change is one thing – learning from the process of change is an entirely different thing. Yet only if we do so can we sustain effective performance for the long term.

Analysed simply, we could divide the concern over the management of major changes into two main questions: 'What changes should we implement?' and 'How may we implement them successfully?' To develop answers to these questions requires specific skills: to diagnose the need for change; to audit performance; to develop a vision of improvement; to describe or define new strategy. Achieving change also requires the skill to get things done, to achieve action. It is often disturbing and disruptive. By definition, change upsets the 'status quo'. Leadership is central because to achieve effective organizational change requires us to elevate analysis over consensus. Easy options are in short supply. The consensus view may reflect the lowest common denominator, the view that no one will oppose. It may not be an appropriate view for the future. Implementing major organizational change demands the combination of action and analysis into a new managerial synthesis.

In this and the next two chapters I propose to discuss this new managerial synthesis necessary for effective change. I propose to develop two main themes as follows:

1 What are the managerial skills required for effective organizational change? We will examine a number of key managerial skills.

2 Change is disruptive and disturbing. How do people experience change and how may they be helped to cope with the pressure of major changes?

Managers in all organizations deploy these managerial and coping skills to lesser or greater extents. Our purpose is to identify these two sets of skills so that managers can more effectively identify strengths and weaknesses and, thereby, further develop their capacities to achieve effective organizational change.

In SmithKline Beecham (page 184) it is clear that 'the simply better way' approach is carefully thought through and relevant. Part of the early learning from the programme has been the role of leadership in energizing a sufficient critical mass of change and commitment to further change that prevents a reversion to past ways of doing things, which contributes to a change in the 'mind-set'. In common with other major corporates, SmithKline Beecham has developed a leadership behavioural role model as a means of defining how it wishes leadership to be displayed and as a development tool and process for the managers involved.

Managerial skills for effective organizational change

To manage change effectively involves the ability to create a new synthesis of people, resources, ideas, opportunities and demands. The manager needs skills rather like those of an orchestral conductor. Vision is essential and creativity paramount. Yet the capacity to create systematic plans to provide for the logistics of resources, support, training and people is central to any change programme. People must be influenced, departmental boundaries crossed or even 'swallowed up', new ideas accepted, new ways of working embraced and new standards of performance and quality achieved. The politics of the organization are crucial. Support must be mobilized, coalitions built and supported, opposition identified and considered. People need help to cope with the stress, anxiety and uncertainties of change. Continuity and tradition must be overturned, in part, as the old is replaced by the new. Yet continuity and tradition provide people with stability, support and meaning and should not needlessly be destroyed. The effective management of organizational change demands attention to all these somewhat conflicting issues and challenges. So in a period of change, synthesis is the key. In this section we shall deal with three skill areas:

1 Managing transitions.

2 Dealing with organizational cultures.

3 The politics of organizational change.

Managing transitions

Company A manufactures a range of engines. It is a wholly owned subsidiary of a US-based multinational corporation. It supplies engines to a small number of end-user companies, each of which incorporates them into its own products. By the 1980s the company was experiencing severe external and internal pressures (see Table 13.1). This is a familiar enough pattern: a cycle of decline creating major challenge for management to find ways of achieving a transition to effectiveness.

Table 13.1 Internal and external pressures in an engine manufacturer

External pressures	Internal pressures
Recession	Inadequate organizational structures
High interest rate	
Falling orders	
High energy and material costs	Lack of confidence and fear of change, including the fear of redundancy
New products/materials technology being adopting in engine design and manufacture	Accustomed to slow change (or paralysis)
Increased competition both from abroad and because some end-users were beginning to switch to building their own engines	Limited managerial competence in managing change
	Lack of experience with new technology
Changes at group level as a consequence of a change in ownership	Low productivity and quality
	Ageing plant with attendant maintenance problem
	Low morale, high absenteeism and industrial disputes
	Cash flow problems

The first and most important challenge was to develop an open attitude towards change at all levels. The company had experienced little or no change in 30 years. Employees were accustomed to stability and managers possessed little or no skill in the management of change. New management at group level, recognizing this company as declining economically, brought in a new top management team – a managing director, engineering director and finance director. The new team moved quickly. The strategy adopted is shown schematically in Table 13.2.

Table 13.2 A strategy for change

Testing reality	New attitudes and structures	Achievements
Threat of closure and redundancy		New technology introduced in manufacturing technology and in materials
Encouraging understanding of the problem	Developing new attitudes to work and to change	
Development new ideas for the future – new products		
Search for new markets and business (including subcontracting)	Training for new technology and to deal with change	Quality control system introduced
Open negotiation communication	Reorganization and contraction	New products
Full involvement of employees and unions	Investment in new technology	Labour flexibility

The first step was to test the reality faced by the company and to draw people into this testing process. Employees at all levels needed to understand the problems the company was facing. Beyond this, it was essential that people be given the chance to seek out and develop solutions. Thus on the one hand openness in negotiations and communications with employees meant that the problems were better understood. On the other hand, through involvement of employees and by bringing in new skills (particularly marketing), new ways of doing things were sought. Employees were drawn into solving problems such as quality, absenteeism, factory layout and so on. Project groups from the design, marketing and production departments became involved in seeking new products. People were given the opportunity to try out new ideas, to experiment, to seek solutions. This, then, initiated a process of attitude change. Recognizing the problems and becoming involved in processes aimed at developing solutions led to a more open approach to the idea of change. Initially seeing it as unavoidable, employees began to recognize the possibility that constructive, albeit not painless, action was feasible. In these ways management and employees were facing the challenge identified in Table 13.3 (based on Argyris and Schon, 1974).

Important in the above was the recognition that involvement of people in examining the problems and seeking to develop solutions was only one part of the approach. Top management involved themselves actively in that process. Moreover, all manner of developments and improvements were discussed in the context of the strategy that management had agreed on in order to turn the company around. By showing people that new products were being developed, that new markets were being actively sought, that new materials were available, a 'vision of the future' was being established. Within such a context, project groups worked effectively and energetically. Thus began a process which led to some quick and some longer-term results. Attitudes changed over time as part of a process of trial and error, experimentation and success. Only when this process developed was training introduced. This process clearly involved personal and management development. More specific programmes of product, technical and skills training were deployed in support.

Opening up the reality-testing process through involvement merely creates uncertainty and anxiety unless those same people really believe that there is a

Table 13.3 Learning from changing: implementing strategic change testing (the problem-solving process)

| Attitudes to change (particularly within top management) | Decision making | |
	Restricted (within the management team)	Extensive (involvement of those affected)
Negative	Little learning or change	Anxiety-creating behaviour
Positive	Learning and change can occur only if not dependent on other people	Learning and change possible

positive attitude to change among those who will make the final decisions. I well remember discussing a proposed involvement scheme planned by a company which faced declining sales in the middle 1970s. A strategy for change and improvement had been articulated. There seemed no future other than decline unless this strategy was implemented. One employee rejected involvement on the grounds that it meant he would be 'conspiring in his own redundancy' – he could see no point to it. Where managers are clearly determined on change and have good ideas, the implementation of change is obviously feasible. People can also learn from changes implemented without extensive involvement as long as there is general agreement over such changes, and care devoted to training and communication. People will then learn new skills and new systems. But what if an important and influential group of those involved is opposed to the changes? Much will depend on the nature of that group, its power and the nature of its opposition. Its members may be capable of persuasion. Other opportunities might be created for them. However, to the extent that this is not so, to the extent that its members feel coerced, then an outcome combining effective implementation and learning becomes more difficult. But we should not see this as a single event; it is a process. Over a period of time some or all of the members of such a group may come to change their mind. We will turn to how this may be achieved in subsequent chapters; for the moment I merely note the problem.

Significant change involves learning. If reality is tested openly, and if open or constructive attitudes to change prevail, then we are most likely to achieve significant changes. Change is possible without open reality testing, but only where people who are excluded from this testing process are not fully engaged in the changes to be implemented. If they are not involved in testing reality they can neither understand the need for change nor feel committed to the changes, let alone learn from them. Public or extensive testing of reality in a declining situation merely creates anxiety unless a constructive attitude to change prevails, particularly within management. Thus to argue that effective communication is enough, without giving people the opportunity and support to seek solutions to problems, will merely sustain the spiral of decline. In this company the reality-testing process led to new attitudes which themselves both facilitated, and were in turn sustained by, training programmes for new technology, improved maintenance and quality control by the emergence of new investment, new equipment and by reorganization (including the formation of a marketing department and the introduction of quality control systems). The spiral of decline was being reversed.

Managing this transition to effectiveness, then, demanded both learning and change, as indicated by the following five criteria:

1 Learning is produced by *exploring dilemmas* or *contradictions* (e.g. improved quality was essential and end-users had to be convinced that they should continue to use company A's product, *but* ageing plant, managerial problems and low morale made this difficult to achieve).

2 Learning is based *on personal experience and experimentation*. People will only learn if they understand the problems and are brought into the process of seeking solutions.

3 Learning can be encouraged in a climate which *encourages risk taking*, doing things and trying out new ideas.

4 Learning requires the *expression of deeply held beliefs* and will involve conflict. Only then can ideas emerge and be properly assessed before being incorporated into new systems, products, strategies, etc.

5 *Learning can be helped by recognizing the value of people and ideas*, developing learning styles which encourage individuals rather than close off discussion (see Argyris and Schon, 1974).

By 1983, company A had reduced staffing, improved the organizational structure, introduced a quality control system for the first time, achieved labour flexibility and developed new products. The leadership challenge faced successfully in this case was that of achieving change in the ways described, while maintaining the business through very difficult times. 'Selling' the solution to the group and 'buying' time were central to this and part of the politics of change, a matter to which we turn below.

■ Dealing with organizational culture: a major financial institution

Company B is a large financial institution with hundreds of branches in major towns and cities in its home country. It operates internationally. In recent years it has been very successful, with growth in profitability and turnover. Yet it faces major challenges. Deregulation, new technology, competition and growing complexity of the services it provides, to both private and corporate customers, are among the challenges that it faces. The company is involved in a major programme of branch rationalization. Some branches are being closed, others remodelled to provide either private or corporate services, others are being expanded as key branches. Early on in this programme of change it became clear that the company's property management department needed attention. Its property management performance was poor and outmoded. Its capacity to plan and carry through the branch rationalization programme seemed doubtful.

Property management was the responsibility of a central department employing 250 professional staff, mainly architects and surveyors, managed by a general manager. The general manager was drawn from the senior management team on a two-year posting. All general managers at that time had mainstream finance backgrounds. Indeed, the culture of company B powerfully sustained the belief that the only important work was finance. All other work, whether property, computing or marketing, was secondary. Career paths for non-finance people were limited, departments being managed by people with finance backgrounds. The extent to which non-finance staff were undervalued may be seen by noting that in the property management department no one could remember anyone having any training and development since the day of their appointment. The morale of the property management department was low and the level of interdepartmental conflict (between the surveyors' group and the architects' group) was very high.

The company was organized into 12 regions, each managed by a regional director. Property management at regional level was uncoordinated. Regional directors took many of the decisions without being properly or formally accountable. Refurbishment decisions were under regional director control yet the costs of refurbishment were a charge on a head office account, and were not on the region's books. Moreover, the lack of cooperation between architects and surveyors diffused any professional input into property decisions taken at regional level.

The organizational culture: a major financial institution

Company B typifies the *role culture*[1] under significant external and internal pressures. Often stereotyped as bureaucracy, this culture is characterized by stability, prescription, rules and standards. Functional departments are clearly specified. This can be a very efficient culture in stable environments. Role cultures emphasize high levels of commitment by individuals, either to a department or, in a professional role culture, to a particular profession. In this culture, position power is a predominant form of power. But in this case the stability of the 1960s and 1970s had been replaced by the turbulence of the 1980s. Property management expertise was now essential if the branch rationalization programme was to proceed.

To detail briefly the organizational changes decided on, a property management professional was brought in to take charge and develop a modern property management strategy. This was only the second time in the history of company B that a non-finance manager had been appointed to this level and the first time such an appointment had been made from outside. Under his control property management was decentralized to regional teams, managed by regional managers. Small teams, closer to the regions, would be more likely to develop improved working relationships both within teams and between the property management team and region. Training and development was initiated for the professional staff. A career path was now opening up for them. All this was moving property management towards a *task culture*. Here, influence is based on expertise, i.e. the expertise needed to carry out the task. Teams of people work together to achieve objectives and tasks. This culture places demands on people but it also provides for the merging of individual and organizational objectives in changing circumstances. It is an adaptable culture in which the needs of the task, rather than systems and procedures, predominate. In this case, architects and surveyors now work together more closely and manage the regional teams. For professional purposes there is a professional development role played by a deputy general manager in the now small head office property management function. Arguably, company B has moved towards a culture that is more appropriate to the challenge that it faces.

Organizational issues which must be faced if more adaptable organizational cultures are to be achieved are outlined by the following criteria:

1 *Management autonomy*, particularly with regard to reward systems: to what extent should local management have the ability to make decisions about gradings and salary dependent on market conditions and personal performance?

---

[1]The terms 'role culture' and 'power culture' are taken from Charles Handy (see Handy, 1984).

2 *Interchangeability*: movement across specialist/professional boundaries by internal promotions, fixed-term secondments or short training periods would help to develop broader knowledge and experience. To what extent should promotion depend on diversity of experience? Moves of this kind can sustain task forces or project teams. It can also reinforce individual autonomy, creativity and knowledge.

3 *Openness* or *public testing* of issues and problems would also be aided by interchangeability.

4 *Recent developments in management information systems* seem likely to bring about systems which managers can interrogate! This will aid *communication* partly through the *access* so provided, partly by the prospect of simplification of procedures and paperwork that such developments promise.

5 *Functional and professional advice* can be provided at a more local level utilizing task-team approaches such as that described briefly in the case where professional development, planning and control are centrally organized. The focus should be on *business needs* rather than on professional demands.

Other organizational cultures have been identified. The *power culture* is worth a moment's thought. It is frequently found in small, growing companies, including property and finance. These organizations are highly dependent on one or more strong leaders. Control is exercised from the centre and decisions are largely made on the outcome of a balance of influence rather than on rational grounds (which the uncertainties of our changing world will rarely allow in any event). An organization with this culture can react well to change but the quality of its top people is crucial. Individuals who are power orientated, risk taking and politically skilled will do well in this culture wherein accountability is personal and direct.

Managing in different cultures

One final thought on culture: we have discussed the links between organizational culture, the tasks to be performed and the rate of environmental change, but culture is a broader part of our affairs. At home and abroad we often find ourselves working with people from different occupational, local and national cultures. Effective management thus demands the capacity to deal with cross-cultural issues and influences. The important skill here is that of *empathy*. Managing change involves the need to influence people. Empathy, sensitivity to cultural differences and the struggle to understand them and to communicate in an intelligible fashion are essential.

The property management professional brought this skill to bear in his work with the professional staff involved in the change process described above. While these boundaries cannot easily be crossed, people responded to the attempt and change programmes were all the more feasible and relevant for a leavening of the cultural sensitivity.

The key issue of organizational culture emerges clearly. To achieve a more effective and professional, yet adaptable, property management department it is necessary to move towards a task culture. This demands openness, learning, good communication and the recognition of people's needs. Relating this to business needs is also important in order to give a clear sense of objectives and contribution.

Implementation

The important thing about the implementation of the above change is that it was carried out in two phases. Full consultation was undertaken over the issue of assigning people to regional teams. No one was given any guarantees, but all were asked to indicate preferences. For most people relocation was involved. Various factors had to be considered in creating teams: the correct mix of skills and people, regional team managers designate, as well as people's preferences for particular teams (and, therefore, particular parts of the country) were all relevant. What this consultation phase allowed was a careful explanation of the proposed changes such that people understood what was involved. The second phase was actually to form the regional teams. Originally, this was to be done gradually when office space was available in the various regions.

In the event the teams were formed at head office, overnight. Doing it quickly had the advantage of creating a clear break with the past. Also, it meant that the teams could form and settle down in the secure head office environment. Relocation could then be more effectively handled by the regional team. The process took three to five weeks to settle down. Over the year the regional teams were all well established in the regions. Regional directors who originally had said that no space would be available for two years now seemed to jump at the chance of getting the new cohesive and more effective regional property management teams in their regions. The management of change is often a matter of the management of image. Create the image of success and it is surprising how quickly stereotyped attitudes can be changed.

■ The politics of organizational change

To understand how organizations are managed, experienced and changed we need to understand the politics of organization. This has become a widely accepted view. (Pettigrew, 1973, 1985; Pfeffer, 1981; Lawler and Bachrach, 1986 – all develop this view.) Moreover, the work of Child (1984) and Hickson *et al.* (1986) elaborates the importance of politics within a contingency theory framework. Organizational structures, technologies, decisions and outcomes are not given but rather are contingent on factors such as the environment (whether or not it is complex and changing, for example). Strategic choice is available. The contingencies limit or constrain; they do not determine. Thus it is that managers may *choose* how to operate, and choice creates the conditions for politics because people will support different views regarding these choices.

One fairly straightforward approach is to focus on the so-called 'dominant coalition'. Senior executives of an organization within such a group may have considerable influence over decisions, the use of resources and other changes. They create rules, policies, standards of performance and procedures which 'channel' employee behaviour. Major decisions on growth products, redundancy and restructuring are made at this level. But we must beware the assumption that 'dominant coalitions' provide a structure to an organization's political process. Coalitions are shifting. Membership varies over time. The concerns which people deem important also vary. To suggest that 'dominant coalitions' are formed and sustained, and then dominate decision making and action, trivializes the problem of understanding organizational politics.

Lee and Lawrence (1985) suggest that 'over and above "dominant coalitions" and "strategic choice" we must study . . . the political situation and political activity, and accept that there will be many interest groups influencing structure . . . as they push towards their own goals'. Whether they prefer a pluralist view (seeing interest groups of equivalent power) is not clear. They suggest the adoption of a 'radical' view. Such a 'radical' view involves making no assumptions that organizations have goals, over which management have the right to decide. Moreover, no interest group has any *a priori* rights, although Lee and Lawrence accept that interest groups might be assumed to have such rights, either by themselves or by others. No set of values is judged as either 'right' or 'wrong'. One is tempted to add that if we suggest that people assume that organizations do have goals, and act accordingly, then the confusion created by these definitions becomes almost complete.

Individual behaviour is viewed as the impetus to all organized activity and emerges from the pursuit of personal interests and goals. Individual behaviour, they say, is essentially active and rational rather than passive, irrational or emotional. Conflict is the very stuff of organizational life. This seems overly simplistic. The distinction between the rational and the irrational has been replaced by the notion of 'multiple rationalities' (see Weick, 1979). Rationality is in the eye of the beholder. While there is much conflict in organizations, all have experienced situations where the absence of conflict is even more worthy of attention. As Lukes (1974) has made clear, one form of power is that of limiting the 'political' agenda such that particular issues or choices are not recognized as being important and are therefore precluded from consideration.

The world of organizational politics is characterized by structures of interests, goals, power and status which are inherently unstable. This does not mean that a given political order (e.g. the power of a dominant coalition) will be overturned. Rather, it seems likely that in a world of changing markets, technology, social ties, population, values and beliefs and politics, the political order in an organization will be necessarily unstable. To understand behaviour in organizations we must understand how that order is sustained or overturned. This may have less to do with the ebb and flow of individual goals and interests at the microlevel and more to do with how a particular organization's problems (say, in a declining market) are conceived, discussed and assessed. This means trying to understand how such a problem is approached through analysis, discussion, the production of reports and papers and so on. Accountants, engineers, marketing and production personnel will be involved. Thus, different professional perspectives will be employed. The emergence of an approach, whether to develop new markets, disinvest, launch new products, seek a higher market share or whatever, does not flow solely from the 'facts' but, rather, from a process in which professional, departmental and individual perspectives, attitudes and interests are involved. Pettigrew (1985) argues for just such an approach. Interest groups have different goals, time scales, values and problem-solving styles. Different interest groups have different rationalities. Change processes in organizations may be understood, in part, as the outcome of processes of competition between these rationalities expressed through the language, priorities and values of technologists, of accounting and finance, or from the perspectives of groups such as operational research, organizational development or personnel.

Proper study of organizational politics involves the examination of political process, activity and skill, and the study of what we refer to as 'professional rationality'. There I depart somewhat from Pettigrew. For me the interest is on professional rationality, being the language which represents the professional technique (whether engineering, accounting, personnel or operational research). It is somewhat simplistic to equate interest groups with professional groups. In our view the professional can be compelled to support one view of a problem through use of the rationality into which he or she has been professionally socialized and yet, individually, may experience feelings which impel him or her to a different view. As I shall argue later, changes in professional technique emerge when the tensions so created lead individual professionals to question their roles. An accountant can thus be aligned with engineers, personnel specialists and others who form an interest group supporting a particular project. Rationality emerges from professional technique, not simply from the emergence of interest groups; the latter are altogether too unstable. Interest groups form around specific interests regarding policies, practices, power, status and authority. Rationality comprises a means of dealing with the circumstances of a particular professional practice and ways of articulating and legitimizing that practice.

Managing change

To understand how organizations are managed, experienced and changed we need to understand their politics. In turn, this involves the examination of political process, activity and skill. Why is the use of power and politics a necessary part of managing change? Partly this is because of the departures from accepted norms:

> **Innovative accomplishments stretch beyond the established definition of a 'job' to bring new learning or capacity to the organisation. They involve change, a disruption of existing activities, a redirection of organisational energies.**
>
> Kanter, 1983, page 21

Of course this is right, but the impetus to the use of power runs deeper. Any significant organizational change demands that existing ways of thinking about and talking about what we do can be overturned. Dominant views must be usurped. Experience tells us that the first attempt to articulate an alternative view, a novel concept, will frequently fall on barren ground. It will probably meet opposition and even outright rejection. To overcome such opposition or rejection, neither logic nor evidence, nor the participation of all concerned, appears to be enough. New ideas can seem unorthodox and even risky. A manager seeking support for new ideas must be sensitive to political processes.

Kodak, once the dominant player in photographic film, saw competitors take significant market share and through the late 1980s and early 1990s the company went through repeated restructuring, losing 40,000 jobs. While substantial refocusing has been achieved, much turns on the success of digital imaging.

A crucial issue is how to achieve the ability to adapt continuously in rapidly changing circumstances. Part of this has been about the realignment of resources away from functions towards customers. Cross-functional teams are seen as a vital building block of change strategy and the teams (some of which include customers) become the focus for organizational learning. Not least Kodak uses benchmarking to build unit goals which it uses to seek improvements within which cross-functional teams operate. This is based on the need for flat structures, more capable people, enhanced collaboration, evidence-based management, customer focus and increased energy and commitment.

Coping with organizational change

Thus far we have considered some of the managerial skills associated with the effective management of change. We now proceed to consider the impact of change on the people directly affected, which will often include many middle and senior managers. We are concerned here with the people who must take on new tasks, develop new skills, be transferred, regraded or retrained. Once changes emerge, people must learn to cope as individuals. I will describe a simple model of how people experience change and, below, we will consider the model in more detail and examine how they can cope with the pressures created by change. Understanding this can enable senior managers to provide practical support to people undergoing change and may better enable them to avoid creating constraints on people, which makes their personal task of coping all the harder.

Coping with the process of change places demands on the individuals involved. Various issues need to be faced either by the individuals or by managers. Note, however, that these issues are of concern to all those who are affected by an organizational change, including managers. I will set down a practical framework for coping with change below, based on ideas from various workers in the field, including Cooper (1981), Argyris (1982), Kirkpatrick (1985), Kanter (1983) and my own experience. Many managers I know arrange two-hour workshops in groups of 10 to 12 people in which the participants are asked to discuss and then report back on those issues that they feel are important in a period of change. This can be a powerful method facilitating a more knowledgeable and constructive approach to a major change, and it can lead to useful ideas. I also remember talking these ideas over with a senior manager in a diversified group who had introduced computerized photocomposition for a newspaper company in the early 1970s. The company had allowed the typesetters to try out the visual display units in a test room but *not* in a training environment. Providing support, they avoided any sense of formal training and were surprised to find that, allowed to learn at their own pace, the typesetters embraced the technology enthusiastically and quickly. This is important; giving people the chance, the time and the support to try things out for themselves is a way of allowing them to build their self-esteem under their own control *and* to solve the problem of change along the way. Only then does formal training have a really effective role as a means of ensuring consistent performance, disseminating best practices and so on. While it is often said that not enough training is done, it is too easy to be beguiled into introducing formal training programmes too early.

■ Rebuilding self-esteem

The ground covered in this section is summarized in Figure 13.1. Simplifying somewhat, it suggests that individuals have four main categories of need if they are to rebuild their self-esteem amidst a programme of organizational change. They need *intelligible information*. They will probably need to develop *new skills*, if only the skills of dealing with new people as colleagues or supervisors. They will need *support* to help them to deal with the problems. Encouragement to try out new systems is important. Provision of short workshops planned to achieve part or all of the work discussed in the preceding section can help. Technical support to aid solution of problems is often needed. Access to people who can help is useful. Control over the rate of personal learning should be possible. All these things can help. First and foremost, *empathy* (understanding) is a key issue and Kirkpatrick (1985) rightly sees it as one of the key skills for managing change. Pierre Casse (1979) defines empathy as follows:

> **Empathy is the ability to see and understand how other people construct reality, or more specifically how they perceive, discover and invest the inner and outer worlds. We all use empathy all the time. We constantly guess what people think and feel. The problem is that in most cases we guess wrongly. We assume that what is going on in somebody else's mind is somewhat identical to our own psychic processes. We tend to forget that we are different. Sometimes, drastically different. To practice empathy is to recognize and take full advantage of those differences.**

We see the skill of empathy as the struggle to understand. We can never fully see a situation as others see it. But we can struggle to try and individuals will respond to that struggle. They will also respond to someone who clearly does not try. Generally their response will be to ignore them if possible, to resist them and certainly to approach dealings with them cynically. Making information intelligible to its recipient requires these skills. We need to try to see things as the recipient will see them in order to communicate. Often we do not try; we

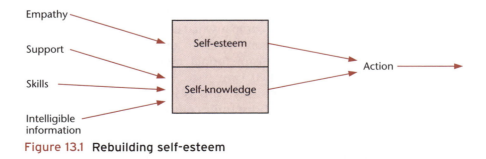

Figure 13.1 **Rebuilding self-esteem**

pass on the information we have. Usually we do so without attempting to make it intelligible, if we pass it on at all.

Thus far in this chapter we have discussed ways and means of introducing major changes effectively. Here I wish to stress one crucial point. Effective organizations are those which introduce change quickly and in which people – employees and managers – learn about the business or organization as this process proceeds. Achieving change without learning is possible, but sometimes not without struggle if powerful groups oppose. Introducing change in ways which do not encourage learning is likely in the future to entrench negative attitudes to change. Only if people and organizations change, by learning from the experience of change, can effectiveness be achieved and sustained. I have attempted to draw together a range of ideas and practical steps to help people manage change effectively.

All these ideas and steps need to be integrated for effectiveness. Only if we manage transitions effectively can learning and change occur. This also acts as a constructive constraint on the politics of change which can so easily run out of control. Moreover, managing change effectively reduces anxiety and helps those individuals who find change stressful to cope with it. This in turn leads to a more positive attitude to change. Thus it is that we come full circle. If these ideas are synthesized in a managerial approach to organizational change, then there would seem to be a better prospect of success and effectiveness. Difficult and demanding in practice, I offer these ideas as the basis of how managers are able to see changes through. Figure 13.2 summarizes the ideas presented here. The key point is that only by synthesizing the management of transition, dealing with organizational cultures and handling organizational politics constructively, can we create the environment in which creativity, risk taking, learning and the rebuilding of self-esteem and performance can be achieved. If we can sustain such a synthesis then learning and change can follow. More important, because people have learned about the business through the process of changing, the organization probably becomes more effective. By creating the conditions for extensive problem solving and positive attitudes to change, future effectiveness is created.

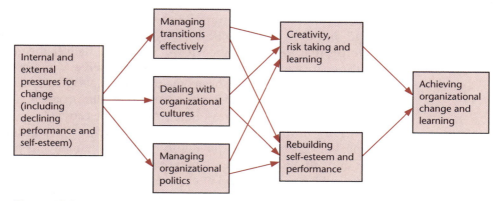

Figure 13.2 Managing major changes

Coping with change

So far we have reviewed some of the processes by which people come to decide on a new strategy, a new product, a new organizational structure, to close down a factory and so on. What then? The easy answer is to say that the changes must be implemented; the resources must be obtained, the constraints considered and dealt with in one way or another. To say this is really to see the problem of organizational change from the perspective of those concerned in its introduction.

Now we consider the process of implementation of change from the perspective of those who are directly affected: the people who must take on new tasks, develop new skills, be transferred, regraded and retrained. Here, then, I refer to middle managers and other employees. Whether or not they participated in the planning, once the changes take concrete form they must learn to cope with them. Our concern is to describe a simple model of how people experience change as a precursor to considering how people come to cope with the pressures created by change. Better understanding of these processes will enable senior managers who implement change to develop a richer understanding of the issues they must face. Thus they will be better able to provide help and support for the people concerned and, perhaps more importantly, avoid creating constraints on the people involved which makes their personal task of coping with change more difficult. I start from the assumption that the individual concerned must be the prime mover if change is to be assimilated and if adaptation is to occur.

Often, the problems of implementing change are discussed largely as if 'resistance to change' is the main concern. In this chapter we see that the situation is, first, more complex than this and, second, is capable of much more positive or optimistic construction. Indeed, it is often possible to encourage 'resistance to change' by dealing with people as if that is the only response one expects. We have discussed various responses to change in an earlier chapter when our focus was on planning and implementation of change. Now we pick up the threads of this argument in order to consider the practical and positive steps which can be taken to support people as *they* cope with change.

Change creates anxiety, uncertainty and stress, even for those managing change, and even if they are fully committed to change. Seldom are there any guarantees that the new approach will work, will deliver the goods. Those who wish the change to be successful often find themselves working long hours, dealing with problems, trying to overcome the doubts of others and doing everything needed to see the changes through. In working life, change and role strain are two important sources of stress. Role strain can be caused by not being involved in decisions, having inadequate managerial support, having to cope with technological or other changes, having to maintain standards of performance even under difficult circumstances, having responsibility for people who are uncooperative – all likely in a period of change. In non-working life 'moving home' is a key source of stress and this sometimes flows from change. Thus we should not be surprised by the links between change and stress.

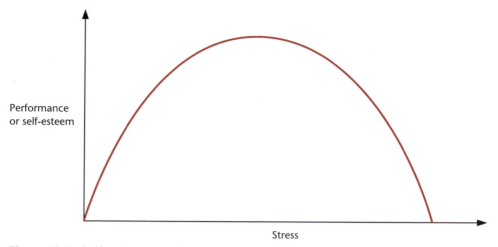

Figure 13.3 Self-esteem, performance and stress

One simple and helpful idea for managers dealing with change involves look-ing at the relationship between self-esteem, performance and stress. This is shown in Figure 13.3. The relationship turns out to apply to both performance *and* self-esteem. The problem is that people are different.

We do not all fit neatly onto the one curve. However, the general nature of the relationship seems to hold. In any event, if change causes stress we cannot be at the left-hand end of the diagram. We must be moving in the direction shown in Figure 13.4 and therefore down the curve. Is there a threshold beyond which

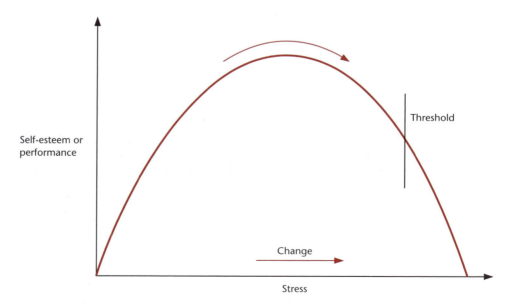

Figure 13.4 Self-esteem, performance, stress and change

behaviour becomes volatile and unpredictable? In fact, people respond differently. Some stress motivates people by providing challenge. But we need to avoid stressing ourselves and others overmuch; it can lead to people feeling 'swamped'.

The coping cycle

Changes which have a significant impact on the work that people do will have a significant impact on their self-esteem. So much is well established (see Cooper, 1981; de Vries and Miller, 1984; Kirkpatrick, 1985). Linked to this impact on self-esteem will be an impact on performance. I suggest that performance will be affected in three ways, as follows.

The new systems, processes, structures, etc. will have to be learned. This takes time. There is a *learning-curve effect* as people build their performance up through learning. There is also a *progress effect* as the new system is commissioned, the snags ironed out and modifications introduced to enable performance to be improved. I remember being invited to a large new factory in Scandinavia 'to see our new robots'. There were 27 of them and on the day of the visit only six were working. In some cases this was because the staff involved had not yet learned to program or maintain them; in others it was because the robot had proved incapable of meeting the task requirements without modification. Thus, while learning-curve and progress effects are interrelated they are, however, quite different in origin. New systems never work 100 per cent to specification first time. Especially if the specification is wrong.

In addition to these performance effects there is also the *self-esteem effect*. I suggest that significant organizational changes create a decline in self-esteem for many of those who are directly affected. This decline has an impact on performance. The link between satisfaction, feelings of well-being, self-esteem and performance has been the subject of much research. Lawler (1978) and Steers and Porter (1979) present excellent reviews of much of this work. Whatever the causal mechanisms involved and whatever the direction of the relationship, there does seem to be a clear link, albeit a small one. Combine the suggested self-esteem effect with the learning-curve effect and the progress effect and we get a significant potential effect on performance. All the effects are interrelated. We propose that the driving force for rebuilding performance subsequent to a major change will be the rebuilding of self-esteem. However, as we shall see, this can be helped by action on the learning-curve and progress fronts. I summarize this discussion with a simple model based on the work of de Vries and Miller (1984) and Adams *et al.* (1976). In the model I propose five main stages. These are capable of more detailed analysis but for both practical and pedagogic purposes I have presented a simplified model. The model is shown in Figure 13.5.

■ Stage 1: Denial

When significant changes are first mooted the initial response may be to deny the need for change: 'We have always done things this way.' 'Why change, we are making a profit, aren't we?' 'Don't change a winning team.' 'We tried that before

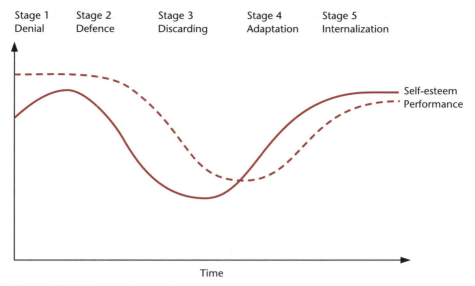

Figure 13.5 **The coping cycle**

but it did not work.' 'You will never make it work.' Faced with the possibility of changes, people will often find value in their present circumstances, often in work situations which they would bitterly complain about at other times. That this is paradoxical should not surprise us. Our actions are impelled by complex and often contradictory motivations. Thus sales staff threatened with the closure of their store can defend their jobs with vigour, yet still believe fervently that working conditions are poor. If major organizational changes come suddenly and dramatically then paralysis can often result. Adams *et al.* (1976) refer to a kind of immobilization or a sense of being overwhelmed, of being unable to reason, to plan, or even to understand what is going on. For the individual a suddenly announced redundancy can have such an impact, but there is often a longish period of gestation as ideas are discussed and the changes are planned. If the changes are not particularly new or dramatic, and if there are obvious opportunities for people, then this paralysis is felt less intensely. The tendency to deny the validity of new ideas, at least initially, does seem to be a general reaction, however. Built into this is the likelihood that self-esteem actually increases in this first stage. The advantages of the present job are emphasized, attachments to the job, the work group and valued skills are recognized. The sense of being a member of a group subject to external threat can lead to increased group cohesiveness. All this may lead to increased self-esteem. A sense of euphoria can develop. We have shown performance to be stable, however. If self-esteem does increase we would guess that performance would not improve, either because the discussion of impending change can absorb energy or because often there are systems in place which may hold back performance improvement (payment systems, for example). If the change is dramatic, novel and traumatic (say, involving a sudden job change or redundancy) then this stage can involve an immediate decline in performance. Generally, however, there is a warning period and performance will not decline immediately. One way of handling the stage is to minimize the immediate impact of the change. This allows people time to face up to a new reality.

■ Stage 2: Defence

Reality obtrudes, however. The early discussion of changes leads to concrete plans and programmes of change. Now the realities of change become clearer and people must begin to face new tasks, working for a new boss or with a different group of people, perhaps in a different department or a new location. Thus they become aware that they must come to terms with the way in which they work, and perhaps with more general changes in life (if, for example, relocation involving a house move is required). This can lead to feelings of depression and frustration because it can be difficult to decide how to deal with these changes. This stage is often characterized by defensive behaviour. People may attempt to defend their own job, their own territory. Often this will be articulated as ritualistic behaviour. I can remember the introduction of computer-aided learning in business schools many years ago. Many embraced these ideas enthusiastically; many simply rejected them: 'My subject is unsuitable.' One colleague provided an impressive show of activity on the computer, finally concluding that after much effort he had failed to make computer-aided learning work for that subject. Years later, computer-aided learning in that subject is commonplace. Was this a ritual? Again, this defensive behaviour seems to have the effect of creating time and 'space' to allow people to come to terms with the changes.

■ Stage 3: Discarding

There now emerges a process of discarding. The preceding stages have focused powerfully on the past. Now people begin to let go of the past and look forward to the future. We do not know how this happens. We know that support can be helpful, as can providing people with the opportunity to experiment with new systems without the pressure of formal training programmes and so on. Now it is possible for optimistic feelings to emerge. It may well be that the discarding process is impelled by an awakening sense that the present anxieties are just too much to bear, or that perhaps the future is not as forbidding as it first seemed. Now we may observe behaviour which appears to identify the individual with the changes involved, who will start to talk openly and constructively about the new system, who will ask questions about it, who in a sense will say: 'Well here it is – we are committed to it – here's how I see it.' People may begin to solve problems, take the initiative and even demonstrate some leadership. Thus it is that self-esteem improves.

Discarding is initially a process of perception. People come to see that the change is both inevitable and/or necessary. It becomes apparent to them. Adaptation starts with recognition. Here we see human courage amidst difficult circumstances as the individual accepts new 'realities'. This can be exciting for individuals and groups. Taking the risks of publicly facing a new reality, there is a sense in which they re-establish their own identity, the identity which may have seemed threatened by the changes being introduced. Thus it is that self-esteem begins to flow back like the returning tide.

The crisis of change creates great tensions for those involved; this much we have seen. It creates a plethora of reasons for people to feel upset and disorientated. The new job we have been assigned to appears to be of lesser status, valued skills seem unnecessary, the new work appears to be frustrating. The new system or machine appears to be unusual, even frightening, although with practice it becomes commonplace. The crucial point is that this process needs time. Discarding involves experimenting and risk. Time is needed for individuals to recreate their own sense of identity and self-esteem as they 'grow' into the new situation.

Stage 4: Adaptation

Now a process of mutual adaptation emerges. Rarely do new systems, procedures, structures or machines work effectively first time. Individuals begin to test the new situation and themselves trying out new behaviours, working to different standards, working out ways of coping with the changes. Thus the individual learns. Other individuals also adapt. Fellow workers, supervisors and managers all learn as the new system is tried out. Finally, technical and operational problems are identified and modifications made to deal with them; thus progress is made.

Significant amounts of energy are involved here. The process of trial and error, of effort and setback, and the slow building of performance can often be a source of real frustration. In these circumstances people can evince anger. This is not resistance to change; rather, it is the natural consequence of trying to make a new system work, experiencing partial (or complete) failure which may or may not be under the control of the individuals concerned. This anger does not result in attempts to oppose but, rather, articulates the feelings of those trying to make the new system work. While managers should ensure that the right training and support is available, we argue that they should generally remain in the background, allowing the people who are directly involved to make it work. By doing so these people will develop the skills, understanding and attachments needed for the system to be run effectively in the longer term.

Stage 5: Internalization

Now the people involved have created a new system, process and organization. New relationships between people and processes have been tried, modified and accepted. These now become incorporated into an understanding of the new work situation. This is a cognitive process through which people make sense of what has happened. Now the new behaviour becomes part of 'normal' behaviour.

It appears that people experience change in these ways, initially as disturbance, perhaps even as a shock, then coming to accept its reality – testing it out and engaging in a process of mutual adaptation and finally coming to terms with the change. Self-esteem and performance vary, initially declining and then growing again. The variation of performance flows from mutually reinforcing individual and operational causes, as we have seen. The 'engine' for rebuilding performance is the self-esteem of the people involved. (Note here that we think of relative levels – notional performance might be improved tenfold as a consequence of new technology – the problems we have discussed may mean that in the early stages following the introduction of the new technology only 60 per cent of notional performance is achieved. While this means that 40 per cent is being lost, it does represent a sixfold improvement.) Finally, it is not suggested that people go through these stages neatly, or that all go through them at the same time or at the same rate. Some may not go beyond the denial of change.

The important point is that people do seem to experience significant changes in these ways *and* that this leads to a number of practical ways in which the problems of coping can be handled.

Coping with the process of change

Coping with the process of change places demands on the individuals involved; various issues need to be faced either by these individuals or by their managers. Note, however, that these issues are of concern to all affected by an organizational change, including managers. In the following pages I will set down a simple framework of coping with change, identifying issues to be faced.

■ Coping with change: issues to be faced

Know yourself

Issues

Would I have chosen this to have happened? Do I accept it? Can I benefit from the changes? What is the worst that can happen to me?

Discussion

Here we are concerned with feelings about the changes to be introduced. In particular, we are concerned with the question of the worst that can happen to the individual. This might be the loss of a job. Alternatively, it might be a transfer to a new job or new department. Or it might mean taking on new skills. It is often difficult for managers to provide this kind of detailed information (see the section on information below). However, it is often possible to provide some level of guarantee at an early stage. Doing so sets boundaries on the problems for the individuals concerned. It provides them with vital data as they try to make sense of how the changes will affect them *and* how they feel about it.

Issues

Do I know what I want? Do I know what I don't want?

Discussion

These are difficult questions to face. How many of us have clear answers to them? Yet answering them (even if only in a tentative way) is essential if we are to come to terms with changes. In essence, individuals can be encouraged to think about these questions through using diagnostic techniques of various kinds. A good example would be the job diagnostic survey (see Hackman and Oldham, 1976), which aims to obtain information about how people react to different jobs, including their present jobs and jobs they might prefer. The approach involves examining responses in terms of issues such as various job characteristics (skill variety, task identity, task significance, autonomy, feedback, dealing with others), experienced psychological states (experienced meaningfulness of work, experienced responsibility for work, knowledge of results) and affective outcomes (satisfaction, internal work motivation and growth satisfaction). An approach of this kind can be used, perhaps as part of a workshop activity (see below), to encourage people to think about their present job and the demands it places on them, their own preferences and the jobs likely to result from the changes. This could allow them to examine work design problems, and could both provide solutions of value and be a process through which individuals begin to think about the new situation in a constructive fashion.

Issues

What skills and abilities do I possess? How might I develop new skills?

Discussion

This issue emerges directly from the preceding one. If we can begin to answer questions about the kind of job we want, then we can go on to consider the skills and abilities we possess and view them in the light of the changes to be introduced. How relevant will they be? What new skills are needed? Can I develop such skills? Can such development be seen as an evolution from my present skills? For example, if we consider the case of an office worker being introduced to a new software package it is clear that some of the existing skills (keyboard skills, layout skills, language usage) will be transferable and some new skills will be needed. Again these issues can be examined by utilizing an instrument such as the job diagnostic survey and approaches more directly concerned with skills analysis (see Carnall, 1976).

Issues

Have I experienced similar changes? How did I cope? Can I take the initiative?

Discussion

Many people have undergone many changes either at work or in their personal lives. What can they learn from those past experiences? What ways did they use to cope with the changes? How long did it take them to resolve issues and make the personal adaptations necessary? Facing questions like these helps us set the present changes in a broader life context. It also enables us to develop ideas about coping with those present changes or of where we need help to do so.

Issues

Can I cope with stress? Am I able to handle conflict? Can I avoid conflict? How well do I manage my time? Do I blame myself?

Discussion

We have already seen that stress is a necessary part of organizational change. Similarly in the section on the politics of change we saw that conflict was a necessary part of change. We need to develop means of dealing with these linked phenomena. In particular, we need to examine how we respond to conflict and whether we are able to minimize or deal with it. Conflict is likely to increase the level of stress that we experience. Can we limit its impact? Perhaps more important, we must face the issue of self-blame. Individuals undergoing changes which appear to make their skills or experience unnecessary will often blame themselves: 'This proves that I am no use.' 'I have been put on the scrap heap.' People say these sorts of things when blaming themselves. If change undermines self-esteem, self-blame merely reinforces that situation. People should be encouraged to face this issue. Do I blame myself? Do I feel useless, paralysed, confused? Can I begin to deal with those feelings? What can I do to overcome them? Will working out a new role in the new situation allow me to do so? Self-blame in these circumstances seems to be unavoidable; making it explicit can be helpful.

Issues

Do I take stock of my situation? Am I prepared to reflect on myself and how I feel about change? Do I expect others (perhaps managers or union representatives) to deal with these issues?

Discussion

Do I respond to change as an independent person or do I allow myself to be dependent on others? What do I define as my responsibilities? We noted earlier that discarding the past had an important element of risk and personal growth attached to it. People handle crises in their non-working lives (divorce, bereavement and so on). There is no reason to suppose that they cannot do so in their working lives.

Know your situation

Issues

Can I describe the situation? Can I explain the new system? For my own work area? For the department as a whole? Can I explain why the changes are necessary?

Discussion

If one does not understand the changes to be introduced, one is in no position to come to terms with them as an individual. There is no better test of understanding than the task of explaining to another. If people cannot understand the changes then this implies a failure to communicate them effectively. While managers often say that they have described the changes to their employees it may be that they have not done so in a manner which those people find intelligible. This means describing it in the listener's own terms, which does not necessarily mean describing it in a lower or simplified form; rather, it means in a relevant form. Kirkpatrick (1985) provides us with a useful approach to this problem focusing on barriers to communication created by the sender and through the receiver emphasizing that feedback is important if effectiveness in communication is to be ensured. In fact, using these coping with change ideas as the basis for short workshops can provide for more effective communication about changes.

Issues

Do I know how I am expected to behave? What standards of performance will be required? Who will I work with? Who will I report to? Who will I be responsible for?

Discussion

If I do not understand the new situation I am unlikely to be able to deal with these questions. Yet if people are to adapt they need to be able to answer them. These questions are really the behavioural element of the questions raised in the last section. They also begin the process of establishing precisely what others expect of us in the new situation.

Issues

Can I try out the new system in advance? Is it possible for me to experiment with the new system? To learn by trial and error?

Discussion

Coming to terms with new systems takes time, requires experiment and risk and involves learning. Very often, the first time that many people face a new system is either on a training course or when the system is installed. Both situations create expectations which can mitigate against risk. Often, training programmes, unless sensitively handled, involve comparisons between people. No one welcomes feeling stupid or ineffective in front of others. If we are trained to handle a new system we may feel that we cannot control our own learning because we are holding back the group, or because the trainer has so much ground to cover and we feel we cannot or should not hold things up. Trying out new systems for ourselves and by ourselves allows us to familiarize ourselves with the system at our own rate. We can begin to come to terms with new systems if our first attempts are not organized in such a way as to make us feel that we are being evaluated. I once discussed this point with a senior manager from a newspaper group which had introduced computerized printing technology. In doing so the company had bought a number of workstations long before they were needed for production purposes. These workstations were placed in a room which operators were allowed to use at any time and unsupervised. Instruction was available but was delivered at the rate that the operator wished and not to a predetermined training plan. Thus the operators controlled their own learning. The company found that people made rapid progress, including many who had been considered unlikely to take on the new technology.

Know others who can help

Issues

Is there benefit in talking things over with family, friends or colleagues? With my manager? With strangers?

Discussion

There is some evidence to suggest that many people do not discuss work 'in their own time'. If change creates uncertainty and stress, this can mean that they lose important opportunities. Simply talking through a problem can be helpful – this of course requires that we understand the changes well enough to be able to describe them to others. It seems to make sense to encourage people to discuss their problems. Discussion with colleagues can be facilitated by running workshops. Much the same applies to talking things over with the manager involved. Sometimes there is benefit to be had from talking things over with a complete stranger.

Working on self-esteem

Issues

Test out ideas and beliefs.

Discussion

Working with our ideas and beliefs about a change can usefully form a basis for building our self-esteem. Consider the case of a hospital within which new roles are being introduced impacting the jobs of nursing staff. Some may fear they will lose their jobs? Is this true? In all circumstances? In these circumstances? What has management said about the issue? Is it the subject of negotiations? Have guarantees been given? People might also think that they are too old to get to grips with the new roles. Is that true? What help can be obtained? Can I try it out now? Work on the issues discussed above will feed into this and help people to make progress. Perhaps the important point is for us to recognize that we need to build our self-esteem as part of dealing with a programmed change. We need to recognize that this is an essential, unavoidable part of this process.

Issues

Talk out issues with yourself!

Discussion

On the face of it this may sound rather silly. Discussing the point recently on a senior management programme, one manager said that he always got his people to write out those issues that they felt were important in a change situation. Talking or writing involves thinking through systematically. Writing creates a publicly available record. To deal with our feelings about changes we need to understand them better. Thus talking them out (or writing them down) is an important facilitating process, and something which could form part of a workshop programme.

Issues

Let go of the past. Accept that this will create a sense of loss.

Discussion

We have already discussed the need, and the processes through which people will discard the past. It is important to recognize that this will create a sense of loss and will cause anger. It is inevitable, and it is important for all of us to recognize that it is inevitable. Managers must ensure that time and space are allowed for people to experience these feelings and that this is legitimate. The temptation to calm people down, to soothe their fears and anger, may be compelling but must be treated with caution. If we are not careful we deny feelings which must be experienced if change is to be accepted. Most important, we should recognize that this process of letting go of the past, while painful, does involve learning and is really part of the process through which individuals choose the future.

Issues

Set goals, act, look for gains.

Finally...

The discussion presented examines issues and questions which must be faced, and ways of doing so. It seems clear that they could form the basis of a series of workshop activities for people who are involved in significant change programmes. While not a 'blueprint' for success, they do provide a basis for constructive work and progress. Problems of layout, work design and work organization often abound with new systems. Problem-solving activities to deal with these matters provide an excellent opportunity for people to get to grips with a new system.

Crafting change for the individual

Simplifying somewhat, I suggest that individuals have four main categories of need if they are to rebuild their self-esteem amidst a programme of organizational change. They need to understand the changes and thus need intelligible information. They will probably need to develop new skills, if only the skills of dealing with new people as colleagues or supervisors. They will need support to help them to deal with the problems. Encouragement to try out new systems is important. Provision of short workshops planned to achieve part or all of the work discussed in the preceding section can help, as can technical support to solve problems, access to people who can help and allowing people to control their own learning. First and foremost, empathy, understanding, is a key issue. Kirkpatrick (1985) rightly sees this as one of the key skills for managing change. We have discussed empathy earlier. In this chapter we have discussed a range of ideas which can be used as a way of developing or practising empathy – of trying to see changes the way others see them and using that as a 'basis for building self-esteem'. If these four needs can be met by appropriate resources then it is possible for people to carry through the personal work needed for them to rebuild their self-esteem and to act. Thus they can adapt to changes and develop new skills, abilities and roles with which to face the future.

However, two problems must be faced immediately. The issues we have discussed are difficult for individuals and groups, whether employees or managers, to face and discuss. The first relates to the provision of information by individuals.

Is that as straightforward a matter as it seems on the face of it or are there problems here? What processes can hinder coping activities? The second problem relates to the problem of ineffective behaviour.

Providing information

At a practical level much of what we have said has been concerned with information. People need to understand the new system if they are to understand their own part in it. Information must be shared if people are to judge the impact of changes on themselves and on 'their' jobs. Does this mean that openness and sharing information is a good thing, and the more the better? Some will say that this is so. We can only make mature judgements if we have the relevant information.

Others will point to the uncertainty surrounding many changes. What if the manager you exhort to pass on information does not have it to share? Then the question of confidentiality is often raised.

In fact, there is a dual problem which must be faced when significant changes are underway. For the individuals concerned, the demands of a change situation can be revealing to themselves and to others. We often respond emotionally because we feel that the new demands, the new situation, strip away barriers and reveal parts of ourselves which we have kept private. One's recent performance, the good and the less so, are now examined as the planners gather data to justify the change. One's skills are examined and explored. One's work behaviour comes under observation and analysis. The individual is asked what he or she feels about the present system, process, job, machine or structure. How well does it work? What are its problems? How might it be improved? What are the best things about it? What are the worst things about it? Thus the individual provides information.

As Bok (1984) makes clear, this is not without problems. To the extent that this probing enters the individual's personal domain (or territory), then it is an invasion of the self. That human beings will use ingenious means to protect their privacy has long been understood (see Roy (1954) for fascinating case material based on well-known observational studies in industrial settings). Should we be concerned about it? Yes, if it is our concern to see these same people actively supporting and committed to the changes. What does this mean? We would suggest that it tells us how important it is to collect information from people *on their own terms*. Only then will we minimize the chances of invading their personal domains. Information is needed, of course, but the more we can get the people involved to collect and interpret their own information, feeding it into the broader analysis of the section, department or organization, the better. Empathy becomes a crucial skill (see above). Do we mean that people should be free to keep poor performance secret, or problems? We do not but we must accept that there is a need for secrecy; the question is one of balance. Secrecy may be indispensable to individuals, to groups and to organizations.

Secrecy for plans is needed, not only to protect their formulation but also to develop them, perhaps to change them, at times to excuse them, even if to

give them up . . . Secrecy guards projects that require creativity and prolonged work: the tentative and the fragile, unfinished tasks, probes and bargaining of all kinds . . . Lack of secrecy would, for instance, thwart many negotiations, in which all plans cannot be revealed at the outset. Once projects are under way however, large portions of secrecy are often given up voluntarily, or dispelled with a flourish.

Bok, 1984, page 181

Some degree of control over information provided may be justified at the individual level to protect identity, plans and action, or choices for the individual. Thus it applies as much to the senior manager as it does to the employee. This, then, is the dual nature of the question.

Openness and sharing of information is valuable as a means of facilitating change. Yet other pressures apply. There are counteracting pressures which create limits for the individual whose job may be changed, for the people who have taken the initiative, planned and gained support for change and who are now seeing it through to implementation. Our concern, then, should not simply be to provide information but, rather, to establish the means by which people involved can control the information to be provided – not a purist answer because there is no guarantee here against abuse. But no such guarantee exists, short of domination and coercion. Making the issue explicit seems likely to create conditions under which valid and relevant information can be established without undermining the identity of those involved. To do otherwise is to be careless of the people involved in a change situation and careless of the quality of information to be obtained.

Give people time

People need time to get through a major change. This is especially true if the change requires them to solve problems. Spend time with people. It is important to listen to their views. They may well know better than you do about the details of a particular job, system or work area. Always reinforce the new situation in your discussion. Empathy is important but remember that the concern should be to help them build energy for change. Encourage people to put off those decisions which are not needed immediately. Recognize that everyone needs to feel their way forward in a period of change. Help them to see personal milestones, jobs to train for, objectives to achieve, systems to get working. Routines and milestones provide stability and structure. People need time to get through change but they also need to structure that time. Do not impose this structure. Encourage it to emerge.

Involving people

Whether, when, to what extent and how people are involved in a change situation needs careful thought because there are both advantages and disadvantages, as discussed in the following.

■ Advantages and disadvantages of involving people

Advantages

1 Improved decisions because people have better detailed knowledge of jobs and systems.
2 People will better understand the aims of the change, and the working of new systems.
3 Creates a feeling of ownership.
4 Redirects energy in support of change rather than against change.
5 Allows us to experiment.
6 Builds a better understanding of change and how to achieve it.

Disadvantages

1 Takes longer, particularly at the planning stage.
2 Therefore requires more time and effort in the early stages.

In addition, involving people may lead to greater uncertainty and instability as individuals or groups use the involvement process as a means of opposing change. However, if the objective is the effective implementation of change, this latter is less of an issue. These same people are likely to oppose the change, whether or not they were involved. If they are not involved the opposition will come out in different ways. Below, I list some useful criteria in planning how people are to be involved in change, and this may depend on the following:

■ The complexity of the changes and the strength of linkage between different parts of the changes.
■ The expected opposition and the level of dissatisfaction with the present situation.
■ The level of credibility of the people promoting change.
■ The impact of change on people, both positive and negative – how many 'winners', how many 'losers'?
■ Where the quality of the decisions is more important than their acceptability alone.
■ Where rumour is likely, whatever happens.

These factors need to be considered. Sometimes changes are probably best imposed by top management. There is no easy answer but, just as important, involvement of top management is not always the way forward. However, there are two further points to add. Because there are real advantages in involvement, some level is always worth considering. Usually there are many details to be resolved in which people can and should be involved. The point here is to make clear precisely how and to what extent involvement is planned. Just as important is involving key power holders and opinion leaders. They will influence the attitudes and behaviour of others and therefore their open support is worth seeking.

Conclusion

The quote at the start of Chapter 11 says it all. The above will take a little time. But if we do it well it will release energy in support of change. We often underestimate the time and energy needed to introduce change. Paying attention to the issues dealt with here will save time in the longer run. The current changes will be implemented more quickly. The organization will become more receptive to overall change.

EXERCISES

1 Can you identify any means by which the method for implementing change in company B (page 229) took account of the coping cycle model?

2 How important is the corporate culture? To what extent does corporate culture affect innovation?

3 Can you apply the coping cycle model to any change you have experienced?

14 Change architecture

Introduction

In this chapter we propose to explore the underlying 'building blocks' of successful change. What are the characteristics of a successful change programme? Is there more to say than the helpful advice one gets in much of the literature? Generally managers are exhorted to 'create a clear vision', to 'engage people in the process', to 'communicate, communicate, communicate', to 'involve people' and so on. All of this is fair enough. But is it enough?

Many people ask me whether or not a total quality management programme is an example of what this book talks about. Similarly people refer to business process re-engineering. When I say 'yes' they then ask me what is different about such programmes of change. To this I answer nothing except that the 'packaging' is different. So far in this book we have been concerned to analyse change and the problems of change. Through such analysis comes better understanding and thus we are able to handle change more effectively.

But is that enough? In the real world change must be defined and 'sold'. It must be controlled (at some level). It must be managed to achieve and sustain momentum. Managers need to attract attention. In this chapter therefore we are concerned with programmes of change. We shall examine some of the important design parameters facing those taking overall responsibility for a major change effort. Our concern will be on how to create a programme of change.

What we deal with here is relevant to generic organization-wide change and to multi-organizational change. Total quality management programmes and business process re-engineering programmes are currently good examples of how to achieve change. A joint venture would be a classic multi-organizational example.

One of the problems each of us experiences when we attempt to relate models of change with our real-world experience of change is that formal models of change generally give an impression of change as a neat, orderly sequence of activities or stages. Conversely, our experience is usually altogether more 'messy'. Activities are often going on in parallel. We often recycle through different stages as we pilot a new organizational design on new marketing policy, only to find that in some respects it does not work. As we shall see, our response is to see change as a spiral process and to view it as comprising three essential characteristics: *awareness*, *capability* and *inclusion* (each of which in turn comprises many detailed ingredients, programme elements, etc).

Cycles of change

Figure 14.1 identifies the three characteristics of awareness, capability and inclusion as necessary conditions for effective change. For change to be successful those involved must understand the change, its objectives, their role and so on. Understanding *and* credibility are vital. Only then will they feel confidence in the likelihood of success and only then is there the prospect of energizing them to act appropriately. Given that, they must have or be helped to acquire the necessary capabilities to handle the new tasks and new work situations. As sketched out in Chapter 13, people must feel that they can cope with the new situation. Finally, they must feel included' in the change process. To be successful those involved need to feel that they value the new objectives (individual and/or corporate) and that they both choose and feel able to choose.

Judson (1990) sketches an outline of five key issues, each of which can be related to one of these three necessary conditions.

Awareness

1 How thoroughly does everyone affected understand the needs of customers, objectives, strategy and timetable, resources required and new behaviour, techniques, systems, etc.?

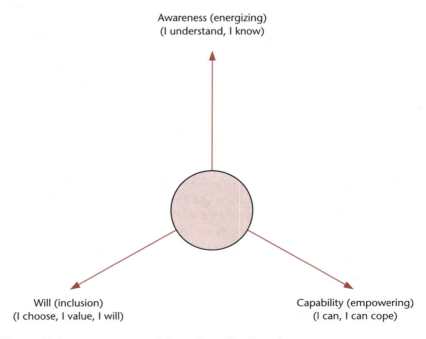

Awareness (energizing)
(I understand, I know)

Will (inclusion)
(I choose, I value, I will)

Capability (empowering)
(I can, I can cope)

Figure 14.1 **Necessary conditions for effective change**

2 How systematic a process has been instituted for tracking implementation and for making corrections while change is in process?

■ Capability

3 How completely have the resources required been identified and provided, including financial resources, skills and time?

■ Inclusion

4 How strong is the commitment of relevant managers and employees to implementing the change, including how credible do they view the change as being, to what extent do they 'own' the approach, how can commitment be sustained, etc?

5 How consistent and credible is the climate of accountability for the implementation period, including to what extent will those involved live up to their commitments, what are the consequences of failure, will reward systems differentiate between success and failure and how visible and consistent is leadership behaviour?

Turning now to Figure 14.2, we can see how to put some 'flesh' on these ideas. At its simplest the figure defines three stages of change: *beginnings*, *focusing* and *inclusion*.

Stage 1: Beginnings

Here the problems are recognized, awareness raising begins, diagnostic studies are undertaken, feasibility studies are begun, we look at the experience of other organizations and so on. This begins to create a new perception of achievable performance in what may be rapidly changing markets, technologies and so on. The main focus of this stage therefore is that of creating awareness but, as we shall see, awareness building continues long into the next stage.

Stage 2: Focusing

We show the first stage as including the establishment of a steering group taking responsibility for the 'problem' and even agreeing the basic approach. The next stage we call focusing. Here, effort at building awareness continues but also people are moving towards decision and action. Task forces may be established. If new skills are needed then the first attempts to seek them, or to attempt to create them internally, will begin. Effort will be directed at building coalitions in support of the changes, both through work with opinion leaders and through other means. Pilot trials and experiments often will be undertaken. Visits will be organized to sites and organizations which have already implemented the changes. Early results will be used to further 'shape' and modify the change programme. Much attention will be devoted to 'selling' the new ideas and dealing with likely opposition.

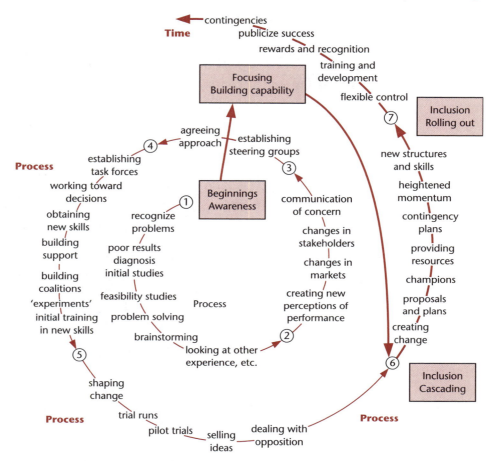

Figure 14.2 Change as a cyclical process

Stage 3: Inclusion

Now the focus of the change activity broadens. We both 'cascade' and 'roll out'. Cascading is about creating and implementing a communication plan. Rolling out is about implementing the change throughout the organization as a whole. The two are often linked. Thus if two organizations are merged the initial announcement is often followed by a process of senior management appointments. This is followed by a process to decide the corporate structure for the merged entity. In turn this is followed by a series of lower-level appointments. Then may follow detailed examination of work organization, information systems, procedures, etc. in which small task forces (for example) are charged with the job of picking the best ideas from the two original organizations to implement in the new. Here we see a process of decision and action both cascading down the organization and rolling out at each level across the organization. This cyclical process is illustrated in Table 14.1.

Table 14.1 **Cycles of management** (from Juch, B., (1983) © John Wiley & Sons Limited. Reproduced with permission)

Stage	Task/activity	Process
1 Thinking	Objectives	
	Policies	
	Forecasts	Preliminary discussion
	Proposals	
	Projects	
2 Addressing	Budgets	
	Targets	
	Commitments	Decision making
	Organizing	
	Scheduling	
3 Doing	Controlling	
	Training	Monitoring
	Reporting	
	Progress chasing	
4 Sensing	Analysis	
	Evaluation	Evaluation
	Problem solving	

Learning and change

We have already noted that learning is a characteristic of effective organizational change possibly best viewed as a consequence of change. This raises the question of whether we can identify any meaningful equivalence between individual learning and the processes of organizational change identified in the above. Juch (1983) has identified what has become a very influential model of learning which sees the learner at the centre possessing levels of sensory, cognitive, contractual (communication) and operational skills. The process of learning comprises a cycle of four stages: namely, thinking, addressing, doing and sensing, with four barriers. He characterizes the four as follows:

1 *'Gate'*, through which ideas are converted to intentions and declared to others.

2 *'Rubicon'*, through which some proposals are considered as attracting commitment.

3 *'Window'*, through which attention to certain outcomes is raised.

4 *'Skin'*, through which new perceptions about, say, possible performance are accepted, leading to a repeat of the cycle.

Clearly it is not difficult to relate these ideas to the processes of change which we have identified. Juch presents a 'cycle of management' which does. So the four stages being linked to typical management tasks or activities are as shown in Table 14.1. Derived from this revision of Juch's presentation and linking the change model with his learning model we get Table 14.2. Juch explicitly includes an evaluation stage which we have omitted – largely because formal evaluation is rarely practised and also because the learning appears to take place throughout the process. There is an equivalence between our beginnings stage and the Argyris (1990) concept of action maps. Argyris contends that, faced with contractions in behaviour, the process of mapping can lead to changes towards more effective behaviour, implying a much more natural process of learning than Juch's model suggests – although in making this point I do not mean that Juch adopted a static view of learning (i.e. that it did not take place until all thinking, addressing and doing were complete). The view offered here is that life, work and managing change were never so simple.

Table 14.2 Cycles of change

Stage		Task/activity	Process
1 Thinking	Beginnings	Diagnosis	
		Feasibility studies	
		Brainstorming	
		Communication of concerns	Getting started
		Problem recognition	
		Establish steering group	
2 Addressing	Focusing	Task forces	
		Training	
		Buying in new skills	
		Building support	Building capability
		Building coalitions	
		'Pilot' trials	
3 Doing	Inclusion	Creating change	
	Cascading	Champions	
	Rolling out	Proposals for change	
		New structures and skills	
		Team building	Building and sustaining change
		Rewards and recognition	
		Sell change	
		Publicize success	

Again one can see how 'personal learning cycles', 'change coping cycles' (see Chapter 13) and the organizational change cycle may fit together. Learning cycles may be 'nested' within the 'change coping cycles' which in turn are nested within the organization's change cycle. Add to that the concept of adoption of innovation, which suggests that people vary in the pace of adoption of new ideas from innovators, early adopters to laggards, and it is possible to suggest some interesting lines of thought both for the practice of organizational change and for research.

Can we, for example, pick out the most likely innovators? Many observers suggest that they are venturesome and prepared to accept risks. De Vries (1980) would probably add that they are prepared to take calculated risks. Kirton (1988), the originator of the Kirton adoption–innovation test or KAI, identifies various differences between innovators and adopters suggesting that both are essential to success. Amabile (1988) identifies components of individual creativity (e.g. product and technical skills and knowledge, cognitive style, work styles, attitudes and motivation) which she sees as emerging from cognitive abilities, perceptual and motor skills, education, training, experience in developing new ideas, the ability to minimize extrinsic constraints, which certainly suggest lines for further research but which *might* allow us to identify potential 'change champions' and 'change agents'. The champion might be the risk taker, strongly achievement orientated, with the capability of ignoring, or at least settling for, one-side constraints until ideas are shaped through the process of early trials. Amabile (1983) suggests that the appropriate cognitive–perceptual style includes the following:

■ the ability to break the existing mind-set;
■ the ability to hold open options for a long time;
■ the ability to suspend judgement;
■ excellent memory;
■ the ability to break out of 'performance scripts'.

All of this appears very similar to the 'block-busting' capabilities we have discussed.

Grundy (1994) adds important insight into strategic learning to the Juch model. For him strategic learning and strategic action are two linked cycles. Set out in Figure 14.3 is a modified version of his idea. Thus strategic learning is a dual process of action and learning. Both loops operate simultaneously but are not often well synchronized. In much the same way the learning loop is often not completed and the learning maximized because formal evaluation is not encouraged. In effect, Grundy supports our original view of this: that it does not require a separate stage but, rather, a linked process aimed at achieving the learning. Thus not least there could be a management development programme used both to roll out and to cascade major changes throughout an organization. Grundy also argues that a key feature of success is the ability to block out distractions (see the discussion of 'champions' above).

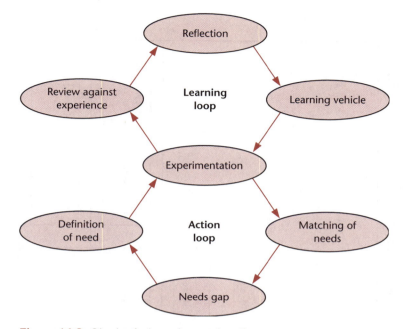

Figure 14.3 **Strategic learning and action**

How do we block out distractions? Well, as we have already implied, this is partly an issue of cognitive style at the individual level. There are things we can do at the team and organizational levels, however. Following Grundy (1994), I include the following:

- Manage personal and corporate agendas in order to meet the needs of stakeholders, your board or other influential people along the way.
- Define some 'givens' to stabilize the process.
- Flexible control to spread learning beyond the top team.
- Build learning into the organization through regular customer surveys, staff surveys, quality assurance, performance improvement, etc.
- Keep task forces etc. involved until implementation is complete.
- Involve top managers at the centre of the process.
- Use communication as a vehicle for learning.

All of this has implications for what and how we manage, which I have touched on at various points in this book.

Programmes of change

Given that major strategic change creates tensions and conflicts, not least within an organization, *and* that many fairly rigidly structured organizations already experience

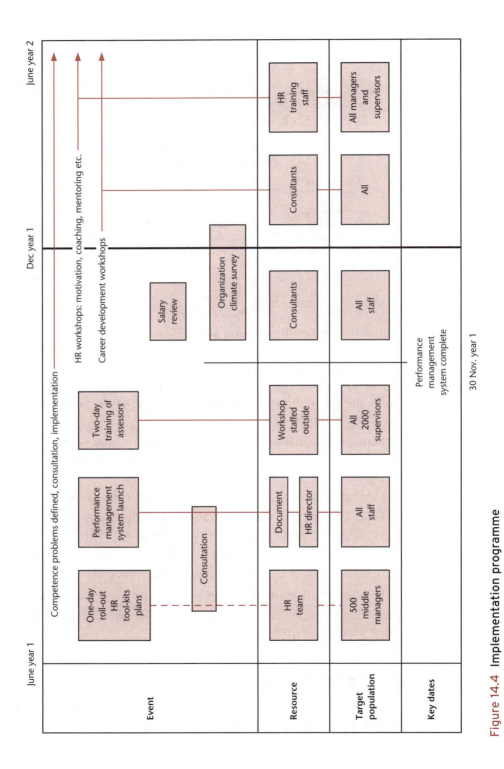

Figure 14.4 Implementation programme

such tensions, how can we encourage at one and the same time integration and learning? Set out below are a series of steps:

1 *Building relationships*: company conferences; cross-functional management; development and functional training; job rotation; building *networks*.

2 *Creating project groups*: solving problems via project groups and task forces; creating *centres of excellence* throughout the organization.

3 *Focused training and development*: total quality management programmes; action-learning-based management development; company-tailored development; business process re-engineering programmes.

4 *Career management*: defining and developing *managerial competence*; performance appraisal; career counselling and planning.

Each of these steps is designed either to link or interface individuals in problem-orientated settings or to link the individual to the organization in an output-orientated way, focusing on achievement of objectives. Thus managing change appropriately can and should create and sustain both learning within the organization and also its integration.

If these are the issues which we must consider in creating a programme of change, and if there are various stages to include, what will a programme look like in practice? Normally it is possible to create a project plan which sets out the key events, including time scales, resources and inputs, target population and key dates/milestones. Set out in Figure 14.4 is such an implementation programme detailing the development of a human resources (HR) strategy within an oil industry 'major' over a 12-month period.

CASE STUDY

Wilkinson Sword

Wilkinson Sword is a well-known fmcg (fast-moving consumer good) and manufacturing group trading throughout Europe and North America. It manufactures razors and other personal care products. With headquarters in Germany, it was valued at US$600 million in 1990. During the period of the change to be described the group was experiencing major operational problems: the owners were moving towards divestment and a wide and complex set of financial arrangements was being refinanced and/or restructured.

Beginnings

The chief executive's initial problem was that in difficult circumstances he was trying to manage the group 'blind'. The most successful product had been launched in too many markets. Demand far outstripped supply. Retail customers were threatening to withdraw business. The group was profitable only in Europe, and there mostly in Germany. The 'star' produce needed specialist equipment to expand manufacturing with an eight-month lead time. Inventory levels were high and on a worsening trend. The monthly report was 60 pages long and unintelligible.

A project was defined, designed to help the board understand the following:

■ How the group had been managed to date using the existing management information.

→

- What the perception was of the three factories and regional sales organizations as to their financial reporting responsibility.
- What 'culture' was predominant in the various financial departments.

The initial conclusions were as follows:

- Local general managers were dissatisfied with management information.
- Financial controllers reported reliably and promptly to the German head office but received no feedback of any kind.
- Each business unit had proceeded independently to develop local internal reporting systems and software.
- Rarely did financial controllers meet each other or visit head office.
- Local computer managers knew nothing of developments elsewhere in the group.
- There was little understanding by group management of local activities, traditions, cultures, etc.

Rethinking the problem, the chief executive recognized the above as consistent with a review he had undertaken of strategy as a whole, and management style in group finance was part of the problem.

Too much emphasis on the detail, overmuch concern with involvement and a concern not to 'upset' others suggest some of the problems Argyris (1990) refers to. The appointment of a new chief financial officer (CFO) delayed progress because the immediate priority was a series of pressing financial problems.

The next major step was for the CFO to visit group operations in Germany, Italy, France, Spain, the UK, the USA and Canada to evaluate local hardware and software and to identify aspects of local software which might be used more widely. From these visits and subsequent discussion, a brief for a common integrated system was agreed, including features such as modular design, European upgrades in facilities, tailored to unit level, capable of being networked to local PCs and of remote access and supplied on the basis of support and training available in local languages.

Focusing

Project groups were created to work toward solutions. Each was international in make-up and each would have a make-up of people appropriate to the study tasks. The tasks ranged from a review of the information needs of the sales organizations and the adaptability of local systems to wider use to a review of local area networks and DOS applications. A senior manager was identified as project manager for the programme of change now unfolding, with the study groups reporting directly, in turn reporting to the CFO.

All of this effort was creating a new recognition of the reality for information systems design in the group including the following:

- Each territory needed to be seen and see itself as part of an international group.
- Needs were essentially *local*.
- Recognition that skills and inputs came from *throughout* the group.

Subsequently the study groups reported to the next of the quarterly 'global conferences' organized by the group with all managing directors in attendance. Also examined were problems of liquidity, profitability, marketing and supply.

In response to the financial problems it was agreed that the group would not impose the budget that year, but rather that local budgets were to be set with 'quantified stretch' beyond the previous year. A new reporting format, with monthly reports and a budget package, was now emerging and sent to local management for consultation. Local management were allowed extra time to complete the budget pack and parallel running of the new pack was organized for the last three months of the current financial year.

Inclusion

As the study groups completed their work, from one group had come proposals for particular hardware/software combinations. Each study group was now briefed to examine this option in detail. This set up a process of local presentations by the supplier, with site visits to see the system operating elsewhere in order to assess customer/user views. A detailed technical evaluation was also undertaken and provided to the study groups. In parallel the CFO and project manager were making local visits reviewing existing infrastructure. A crash programme of PC replacement, upgrades, laser and desktop colour printers, etc. was implemented. Local choices were encouraged where compatibility was broadly available. Training plans and budgets were emerging from the study groups. Again a sense that local views mattered began to emerge.

Now a systems proposal was made to the group board. The plan set a date for installation, progressive roll-out, existing systems in place for a period but with a 12-month plan to install, pilot, test, train, etc. and bring the new system online.

■ Learning

The main lessons were as follows:

- An effective change project brings together the people who need to be involved in a well-structured way, with clear reporting and accountability but with sufficient freedom to encourage the sharing of skills, experience, needs, etc.

- It is vital to avoid preconceived ideas on options.

- It is important to minimize 'fear of change' by having those affected by change involved in the process of change.

- It makes sense to allow *time* for learning to develop to allow people to select the right solution for local needs. It was more important to get the right solutions than to get quick solutions.

If you were the CEO of a global business facing a radical change within tough constraints of competitiveness, revenue instability, dramatic technological change, a rapidly falling share price, investor pressure, legislative issues and so on, what would you do? How do you put together a major change programme if, say, you are ABB employing tens of thousands of people in hundreds of units, businesses etc. across the globe?

Consider the case of Technology Associates, a fictional information management consulting business wholly owned by a group committed to the manufacture of PCs, other peripherals and software. In recent years the group has dramatically increased the output of its factories and its software development capacity by going to a 24 × 7 regime. Despite the growth of the industry in recent years, this creates substantial pressures on the sales side. Technology Associates, while notionally pursuing a vision of 'customer service', is in fact under pressure to sell solutions to maximize group sales of hardware and software.

This does not mean that its consultants wholly ignore customer needs, but nevertheless their bonuses are linked to the sales of group products. Competitors outsource and are therefore less committed to particular configurations. Thus Technology Associates' position has deteriorated.

The board review the situation at a strategy conference. It decides on the need over a period of two years to shift the 'business model' toward the idea of 'outcome–based consulting'. A simple enough idea, the change involves focusing the objectives of any consulting engagement more directly on the *outcomes* defined by the client. The board recognizes that at its core the change involves switching the focus of the engagement away from the pursuit of selling IT configurations. This requires less attention on selling particular combinations of hardware and software and more toward jointly defining 'solutions', working with the client on defining and understanding client needs. Ironically in any event this also means changing the focus of the engagement from enhancing low value-added sales because competitive pressure has led to the commoditization of hardware and software. Instead the focus was to be on higher value-added outputs–solutions, facilities management, development work, training and so on.

But this change represents first and foremost an intellectual challenge of huge proportions. How to achieve this shift while at the same time continuing to make a valued contribution to those group sales targets is the issue. It is all very well identifying the 'paradigm shift' which is needed. But it is another thing entirely to make that change without destabilizing the parent group.

Moreover to achieve the change, a 'mind-set' shift is needed by the consultants themselves. They need new ways of working, new tools and techniques and they must embark on a new world of 'relationship building' and client management.

So how do Technology Associates go about this challenge? There are various tasks to undertake:

1 Develop a competence model defining the skills, capabilities and characteristics needed of consultants in order to deploy the new model.

2 Develop a consulting skills workshop as a training and development intervention.

3 Ensure the commitment of managers and consultants to the new business model.

4 Look at existing systems of performance management, people development, coaching, appraisal and rewards to ensure alignment to the new approach.

Let us look at the approach adopted. The board strategy forum was followed by a conference of the board and the regional management teams. With inputs from group, key customers and others, the focus of the conference was on understanding the new vision and working up both a new business model (in outline at least) and an implementation task.

Regional management teams were tasked to work on the various systems which would need to be realigned, making proposals to a project team. The project team was led by a main board member and reported directly to the board. Each regional management team was represented by the team member deputed to drive forward its own alignment work. A senior HR manager from the group was appointed project director on a two-year secondment. The team had a number of consultants involved and through them involved other consultants via a focus group process. There was also outside membership in that project team.

The first task of the project team was to define the competence model. It did so via an open process, seeking inputs from consultants in the field and looking at other experience outside the business. Its initial formulations were then tested via panels (internal and external people), focus groups and regional conferences. As the project team was undertaking this work, the regional team alignment projects acted both as inputs to the process (via the project team process and representation of the regional team member) and took value from the work on the development of the competence model.

The competence model developed; the project team now turned to development of the consulting skills workshop. Several very important decisions were made before any attention was devoted to content.

First, it was decided that the regional teams would find (from among themselves) the members for the pilot. Also, it was agreed that those participants would become the tutors on the consulting skills workshop once it rolled out – accepting that workloads meant that other consultants would also become involved as tutors downstream.

Second, a database was designed to support the workshop and activity following the workshop. Participants were committed to making three-month reviews of progress with the new model. In addition a process of best practice exchanges was created using the database and focused activity at regional level incorporated in the existing performance management process.

In outline, then, let us look at some features of this change architecture:

1 Direction from the top is clear enough. The board went into strategy-forum mode to work up a new vision and then worked that up into a new business model and implementation plan.

2 The project team is clearly accountable to the main board. Its chair is a member of that main board. It utilizes members of the regional teams. The regional teams work on alignment projects, which in turn are linked into the work of the project team.

3 Regional team members both pilot the consulting skills workshop *and* become tutors on the roll-out. Thus the company defines its new approach, develops it *and* works on the changes directly. Outsiders play a role but in that of providing benchmarking, advice and questioning – they are not central to the achievement of change.

4 A well-established process of follow-up is put in place. In particular the database is used to leverage best practice and to target follow-up. It is vital to the

achievement of this change that Technology Associates achieve *consistency* of account management practice. Many of its customers operate globally and may well be dealing with more than one region. In any event inconsistency of account management practice will lead to confusion, inconsistency and poor quality/higher cost in delivery. It seeks to pursue this consistency through the follow-up process.

However, the project team is also very aware that the initial business model and the consulting skills workshop will be imperfect. Both need revising in the light of experience. The follow-up process provides for the sharing of best practice as a means of doing so. Admittedly not easy to pull off, nevertheless the chances of this follow-up process working effectively is enhanced by designing it as a transparent process and by having the project team responsible for overseeing the process.

More formally then, how would we define the change architecture? Let us look at the following:

1 *Governance* is in place. We are clear how the main board is overseeing the process and we are clear about the mechanisms through which change is to be implemented.

2 *Accountability* is defined. The project team is accountable to the main board. The regional teams are tasked to work up alignment proposals in support of the project team and therefore...

3 Regional teams are engaged but so are other consultants via the process used to develop the competence model.

4 Regional team members are engaged in the delivery of consulting skills workshops.

5 The follow-up process seeks to ensure *consistency* in both the application of account management practice and to provide for the *leveraging* of best practice.

6 By using regional team members and other consultants as tutors, the consulting skills workshop process was *scaleable* – in fact, in year one the number of consulting skills workshops rolled out was doubled because of demand from consultants.

7 Overall there is a high degree of *connectivity* between those driving the change, those managing the change processes and those directly affected.

8 There is also a considerable degree of *transparency* of process.

9 While it is not completely clear from the above, some attention has been given to the *management of expectations* throughout the process. In particular, the various stages in which internal stakeholders, group (via the project director) and external advisors have been involved, alongside the follow-up process, benchmarking and best practice exchange, all provide for *reality checking* in terms of the appropriate balance between the external imperatives which must be faced and a realistic view of how quickly change can be achieved within the business.

But note that this external *vs* internal contrast is far from straightforward. Thus, while competitive pressure on Technology Associates argues for rapid change, this must be balanced by the view that too rapid a change risks destabilizing the group. Yet, as we have already seen in the context of GE not least, too much concern about that can lead to the company going down. Interestingly enough, the pace of change was ultimately determined by demand from consultants. The original plans were doubled in year one and the roll-out from Europe to the rest of the world was dramatically accelerated. Would this have happened without the transparency of process, level of engagement and connectivity and so on?

Thus we are beginning to see a model of change architecture emerging. Before we proceed, let us look at another issue of importance in planning change programmes. How should we balance centralized and project-changed change against local management? How should we balance leadership from the top with approaches to change relying on the drive from customer-facing staff?

I set out the arguments in Figure 14.5.

Central management

The position *vis-à-vis* central management may be summarized as follows.

Advantages

- Scale economies.
- Development of a critical mass of skills.
- Standardization.

Disadvantages

- Lack of flexibility.
- Undermines business unit control of overheads.
- Business units may be unresponsive to change.

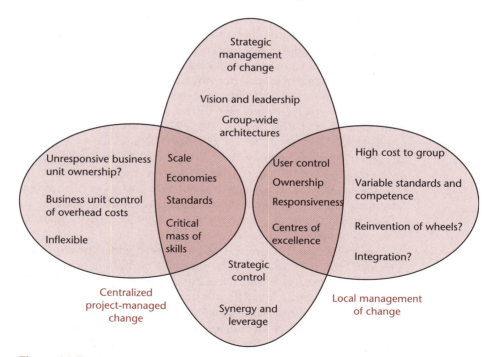

Figure 14.5 Strategic management of change

Local management

The position *vis-à-vis* local management may be summarized as follows.

Advantages

- Users more fully involved.
- Development of centres of excellence at local level.
- 'Ownership' and 'buy-in'.
- Market-focused.

Disadvantages

- Higher costs due to duplication.
- Lack of integration and consistency.
- Variable standards and competence.

Overall change architecture seeks to create a framework within which the central and local approaches can be more effectively balanced.

CASE STUDY

Lufthansa

In the eight years to 1999 Lufthansa proceeded from the verge of bankruptcy to record results and being a founder member of the Star Alliance – a global network of airline companies and others. Following the initial restructuring to avoid financial collapse, the executive board and the supervisory board decided on a process of strategic renewal, fundamental to which was a process of 'mental change'.

In early 1992 Lufthansa found itself with only 14 days of operating cash available, with little prospect of support from the banking system. Having engineered a short-term solution, it embarked on a four-week change management programme for executives out of which emerged a grouping committed to radical change. This became known as the 'Samurai of Change'. In mid-1992, 20 senior managers participated in a meeting initially known as 'Mental Change' but which became known as the 'crisis management meeting'. This created Program 93, comprising 131 projects or actions leading to 8000 job cuts, fleet downsizing, revenue enhancement efforts and so on.

The executive board appointed task forces to implement these projects, mostly headed by members of the 'Samurai of Change'. To communicate this, Lufthansa adopted General Electric's 'town meetings'. By mid-1999 the CEO had participated in over 200 such meetings.

Progress of the 131 projects was monitored under the direction of the corporate financial controller using explicit measures of revenue growth, cost reduction, etc. By 1995 the results were apparent throughout the group, setting the scene for more fundamental restructuring from a functional structure to a federal structure comprising decentralized business units. Subsequently Program 15 was implemented (from 1996) focusing on strategic cost management aimed at cutting costs by 20 per cent in five years. The Program 15 task force emphasized the vital need for transparency and measurement as a means of progress-managing major change. Line managers are responsible for the implementation of Program 15 cost reductions, all of which are integrated within their objectives and form part of their performance evaluation.

The underlying principles of this change effort were as follows:

- Reduce communication costs and simplify decision-making.
- Support corporate-wide task force working.
- Support for the Lufthansa Service Initiative via service-focused workshops.

Perhaps more important is the 'change architecture' implemented around the various change projects. Performance management was used explicitly to drive change forward. Feedback systems – customer surveys, employee commitment surveys, 360° feedback tools and customer and employee short surveys ('pulsetakers') – were used to get feedback around the group. Programmes such as Explorer 21 and Climb 99 initiatives, run within the Lufthansa Business School, became an explicit part of the culture change process. Involving 210 and 160 managers/young professionals, respectively, these programmes represent both investment in learning and development *and* in culture change. The vital word is integration, or leverage. Such activities became seen as 'transformation platforms' for change providing the prospect of achieving a critical mass of change. Starting from self-assessment using customized leadership tools, the programmes are a means of learning by 'contributing to the future of the business'. By the year 2000 many thousands of Lufthansa employees had been involved in one or more activities related to strategic changes.

Source: Bruch and Sattelberger (2001)

Let us turn to the Lufthansa case study. Here again we see an elaborate process early on which seeks to engage key players but also define credible vision and clarify accountability, governance and change process. In summary the 'Samurai of Change', the 'Mental Change' conference and the subsequent projects, task forces and so on are clearly overseen by the CEO and main board. Restructuring to accountable business units is also a prime example.

Connectivity is very high. The initial changes are communicated via 200 'town meetings'. Since 1994 some 24,000 employees have been involved in at least one change event. Feedback is sought via 360° feedback, employee surveys and customer surveys. The Program 15 task force focuses on improvement targets which in turn are fully integrated with the established performance management system.

But other initiatives are also tightly integrated. Thus the Lufthansa School of Business and the Lufthansa Service Initiative created activities which contribute directly to the change programme. Explorer 21 and the 'climb programme' together involve 370 executives each year. No doubt these initiatives pursue talent management and development objectives. But they are also leveraged as part of a total process in pursuit of strategic change.

Overall the vital point being made here is that the strategic management of change via a change architecture approach seeks to bring change to the centre stage. Too often change projects are treated in isolation from the management of

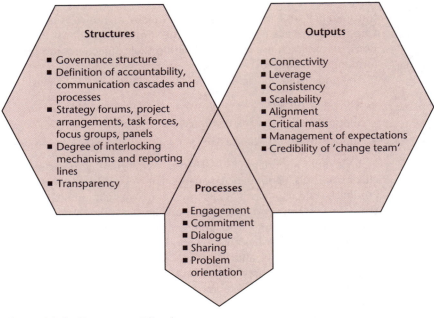

Figure 14.6 Change architecture

the business today. Change is something we do in isolation from 'business as usual' – in isolation in terms of how change is monitored and measured, not of course in terms of pressures on people.

In the change architecture model (Figure 14.6) I posit a need to focus on structure processes and outputs of any change process. This is particularly relevant if a change is radical or wide-ranging. Or perhaps more sensibly we should say that structures=processes=outputs of change architecture is always relevant but big projects demand close attention to these design considerations. Doing so can significantly lift the degree of confidence in success.

In particular, processes and outputs which include dialogue, problem orientation, connectivity, leverage, alignment, consistency, scaleability and so on create positive pressures for change (see the force field technique in Chapter 7). This can build confidence in the outcomes which can, in turn, reinforce the problem orientation – a virtuous rather than a vicious circle.

Change architecture: blocks

So far so good! But what can get in the way? We have already seen two problems or blocks. Our corporate culture can create blocks to a successful change architecture. Simplifying somewhat, the crucial issue is not which is the most appropriate corporate culture but, rather, is it a positive or negative culture – following Goffee and Jones (1998). What does this mean? If you look at the simple pro forma tests these authors propose, it seems clear that the key issue

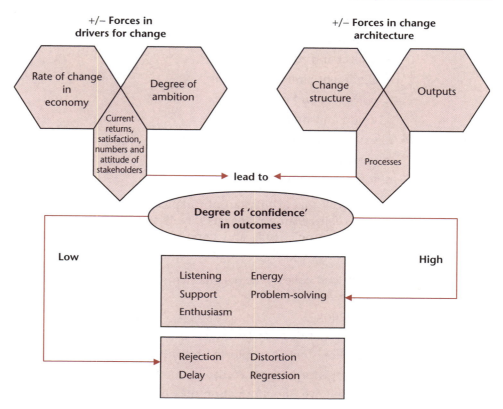

+/− **Forces in drivers for change**

+/− **Forces in change architecture**

Rate of change in economy

Degree of ambition

Current returns, satisfaction, numbers and attitude of stakeholders

Change structure

Outputs

Processes

lead to

Degree of 'confidence' in outcomes

Low

High

Listening   Energy

Support   Problem-solving

Enthusiasm

Rejection   Distortion

Delay   Regression

Figure 14.7 **Energy for change**

is that of problem orientation. A positive culture is one that is characterized by openness to issues, problems and new ideas and within which people are, and feel they are, valued for the contribution they make. One in which the energy for change is often high, depending on both forces in the internal and external environment and on the adequacy of the change architecture – see Figure 14.7.

The second block relates to inadequate measurement and linked to that a lack of transparency in performance management. As we saw when discussing the balanced scorecard (see Chapter 7) organizations often rely on inadequate and poorly balanced performance measurement frameworks. In particular this is true in the context of radical change. Almost certainly existing measurement focuses on finance and activity and on past performance. Clearly this is particularly problematic in the context of change.

But this point goes further. Look at the work of Sweet and Heritage (2000). These authors report a survey of UK executives undertaken in 2000. They focus on questions in the following 12 areas:

- workload and efficiency;
- training and development;
- improving and innovating;

- communication and involvement;
- help and feedback;
- respect and recognition;
- alignment and commitment;
- objectives and performance;
- vision and strategy;
- working practices and procedures;
- planning and monitoring;
- roles and responsibilities.

Let us recall that at the start of Chapter 1 we rejected the simplistic notion that changes fail because managers devote too little attention to the so-called soft issues, the people issues and so on. These data support that view. If you look at the data the following relative weaknesses emerge:

1 Workload issues – the balance across teams, waste, lack of resource, unnecessary work.
2 Coaching.
3 Time set aside to review and plan for improvement.
4 Conflict is openly explored and addressed.
5 Underperformance is confronted.
6 People have the information they need.
7 Working methods are documented and accessible.
8 Systems are simple and helpful.
9 Problems are quickly spotted and corrected.
10 Regular, effective planning meetings.

I am reminded of something Dwight D. Eisenhower (Commander of the Allied Expeditionary Force, D-Day and beyond) is famous for saying:

Before a battle planning is everything: as soon as battle is joined, plans are worthless.

The most compelling point relates to performance management. To the extent that performance management involves handling conflict, challenging underperformance, reviewing performance and planning improvements, these executives report weakness in their own organizations. But even more telling they report weakness in systems, documentation, methods and so on. If this is true how can we achieve consistency in anything? And if we cannot achieve consistency how can we possibly align systems, processes and so on? In practice what we align is behaviour. How can behaviour possibly align in the circumstances suggested by that data? Interestingly enough I have used that data on 30 or 40 strategic change workshops since mid-2000. Senior executives in the major corporates with which I have worked all too readily recognize how closely those data match their own company.

If plans are worthless once battle is joined, what do we need? A problem-oriented process which seeks to deal with the inevitable gaps between the original plan and current performance. This demands the training and follow-up we have referred to above.

These ideas find powerful reinforcement in the work of Manzoni (2000). In a study of managerial behaviour towards better performers (BPs) and weaker performers (WPs) Manzoni reports the following:

1 Toward BPs managers tend to:
   - discuss the what and why of tasks/projects;
   - be open to ideas from BPs;
   - spend more time with them;
   - give them more challenging tasks.

2 Toward WPs managers tend to:
   - discuss how;
   - push their own ideas;
   - monitor actions and results systematically;
   - be less patient.

3 Various studies show that bosses have 'in-' and 'out-groups' and that they probe failure differently.

But does this surprise you? Does it matter? Manzoni argues that subordinate performance tends to adjust to superiors' expectation. Thus the danger is that a vicious circle is created. We expect the weaker performer to underperform. Therefore the boss tends to get involved, to question, to be impatient and to provide less positive reinforcement. In turn this is perceived by the boss as 'doing the job for the WP!' and by the subordinate as 'He doesn't listen/care'. Overall the subordinate feels undervalued, lacking in confidence and esteem and therefore withdraws, behaves mechanically, avoids contact with the boss and so on.

Manzoni calls this 'the set-up-to-fail syndrome' and brings various 'costs', as follows:

- worsening performance of WPs;
- time and energy of boss;
- weaker team;
- negative energy;
- BPs get increasingly loaded with additional work.

And the syndrome seems more likely to emerge if there is:

- pressure for results;
- short tenures in post;
- performance review systems emphasizing a limited range of objectives;
- flatter organizations and larger spans of control.

We have already seen that much of these conditions are either a consequence of value-adding organization structures (see Chapter 7) and/or a clear consequence of radical change.

Gratton (2000) identifies a similar 'cycle of despair' and indicates that she has observed the converse in place at Hewlett-Packard. This 'cycle of hope' is created by providing people affected by change with voice, choice and what she describes as 'interactional justice'. This latter may be about treating people with respect and creating a perception of fair treatment (but see Carnall (1982) for the complexity of this concept in practice). Be that as it may, we are clearly operating at the intersection between the 'hard' and 'soft' world of organization. Just as clearly many of the problems in handling change emerge out of inadequate management and infrastructure and thus it is that we argue for change architecture to deal with these problems among others.

Gratton's book is of relevance because she develops an idea of strategy methodology which relates closely to the change architecture thinking presented here. For Gratton, creating a 'living strategy' requires five steps, as listed below.

■ Step 1: Creating a guiding coalition

Here she identifies five key sets of stakeholders, namely senior managers, HR professionals, young people, line managers, front line staff. Each brings a unique perspective.

■ Step 2: Visioning the future

But here she limits herself to visioning the people issues. Thus she recounts how at Phillips Lighting the senior executives team presented strategic goals (e.g. grow to 25 per cent market share, no. 1 premium choice in Europe, no. 2 in the rest of the world, no. 1 in customer satisfaction and so on, which became a frame of reference for visioning teams. In turn these visioning teams identified the organizational factors with a high impact on the delivery of that vision, namely a structure capable of delivering new business and a network-driven organization.

■ Step 3: Identifying gaps

In essence, understanding the current position and identifying gaps. Here she presents a risk matrix – essentially a two-dimensional model mapping strategic impact against current alignment.

■ Step 4: Mapping

She identifies key themes (e.g. customer focus, innovation, globalization and market share), identify change levers (e.g. selection, rewards, training, development, etc.), identify desired end states and model the dynamics.

■ Step 5: Modelling the dynamics of the vision

This final step looks at implementation. Gratton identifies two principles of interest to us, namely:

1 *Leverage with processes and behaviours and values will follow*. Here she argues that values and 'meanings' are outcomes of change, not levers to create change.

2 *Understand the forces for and against change*. In essence the force field idea.

Interestingly for this review of change architecture, Gratton argues that the journey forwards to create new strategy includes four further guiding principles:

1 Continue to build guiding coalitions.

2 Build the capacity to change.

3 Keep focusing on the themes.

4 Build performance measures noting that *leading measures* are in the field of people development, behaviour and attitudes, *living measures* are of performance and *lagging measures* include financial performance.

This is too simplistic. To argue that leading measures are to be found only in measures to do with people is wrong. If you are looking at an engineering business, quite obviously technology capabilities are important as leading measures. Could the success or failure of the Wellcome Trust-funded Human Genome project be judged at the point of committing funding only, or even largely, on the characteristics of people – many of whom were not yet involved? Could you assess whether or not to fund a Mars project with NASA by looking only at people issues? This is just too narrow. It argues that we replace one extreme with another. Nevertheless there is a sense running through the approach that you do need to have regard to the design of the strategy and (by implication) the strategic change process.

CASE STUDY

The BBC

This case study outlines what was a radical change at the BBC – an initiative known as 'Producer Choice' which was implemented in the 1990s. For us it is of interest because:

1 It was a logical extension of various resource utilization studies and change programmes which began to be implemented in the late 1980s.

2 The change was based on an explicit theoretical model (Burke and Litwin, 1992).

3 We are able to assess the changes in terms of 'change architecture'.

Producer Choice was adopted in spring 1993 and represented a radical shift of culture and ways of working. Before Producer Choice, all budgets were held centrally and delegated to departments. Programme makers did not have budgets, rather they accessed resources with which to make programmes. The underlying idea, therefore, was to assign budgets to programme makers and allow them to utilize outside resources – this was intended not least to focus attention on the true cost of programmes, on value for money and on market comparisons of efficiency, quality and so on.

Announced late in 1991, it was proposed that the period to April 1993 be devoted to preparatory work – of which much was needed. Training and development programmes

→

would be included. A steering group was established to oversee the changes, and an implementation plan comprising 107 key activities was agreed. A comprehensive communication programme was established including the formal launch attended by 170 key BBC staff. This was followed up by staff meetings, workshops, question and answer forums and the distribution of a Producer Choice brochure.

A series of one- and two-day courses was implemented over the 18 months to spring 1993 involving 1800 staff from different levels. In parallel, workshops were arranged for all levels of BBC staff to discuss and debate Producer Choice, not least to continue the process of raising awareness.

In parallel with these activities, an overhead review, a resource utilization review and a market testing process were also underway. Headcount was reduced by 19 per cent between 1990 and 1993.

Producer Choice commenced with a pilot period. This opened with groups of senior BBC managers attending workshops in which a custom-designed simulation of the BBC under Producer Choice was used as a vehicle for 'piloting' the model. Seventy-two senior managers were involved.

There were myriad implementation problems associated with this change, many of which were predicted by the pilot exercise. Many junior staff noted that the 481 business units created under the new regime was unnecessarily high, creating a large 'paper chase'. Nevertheless, by 1994, survey and other data suggest that value for money had improved and, moreover, the BBC now had credible measures of its market performance. The number of business units had been reduced to 200. While not ever anything but controversial, Producer Choice appears to have been part of a process of culture change needed by the BBC as it moved into the era of global competition for media and the digital age. But results from staff surveys (based on the Burke–Litwin model) undertaken in 1994 and 1995 suggest that staff were not opposed to the ideas of Producer Choice, but rather that they believed the pace of change was out-running the ability of management to create the infrastructure needed to deploy the new ways of working. Thus, while issues of resistance to change commitment, stress and anxiety were all too apparent, a crucial question related to infrastructure. Would it be in place? If not, the new approach would not work. If so, staff would prefer the old, comfortable ways. If yes then, given the tools, they felt able to work in new ways. On this view, success in change is about whether people involved see a 'change architecture' which looks able to deliver that infrastructure, and resistance to change is as much about resistance to half-hearted changes which look likely to fail – not resistance to change as such.

Source: Felix (2000)

Conclusion

Is there a difference between engagement and involvement? I argue that this is so. For example, if I ask someone to send me their views on a particular topic I seek to gain their engagement with the topic and the issues involved. But I have not sought to involve them in the process of debate, dialogue, decision making and so on. We could only describe this as an example of involvement by defining the latter too widely to be useful. Again, if I ask someone to think about the implications for them of a particular change before a career counselling discussion I am seeking to engage their thinking about the change without involving them.

The distinction is important in this sense. When we talk of the need to communicate during a period of change we often argue that communication must be two-way. In practice this is often not the reality because we provide little real opportunity for the feedback process. However, modern practice increasingly provides for feedback (e-mail 'speak-ups', 'town meetings', etc.). Thus, we suggest that one can think of communication as a process for cascading messages about vision, objectives, plans and progress. Engagement refers to attempts to get either feedback or ideas, i.e. we seek to stimulate thinking about the changes. Involvement relates to bringing people into task forces, working groups, focus groups and the like. Ghosal (2002) captures the difference in discussing turn-around at Nissan. They did so via the work of some cross-functional teams developing a revival plan. But crucial to success was 'building trust through transparency'. Every number was to be thoroughly checked. All accountabilities were to be clear to everyone. Everyone was to know how everyone was involved. Thus, via transparency everyone was to be engaged so that confidence and trust could be built. There lies the real difference.

EXERCISES

1 Apply the various methods introduced in this chapter to change situations with which you are familiar.

2 Apply them to the BBC case study.

15

A strategy for organizational effectiveness

Introduction

Throughout this book we have dealt with a range of concepts and techniques dealing with organizational structures, diagnosis, effectiveness and the management of change. Throughout, I have identified guidelines, techniques and 'role models' for more effective management practice. This chapter sets out two practical ways of organizing your own application of the ideas covered in the book in *your own organization*. We go on to summarize the practical ideas considered in other chapters.

A project approach is something that organizations adopt more and more often when major changes are in preparation, or are being implemented. Whether or not one adopts a 'full-blown' project management approach, it makes sense to prepare for, and manage, change in the more professional ways we have identified here, always taking full note of the comment: pragmatism above theory, but never 'adhocracy'!

Here are three exercises which can be used by yourself, your management team, colleagues and employees as part of the planning and management of change. The first is force field analysis, and sets out how this technique can be used more fully. The second is a simple implementation exercise. The third is a self-assessment exercise which will help you to review your own personal strengths and weaknesses in this area.

Force field analysis

Force field analysis provides a technique for analysing complex problems. It is based on the idea that any situation can be analysed as a balance between two sets of forces, one set opposing change and one set prompting or supporting change.

The analysis proceeds in a number of stages, as follows:

- *Stage 1*: Define the problem in terms of the present situation, with its strengths and weaknesses, and the situation you would wish to achieve. For example, in International Engineering (see page 142–4) management may wish to achieve contracts with high staff-hour rates and a more commercially focused approach at all levels of the organization.

- *Stage 2*: Identify the forces working for and against your desired changes. They can be based on people, resources, time, external factors and corporate culture. Draw a force field diagram.

- *Stage 3*: Underline the forces that you believe to be most important. For each force opposing change list the actions you could take to reduce the strength of this force. For each supporting force list the actions you could take to exploit or build on this force.

- *Stage 4*: Agree on those actions which appear most likely to help solve the problem of achieving change. Identify the resources you will need. Identify how those resources can be obtained.

Again taking International Engineering as an example, designing and implementing a new performance appraisal system will help to support moves to a more commercially orientated culture, but it will take time. The first set of actions required involves restructuring the organization to achieve a more effective input of marketing, engineering and project engineering into the organization's top management. This can then be supported by a new appraisal system.

The implementation exercise (checklists 1 and 2)

This exercise comprises two checklists (Tables 15.1 and 15.2), which are designed to help you think about aspects of the organization which might help or hinder the implementation of change. Please complete the two checklists by focusing on a significant organizational change in which you have been or are now involved.

In this exercise the two checklists deal with five and six areas respectively. For each area there are potential problems dealt with by the checklist. Below are set out these problems and *some* possible solutions.

Problems and solutions

Checklist 1: Readiness for change

Company 'track record' of changes (questions 1–3)

The potential problems are:

1 Have past changes met with resistance?

2 Were past changes poorly understood?

3 Are employees too cautious?

4 Did recently introduced changes have limited or little success?

The solutions are:

1 Keep everyone informed by making information available, explaining plans clearly and allowing access to management for questions and clarification.

2 Ensure that change is solid realistically by making a practical case for it. Explain change in terms which the employee will see as relevant and acceptable. Show how change fits business needs and plans. Spend time and effort on presentations.

Table 15.1 Checklist 1: Readiness for change

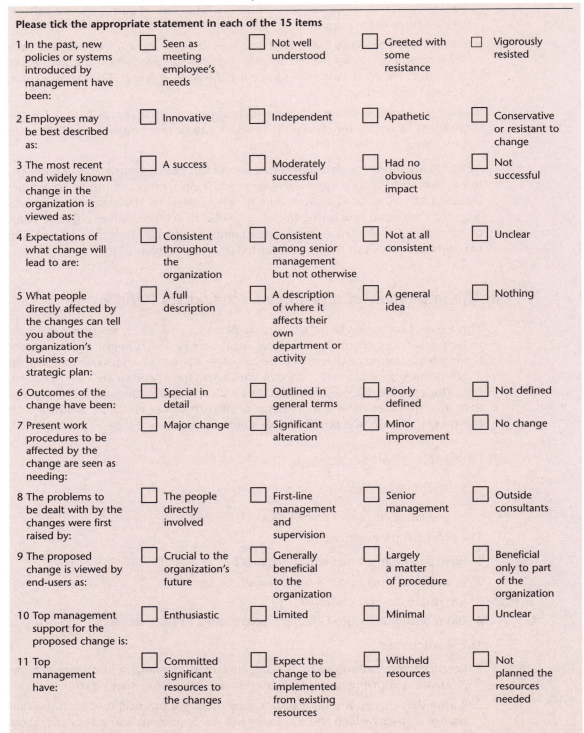

Please tick the appropriate statement in each of the 15 items

1 In the past, new policies or systems introduced by management have been:	☐ Seen as meeting employee's needs	☐ Not well understood	☐ Greeted with some resistance	☐ Vigorously resisted
2 Employees may be best described as:	☐ Innovative	☐ Independent	☐ Apathetic	☐ Conservative or resistant to change
3 The most recent and widely known change in the organization is viewed as:	☐ A success	☐ Moderately successful	☐ Had no obvious impact	☐ Not successful
4 Expectations of what change will lead to are:	☐ Consistent throughout the organization	☐ Consistent among senior management but not otherwise	☐ Not at all consistent	☐ Unclear
5 What people directly affected by the changes can tell you about the organization's business or strategic plan:	☐ A full description	☐ A description of where it affects their own department or activity	☐ A general idea	☐ Nothing
6 Outcomes of the change have been:	☐ Special in detail	☐ Outlined in general terms	☐ Poorly defined	☐ Not defined
7 Present work procedures to be affected by the change are seen as needing:	☐ Major change	☐ Significant alteration	☐ Minor improvement	☐ No change
8 The problems to be dealt with by the changes were first raised by:	☐ The people directly involved	☐ First-line management and supervision	☐ Senior management	☐ Outside consultants
9 The proposed change is viewed by end-users as:	☐ Crucial to the organization's future	☐ Generally beneficial to the organization	☐ Largely a matter of procedure	☐ Beneficial only to part of the organization
10 Top management support for the proposed change is:	☐ Enthusiastic	☐ Limited	☐ Minimal	☐ Unclear
11 Top management have:	☐ Committed significant resources to the changes	☐ Expect the change to be implemented from existing resources	☐ Withheld resources	☐ Not planned the resources needed

Table 15.1 *(Continued)*

12 The management performance appraisal review and process is:	☐ An important part of management development	☐ A helpful problem-solving process	☐ Routine	☐ An obstacle to improvement
13 The proposed change deals with issues of relevance to the business plant:	☐ Directly	☐ Partly	☐ Only indirectly	☐ Not at all
14 The proposed change:	☐ Makes jobs more rewarding financially and otherwise	☐ Makes jobs easier and more satisfying	☐ Replaces old tasks and skills with new ones	☐ Makes jobs harder
15 The proposed change is technically:	☐ Similar to others already underway	☐ Similar to others undertaken in the recent past	☐ Novel	☐ Technically unclear

3 Prepare carefully by making a full organizational diagnosis, spending time with people and groups, building trust, understanding and support.

4 Involve people by getting feedback on proposals, getting people to fill out the checklists, discussing the data from these checklists.

5 Start small and successful by piloting, with a receptive group of employees, in departments with a successful track record. Implement changes in clear phases.

6 Plan for success by starting with things that can give a quick and positive pay-off. Publicize early success. Provide positive feedback to those involved in success.

Expectations of change (questions 4–6)

The potential problems are:

1 Do different people hold different ideas about the change?
2 Do people know what to expect?
3 Are objectives clearly defined?

The solutions are:

1 Clarify benefits of changes by emphasizing benefits to those involved, i.e. to the company.

2 Minimize surprises by specifying all assumptions about the change. Focus on outcomes. Identify potential problems.

3 Communicate plans by being specific in *terms* that are familiar to the different groups of employees. Communicate periodically and through various media. Ask for feedback. Do not suppress negative views but listen to them carefully and deal with them openly.

Table 15.2 Checklist 2: Managing change

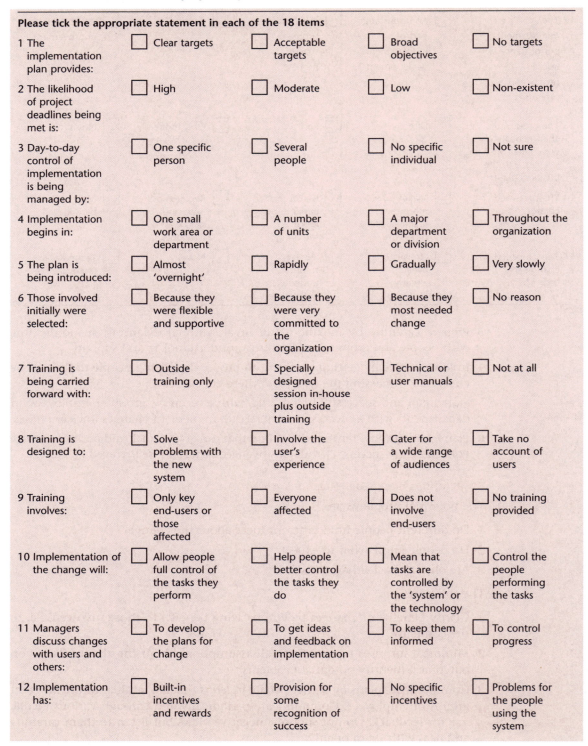

Please tick the appropriate statement in each of the 18 items

1 The implementation plan provides:	☐ Clear targets	☐ Acceptable targets	☐ Broad objectives	☐ No targets
2 The likelihood of project deadlines being met is:	☐ High	☐ Moderate	☐ Low	☐ Non-existent
3 Day-to-day control of implementation is being managed by:	☐ One specific person	☐ Several people	☐ No specific individual	☐ Not sure
4 Implementation begins in:	☐ One small work area or department	☐ A number of units	☐ A major department or division	☐ Throughout the organization
5 The plan is being introduced:	☐ Almost 'overnight'	☐ Rapidly	☐ Gradually	☐ Very slowly
6 Those involved initially were selected:	☐ Because they were flexible and supportive	☐ Because they were very committed to the organization	☐ Because they most needed change	☐ No reason
7 Training is being carried forward with:	☐ Outside training only	☐ Specially designed session in-house plus outside training	☐ Technical or user manuals	☐ Not at all
8 Training is designed to:	☐ Solve problems with the new system	☐ Involve the user's experience	☐ Cater for a wide range of audiences	☐ Take no account of users
9 Training involves:	☐ Only key end-users or those affected	☐ Everyone affected	☐ Does not involve end-users	☐ No training provided
10 Implementation of the change will:	☐ Allow people full control of the tasks they perform	☐ Help people better control the tasks they do	☐ Mean that tasks are controlled by the 'system' or the technology	☐ Control the people performing the tasks
11 Managers discuss changes with users and others:	☐ To develop the plans for change	☐ To get ideas and feedback on implementation	☐ To keep them informed	☐ To control progress
12 Implementation has:	☐ Built-in incentives and rewards	☐ Provision for some recognition of success	☐ No specific incentives	☐ Problems for the people using the system

Table 15.2 *(Continued)*

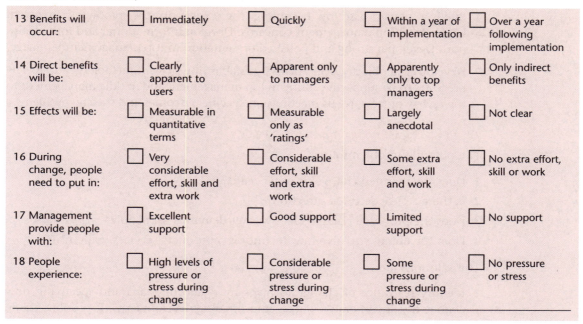

13 Benefits will occur:	☐ Immediately	☐ Quickly	☐ Within a year of implementation	☐ Over a year following implementation
14 Direct benefits will be:	☐ Clearly apparent to users	☐ Apparent only to managers	☐ Apparently only to top managers	☐ Only indirect benefits
15 Effects will be:	☐ Measurable in quantitative terms	☐ Measurable only as 'ratings'	☐ Largely anecdotal	☐ Not clear
16 During change, people need to put in:	☐ Very considerable effort, skill and extra work	☐ Considerable effort, skill and extra work	☐ Some extra effort, skill and work	☐ No extra effort, skill or work
17 Management provide people with:	☐ Excellent support	☐ Good support	☐ Limited support	☐ No support
18 People experience:	☐ High levels of pressure or stress during change	☐ Considerable pressure or stress during change	☐ Some pressure or stress during change	☐ No pressure or stress

Who 'owns' the problem or the idea for change? (questions 7–9)

The potential problems are:

1 Are the procedures, systems, departments, products and services involved seen to be a problem?
2 Was the change planned or introduced by top management or staff departments?
3 Is the change viewed as a matter of procedure?

The solutions are:

1 Specify plans in terms that people understand. Ensure that employees' problems are addressed explicitly as part of the change. Arrange for visible outcomes.
2 Clarify employees' views by exploring their concerns about the changes and examining the impact on the day-to-day routines.
3 Present a clear case by specifying who wants change and why. Explain longer-term advantages. Identify common benefits. Present potential problems clearly. Listen to problems.

Top management support (questions 10–12)

The potential problems are:

1 Does top management support the change?
2 Will top management provide resources?
3 Is the management performance appraisal process an obstacle to change?

The solutions are:

1 Build a power base by becoming the expert in the problems involved. Understand top management concerns. Develop informational and formal support. Develop a strong and polished presentation in top management language.

2 Develop clear objectives and plans by establishing a clear timetable. Set up review processes to be supportive. Bring in top management and middle management to the review process. Focus meetings on specific outcomes and specific problems.

Acceptability of change (questions 13–15)

The potential problems are:

1 Does the planned change fit other plans?

2 Is there a clear sense of direction?

3 Does the proposed change place greater demands on people?

4 Does the change involve new technology, products/services, expertise?

The solutions are:

1 Identify relevance of change to plans by reviewing plans and specifying how change fits. Incorporate changes into ongoing developments. If possible, frame changes in terms of the organization's style.

2 Clarify plans for change by communicating simply and openly.

3 Implement with flexible or adaptable people, people familiar with some or all of the change, in a part of the business where there are strong supporters for change. Recognize why people support change (career, rewards, company politics).

4 Do not oversell change by being adamant about conflicts with present practices. Encourage discussion of these conflicts.

Checklist 2: Managing change

Clarifying plans (questions 1–3)

The potential problems are:

1 Does the plan identify clear phases and deadlines?

2 Is the timetable realistic?

3 Is responsibility for change clear?

The solutions are:

1 Assign one person to be accountable for change.

2 Define goals carefully by checking feasibility with people involved, experts, other companies, using measurable goals where possible but always looking at broader goals and outcomes.

3 Define specific goals by defining small, clear steps, identifying and publicizing critical milestones. Assign firm deadlines.

4 Translate plans into action by publishing plans. Build in rewards for performance. Give regular feedback.

Integrating new practices and procedures (questions 4-6)

The potential problems are:

1 On how wide a scale will the change be introduced?
2 Is the speed of implementation too fast?
3 Are people involved supportive, informed, prepared?

The solutions are:

1 Plan the rate of change carefully by piloting to learn from experience, implementing for success, small steps and specific milestones. Allow *more* time.
2 Enlist firm support. Ensure that new procedures, products, services are well understood.

Providing training and support (questions 7-9)

The potential problems are:

1 Are we providing specific training?
2 Is the training flexible and geared to people's needs?
3 Are we targeting the right people for training/education?

The solutions are:

1 Clarify objectives of training. Use existing skills and knowledge. Depend on people as part of implementation. Use suggestions as part of the training.
2 Allow people to learn at their own pace. Provide opportunities for 'hands-on' experience. Make training relevant to the job. Have line managers 'project-manage' training.
3 Use different learning approaches. Respect and use people's experience. Allow people to solve problems and utilize their solutions.
4 Incorporate feedback into the training programmes.

'Ownership' and commitment (questions 10-12)

The potential problems are:

1 Does the change impose controls on people?
2 Does the change reduce managers' (or others') discretion or initiative?
3 Are those people who are affected being consulted?
4 Are there incentives and benefits?

The solutions are:

1 Plan change to bring benefits by using it to increase personal control over the job (and accountability). Enhance people's jobs and status. Ensure quick, visible benefits. Provide incentives for people to opt for change.
2 Involve people by asking for suggestions. Specify milestones and ask for feedback. Publicize ways in which suggestions and feedback are utilized.

Providing feedback (questions 13–15)

The potential problems are:

1 Do visible benefits occur only over the long term (1 year)?
2 Are benefits visible to top management?
3 Is the impact on cost, productivity, resource utilization, market share (etc.) well documented?
4 Are benefits clear and direct for the people involved?

The solutions are:

1 Make sure that results are well documented, accessible, quickly available, positively described, relevant, achievement of milestones recognized.
2 Arrange wide recognition of success of people involved throughout the organization. Specify how the change has helped the organization to achieve its goals.

Managing stress (questions 16–8)

The potential problems are:

1 Are people overstressed?
2 Is performance declining because of the level of stress?
3 Is there a higher incidence of 'people' problems, volatile behaviour problems between groups of people?

The solutions are:

1 Plan change to control the impact on people. Seek ways of controlling the pressure.
2 Allow more resources and time where the changes are novel.
3 Adopt a rapid implementation plan where people have been consulted *and agree to change.*
4 Empathy – constantly reinforce change – communicate and listen.

The self-assessment exercise (checklist 3)

Checklist 3 (Table 15.3) is designed to help you review your own skills in the area of planning and managing change. You should also consider the management-style exercise included earlier and review your own management approach against the various guidelines, checklists and 'role models' provided in the book.

Having gone through this exercise, identify the main areas where you feel you need to improve your skills and performance. Then identify three or four priority areas for improvement. In doing so you may care to consider the typical problems of change that people in your organization experience, as identified in the implementation exercise. Finally, look for practical ways in which you can improve your approach and style.

Table 15.3 Checklist 3: Self-assessment – management skills for change

	Where I need to improve my performance	Where my performance is moderately good	Where my performance is good	Action plans to improve performance
A Preparing for change				
1 Identifying problems and causes				(i)
2 Remaining calm under pressure				
3 Involving others where appropriate				(ii)
4 Building an open climate				
5 Setting and agreeing objectives				(iii)
6 Drawing out the inputs and contributions of others				
7 Checking for agreement				(iv)
8 Reviewing objectives regularly				
9 Seeking new information				(v)
10 Presenting ideas				
B Planning changes				
11 Identifying opportunities and solutions				(i)
12 Critically evaluating options				(ii)
13 Communicating information clearly				
14 Leading brainstorming meetings				(iii)
15 Identifying problems of implementation, resources needed and appropriate priorities				(iv) (v)
C Implementing changes				
16 Identifying what needs to be done				(i)
17 Identifying priorities and deadlines				(ii)
18 Identifying the impact of change on people				
19 Identifying and dealing with the impact of stress on myself				(iii)
20 On others				(iv)
21 Allocating tasks				
22 Coordinating plans and action				(v)
D Monitoring changes				
23 Making the time to review progress				(i)
24 Discussing problems openly				

→

Table 15.2 *(Continued)*

	Where I need to improve my performance	Where my performance is moderately good	Where my performance is good	Action plans to improve performance
25 Giving feedback				(ii)
26 Identifying areas for improvement				
27 Building on success and keeping motivation high				(iii)
28 Building team spirit				(iv)
29 Improving the use of resources				
30 Allowing enough time for change				(v)

Conclusion

Throughout this book we have discussed management skills for managing change in two contexts: first, we have looked at the context of a significant change being introduced within an organization; second, we have looked at the changing demands of the organization of the future. There is much in common between the skill sets needed in each context.

The future organization seems likely to require adaptive behaviour, will have fewer levels of management and therefore fewer managers, and flexible and more open boundaries. It will be customer-focused and knowledge-based; value-added will be a key determinant of performance, and learning will be a measure of longer-term effectiveness. Facilitating and team-building skills seem appropriate both to the new organizations and to change in organizations. In addition, however, the new organization demands more interfacing skills, negotiation skills and networking skills. All are needed within the organization when change is needed. Multi-organizational changes demand them. The future organization may make these skills a particular priority.

In this book we have examined management issues such as the need for 'productive reasoning', the need to bring 'human scale' to organizational leadership and change and to the characteristics of successful innovators. Central to this treatment is the thought that being an effective manager of change is not about being 'nice' to people. While many of the skills needed are in the domain of so-called 'soft' management skills they are difficult to acquire and to deliver in practice. Ultimately, being 'nice' is a recipe for being ineffective.

EXERCISES

1 Consider a change situation with which you are familiar. Analyse it using force field analysis.

2 Complete the implementation exercise on that change situation. What key implementation issues emerge?

3 Complete the self-assessment exercise. What issues arise for your own development of change management skills?

Part V

STRATEGIC CHANGE

16 Learning from change

17 Culture models and organization change

18 Strategic convergence: a new model for organizational change

19 Strategies for corporate transformation

Learning from change

Introduction

What, then, can be learned from the process of introducing major organizational changes? How can we ensure that we do learn from our experience? Throughout this book the answers to these two questions have been consistent. Developing a more open process for managing change will create the conditions for learning. Planning, implementing and monitoring change more systematically will allow us to consolidate that learning. Let me repeat an earlier point. This is not a prescription for an ideal approach; rather, I would argue for pragmatism combined with the capacity to learn rather than pragmatism driven by an *ad hoc* approach.

CASE STUDY

ABF Ltd

Let us return to the case study outlined in Chapter 11 (see page 178). The reader will recall from the detail provided that there was considerable evidence of both managerial ineffectiveness and the need for specific changes. Top management did not understand the causes of this managerial ineffectiveness, nor how to tackle it. The managing director, who had held the post for some years, adopted an autocratic management style. After an early period of profit growth the company had stagnated, profits remaining stable despite growth in sales. Consultants had been used to review systems and procedures and to help with the introduction of techniques such as materials requirements planning (MRP) systems.

As we saw, the finance director had played a major role in the changes. Let us look at what was learned from the changes, using his own assessment, made subsequently (Keeley, 1988). He reviews the approach he had adopted with individual managers, linking this to the specific changes made and to how he has used approaches such as those discussed in this book to learn from the experience. For our purposes two examples will suffice; many such assessments have been made.

Tony, the company accountant

Tony is the company accountant and reports directly to me. He is a qualified accountant who joined the company late in 1986 and is an experienced man. He is very competent, particularly in the field of computers where his knowledge exceeds mine, and is also highly self-motivated. I have therefore used a delegating style with him and have gone out of my way to let him do things his way. Consequently, he has been able to make a substantial number of changes and introduce many new systems. In many cases replacing systems which I installed when I was doing his job. This leadership style appears to have been effective with him and he has achieved a great deal in terms of systems development.

Despite a high level of achievement on Tony's part, problems do occur. Deadlines are frequently missed. On several occasions he has got into a problem by devoting a substantial amount of time to new work, such as developing the computer system, while being over-optimistic regarding the amount of time necessary to set aside to accurately produce the routine work. It appears that he has not placed a high enough priority on current work such as getting the monthly accounts prepared on time. He tends to work very hard towards those goals which he perceives as his own (e.g. new systems) while assigning the company goals a slightly lower priority.

Missing these goals has been very personal, very difficult for Tony. He has been embarrassed by people such as the auditors, the group chief accountant, Mike, and myself waiting on his promises and he has had to explain on many occasions that he was unable to deliver. I have therefore reverted as quickly as possible to a participating style. In as low key manner as possible, I have discussed with him future priorities such as accounting deadlines. I have shown as much sympathy as possible with his problems and avoided criticism but have not in any way avoided the subject of missed deadlines. I have initiated a two-way discussion on how we can meet deadlines in the future 'now that you have developed a computer system that is so much better than before'. I try to emphasize 'our' difficulties and 'our' failures while referring to 'your' successes. I have made particular efforts to engage in active listening and to try to accept all of his suggestions while avoiding my own suggestions except when he has not had any of his own. My general objective is to motivate him to organize things in his own way but to slightly increase the emphasis on the company's objectives so that these and his own are as closely matched as possible.

Recently I have noticed some improvement which seems to be sustained. I am gradually reducing my involvement but keeping some pressure on him, requiring regular updates on progress and future plans.

John, the production director

One of the major constraints was what I perceived to be the problem with John, the production director. Following an investigation by consultants, a number of significant changes were to be introduced in the production department. These changes included the introduction of just-in-time techniques, MRP systems, total quality concepts and changes in the method of organizing technicians and production managers. John had shown continued opposition to these measures, although they eventually proved to be popular with the rest of the management. In view of John's intransigence towards change, the consultants had recommended that he be dismissed but at the last moment he voluntarily agreed to support the changes. At the suggestion of the consultants he agreed to use me as a supporter/counsellor. I was unavoidably absent from this meeting. Shortly afterwards I was away for two months for business reasons.

In view of the long delay and the fact that I was not present at the original meeting, I thought it inappropriate to broach the question of ongoing collaboration between

John and me. I felt that John was suffering from the dilemma of having problems in his department which he was unable to solve, particularly those that required some degree of interpersonal skills. In the long term I think that John needs training to help him improve his interpersonal skills but in the short term I thought that it would be helpful if I were to try to alleviate some problem areas for him.

Improving the performance of John's production managers in dealing with disciplinary problems seemed to be the most obviously profitable area. I therefore asked him if he would be happy with me trying to sort out some ongoing personnel problems by direct contact with his staff. As I am personnel director, and closely involved in general management, this could be done in a reasonably natural way. For somewhile there had clearly been disciplinary problems with the shop-floor and these had not been properly addressed by management. Absenteeism was running at a very high rate and a number of people were taking 20–40 days off per annum on a regular basis; there were complaints from the production managers that some people, notably on the nightshift, were very difficult to supervise.

Somehow, the production managers had been unable to get to grips with discipline on the shop-floor. A fair amount of aggression had been used by them but no improvement had been seen and shop floor morale was low. There had been claims from them in the past that these problems would be sorted out 'if the managers got enough support from the directors'. It was never entirely clear what was meant by this statement. However, I agreed with John that I would try to sort out whatever personnel problems there were and keep him generally informed about what I was doing. We agreed that he would let me know if he thought that I was interfering over much. I determined to talk to each relevant manager and to discuss their problems with them.

Initially their reaction was as it had been in the past. They said that if they were left to get on with their jobs, take whatever decisions were necessary and dismiss whichever people they felt fit, there would be no problems. They said that the personnel department had restricted management action on discipline in the past. I said that what I wanted to do was to examine each individual case and follow it through to its conclusion – hopefully an improved performance on the part of the employee.

My initial approach was to examine each employee file to see who had been issued with written warnings that could be followed up. When I produced a list of which employees needed to be spoken or written to again, two of the production managers admitted that they had each had a number of written warnings for their department on such things as unexplained absence, excessive sickness and bad discipline and that they had failed to hand them out. They each said that they had forgotten to do so. This seemed extremely unlikely and on further discussion it transpired that none of the production managers was sure what to do in any given disciplinary situation.

One of them had developed an extremely aggressive personal style over the years and tended to shout at people when they did something wrong. He did not really know how to follow up this approach, especially when the employee concerned seemed willing to enter into a reasoned discussion. The other two confessed that they found it very difficult to enforce discipline and were not sure how to go about it. With these admissions in the open, it was a relatively straightforward business from then on to tackle the situation.

We decided to start from scratch. I saw each of the worst offenders personally with one of the production managers present and explained the situation stating that their performance had to improve. Some employees said that a large contributory factor was

→

the attitude of management and that they did not respect them. My response was to say that we were aware of our shortcomings throughout the company and that all managers, including directors, would be receiving training, but that I expected an immediately improved performance from the employees as well. Also, the company was looking for a situation in which genuine problems could be discussed between management and employee. However, failure to meet a satisfactory standard would not be tolerated in future. In other words, we wanted a frank and open atmosphere in which problems were discussable, but we did not intend to be soft.

Most employees seemed to warm to this attitude, who although over the course of the months it was necessary to dismiss several did not improve. After a fairly short while I found that the production managers were becoming enthusiastic and coming to me with progress reports. They also seemed to be happier in what they are doing now that they had some direction.

During those months I rewrote and substantially expanded the company handbook, a publication which I introduced only last year. I took the opportunity to call a meeting of all production managers and supervisors so as to ask their opinion of the section relating to disciplinary procedures. This was an excuse to discuss how to act in different situations and quite a lengthy and lively discussion ensued. It was surprising how many people were pleased that they had the opportunity to ask how to act in various situations. Having a set of rules to discuss relieved some of the embarrassment of their admitting that they did not know how to act – they were able to ask what was expected of them in enforcing each rule.

All this indicates that frank and open discussion of problems helps to motivate staff. The managers and supervisors referred to above were very grateful to be treated in the 'telling' and 'selling' styles and had previously found themselves uncomfortable with John's delegating style because they lacked the maturity to deal with the situation in which they found themselves. It must be remembered of course that John had delegated by default, not because of a conscious opinion of the proper way to react to his subordinates. Although I do not envisage a situation in which I will continue to instruct managers and supervisors in this manner, I believe that they have been given more confidence to work under John with his delegation style.

A further example of increasing motivation by increased communication is the training course which many of our managers and supervisors attended several months ago. This was agreed with the consultants although Mike, who is very cynical about training, agreed that it could be run partly because the consultants supported it and partly because it was included in their original fee. It was a fairly short course at a local hotel and covered basic aspects of supervision and work planning, but I felt that the biggest benefit was the opportunity it created for managers and supervisors to talk together about their work. While there was little discussion afterwards regarding the individual topics dealt with on the course, there was a noticeable increase in *esprit de corps* on their return. It also created an expectation of further change and support and there has been substantial agitation from them for the board to attend a fairly similar course – this has now been agreed.

Simultaneously, there was a change in the work pattern of the production managers. There was previously one nightshift manager with two dayshift managers splitting their duties but without the two shifts overlapping. Problems occurred in both areas on days and there had been severe disciplinary problems on the nightshift for years. With the three managers working rotating shifts and covering the whole 24 hours, there was substantial opportunity for improvement. For example, whereas the nightshift manager could previously hide from his problems at night, it was now necessary for him to discuss them openly with the manager who was about to take over from him and problems had to be faced because they would be noticed by the next person working on that shift. This enhanced the atmosphere of having to address problems frankly and openly. It was interesting to note that whereas previously they had failed to hand out warnings, there have recently been instances where they have gained such confidence and enthusiasm that they have been competing to be the one to hand out the warning. One manager even insisted on coming in from holiday in order to see a particularly difficult employee who had worked exclusively for him before the rotating shift system had been introduced.

By working hard to create an atmosphere in which managers could take the task of changing their approach without fear of reprimand, it was possible to encourage behavioural change. This was enhanced by ensuring that frank admissions (e.g. regarding the written warnings) were not 'punished' but at the same time it was necessary to ensure that the proper approach was discussed.

Managing change for management development

It was clear from Chapter 11 that significant changes were introduced and important performance improvements achieved at ABF Ltd. The two examples given above demonstrate how important management style and management development can be in a period of change. Developing a more open and positive management style was seen in Chapter 11 as a precursor of other much needed changes. Here it becomes clear how important this is for development and learning by these managers during the process of change. Turning back to Table 13.3, it is now all too obvious that learning and change will only be possible given a positive attitude to change (from top management) and an open approach to developing changes, ideas and solving the problems along the way. Without both we have some combination of stagnation, anxiety and resistance to change.

It is important for us to recognize that significant change programmes are not discrete events. The objective is not simply profitability or increased effectiveness, crucial as these are to all of us; rather, it is about increased adaptability and effectiveness and we assess these qualitatively. But do not leave this book with the view that this is about increased satisfaction as such; rather, it is about increased openness, a greater willingness to face and deal with problems, more openly handled conflict. The net result may, superficially, seem less happy. There will be more analysis, more debate and greater effort directed at improving performance and cost-effectiveness.

All this needs patient and sustained effort. There is plenty of room for misunderstanding along the way. Many people's assessments may appear to be contradictory. Take an example I know of change in a social services organization. Specifically, the changes were aimed at alleviating the problems so often associated with the institutionalized care of the elderly mentally disturbed. Among many changes introduced was a residents' council for each 'home'. A comment from the minutes showed one patient saying: 'There's been a fall in the discipline.

I don't like it.' The changes included movement towards giving residents influence over their own care, including the right of access to their own files. Unless handled sensitively such changes can create anxiety and uncertainty. This is partly a direct consequence of the 'fear of freedom'.

Thus leadership, sensitivity and empathy, along with involvement, openness and the rest, are the order of the day in a period of change. We need to recognize that people do need time to go through stages in the experience of change identified in the 'coping cycle' (see page 240), that people go through change at different rates. The coping cycle then becomes a reasonable basis against which to monitor change. Where are people on the 'coping cycle'? Does this explain their attitudes and behaviour?

The resident quoted above may well have been somewhere in the second or third stages of the coping cycle. That would make the resident's assessment entirely predictable. Once people are coming through the coping cycle then we can seek evidence of improvement, both quantitatively and qualitatively.

How can we decide that people are coming through the experience of change? We look for two main things: first, we look for motivated and enthusiastic attempts to make the changes work well; second, we look for people who no longer talk only about the past. If people talk about changes in terms of the future and how they (and the organization) can benefit then it is a reasonable guess that they are through the 'discarding' process that we described in Chapter 13. Now we can monitor improvements and *feedback, feedback, feedback* to build self-esteem, to build success through improved self-esteem. Effectively managed change turns out to be more a matter of ongoing process, of building the capacity to improve into the organization.

Developing the facilitative management style *as part of manager development* is important in this process. We can identify a typical 'role model' of the manager, using this style, drawing again on Argyris (1982) and Argyris and Shon (1974, 1978). The manager concerned to facilitate the process of change adopts the following methods:

■ Seeks 'clients' with problems, demonstrating the intention of helping people to resolve the problems that they recognize as such.

■ Views problems broadly and seeks both organizational and technical means of dealing with them.

■ Adopts changing, broad-based criteria for success.

■ Develops solutions drawing on information, knowledge, experience and views from the people involved in the system, department or organization under consideration.

■ Recognizes that some technically sound solutions may well have to be rejected on interpersonal or organizational grounds.

■ Recognizes that the application of professional technique can remove control from people. This can often impede commitment to change and lead to poor solutions. Joint control between the specialists, line managers and others involved (e.g. unions and professional associations, group managers in a multi-divisional organization) will build a greater willingness to collaborate.

- Clients/line managers/staff/users are becoming more willing to accept professional, specialist advice *but* they increasingly *expect* to be more active and involved in the processes of diagnosis and implementation of change.

- Expects challenge and criticism from line managers/users and others involved. Recognizes that people will employ a range of criteria in evaluating choices. Sets out to develop informed choice and internal commitment for everyone involved.

- Recognizes that planning, implementing and establishing change is a corporate activity and responsibility.

All this is fine if there is the time, energy and money to allow for it, but what if the organization is in, or close to, crisis? It is to looking at recent experience of managing in the crisis situation that we now turn to see whether this situation demands different management styles.

The management of crisis and turnaround

We often say that we learn more from our failures than from our successes. Our understanding of organizational effectiveness can be enriched by examining the causes of failures. Whether a failure is associated with the use of technology, or the collapse of a business, a close examination of the events leading up to the failure will identify opportunities which might have been used to forestall the failure. The lack of prior intervention is clearly 'ineffectual' behaviour. Failures may appear to be caused by changes of environmental conditions that organizations cannot control; events may cause severe difficulties for any organization, and nothing can change that. However, in so far as failures are caused by problems within organizations, these causes are both deep rooted and important. Environmental change raises questions of how to respond. Competitive pressures may require innovation in product design or production processes. Managers are not simply subject to environments but can also respond to them to ensure continued effectiveness.

Increasingly, the study of failures is becoming a part of organization studies. Much credit for this development must go to Hall (1980) and to Bignell *et al.* (1977). Both Child (1984) and Bignell *et al.* (1977) identify some of the indicators or conditions of failure.

Child (1984) identifies a number of 'warning signs of a structural problem'. These include overloads of work, poor integration between departments, a reducing capacity for innovation and weakening control. Bignell *et al.* in their introduction also develop a number of 'conditions of failure'. Typically, the background to a failure will be characterized by the following five factors:

1 A situation or a project in which members of several organizations are involved.

2 A complex, ill-defined and prolonged task which gives rise to information difficulties.

3 Ambiguities associated with the way to handle the situation or project (relevant regulations being out of date or not enforced).

4 Members of the organizations concerned operate with stereotyped attitudes with respect to the behaviour of other people and treat complaints from the general public or members of other organizations in a fairly cursory manner, believing them to come from non-experts who do not fully understand the issues involved.

5 Where signs of possible hazards emerge, some will be recognized and planned for but others will be neglected because:

(a) they are not recognized by those working within a particular occupational or organizational stereotype;

(b) of pressure of work;

(c) recognizing them and taking action would require the investment of time, money and energy;

(d) few of the individuals concerned feel that quite probably it will not happen anyway.

Thus, in general, 'failures' are characterized by problems of communication, problems of perception and attitudes, problems of uncertainty, inadequacy of procedures for handling the situation and, therefore, of training. While there is some overlap with Child's list, important additional factors are identified here. We should note, however, that Child was concerned to identify signs of problems stemming from the structure of an organization whereas Bignell *et al.*'s list deals with conditions for failures generally. We should also note that not every failure will be caused by all the problems previously identified. Lorange and Nelson (1987) identify the following four signs of organizational decline:

1 *Entrapment*: blinded by their own previous success, people can demonstrate a powerful tendency to self-deception. Upturns can follow downturns and we can delude ourselves into not recognizing the message that more and longer-lasting downturns indicate – that of being out of date.

2 *Hierarchy orientation*: where decisions are made more on issues of internal politics than in terms of market and competitive goals.

3 *Desire for acceptance, conformity*: already discussed as 'group think' in Chapter 8.

4 *Too much concern for consensus and compromise*: all decisions being turned over to teams, working parties and the like.

Lorange and Nelson also identify a number of early warning signals of decline, as follows:

1 Excess personnel, particularly of staff and line management.

2 Tolerance of incompetence.

3 Inflexible and time-consuming administrative procedures.

4 Process dominates substance; for example, where the process of corporate planning leads to the production of thick binders full of numbers and strategic options which do not get implemented.

5 Lack of clear goals.

6 Absence of and fear of conflict.

7 Poor communication.

8 Outdated organization structure.

There are similarities between the signs of organizational decline given above and the syndrome of ineffective leadership and change management discussed in Chapter 3 (see Figure 3.2) and the various ineffectiveness – effectiveness patterns identified in Table 8.1 and Table 16.1.

Table 16.1 **Organizational syndromes** (from Miller, D., and de Vries, K., (1984). Reprinted with permission of © John Wiley & Sons, Inc.)

Syndrome	Characteristics	Symptoms	Strengths	Weaknesses	Examples
Tight control	Distrust Analytical Centralized Reactive Sophisticated Information systems	Incremental change 'Muddling through' Too much con-sultation Too many meet-ings Poor innovation	Good knowledge of threats and opportunities Diversification	Lack of clear strategy Insecurity	Dramatic loss of market or market share
Systems focus	Tight, formal controls Standardization Hierarchical structures Conformity	Lack of innovation Ritual Low involvement Inflexibility Fixation Distinctive competence	Efficient operations Well-integrated product–market strategy	Traditional structures predominate Managers dissatisfied over influence and discretion	Achievement of dominance from a relatively weak position Frequent loss of control during history
Personal style	Highly centralized Inadequate structures Poor information systems	Unbridled growth Inconsistent strategy into and out of markets Decisions without analysis Little consultation	Change	Wasted resources Problems of control Inadequate role of second-level managers Rash expansion policies	Rapid growth Chief executive wishing to 'prove' him- or herself
Paralysis	Lack of confidence Leadership vacuum Bureaucratic Hierarchical	Insular Decisions avoided Change difficult	Efficient operations Focused strategy	Limited to tradi-tional markets Apathetic man-agers Weak competi-tive position	Well-established, same technol-ogy, customers and competition for many years

→

303

Table 16.1 *(Continued)*

Syndrome	Characteristics	Symptoms	Strengths	Weaknesses	Examples
Leaderlessness	Leadership vacuum Power struggles	No involvement Incremental change Poor information flows Effective power in shifting coalitions of second-level managers	Creativity	Inconsistent strategy Lack of leadership Climate of distrust Poor cooperation	'Withdrawn' chief executive

If we can identify some of the origins of and signs of crisis and decline, how can such situations be managed? The need to turn an organization around creates pressure to achieve sustainable changes quickly but without the resources that are often available in periods of growth. The organization must reorganize and rationalize either at the level of the firm or, sometimes, at the level of the industry in order to cut overcapacity. Difficult decisions must be taken and implemented. Pulling out of traditional areas of activity is easier said than done. Building up new areas of activity may require new skills and new people. Redesigning products, updating processes and revitalizing services takes massive effort. Taking advantage of new technologies quickly enough to capitalize on them is often a key issue. It must be done quickly enough to turn them to advantage, but not so quickly that the firm becomes overexposed with an ill-developed technology. For Taylor (1983) these challenges require a new style of management, incorporating the following eight features:

1 *Decisiveness*: the situation calls for a speed of decision and ruthlessness in decision making: a willingness to take unpleasant decisions and to face public criticism in order to ensure the continuation and recovery of the overall business.

2 *Direct communication*: management must rely more on personal face-to-face meetings and telephone conversations, rather than on formal committees and paperwork systems.

3 *Personal responsibility and accountability*: there must be a greater emphasis at all levels on personal responsibility and accountability for meeting the targets and deadlines which are necessary if the business is to survive.

4 *Central control of funds*: this accountability is accompanied by a tighter central control of cash and an assumption by top management of the right to reallocate cash among divisions.

5 *Investment and disinvestment*: there is a need to rethink the future prospects for each product and market segment – in terms of the growth and profit potential and how to stay competitive in price, quality and service, often on a lower level of business, and take radical decisions to invest or disinvest.

6 *Expansion internationally*: as growth slows down in traditional markets, it is necessary to expand internationally, sometimes into politically risky areas.

7 *Personal negotiation*: the restructuring and rationalization that is taking place demands political skills of a high order and the ability to negotiate with employee representatives, with pressure groups and with government bodies both at home and abroad.

8 *Innovation and risk taking*: there is a recognition that firms must adopt and develop the new technologies or 'go under' – introducing new products and processes and pioneering new businesses. With the above this also forms part of the management of turnaround.

The key problem is to manage the contraction of traditional activities while at the same time expanding new activities. This must be achieved quickly and with limited resources, often under significant pressure from curious, demotivated staff and problems with the media. Turnaround strategies often include the following:

- Mergers and cooperative supply, design or manufacturing/assembly agreements.
- Sales of assets.
- Programmes aimed at reducing overheads.
- Improved systems of cost and budgetary control.
- Value-for-money programmes.
- Productivity improvement programmes including closing old-fashioned plant, concentrating on few facilities, automation, quality improvement and new technology.
- Developing new corporate strategies.

While 'turnaround' is often discussed in connection with private sector companies, it is worth noting that similar pressures have been faced in the public sector. Strategies for change in the public sector may include the following:

- New systems of management (e.g. the introduction of general management in the health service in the UK).
- New strategies and approaches (e.g. the development of commercialization programmes and marketing in higher education).
- New systems for human resource development (e.g. appraisal systems in education).
- Rationalization, simplification, automation and reorganization (across organizations, both public and private).

From what I have said so far it is clear that crisis situations are likely to have had a long and identifiable history, with clear signals of decline along the way. It is also clear that decisive action is needed and that turnaround strategies include a characteristic range of techniques, systems and approaches. Does the time and resources pressure created by crisis mean that the 'role model' for facilitative management is not relevant?

There are two points to make in dealing with this question. First, throughout this book I have made very clear the point that managing change demands a complex set of skills and styles within which both effective leadership and facilitative management styles are equally important; second, turnaround management still requires commitment. As Taylor (1983) makes very clear, it demands a high level of interpersonal skills. If the organization wishes to avoid the present crisis and the next one, managers and employees need to learn from the changes being made. The very fact of the crisis, if clearly communicated, can impel support. If so, the learning we are talking about can follow. I re-emphasize: managing change effectively is not about being 'soft' with people – it is about making demands of them.

Turnaround situations bring the prospect of sudden and dramatic changes. The impact of these changes can create the stresses referred to in Chapter 13. But if managers are seen to be dealing with the long-ignored fundamentals (the fact they have been ignored leading to crisis) then this can motivate commitment and energy for change. Even so, the lessons of Chapter 13 need to be considered along the way. Under pressure people can achieve a lot, but the quality of decisions and actions can also flag and fail. Thus a careful watch for the signs of stress should be a part of senior management's 'agenda'. In summary, then, even in crisis situations attention needs to be given to longer-term effectiveness by being careful over the process of managing change.

Conclusion

The starting point adopted in this chapter was to ask what can be learned from the process of change. This has been examined through a continuation of a case study introduced in an earlier chapter of the book. The analysis here is extended by reference to the learning organization ideas reviewed in the book. The chapter continued with a review of what we can learn from crisis and turnaround situations. These represent a real challenge because the need for change is dramatic. While some of what is required turns out to be distinct, much derives from general change management approaches.

EXERCISES

1 What now is your assessment of the approach to change adopted by ABF? To what extent is ABF really focused on mind-set change?

2 To what extent do crisis and turnaround generate special change characteristics and demands?

3 What is the role of the leader in change as far as promoting learning and development is concerned?

17 Culture models and organization change

Introduction

Throughout much of the twentieth century, research into organizations looked at how most effectively to increase performance, productivity and profitability. Latterly client/customer satisfaction and the satisfaction of employees came to be seen as central to improved performance, and public service organizations were increasingly the subject of study. It is worth noting that in the USA and in Europe major wars led to rapid increases in research efforts as attempts were made to solve the novel problems presented by such conflicts. These included learning how to select candidates for officer training in rapidly expanding armed services and looking at the factors affecting productivity in factory systems being rapidly expanded to manufacture weapons on a vast scale.

After the end of the Second World War in 1945 many observers argued that the Cold War, other incipient conflicts around the world and the growing pressures of global competition, alongside the demands of what Eisenhower famously called the 'military–industrial complex', added substantial and continued impetus to this research effort and to the related and impressive growth of business schools in the USA and elsewhere. (Professional schools such as law schools, medical schools and the like were established earlier but the emergence of business schools was a feature of the educational 'landscape' during that period.)

The twentieth century has been labelled as 'the American century' as America's capitalist organizations came to be dominant in sectors such as automobile and aircraft manufacture. Moreover, American culture came to be almost the defining culture for big cities around the world. American business, diplomacy and military power eventually evolved into such a position that led scholars to cite the USA as the world's only global superpower, at least for the moment. Yet even as this position emerged there were clear signs of change in the position of business in the USA relative to the rest of the world. More particularly it is clear that while US businesses continue to deliver economic success there are, nevertheless, US businesses struggling to survive and prosper in mature sectors such as automobile manufacture. This has led many thoughtful business leaders to raise new questions.

As long ago as 1986 Turner (1986) traced the emergence of interest in corporate culture to both the decline in standards of manufacturing quality and design in the

USA and the challenge to the economic supremacy of the USA from Japan in particular. He argued that the culture concept offers a new way of understanding organizations. The use of corporate culture appeared to offer analytical possibilities for explaining the success of Japanese companies, at least in the 1960s and 1970s. Of course, there were other feasible explanations, not least the need for Japan and Germany to re-equip their industry after the war, but these were deemed to be insufficient in themselves to explain the observable differences in performance and success. It is worth noting that literally hundreds of research studies seeking to explain organizational performance by looking at structure, innovation, technology, size, adaptation and so on tended to reveal statistically significant correlations. However, it was also true that the factors studied provided an explanation of only part of the variance in the dependent variable, commonly a 'bundle' of performance measures. Researchers concluded that some other factor, not being measured, was at work. It was not a long stretch from that position to conclude that the missing variable was culture.

Of course, such a view possessed powerful 'face validity'. Just as the 'frontier spirit' thought to engender values of self-reliance, independence and enterprise was thought to have been instrumental in the growth of American business, so observers now sought similar explanations for the success of Japanese enterprise in 'consensus management' Japanese style, alongside the adoption by Japanese corporations of American ideas such as total quality management combined eventually with the 'Toyota Manufacturing System' incorporating ideas which came to be known as 'lean thinking', 'Kanban' and so on. While the explanation ultimately relates to changes in the way work is arranged, the argument for why Japanese enterprises achieved advantage by making these changes first was seen to include culture as one important source of explanation.

What is organization culture?

Organization culture is commonly defined as the attitudes, values, beliefs, norms and customs which distinguish an organization from others. Organization culture is intangible and difficult to measure. In fact there are many ways of defining organization culture. Elliot Jacques (1952) referred to 'customary and traditional ways of thinking and doing things ', noting that new employees must learn to adopt them sufficiently to gain acceptance in the organization. Schwartz and Davis (1981) note that culture is both about beliefs and expectations while Lorsch (1986) refers to the beliefs of 'top managers'. Conversely, Kotter and Hesketh (1992) note the importance of community and its preservation within any definition of culture, effectively arguing that the urge to create identity and ensure survival are what gives a culture impact.

Johnson (1988) sets out a 'cultural web' noting a number of components which help in the definition of organization culture:

1 *The organizational paradigm*. What an organization does – its mission, its values and how it defines itself.

2 *Control systems*. Processes in place to monitor performance and/or behaviour. Role cultures have many formal controls, rules and procedures, for example.

3 *Organizational structures*. Reporting lines, hierarchies, work flows.

4 *Power structures*. Who makes the decisions, how widely spread is power and on what are power and influence based?

5 *Symbols*. Logos and designs, office allocation, car parking and other tangible and intangible means of differentiating people.

6 *Rituals and routines*. Meetings, reports, budget and performance review processes.

7 *Stories and myths*. Convey messages about what is important and valued in an organization.

While not denying that organizations are cultural entities, it ought to be noted that the underlying consequence of there being such cultural assumptions could be to stifle dissent and limit innovation. In any event organizations are certainly only rarely capable of being understood as a single, homogenous culture. This brings with it the prospect of cultural differentiation and adaptation via what would in effect be a process of evolution. Evolutionary explanations of change attract some interest (see below). For the moment, however, we need to note that the idea that a leadership team can change the culture of an organization is very contentious. Parker (2000) observes that many of the ideas behind organization culture theories are not new depending as they do on the well-known tensions between cultural and structural or informal and formal explanations of behaviour in organizations.

With this in mind note that one of the often contending explanations for the famous Hawthorne research lies in a cultural explanation different to those offered by Mayo, Roethlisberger and Dickson and others. You will recall that the Hawthorne experiments started in consequence of an earlier study in the same factory looking at the impact of lighting on the productivity of workers engaged in tasks demanding physical skills. Gains were observed as lighting levels were increased. Then lighting levels were reduced. Even so further gains were recorded, only stemmed when lighting levels were reduced to the level of moonlight. Social factors were believed to be the explanation. The famous 'relay assembly test room study' was set up to investigate these factors in greater depth. The results of this latter study were reported in great detail (Roethlisberger and Dickson, 1939). Taken together, the results of this and later studies at Hawthorne were taken as a demonstration that social factors explain performance more fully than various economic explanations including the operation of incentive schemes. These social factors were in-group factors such as 'group pressure'. Thus the social explanation did not relate to factors we might associate with corporate culture as such.

There have long been various contending explanations for these results (see Sofer (1973) for an excellent summary). But Zinn (1980) offers an explanation of interest to those interested in cultural factors. The relay assembly test room operators were female workers in the Hawthorne factory, a Western Electric factory in outer Chicago. The majority were recent immigrants whose English language skills were relatively poor. They were often the main income earner in their family. Economic pressure, mediated by the experience of being a relatively recently arrived immigrant and therefore not fully socially adjusted, may well offer an explanation as to why group pressure was so important. The group incentive scheme was clearly an important part of the reasons for the group pressure so it is difficult to conclude that no economic explanation applies. Certainly output increased in the relay assembly test room. However the Roethlisberger and Dickson book, although published in 1939, shows the data only to 1929. Whitehead (1936) publishes the relay assembly test room data to 1934. From the advent of the Great Depression of 1929 output fell away thus reinforcing the likelihood that while social factors were important there is the possibility that these factors mediate the operation of a group incentive scheme, and that from 1929 onwards the key motivation was that of limiting output. Note, however, that other, operational factors may explain falling output from 1929 onwards. We cannot tell from the available data but what we can conclude is that a combination of social, cultural and economic explanations are needed.

We note here the intersection of various economic, social and contextual variables, as well as social group factors related to the 'informal' organization idea. Of course, we have long known that the 'real world behaviour' in an organization operates differently from the formally proscribed rules, procedures and so on. In order to 'get things done' people develop 'short cuts'. From there it is not difficult to see how corporate cultures may emerge. A combination of the operation of formal systems and processes and informal organization could reasonably be expected to result in the development of tacit understandings about what is and is not 'acceptable behaviour' in any given organizational situation. The important point to note here is the intersection of factors at different levels, individual, organizational and contextual. If this is how culture arises we should also note the Deal and Kennedy (1982) observation about 'strong' and 'weak' cultures.

A strong culture exists where employees respond to changing situations consistently with their alignment to the values of the organization. There is a high degree of predictability in this regard. Conversely, a weak culture exists where there is little alignment with organizational values. Here control must be exercised through extensive procedures, rules and formal systems. Where the culture is strong we have the possibility, identified by Janis (1972), of 'groupthink'. This happens when people do not challenge current thinking but also where the group will take riskier decisions than would any individual member acting alone. There is a strong belief in the organization's values and a tendency to create negative stereotypes of competitors, the latter leading to a belief in the inherent advantages of the organization on the part of its members. In turn this leads to the riskier decision making. It is worth noting that strong cultures tend to outperform weaker cultures (Kotter and Hesketh, 1992; Burt *et al.*, 1994).

Are strong cultures likeliest to emerge in a period of growth? Is that when organizations with strong cultures perform best? Could the Hawthorne research not be an example of a strong culture in operation but one in which the contextual factors were both conducive to the development of a strong culture and likely to support effective performance due to the congruence between employee objectives and needs and corporate goals. Does the very predictability of predictable performance limit the differentiation most likely to help innovation and adaptability? I cannot provide final answers here but the questions are intriguing to say the least. We turn now to various well-established models of organizational culture before considering these questions more fully.

Models of organizational culture

Various influential models are identified, as follows.

■ Hofstede

Hofstede (1968) identifies five characteristics of culture in his study of national, cultural influences:

- *Power distance*. The extent to which, in a given national context, people expect there to be differences in the level of power across groups and between individuals. A high power-distance score represents an expectation that some people can wield substantial power. A low score is an expectation of equal influence over decisions.
- *Uncertainty avoidance*. In essence a national attitude to risk taking and coping with uncertainty.
- *Individualism vs collectivism*. People are either concerned for themselves primarily or act as a member of a group, subordinating individual to group goals.
- *Masculinity vs femininity*. The contrast between male values of competitiveness, aggression and ambition with feminine values emphasizing the value of others and of developmental rather than simply economic goals.
- *Long-term vs short-term orientation*.

Using attitude data from a major multinational organization Hofstede was able to show national differences on these factors.

■ Deal and Kennedy

Deal and Kennedy (1982) defined organizational culture in a more pragmatic way, which turns out not to be very helpful. They define it as 'the way things get done around here'. On the face of it this is based on organizational reality. However, it seems likely that we can hardly explain why different organizations do things differently as being definitive of the organization's culture. The organizations concerned may deploy different technology and therefore do things differently. Does that mean they had different cultures at the outset. Of course, different cultures may emerge over time in those circumstances.

More helpfully, they go on to define measures of corporate culture depending on two factors:

- *Feedback*. The speed of feedback and the scope of it have an impact on behaviour in an organization.
- *Risk*. The level of uncertainty applying to an organization.

Using these factors Deal and Kennedy propose four culture types. In turn, these are the 'tough-guy' or 'macho' culture in which rewards are high and feedback immediate. Fast moving financial and investment companies might be typical but Deal and Kennedy note that this culture can emerge in hospitals, sports organizations and police forces. Next is the 'work-hard/play-hard' culture, emerging where risks are high but more typically in large organizations as compared with the previous culture type.

Then they identify the 'bet your company' culture in which big decisions are taken but it may be years before the results are known. Power utilities may be one sector in which such a culture might emerge. Oil exploration may be another alongside aviation, space and all forms of mining. Finally the 'process' culture is one in which people get little or no feedback. Often this is because services delivered to clients are complex with many departments and individuals involved. Social services organizations are typical examples but retail stores may be another.

The strength of this model is that it deals with corporate culture in a relatively pragmatic way. The key problem is that if you are seeking to define culture types then the types should be independent each of the other. Here the first three overlap substantially thus weakening the analytical power of the model. In practice it will be difficult to define particular organizations using these culture types. However, the focus on feedback is very useful, not least because it relates to discretion.

■ Handy

Handy (1984) builds on the work of Roger Harrison in developing a model of organizational culture in which he describes four culture types. First, the 'power culture' in which power influence and decision taking is concentrated on a few key people and positions. The organization is controlled from the top through networks and teams rather like a web. Decision and action are quick and decisive and there are few formal systems, procedures and rules. Next is the 'role culture'. Here people as role incumbents or role holders have clearly defined authority within previously defined parameters. Power derives from position and/or expertise, so long as the expertise is recognized and legitimated organizationally. Third, a 'person culture' comprises an organizational setting designed around individual performance. A ballet or opera company would be one example, law firms, consulting firms and the like are others. Handy suggests person cultures exist where each individual ranks their own performance as superior to the organization. Finally, a 'task culture' exists where teams are created to work on and resolve particular problems. Power derives from expertise so long as that expertise is needed. Organizations with matrix structures and multiple reporting lines will often be characterized with this culture.

Here at least the culture types are defined independently of each other and linked to a questionnaire Handy reproduces. However, there is a real problem in practice. The day before writing this section I met with senior executives of a global technology services group. It is organized into 'sector groups' to win and manage business, 'capability groups' to facilitate solutions development and central functions (including information services, marketing, finance, human resources, to provide shared services) and a further 'business transformation group' to provide thought leadership. It brings together teams to serve clients. The key point is that it seeks to maintain a 'task culture' for clients alongside a 'role culture' elsewhere. Is organization reality too complex for these models to be the basis of useful solutions?

The work of Ed Schein

Schein (1996) defines organizational culture as 'the residue of success'. Of all organizational attributes it is the hardest to measure and therefore the most difficult to change. Once changed, Schein argues that the impact of that change will be long lasting outliving products and services, leaders and founders, buildings and other physical attributes.

Schein describes culture at three cognitive levels. The first and simplest are those aspects of the organization which can be directly observed and experienced by anyone. The second level deals with those aspects of culture professed by participants only. Here we talk about mission statements and the like but also about employee and client surveys. At the third level we deal with tacit assumptions, 'unspoken rules' and the like. Much of this is taboo. It cannot be discussed openly in the organization. Schein suggests that much of this exists without the conscious knowledge of those involved. This seems likely only in the sense that we are talking about unspoken rules which are so deeply embedded that we do not think about them.

Here Schein is offering a line of analysis also developed by Argyris and Schon (1978) in their discussion of 'espoused' theory and 'theory in use'. The latter distinction derives from observing differences between what senior executives and others say is important and what their behaviour actually signals to be important. Often in this sense behaviour in organizations is paradoxical. Thus it is that newcomers to an organization may take a long time to settle into the culture. More important, it explains why culture change is so difficult in practice. We shall see that writers working within the critical theory perspective are also deeply sceptical about whether culture change can be achieved. Nevertheless, recognizing the complexities ought not to allow us too easily to ignore the point that many organizations certainly report successful culture change.

Trompenars

For Trompenars (1998) each organization has its own unique culture, probably created unconsciously, based on actions and behaviours of senior executives, founders and other core people such as those who built it originally and any who subsequently changed it. Culture is an acquired body of knowledge about how to behave and shared mind-sets, and includes cognitive frameworks. His model utilizes the sources of national cultural differences in corporate culture on a number of dimensions:

- *Universalism vs pluralism.* Do we focus on rules and procedures or rely on our relationships when we seek to get things done?
- *Individualism vs communitarianism.* Do we think organizations should focus attention on individuals or on groups?
- *Specific vs diffuse.* Are relationships superficial and transactional or deep and go beyond the workplace?
- *Inner directed vs outer directed.* Is action focused inside the organization or externally?

- *Achieved status vs ascribed status*. Value is seen in who people are or in the position they hold.
- *Sequential time vs synchronic time*. Attention to people and problems in sequence or jointly.

The connections between this study and the Hofstede work are evident enough but it seems clear that Trompenars' work has application to corporate culture generally. Thus, for example, where ascribed status is important in defining people's worth in a given organizational setting there have to be real questions about how easy it would be to introduce change because change would be likely to undermine those definitions of worth. While his concern was with the sources of national cultural difference it seems clear that the model reveals much about corporate culture.

It is clear that attitudes to risk, the feedback people get and the timescales associated with feedback are all important factors in understanding the emerging complexity to which Schein also directs our attention. It is also probably true that we ought to examine the mechanisms through which cultures are formed because while these factors clearly are important they can hardly be used to explain the emergence of long lasting cultures. For example, it would stretch incredulity to claim that the attitude to risk remains stable over time, as between generations of employees, but we would need to believe that to be true if we were to explain the emergence of a particular culture on that basis.

Both the ABF Ltd and International Engineering cases (see pages 178 and 142 respectively) provide examples of this more detailed analysis. Particularly interesting is the point about 'fear of failure'; the pressures are dual in nature. On the one hand the short-term approach combined with a functional or departmental orientation, centralization and autocratic management styles creates a powerful tendency to limit risk taking. On the other, managers moving rapidly through careers and not having to face up to their mistakes do not learn the interpersonal skills needed to do so. They find facing up to performance issues difficult. Therefore, when forced to do so by those same short-term pressures, they often do so inadequately and in a volatile, even primitive, fashion (ABF Ltd). This further reduces risk taking, over time creating an organization within which the 'fear of failure' is very high indeed. Thus, where a problematic culture emerges it may be difficult to change. Indeed it seems clear that to change culture we must work on the mind-set or mental programming within the organization. However, it does appear that we can do so. The key seems to be that of getting people to focus on shared problems. Developing new solutions and supporting their successful implementation helps. Most importantly we can aid the creation of new mind-sets by identifying 'tacit' knowledge which already exists in the organization, converting it to new explicit knowledge and encouraging its use in problem solving. Thus new possibilities are created – engendering mind-set change not by seeking to destroy the current mind-set but, rather, by adding new ideas; by focusing on solutions and not on failure.

■ Goffee and Jones

Goffee and Jones (1996) offer another approach to the analysis of culture. For them culture is about the presence (or absence) of community. Building on the ideas of social theorists such as Durkheim they argue that sociability (the

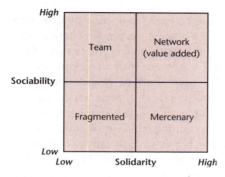

Figure 17.1 **Two dimensions, four cultures**

extent to which people like each other, mix with each other in and out of work) and solidarity (the extent to which there are shared goals) are important components of corporate culture. These two dimensions lead to the identification of four cultures – see Figure 17.1.

Note that I have modified the Goffee and Jones model here. In my version, where sociability is high but solidarity is low we have a team culture. Of course the solidarity within the team may be high while solidarity for the organization as a whole is low. Where sociability and solidarity are high we see a network culture emerging. These are characterized by easy and effective vertical and horizontal communication and relate to the value-added model described earlier in the book.

More importantly, for these authors the issue about culture is not only about changing culture but rather about identifying whether an organization has a positive or negative version of that culture. A positively oriented culture is more likely to be an adaptive culture. Here they rely partly on Kotter and Hesketh (1992) who identify values and behaviour common in adaptive versus non-adaptive cultures, as follows:

- *Adaptive cultures*. Customer focused, value people, value change and improvement, focus on needs of stakeholders.
- *Non-adaptive cultures*. Value orderly decisions and risk averse processes, silo mentality prevails.

How far we could take this argument is unclear but it does at least offer a prospect of culture change through incremental steps, initially seeking to move toward a positive culture rather than seeking to change the culture in one 'heave'.

CASE STUDY — Philips

As a case study we may examine Philips NV – Operation Centurion. From 1990 onwards Philips has sought to transform itself as a business. The company has tried hard both to build current performance and to become more innovative. Combining cascade communications with taskforces working on a range of issues deemed important to the →

future success of the business, the company has attempted to engender a sense of urgency about the need for dramatic change. Also much attention has been paid to the need to create new values based on trust, openness and honesty. Early on it was recognized that culture change cannot be achieved without fundamental change to how the business operates. Projects have been used to change the way people manage. However, it is also recognized that mind-set change lies at the core of the needed changes. In particular, the attempt to create a new and shared mind-set requires attention to creating a sense of urgency, opening minds to what the competition is doing but most of all focusing effort on action projects which can have an impact on the business and which over time may lead to the growth of solidarity.

Here we see an attempt to use changed behaviour as the basic building block of culture change. In summary, the new behaviour includes cascade communications, dialogue across all levels of the business, cross-boundary working, a new focus on asset management, benchmarking and so on. Not least of Philips' ambition is to reinvent its culture to emphasize behaviour such as risk-taking, creativity, etc.

Managing corporate politics

We have now seen that achieving change requires us to manage effectively in circumstances which include problems of organizational culture, organizational politics and the need to help people to cope with the pressures and anxieties created. All this creates great uncertainty. In this chapter, we extend our discussion by looking at the politics of change and how they can be managed.

Before commencing this task there is one point which deserves emphasis. Changes in organizations are rarely, if ever, neat. One can rarely identify a clear starting point or a clear end. The trends and pressures to which we respond are ongoing. Discussion moves forward at varying speeds and in different arenas. There is nothing new under the sun! The ideas incorporated in any particular change will have been considered elsewhere, for other purposes, by other people. Thus it is that organizational change is more process (and muddy process at that) than event.

To organize our discussion of the use of political skills in the management of change I present a simple model in Table 17.1. Managers and others utilize a variety of resources as they engage in the politics of organization. They may have formal authority (or may be perceived as having such) by virtue of their positions in the organization. Moreover, they may have direct control over resources. The use of resources to negate change efforts is widely observed. If a change programme needs engineering resources, and if the engineering manager can withhold those resources (perhaps by claiming that other priorities must prevail), then the change programme will be delayed.

Control of information, agenda and access are all important political resources. It is commonplace to state that 'information is power'. This applies in two main senses: power to control the organization internally, and power in regard to the development of policies for the future. Control over the organization is essential for control over policy. This point is made eloquently by Henry

Table 17.1 Political skills and the management of change

Resources	Process	Form
Formal authority	Negotiation	Politics of:
Control of resources	Influencing	Budgets
Control of information	Mobilizing support	Careers
Control of agenda	Mobilizing bias	Succession
Control of access symbols	Use of emotion	Information
	Ceremony and ritual	Organizational structures
	Professional 'mystery'	Appraisal

Kissinger (1979) when he discusses the new role that Nixon and he had agreed for the National Security Council at the beginning of Nixon's first term:

> A President should not leave the presentation of his options to one of the Cabinet departments, or agencies. Since the views of the departments are often in conflict, to place one in charge of presenting the options will be perceived by the others as giving it an unfair advantage. Moreover, the strong inclination of all departments is to narrow the scope for Presidential decision, not to expand it. They are organised to develop a preferred policy, not a range of choices. If forced to present options, the typical department will present two absurd alternatives as straw men bracketing its preferred option – which usually appears in the middle position. A totally ignorant decision-maker could easily satisfy his departments by blindly choosing Option 2 of any three choices which they submit to him. Every department, finally, dreads being overruled by the President, all have, therefore, a high incentive to obscure their differences. Options tend to disappear in an empty consensus that at the end of the day

We have already noted that Deal and Kennedy (1982) define corporate culture as encompassing how people in a company are likely to act in given situations both inside and outside the organization. It includes a set of beliefs, a code of behaviour and minimum standards of performance and ethics. It will influence service quality and the way in which people are treated, whether customers or clients.

Deal and Kennedy go on to argue that organizations with 'strong' cultures (i.e. clearly identifiable) are likely to be more effective, basing the conclusion on evidence collected on 80 or so corporations in the USA. They believe that a strong corporate culture comprises the following key features:

- *Characteristic and clear approach* to the corporate environment – markets, clients, stakeholders and so on.

- *Values* – shared by the people who make up the organization.

- *Heroes* – people who represent and communicate these values, people who provide others with 'role models'.

- *Rites and rituals* – systems and procedures which it is expected that people will follow.

■ *Networks* – the informal means of communication often known as the 'grapevine'.

A strong culture is one in which people may have a clearer idea of what is required of them, a clearer sense of the objectives being pursued. Following Itami (1987), it is an important 'invisible asset'. Organizations with weak cultures may be less effective, less productive and less satisfying places in which to work.

If all this is true can we then change the corporate culture? This is what is being attempted at International Engineering, for example. The evidence suggests that one can change a corporate culture, but only slowly and through sustained effort and hard work.

Deal and Kennedy (1982) conclude that an attempt at corporate culture change can only be justified where any or all of the following various conditions apply:

■ Where the environment is undergoing fundamental change (say, in healthcare or banking).

■ Where the industry is highly competitive and the environment is characterized by rapid and often turbulent change (e.g. the computer industry).

■ Where the organization is growing rapidly, particularly where the organization is becoming very large.

■ Where performance has been in sustained decline.

In such conditions sustained changes to attitudes and behaviour will be essential. New 'role models' will be needed; new management styles will be emerging. The 'lists' of change are such that people will need to understand why the changes are needed. Deal and Kennedy identify the following guidelines for those engaging in culture changes; these are worth examining:

■ Peer group consensus will have an important influence on acceptance of change. Typically, people do not feel strongly opposed to a given change. However, social ties can be such that resistance to change can build within social groupings and networks. It is important to build support within these networks.

■ It is important to convey and build on trust in communication and in how problems are handled.

■ Changes need to be treated as opportunities within which to build skills and develop people.

■ Allow enough time for changed behaviour to become the norm. This point is often ignored, with naïve estimates of how much time is needed.

Encourage people to adopt new approaches, new behaviour patterns and new systems to match their needs more effectively and these can be built on. Stronger relationships and a more open decision-making style will be a better basis for dealing with the ongoing conflicts of views and ideas which will inevitably exist.

Conflict and organizational politics are inevitable. Moreover, both are likely to be heightened during a period of change. The Philips case study summarizes one example of how it is possible to develop a more open approach to management. The purpose is not to avoid conflict but, rather, to create a more open and collaborative approach in order that conflict and politics can be handled constructively. That is not to say that this always happens. Often, individuals (or even coalitions of individuals) and departments pursue narrow interests. This seems to be inevitable and even desirable. Without it people might lack the energy to argue, question, put forward ideas and so on. What is needed is a credible way of moving forward amidst conflict. As we have already suggested, it seems likely that longer-term credibility and organizational effectiveness flow from the ability to establish a more balanced, constructive approach to conflict.

Leadership and corporate politics

The style and approach of the finance function is to be changed and this demands leadership, partly to 'sell' the ideas throughout the function; partly to provide 'role models' for other staff, i.e. leading through example; partly to manage the relationships between finance and other functions. No matter how gradually the changes are made, people from other functions will recognize the different approach and may exploit the new situation. Years of low trust and interdepartmental conflict leave a legacy.

The task of the leader in this situation is multi-faceted. We shall be dealing with leadership, but because of the obvious relationships between leadership, the constructive management of conflict, corporate politics and power I will deal with these aspects briefly.

Few, if any, prescriptions for effective leadership can be offered. Leadership has been linked to individual traits (e.g. intelligence and charisma) and to specific types of behaviour (e.g. focus on the tasks, focus on the people). Currently, much attention is devoted to contingency approaches to leadership, which link effective leadership to features of the situation in which leaders and others operate, such as technology, organizational structure, the environment, characteristics and needs of subordinates, etc. This approach leads us to suggest that leadership style should be varied to meet the varying circumstances in which leaders lead.

Effective leadership is an elusive concept. In practice, it is also difficult to determine the criteria underpinning effective leadership. It is clearly linked to power. The following concepts seek to identify the following five social bases of power:

1 *Legitimate power*: deriving from the manager's position and therefore formal authority.

2 *Expert power*: deriving from the knowledge and experience of the individual (thus a doctor can influence the patient's behaviour because he or she exerts expert power when giving advice).

3 *Referent power*: deriving from the ways in which people identify with others (often involves a charismatic individual).

4 *Reward power*: deriving from the individual's control over rewards such as pay, promotion and task assignments.

5 *Coercive power*: deriving from the capacity to sanction individual behaviour.

Thus power is not simply a matter of position; people appear to vary in their motives for power and can thus exert personal power. Power is inherent in bargaining, negotiation and political processes. The effective use of power is central to effective management and leadership. Kotter (1978) suggests that individuals who make effective use of power are likely to possess the following characteristics:

- Be sensitive to what others consider to be legitimate behaviour acquiring and using power.
- Have good intuitive understanding of the various types of power and the methods of influence.
- Tend to develop all the types of power to some degree, and use all methods of influence.
- Establish career goals and seek out managerial positions that allow them to develop and use power successfully.
- Use all resources, formal authority and power to develop more power.
- Engage in power-orientated behaviour in ways that are tempered by maturity and self-control.
- Recognize and accept as a legitimate fact that, in using these methods, they clearly influence other people's behaviour and lives.

Coping with conflict

What can managers do to cope with conflict? We can look at this question by considering first what a middle manager can and cannot do, what top managers can do directly and how top managers can support implementation indirectly.

Some things that managers cannot do much about

Decision making is neither a rational nor an orderly process

This is particularly so in periods of change, characterized as they are by uncertainty and involvement of emotions. We now know a considerable amount about the process of decision making, enough to know that a wide range of individual, group and organizational factors can affect the process (see Janis and Mann, 1976; Hickson *et al.*, 1986). Selective perception, uncertainty, organizational politics and time pressures are but some of these factors. Moreover, decisions are not discrete events; they are fluid. A group of people 'decide' but in implementation the decision is often modified, scaled down or delayed. Decisions have both intentional and unintentional consequences. These may occur rapidly and the latter may lead to changes to the original decision. Decisions are part of a 'stream of decisions', connected either directly or indirectly, because they are part of the same programme or project or because implementation demands that those involved compete for scarce resources. Add to this the tendency of many to dissociate themselves from failure and we begin to get a picture of the real-life complexity involved.

CASE
STUDY ## Oticon

Oticon, the Danish manufacturer of hearing aids which we came across in the case study in Chapter 10 (page 167), is famous for having created 'the Spaghetti organization' through which it seeks to create new ways of working in pursuit of innovation and reduced time to market. It has a record of substantially improved financial performance since restructuring in the early 1990s.

In the midst of a turnaround strategy begun in 1989–90 a proposal came forward to relocate head office to western Denmark so that it would be located with Oticon's principal factory. The new design provided for appealing working conditions, paperless offices and so on. There was considerable opposition. Eventually this change was not forced through over the opposition of staff. At the same time top management pressed forward with the reorganization plan – once staff were settled into the new head office the change was widely publicized in the press, on television and eventually on CNN. Was this about creating a sense that there could be 'no turning back'? To what extent was all of this about managing perceptions? To what extent was the concession on location as much about recognizing that some battles are not worth fighting and that ensuring that people felt engaged in the process and *listened to* was important in focusing attention on the future? If change requires that new routines be accepted and problems be solved, then a platform of high self-esteem is needed. To what extent is the management of the politics of change about managing perceptions and expectations to that end?

CASE
STUDY ## Union Carbide and the Bhopal disaster

On 3 December 1984 a cloud of deadly gas was released into the atmosphere around the Union Carbide Corporation's pesticide plant in Bhopal, India. With a death toll of over 1200 people, and many more injured, this was the world's worst industrial accident.

On the other side of the world, in Connecticut USA, Union Carbide managers faced the prospect of coping with the disaster. A complex set of issues had to be dealt with quickly: how to establish the cause; how to ensure it could not be repeated; how to help the victims; relief agencies; how to reassure investors; how to control the issue of legal liability; what to announce.

With only two telephone lines into Bhopal and the plant supervisors under arrest, hard information was difficult to come by. Much of the information coming through seemed barely credible.

Hellreigel *et al.* (1986) quote this as a case of complex decision making. They describe it as a convoluted action process because of the following four points:

1 The nature of the problem was unstructured – the managers had never faced a disaster of this magnitude before.

2 The problem will go on for years – litigation alone is likely to continue over a period of years.

3 Many vested interests were involved – the company, the Indian government, the USA, the heirs of the dead, the injured and the shareholders of the company.

→

4 Many people were involved in different ways – to fix responsibility, report the story, compensate victims, avoid repetition of this type of accident and look at the future of the Bhopal plant.

In this process all manner of trade-offs, bargains, compromises, misunderstandings and conflicts were likely.

Conflicting demands

In a world in which resources are finite, there will always be conflicting demands for resources, attention or priority. Moreover, it seems likely that managers and others will be in conflict over the goals to be pursued and the means of use. Finally, disagreement will have both cognitive and emotional dimensions. While conflict can be a positive force for change, the first point to note about it is that it cannot be (and indeed should not be) eliminated. For example, in the Bhopal disaster described in the case study it was always clear that the demands of victims, the governments concerned and the company would be in conflict – the interests were so different.

Uncertainty

This point hardly needs emphasizing. We live in an uncertain world. Managers must necessarily deal with uncertainty.

Bias

Again, the point hardly needs emphasis. We all have incomplete perceptions and stereotyped attitudes, and this can lead us to adopt biased views. Moreover, departmental as well as personal bias needs to be considered. The different departments reflect the concerns and views of that department, which are not necessarily a corporate view.

External forces

The changes in markets, technologies and legal frameworks external to the organization need to be dealt with by managers. While companies can set out to influence these external factors by lobbying, advertising and so on, they tend to be insurmountable at any given time.

■ Some things that top and middle managers can do

If these are the things managers can do little about, what are the things *that managers can do*?

1 They can *choose the problems to work on*, the battles to fight, when to act and when to wait. Timing can be an important skill (see below).

2 They can develop a broad and detailed *knowledge of the organization, its clients or customers and its people*. Knowledge is power.

3 They can try to *develop their own self-awareness*. What are my strengths and weaknesses? What do I wish to achieve? What does all this tell me about 1 and 2, but about 1 in particular?

4 They can set out to *develop their own skills* in order better to influence others.

Set and sustain values

By setting appropriate values top management can influence people throughout the organization. The chief executive of International Engineering constantly discussed, communicated and supported people working towards a more commercial set of values for the company. The traditional values of engineering excellence were insufficient as a basis for meeting increased and global competition.

Support problem solving and risk

Once again taking the example of International Engineering, here we had a low-risk-taking culture, an engineering culture which had been managed in a fairly authoritarian way and in which the operations department dominated, and had reinforced the 'fear of failure' very powerfully indeed. People were afraid to take risks because the price of failure was known to be high. Directly or indirectly, people who 'failed' felt that they were being punished. Typically, this was carried out by assigning them poor jobs on 'low-profile' work or projects. Such assignments have a powerful impact on career, promotion, job interest and even pay. This was a 'reality' that many managers were not prepared to face. After 10 to 15 years of that style of management, present-day senior managers bemoan the fact that managerial succession is a problem. Why so? It is clear how that came to be. Under the circumstances described, the better people try, fail and leave.

Design systems to support action

The most important thing is to get on and do things; to get action. Only then can people try out new ideas, learn and develop. Pilot schemes can allow for this approach. Reporting systems should be designed to encourage it. The attention of managers should focus on action. Plans, targets and milestones should be clearly defined and consistent with a well-understood longer-term strategy.

Q: How do you eat an elephant?
A: In slices.

Focus on the manageable

The excellent is the enemy of the good. Managers rarely start from an ideal position and rarely have enough time, resources or knowledge about what they either can or should do. Thus it is crucial to focus on manageable issues. Managers can communicate these to their own people; they will be credible and will support action and progress. It is important to have and to articulate a clear longer-term vision. But people need to work out how *they* are going to get there.

In an uncertain world managers cannot be everywhere

They must rely on others. This means that they must create opportunities to help people develop. *They need to support learning and development.*

Spend time on the problem/project

There is no better way of focusing attention, effort and energy in support of change than by top management devoting time. This needs to be done carefully. Top managers should provide support, interest and resources. They should not interfere because this will demonstrate lack of trust in the manager on the spot.

This is a difficult balance to draw because to ignore change may well be taken as a signal of low priority.

Interpret the traditions of the organization around the new systems, procedures and solutions

Give powerful emphasis to how the traditions of the organization support and are sustained by changes. I work for a business school which pioneered distance learning in management education in Europe. One of the school's key traditions has always been its concern to deliver and establish learning situations which meet the needs of course members, in a practical way. Throughout the early development of distance learning, the need to design the new material on this principle was always paramount. Also emphasized was the idea that distance learning was a practicable and flexible means of providing management education to the large numbers of managers who never attend business schools. The rapid growth of distance learning clearly demonstrates that this was not because the managers had no need or desire for management training. For us the point is to note how the traditions of the school were linked to the development of new systems for delivering management education.

Manage the timing effectively

Managing the timing of change is very important. A number of considerations apply. How much expertise does the organization possess? The more established the necessary knowledge and expertise, the quicker will be the changes. To what extent is there opposition? How powerful is it and what control does it have over resources and decision making? Are other significant changes likely? If change creates disruption, then it is worth looking at how to time various changes so that they occur together. Managing the timing to manage the stresses induced also deserves attention to balance this latter point. Finally, attention must be given to logistics, resources and other commitments. We tend to underestimate the time, resources and energy needed to achieve change. More attention to these issues is invaluable, particularly if realism prevails.

Managing corporate politics

Managing the politics of change requires us to consider the interests of the various groups involved in the changes, but it also requires much more than that. Ultimately, it involves us in finding ways of making sense of the 'booming, blooming confusion' around us. Creating effective organizations is not about eliminating corporate politics. There is too much uncertainty for that to be feasible. It is about finding principles of action which allow politics and conflicts to be handled constructively and thus harnessed for corporate change.

Conclusion

The culture and the politics of any organization are both distinctive and important. Without understanding both it is much more difficult to predict the outcomes of any action or intervention as a leader or manager. Thus both need to be considered during attempts to achieve change. In this chapter we have considered the most influential work on corporate culture and examined a means of analysing corporate politics. Can corporate culture be changed? 'Only in the long term' seems to be the most likely answer to that question. Can we therefore ignore the culture? Only at the peril of seeking to introduce changes that are more likely to fail.

EXERCISES

1 What core competencies will be important for Philips NV in the next five years?

2 Do corporate politics play a positive role in change?

3 How would you characterize the culture of your organization? What implications does this carry for successful organizational change?

4 Refer back to the KPMG case study in Chapter 1 (page 9). How did KPMG set about changing the corporate culture?

18 Strategic convergence: a new model for organization change

Introduction

This chapter introduces a new model for strategic change. The model seeks to develop the concept of change architecture into a practical model for change management. In particular, the model starts from the assumption that any serious model of change must take account of the reality of multiple and concurrent change.

The outline model here takes as a starting point the idea that the more ambitious the change the more likely it is to be successful so long as a robust change architecture is in place. Two immediate qualifications are needed. First, we assume that change proposals with insufficient ambition fail before they start because they do not meet the challenges faced by the organization. Second, we accept as a general point that it is possible to propose changes which are overly ambitious and which fail in consequence. As a general rule our position is that changes more often fail because senior managers have not willed the means to success. However, we do need to provide for the possibility that the proposed changes were not feasible. We will see that such a judgement is in practice often quite controversial, not least because if I suggest a particular change is not feasible, is that because I wish to resist that change?

In reality, change models have tended to duck these issues focusing mostly on leader behaviour and the level of stakeholder engagement (both important issues) devoting little or no attention to either the inherent quality of the decisions, underpinning assumptions or intended means of implementation as articulated in change plans, nor to the level of ambition involved. Given the possibility of controversy it appears that generating an adequate change model will require us to be able to assess both the decisions and the level of ambition independently of stakeholder views. Unless we do so we cannot triangulate stakeholder views.

Yet managers find themselves facing the need to handle complex and challenging changes often imposed on them from either a higher level in a large international organization, or as a consequence of political choice and new legislation in the public service. In these situations it is just not enough to argue that leadership, team building, communication and involvement of colleagues provides a sufficient

326

basis for designing and managing big changes. Each of them is important. They are necessary conditions for successful change but in themselves they are not sufficient. This is why practitioners and researchers in the change management field are showing increased interest in project and programme management techniques and disciplines as a means of achieving higher levels of professionalism in change management in practice.

Finally, we need a model which helps us to identify what is planned and how those plans are intended to be achieved but also enables us to ask how effectively those implementation arrangements are being handled. Take a simple example. During an interview with a senior executive in a large organization engaged in a major reconfiguration of service delivery it became clear that governance of the planned changes was being handled by a newly constituted change board. But when I explored the powers of that board I found that it could only refer an issue of difficulty to the executive board and that several members of the executive board claimed not to understand the principles behind the proposed reconfiguration. Whatever the real explanation (and that is likely to be complex) the immediate point here is that governance is unclear. We cannot possibly understand that through merely observing that a governance process is in place. That must be followed by looking at how clear and how effective those processes are in practice.

The imperatives of professionalism, specialization, scale, geography and delivery to customers require those managing corporate organizations to divide them up. Thereby directorates, divisions, groups, units, 'strategic business units' and 'spin-offs' are created. In practice this is further complicated by the many 'partnerships', joint ventures, out-sourcing relationships, etc. so characteristic of modern conditions. Thus the management of change requires the 'management of boundaries' both internal and external. Vital to this is an established process of reporting, accountability and decision which is positioned such that governance of changes can be effective in terms of the ability to influence and call to account all those engaged in the change process. In practice, therefore, we seek to establish whether change is structured effectively. All stakeholders need to be engaged, made aware of their contribution to the changes, aware of the processes of reporting, have access to that process and be capable of being called to account within that process. This is partly a question of the structuring of the change implementation process but partly to do with how that change implementation process is handled within the context of the organization itself, looking at the capability of the organization to handle change, focusing on issues such as culture and leadership among others.

To that end the model comprises three stages. First, we ask how ambitious the change plan is. Next, we seek to identify whether a number of key components of change architecture are in place. Finally, we look at how effectively those components operate through looking at structure, positioning and at various behavioural and/or cognitive aspects. The core of the approach is an aspiration to achieve a better balance between the decision–action sequences which are the core of change plans and the behavioural dimensions.

The model is shown in outline in Figure 18.1. It comprises the linked ideas of ambition and change architecture, in effect proposing that an ambitious change

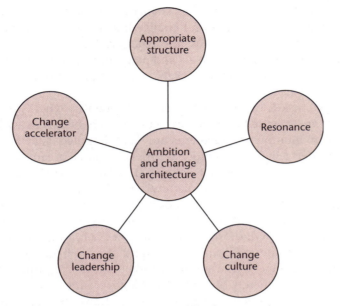

Figure 18.1 **The change capability framework**

and appropriately comprehensive change architecture, while needed for success in change, are nevertheless insufficient of themselves. What matters is how the change architecture is operated and whether certain performance characteristics of change architecture are being established. These performance characteristics are grouped into five dimensions, namely appropriate structure, resonance, change culture, change leadership and change accelerator. I propose a series of questions to address any change situation in order to assess the change capability of the organization involved. This leads to the establishment of a change capability framework (see Figure 18.1 and the appendix on page 336).

Ambition in change

At one level this cannot be defined absolutely. The level of ambition must always be relative. Relative to 'need', where need is socially defined. True enough, but where expenditure, market or competitive pressures apply there exist some pretty compelling definitions of need. But we are also concerned to ask if a given set of change plans and objectives are achievable. What does that mean? Achievable given current skills, capabilities and resources? Or achievable given the organization's ability to fill gaps in its profile of the aforementioned?

Defined relative to 'need' even where the latter is imposed by political leaders . . . but note that corporate leaders are just as likely to impose cuts in order to reshape a business in view of current market size, market share and revenues and in practice are not free of the need to ensure income flows for the organization. Thus, in practice, changes can be imposed in any organization.

We can also define ambition in relation to former achievements. So a given set of change objectives may outstrip any attempted in the past. This clearly can present a challenge to the organization and its people. But does it? What if the past saw little change? What if competitors are not engaged in transformational or breakthrough change? What if political leaders are not pressing on with rapid change? In the current era none of these statements seem likely to be true on the face of it, but there is a kernel of truth here. We need a definition of ambition which goes beyond the relativist position because only with such a definition can we judge ambition on a reasonably consistent basis. Of course, any definition will certainly be socially constructed . . . our point here is that we seek a means to avoid accepting the view of those directly involved merely at face value.

In most cases ambition is also defined relative to what competitor organizations are or seem likely to achieve. This is one level of benchmarking. Another is to take a particular category of activity in the organization and then judge ambition in comparison to 'best in class', comparing an organization to its equivalents elsewhere or comparing it to the world's best, always assuming you can identify either.

With this in mind we propose that ambition can be recognized by various characteristics. Just as you can recognize an 'old master' by characteristics of composition, brushwork and so on, so can we recognize an ambitious programme of change by the extent to which we can identify the presence of the following characteristics:

- *Creative destruction*. To what extent are existing infrastructure, departments, and activities being taken out to enable a significant shift of resources towards new priorities?
- *Distinctive value*. To what extent are the changes planned judged likely to deliver a clear and distinct growth in the value of the business or in the organization's activity?
- *Distinctive operational efficiency*. To what extent are the changes planned judged likely to deliver clear and distinct operational efficiencies?
- *Integration*. To what extent does the change planning/implementation process depend on the integration of internal and/or external knowledge sources about the organization, its clients, its market space, competitors and so on? Are processes in place to do so? Are we engaged in internal and external benchmarking for example?
- *Simultaneous change*. Can we observe many changes going on concurrently?

To repeat, any definition of ambition based on the above ideas is socially constructed . . . not least because stakeholder judgements will often be involved. But some of the above is observable and therefore we have the prospect of triangulation based in part on observable data, rather than on the various views of those stakeholders.

Components of change architecture

Here I simply argue that arrangements need to be in place to achieve certain tasks common to any typical change programme. Again we can observe whether or not they are in place as a first step. These components are as follows:

- Engagement of the top team.
- A steering process is devised to ensure effective leadership and governance.

- A process exists for integrating 'work streams'.

- Appropriate work streams are defined, tasked, constituted and resourced.

- Any needed infrastructure enablers are in place.

- A human resources transition policy and process is in place.

- Support for implementation planning and activities are provided from within operational and other departments.

Of course, judgements about the extent to which these components are in place are again socially constructed but nevertheless observational methods can give some triangulation. Initially we are concerned only to assess whether a comprehensive architecture has been established.

Performance characteristics of change architecture

We now turn to what I call the performance characteristics of the change architecture. We need to go beyond a 'tick box' approach, merely identifying whether a particular component is in place, to looking at how effectively each operates. It is one thing to have a system in place, quite another to operate it effectively. We start by observing that this is the most controversial part of the change management field because there are no final answers to the central question which concerns us. How can we balance the provision of sufficient structure with the necessary freedom to allow local level responsiveness to particular circumstances? Structure ensures alignment, common language and frameworks. Freedoms allow people, operating in the often quite different circumstances as compared to other colleagues, the 'space' to implement changes in ways responsive to those needs.

In looking at these various characteristics in more detail we seek to establish whether a given change programme can be delivered in an organization. In effect we seek to make a judgement about the *change capability* of that organization, looking at both its normal systems and behaviour where relevant and at the arrangements it puts in place to handle change. It is one thing to have a change implementation plan in place, it is quite another to operate it effectively. Our starting point is the observation that this is probably the most problematic and controversial part of the change management field. This is because there are no definitive answers to the central question. How can we provide sufficient structure to give effect to changes while allowing the necessary freedoms to allow local determination in response to particular conditions? And obviously, the more ambitious the plan the more likely is this a difficult balance to strike in practice. Structure to ensure alignment, common language and frameworks, and the sense to change is directed towards a greater set of purposes than those reflected locally. Freedoms to allow people, operating in often quite different circumstances to others, the scope to meet local needs without compromising the integrity of the plan overall.

Ensuring appropriate structure

Here we are looking at whether particular management processes are in place, at how effectively they are deployed as part of 'business as usual' and at how well they are operated in support of change. Specifically we look at the following processes:

- *Performance management.* Most significant organizations have performance management systems in place. These typically comprise some mix of budgets, monthly reporting, KPI's, balanced scorecards, performance appraisals, etc. The real question is how well are they operated? There is a long list of studies showing that the answer here is not particularly positive. Often poor performance is not explored, challenged and resolved. Also we need to look at how well the measures used to track a change programme are integrated into the performance management framework in place. In turn we need to know whether the change objectives have been defined, and if they are measurable in the first place.

- *Governance.* This relates to the arrangements in place regarding accountability for change. Poorly managed changes are often characterized by unclear accountabilities. In turn we observe behaviour which appears to be indifferent to the achievement of intended outcomes. People suggest that change is out of their control. 'What can you do?' cry some. 'Resistance is inevitable' say others. But a robust governance arrangement will define board-level accountability for change and for benefits realization, programme management structures and processes, and reporting arrangements.

- *Risk management.* Naturally our concern here relates to assessing risk both in terms of change outcomes but also in terms of the risk of disruption associated with implementing change. Simply put, does the organization both assess those risks and provide appropriate risk mitigation strategies?

- *Unintended consequences.* In effect a special case of risk but deserving of separate treatment. Here we seek to assess whether the decision process associated with any set of change initiatives has taken a thorough look at all possible consequences of any proposed changes.

Resonance

Here we are building on the ideas of Gardner (2004) and Kelman (2005). In his recent book, *Changing Minds*, Gardner defines resonance (of an attempt to change someone's mind) as relating to the affective component of the human mind. An idea, view or perspective resonates to the extent that it feels 'right' to individuals, seems to fit the situation and the prevailing need and therefore convinces people that further consideration is not needed. While ideas gain resonance often because there is evidence to support them and/or because the proponent of the idea is credible, nevertheless the concept is more than an idea based on rational judgement. It allows for an affective component. In the model we seek to judge resonance in the following terms:

■ *Felt need*: the extent to which change proposals respond to the felt needs of key stakeholders. We are interested in both organizational level and local needs, problems and issues.

■ *Convergence*: the extent to which change initiatives are convergent or mutually reinforcing in terms of purpose, objectives and consequences.

■ *Adaptability*: the extent to which the implementation of proposals allows sufficient scope for local-level response to need or circumstances as experienced in the locality concerned.

■ *Willingness to experiment*: the extent to which the implementation process is explicit about the need to experiment with solutions and learn from experience.

■ *Customer primacy*: the extent to which the proposals will provide for needed developments of customer service/delivery.

Change culture

In many ways the most complex of issues because the word 'culture' covers variations in national, occupational, organizational and often local belief systems about appropriate ways of operating and about behaviour. For our purposes we are setting to one side national, and to some extent occupational, variation in pursuit of a simpler model to guide our analysis of change in a particular organizational setting. In doing so note this as a key limitation of the model. There is no doubt that a fuller treatment of these issues would be needed to allow for a comprehensive analysis of multinational organizations. Also we are clear that occupational aspects will need to be examined in some cases. For example, we would certainly need to deploy an understanding of occupational variation when looking at a hospital for example, or at, say, regiments in the British army or particular departments of central government, law firms and many others. That said, no other change model deals with these issues comprehensively and this model provides a more comprehensive treatment than existing models in any event. We examine change culture as follows:

■ *Evidence-based leadership*. This is a development of the 'willingness to experiment' idea above. Here we ask the extent to which, in general, leaders are prepared to learn from experience, codify that learning and thereby build on it. To what extent is the organization a 'learning organization'?

■ *Informed choice*. In essence this bears on the credibility of decisions for change. In part it relates to the extent to which choice and decision making is based on valid data. To the extent that judgement, experience, insight and intuition is involved it is about the extent to which this is clear, unavoidable and undertaken by those who are trusted to do so. We are, therefore, really looking at whether an authentic process of decision making is in place. If so, then stakeholders will perceive decisions as necessary, timely and appropriate.

- *Problem orientation.* Is management a search for a solution or a search for the guilty? In the event of problems and setbacks, is the organization likely to be focused on blame or on how to progress? Cultures are problem-oriented to the extent that activity and effort is constructive and focused on solutions and achievement rather than failure and blame.

- *Transparency.* Nothing is more likely to encourage a problem orientation than greater transparency of process. 'Blame cultures' thrive in secrecy and obscurity.

- *Management of expectations.* People respond to expectations of change as much as to change itself. Predictions about 'what's in it for me?' will abound, as will fears or enthusiasms about the demands and opportunities in the new ways of working created by the proposed changes. For example, faced with a proposal for 'downsizing' people will conclude that those who remain will have to work harder. Even so, many will predict that others will not be affected. In the absence of hard information people will predict consequences and those predictions will reflect existing stereotypes, including views about who wins and who loses. So here we are looking at the extent to which expectations are provided for in terms of the provision of information about impact and of a process in which they are to be engaged to work on developing new jobs and so on.

Change leadership

Leadership cannot be examined other than as an interactive process. Leaders must have 'followers' so, logically, if we are to understand change leadership we need to say something about followers. One of the limitations of many models of change is that each 'stakeholder' group is treated as if it could be considered as a homogenous group in the context of change. In this model we seek to go beyond that simplification by relying on the diffusion of innovation literature (essentially the work of Rogers (1995)) identifying four categories of responses to change within any group impacted by a given change. There are early and late adopters, to make a simple distinction. The early adopters are likely to be more venturesome, more able to cope with ambiguity, uncertainty and risk. They are also more likely to be 'well adjusted' in the organization. Most interestingly, research by Kelman (2005) shows that 'most respected co-workers' are most influential with peers once the initial case for change has been made, just when we are seeking to consolidate and deepen change implementation. One role for leaders during this deepening period of change is that of providing support and 'cover' to people seeking to come to terms with the changes, including working out the problems and local solutions in order to reach a sensible outcome at local level. Rather than specify the solution in rigid detail it is better to encourage local-level problem solving led by the most respected co-workers, supported by local leaders with senior leaders focused on the overall integrity of design and on the intended outcomes. Down that route lies the possibility of a sense of 'ownership'.

Moreover, the sponsorship of those 'most respected co-workers' group by group as 'early adopters' would become a key leadership task. Not that all will respond.

But that is not the point. If we can identify respected group members who will embrace change, sponsorship of them to be engaged early in the change process and to get early training, may pay dividends later in terms of problem solving, ownership and the desired attitude changes. Thus one key task of the 'senior leader' is to work with 'local' leaders to identify people along these lines and then encourage their engagement in the change process. Later it is to provide support and 'cover' to the group as it adjusts to the new situation.

Now setting out the change leadership idea in detail:

- *Credibility*: the extent to which the leader has a successful track record of change management experience.
- *Visibility*: the extent to which the leader has been and is still accessible to people.
- *Learning orientation*: the extent to which leaders display an orientation to be open to new ideas and to learning.
- *Sponsoring early adopters*: the extent to which leaders sponsor and support early adopters.
- *Organizational slack*: the extent to which leaders can buy time for problems to be resolved, while providing people with 'cover' as they adjust to change and adjust the new arrangements to local conditions.
- *Encourage learning through change*: building on the above, the extent to which leaders use change as an opportunity for learning within their teams, partly by coaching but also by the leadership practices just identified. That is the extent to which leaders encourage learning through change.

Accelerator effect

In a sense this category represents a recognition that we need to view change management as a special case of programme management. We need to identify whether or not project and programme management tools and processes are in use. More to the point, we need to understand whether these tools are used to focus on the particular needs of change situations, as follows:

- *Connectivity*. Here we refer to the extent to which change initiatives are connected explicitly to existing organizational processes. One example could be performance management processes. To what extent are the measures of success engineered into the existing performance management system? Another might relate to IT infrastructure. Another might relate to reward systems.
- *Leverage*. This relates to the extent to which change initiatives are managed appropriately, particularly regarding timing to ensure that those designed as 'platforms' to be in place before others can be implemented are taken forward to delivery in good time. Also, leverage derives out of the effective programme management of a portfolio of initiatives to create impetus, energy for change and a sense of purpose and momentum. Each initiative will need to be co-ordinated with others. As we indicate, platform initiatives must precede others which depend upon them. But all initiatives use resources and conflict over resources will often need resolving through a process of prioritization.

■ *Integration*. Here we mean the effective management of initiatives as an overall portfolio with a set of overall objectives in view. Also known as a 'solutions' approach, we are seeking to assess the extent to which the management of change takes an integrated view of objectives and purposes.

■ *Critical mass*. The result of high levels of connectivity, leverage and integration but, in particular, a perception of confidence in outcomes flowing from the degree of coherence in the overall design of the change programme and of the levels of engagement of key stakeholders.

A framework for assessing capability to change

The balance between appropriate structure and local determinism represents both a tension between central control of change and local autonomy, and tension between strategy, ambition and centrally determined objectives and emergent or organic change. The framework will need to take this into account as part of the judgement of organizational change capability.

The logical thinking behind the framework may be summarized as follows. The more ambitious the change the more likely it is of success given the operation of a robust change architecture achieving high levels of the characteristics described above. However, this holds only if the benefits sought are both delivered via that change architecture and outweigh the costs of change, including the likely destabilization of the organization. But note that the change architecture provides directly for that risk management issue to be addressed.

It follows that we need to consider the rate of change being attempted. Are we looking at radical, or so-called 'big bang', changes or is a more incremental approach envisaged. In reality this forms part of the judgement about the level of ambition in change but just as obviously radical change demands more of all stakeholders. Actually it may be that the more important distinction is between imposed change and those developed within the organization. There may well be more to do in the definition of the level of ambition in change with these distinctions in mind, but at the moment the approach seems sufficient. In any event the managerial issue relates to making a judgement about whether the proposed changes are achievable and it is to that end that this model is proposed as a means of helping managers to handle major changes.

Using the questions shown in the appendix which follows, the model is deployed through assessing whether the five 'performance characteristics' of change architecture are sufficient to provide for the level of ambition in any given set of change proposals given that a comprehensive change architecture has been established. A robust change architecture is therefore defined as both comprehensive in scope and one which is operated to a high performance level as assessed through the performance characteristics. Each is important but each can be worked on in different ways and on different time horizons. Thus resonance and appropriate structure is about decision making. Resonance relates to the decisions being taken as part of the immediate change initiatives. Appropriate structure is rather longer term. It is about whether decisions around performance over time have been soundly based. However, some elements are more immediate, not least decisions relating to both governance and the analysis of consequences.

Similarly the change accelerator dimension derives from the quality of the design of the programme of change. These are immediate decisions. Conversely, change leadership and change culture are rather longer-term dimensions. The central point here is that some of the dimensions examined can be developed by decisions which can be made as part of the change programme design. In turn, getting those immediate choices right will help with some of the longer-term issues, for example getting change decisions right which have a high degree of resonance throughout the organization concerned will be likely to ease the management of expectations and build a perception of informed choice.

Conclusion

In summary then, establishing comprehensive change architecture is a first step when faced with ambitious change. Getting the immediate decisions right should be the next priority. These will vary across organizations and change situations but certainly the resonance of change proposals, change accelerator decisions and some aspects of leadership (for example the early briefing, training and engagement of 'early adopters') are each capable of immediate decision and often of local-level decision and action. Getting these 'change levers' understood and actioned can then create a positive impact on some of the longer-term leadership and culture issues. Does such an approach guarantee success? No, of course not, but it does seek to equip those involved with a framework within which decisions can be made, which will help. If, as a leader, I am told that to lead change successfully I must change my leadership style then that feedback may be valid and could help . . . but there is much that can and should be done immediately which will help, and thereby help me to feel positive about leadership style change. All too often managers go on a succession of leadership programmes without moving leadership forward because it is being viewed in isolation. Here we seek to provide tools to help people to use change programmes as a real opportunity to develop their own and others' leadership.

Appendix: The change capability framework

Ambition

Our plans are ambitious compared to the past

Our plans are ambitious compared to those of our competitors

Our plans will meet the changes demanded by our customers

Our plans require us to acquire new skills

Our plans require us to deploy new technology

Our plans require that we expand the existing resource base

Implementation will require us obtain knowledge we do not currently possess

Change requires simultaneous implementation of multiple initiatives

Our people believe that these changes are ambitious

Key stakeholders view these changes as a challenging agenda

We are shifting resources to new priorities

These changes offer distinctive value to the organization

These changes offer distinctive operational efficiency gains to the organization

Change architecture

To be comprehensive you would expect to see in place:

The top team is fully engaged

A steering process is in place

The steering process is led from within the top team

There is a process in place to coordinate 'work streams'

Work streams have been organized (defined, tasked, constituted and resourced)

An appropriate infrastructure is being provided (information and IT, training, advice and support)

An HR transition policy is in place

There is support for implementation in operational and other departments

Effective and two-way communication is in place

Ensuring appropriate structure

The organization has effective performance management systems and processes in place

Variations in performance are identified and measured in order to drive performance improvement

Management constantly seeks improved performance

There are well-defined project management arrangements in place for each change initiative

Management views each change initiative as part of a portfolio of change initiatives

There is clarity of accountability for benefits realization

Risks are identified and assessed

Risk mitigation is in place

Resonance

Changes are seen as meeting real problems

Changes meet customer needs

Change initiatives are mutually reinforcing

There are no obvious gaps in terms of platforms for change, preparation to achieve change or lack of alignment between change plans

Sufficient scope is available for local-level adaptation

Managers are open to learning as implementation proceeds

Changes are based on an understanding of customer needs

Changes are planned with local circumstances in mind

Customers are a key priority

Change culture

Decisions are based on facts and information

Senior managers learn from experience

There is a real attempt to learn from mistakes

Decisions are viewed as relevant

Decisions are viewed as timely

The organization seeks solutions

When things go wrong senior managers' focus on solutions rather than blame

Management processes are transparent

Employees are well informed of progress, performance and problems

Employees are involved and informed about changes

It is possible to judge how change will impact on people, jobs, roles and structures

Change leadership

Leaders are credible as people who achieve change

Leaders are involved with people as they seek to resolve problems with changes

Leaders see themselves as accountable for change outcomes

Leaders manage conflict constructively

Leaders manage colleagues' expectations constructively

Leaders are accessible

Leaders sponsor people to take the lead in their work groups

Leaders are open to new ideas

Leaders work with colleagues to help them to cope with change

Change accelerator

All those involved in change initiatives are aware of progress, problems and plans

It is possible to align existing systems and processes with change initiatives

Where intended, leverage between specific change initiatives is achieved

We are able to scale up initiatives to impact on the whole organization quickly

Change initiatives are effectively integrated

It is possible to see how change initiatives fit with broader organizational purposes and objectives

The organization achieves a critical mass of engagement of key stakeholders

This concludes the capability to change assessment but for completeness we include something on outcomes and on the organization.

Change outcomes

Most change initiatives fail

Changes in the past have often exceeded planned objectives

People are never really sure whether change delivers planned outcomes

Changes often overrun in terms of time and budget

Organizational background

Sector

Size

Rate of change in sector

Rate of change in organization

Strategies for corporate transformation

Introduction

Any book dealing with change needs to address the issue of transformation. The very nature of our organizations is being recreated. The command and control mind-set has been reformulated, albeit not necessarily to empower people. Oddly enough, while we increasingly seek to empower people with sufficient information and flexibility to allow them to resolve issues locally, this combines with other pressures in the opposite direction.

Supply chain pressures push the need for predictability in the process. Even a small business can be affected. Thus a small firm supplying timber to a national do-it-yourself chain such as Sainsbury Homebase (in the UK) or to manufacturers of furniture for IKEA must deliver 'right on time' and 'right first time' – by which is meant the right quantities of various sizes between, say, 8 and 9 p.m. on a set delivery day later in the week in which the weekly order arrived electronically over the previous weekend. Similarly structures based around the value-added concepts explained in Chapter 7 are more 'transparent'. There is no place to hide in the value-added organization.

Alongside these new pressures has come a recognition that planned change does not always deliver and that, in pursuit of rapid change and achieving shorter time-to-market lead times, market mechanisms have a role to play in creating more innovative and adaptable organizations. For many of the changes we need it is more effective to achieve change through creating the conditions for adaptability upfront. Increasingly, therefore, organizations seek to utilize 'market-induced' change.

'Market-induced' change

In essence 'market-induced' change is an organizational change strategy relying on ensuring that market pressures and changes are recognized early, and that those close to the marketplace are also influential over product–service decision making. Reuters is a good example.

| CASE STUDY | Reuters |

Reuters provides a broad range of information and news services for global markets. Formerly a newspaper news agency, it is part of a rapidly changing business sector experiencing rapid changes in technology, merging of formerly separable sectors (print, radio, video, information services), globalization of TV services including news in particular, new competitors and so on.

Clearly there is a need to manage creative people and creative *output*. Like many of its competitors it has sought to create a highly flexible and organic structure. It operates on the basis of 'front-line business units' supported by corporate control, dealing with finance, legal, tax, etc., and global supplies, offering marketing, development and operations support services.

In the business units, rapidly changing demands have meant that teams must be built and reformed rapidly. Decision making is widely dispersed and there are few levels in the structure. The demands of the task in hand take priority; there are few organizational rules other than those related to schedules and the technology in use. The issue is that of balancing the need for creativity against the need for structure, schedules, etc. Thus two points emerge from this case study. In rapidly changing markets, overly elaborate corporate structures can inhibit creativity and market responsiveness. Conversely, however, providers of information services must place high value on service reliability including availability. Thus *time*, from the client's perspective, is a key issue. Moreover, investment levels are often substantial and this latter point argues for planned change. One cannot justify and manage multi-million-dollar investments as market-induced changes. Thus balance between planned and market-induced models of change is very important.

However, this should not mislead us. We are discussing much more than structures and explicit planning models. The culture and style of the organizations are a much more important aspect for our purpose.

For example, McKinsey, the world-famous consultancy known as 'The Firm', is seen by some as the supreme example of networking. Access to key decision makers via interlocking networks of contacts and shared experiences is a pivotal resource. As an example of the value of discipline, reputation and access, it is a leading light. But still we must explore the point about discipline. What has been one of the oft-quoted models of change in the last 10 or 15 years – the McKinsey 7S Model, which comprises systems, structure, style, strategy, skills, staff and superordinate goals – reflects the influence of the company. The point is that McKinsey achieves much through its access but can do so only through the value it attaches to the intellectual power of its people and that built into the consulting models it deploys. Not least therefore, 'The Firm' projects an image of success, access, being 'in the know' and internationalism, but mainly value through the intellectual reputation it has acquired. The crucial point is to note the symbiotic nature of its approach. Access is vital and remains a necessary but not sufficient resource for success. McKinsey stays close to its market by networking with key decision makers through the way people move between it and key corporates globally. But its reputation flows from providing value through intellectual rigour. All of this is articulated through the style, culture and reputation of the organization.

As we have seen earlier, all of the above turns on two transformation strategies. The first demands that we reconfigure resources around value to the customer and that we put in place credible measures of value at all levels of the company. Transparency becomes a key attribute of transformation therefore, but focused on improved performance. The second is to make the ability to learn a central resource for strategic change.

Learning as a transformational resource

It is obvious that learning and transformation are part of the same process. We have shown how strategic or transformational change both involve and demand learning. As we have seen, the learning organization must find ways of 'capturing knowledge' and converting 'tacit' into 'explicit' knowledge. While the organizational mind-set to create a learning organization needs to shift to one in which we assume that everyone thinks before they act, a key point is the ability to capture and convert knowledge. This point can readily be illustrated by looking at the retail sector.

Here, large out-of-town stores sell groceries and electronics. Stores like Toys "Я" Us, PC World and Waterstones dominate particular niches. Growth in catalogue shopping increasingly focused 'up market' is a feature, as is direct selling of financial services (cutting out traditional players in the sales channel). Telephone banking becomes more important and who knows how huge internet commerce will become.

All of the above has required increasingly sophisticated IT. This technology allows organizations to provide advanced logistics, real-time inventory control and just-in-time restocking. But it also allows a company like Toys "Я" Us to analyse sales patterns in order to identify the toys likely to 'win' in the Christmas shopping period. Immense quantities of scanned data, matched with demographics, through store cards give large retailers key information about the value chain. Thus it is that the design and deployment of IT infrastructure can serve a multiplicity of purposes including that of learning. In a similar way IT infrastructure can facilitate what is known as the 'whole-life' approach to asset management – wherein the full costs of capital assets, from acquisition to disposal, are looked at, measured and managed.

Strategy for corporate transformation

If we see strategic or transformational change as a learning process, then strategies based around Figure 19.1 appear to be relevant. The figure seeks to show the relevant elements in the process of transformation. The change situation or context will certainly include an environment of radical changes impacting on the organization concerned. Within the organization we need to be concerned with the management systems driving the organization towards greater adaptability.

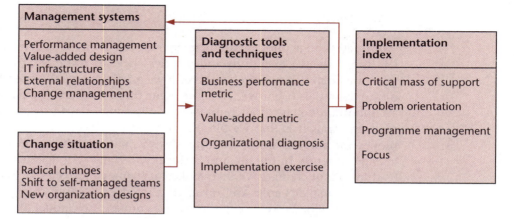

Figure 19.1 Building blocks for corporate transformation

These will include performance management systems, for example. To what extent is performance management focused on outputs? To what extent are those outputs linked to key result areas identified in the strategy and the budget process? To what extent does performance management present a framework for market-induced change?

Similarly, value-added design represents a set of design principles and approaches using the balanced scorecard, activity-based costing, value chain principles and output models which focus on creating highly responsive organizational arrangements. Both approaches require an external focus and good change management skills.

These management systems can be complemented by the diagnostic tools and techniques included in this book, not least because the use of these tools and techniques will help to develop our management systems to cope better with the radical environmental changes to which we have referred. These elements taken together leave us with some capacity to implement transformation. In broad terms we look at this in terms of four main elements in an implementation index:

1 Critical mass of support.

2 Problem-solving orientation.

3 Programme management skills.

4 Clarity of strategic focus.

If these elements are positive the conditions are more likely to be conducive to strategic change.

In my view for too long the discussion of change has been hijacked by those arguing that it was a behavioural issue. If only we could deal with the people issue in change, all would be well. My view is that this is dangerously misleading. If people need to see changes as relevant and critical before they commit themselves – and that appears to be a non-controversial point – then strategic or transformational change has an important cognitive component. If 'mind-set' change is a vital component then the same point holds.

Conclusion

'Mind-set' change implies paradigm change. A 'paradigm' is defined as a constellation of values, perceptions and practices held in common. Clearly there is a powerful cognitive component here. If we are to change the 'mind-set', by definition the task is cognitive. Thus, we argue that while strategic change does have an important behavioural component, no less important is its cognitive component and thus it is that we place significant emphasis here on tools and techniques for analysis. Most importantly, we have sought to review theories of change currently in the literature critically in order to judge how they can help us think about change. We then looked at themes and issues facing practitioners seeking to make change and reviewed a range of existing change management techniques. Finally we brought forward a convergence model of change as a further contribution to thinking about change management in practice.

Anyone who objects that it is the *way* the tools are used which makes the difference is not arguing against this point at all. For me, however, the starting point of change is about vision – a cognitive process. Someone once said:

If the rate of change outside the organization is faster than the rate of change inside, the end is nigh.

I see this as the enduring challenge to anyone seeking to understand and manage change. I hope that this book contains ideas, concepts, tools, techniques and case studies which will help you make sense of this changing world.

EXERCISES

1 Overall, what have you learned about major change through your work on this book?

2 How would you go about change given that learning?

3 Is radical transformation possible?

References

Adams, J., Hayes, J. and Hopson, B. (1976) *Transitions – Understanding and Managing Personal Change*, Oxford: Martin Robertson.

Adams, J.L. (1987) *Conceptual Blockbusting*, Harmondsworth: Penguin.

Alexander, L.D. (1988) 'Successfully implementing strategic decisions', *Long Range Planning*, 18 (3).

Alvesson, M. and Willmott, H. (1992) 'On the idea of emancipation in management and organization studies', *Academy of Management Review*, vol. 17, no. 3, 432–464.

Amabile, T.M. (1983) *The Social Psychology of Creativity*, New York: Springer Verlag.

Amabile, T.M. (1988) 'Creativity to organizational innovation', in Gronhaug, K. and Kaufman, G. (eds) *Innovation: A cross-disciplinary perspective*, Oslo: Norwegian University.

Ansoff, I. and McDonnell, E. (1990) *Implanting Strategic Management*, New York: Prentice-Hall.

Argyris, C. (1962) *Integrating the Individual and the Organization*, New York: Wiley.

Argyris, C. (1982) *Reasoning, Learning and Action*, San Francisco: Jossey-Bass.

Argyris, C. (1985) *Strategy, Change and Defensive Routines*, New York: Pitman.

Argyris, C. (1990) *Overcoming Organizational Defences*, Needham Hts, MA: Allyn and Bacon.

Argyris, C. (2004) 'Double Loop Learning and Organizational Change', in J. Boonstra (ed.) *The Dynamics of Organizational Change and Learning*, London: Wiley.

Argyris, C. and Schon, D. (1974) *Theory in Practice: Increasing professional effectiveness*, San Francisco: Jossey-Bass.

Argyris, C. and Schon, D. (1978) *Organizational Learning: A theory of action perspective*, Reading, MA: Addison-Wesley.

Bachrach, P. and Baratz, M. (1963) 'Decisions and nondecisions: an analytical framework', *American Political Science Review*, 57, 532–42.

Barnatt, C. (1995) *Cyber Business*, New York: Wiley.

Barnett, J.H. and Wilstead, W.D. (1988) *Management: concepts and cases*, PWS-Kent.

Barnett, C. (2002) *The Collapse of British Power*, London: Pan Books.

Bartlett, C.A. and Ghoshal, S. (1989) *Managing Across Borders: The transnational solution*, Boston, MA: Harvard Business School Press.

Barry, D. (1997) 'Telling Changes: from Narrative Family Therapy to Organisational Change and Development', *Journal of Organizational Change Management*, vol. 10, no. 1, 30–46.

Bate, P. (1994) *Strategies for Cultural change*. Oxford: Butterworth-Heinemann.

Bate, P., Bevan, H. and Robert, G. (2004) *Toward a Million Change Agents, A Review of Social Movements Literature*, London: The Modernisation Agency, Department of Health.

Beckard, R. and Pritchard, W. (1992) *Changing the Essence*, San Francisco: Jossey-Bass.

Beer, M., Eisenstat, R. and Spector, B. (1988) *The Critical Path to Change*, Boston, MA: Harvard Business School Press.

Beer, M. and Nohria, N. (eds) (2000) *Breaking the Code of Change*, Boston: Harvard Business School Press.

Bennis, W. (1984) 'The four competencies of leadership', *Training and Development Journal*, 38, 15.

Bennis, W. and Nanus, B. (1985) *Leadership: The strategies for taking charge*, New York: Harper and Row.

Bignell, A., Peters, G. and Pym, C. (1977) *Catastrophic Failures*, Milton Keynes: Open University Press.

Birchall, D.W. (1993) 'Information technology survey', Henley Management College Working Paper.

Bobbitt, P. (2002) *The Shield of Achilles*, London: Allen Lane.

Bok, S. (1984) *Secrets*, New York: Random House.

Bones, C. (1994) *The Self Reliant Manager*, Henley-on-Thames: Routledge.

Boonstra, J. (ed.) (2004) *The Dynamics of Organizational Change and Learning*, London: Wiley.

Bowers, J.L. (1970) *Managing the Resource Allocation Process*, Boston, MA: Harvard University Press.

Brooke, M. (1984) *Centralization and Autonomy*, London: Holt, Rinehart and Winston.

Bruch, H. and Sattelberger, T. (2001) 'The turnaround at Lufthansa', *Journal of Change Management*, 1 (4), 344–65.

Bryman, A. (1983) 'Organization studies and the concept of rationality', *Journal of Management Studies*, October, 391–408.

Bryman, A. (1987) *Leadership*, London: Heinemann.

Bullock, R.J. and Batten, D. (1985) 'It's just a phase we are going through: a review and synthesis of OD phase analysis', *Group and Organization Studies*, 10, December, 383–412.

Bunker, B.B. and Alban, B.T. (1996) *Large Group Interventions: Engaging the Whole System for Rapid Change*, San Francisco: Jossey-Bass.

Burke, W.W. and Litwin, G.H. (1992) 'A causal model of organizational performance and change', *Journal of Management*, 18 (3), 528–34.

Burnes, B. (2004) *Managing Change*, 4th edition, Harlow, Essex: Pearson Prentice Hall.

Burns, J.G. (1978) *Leadership*, New York: Harper and Row.

Burns, T. and Stalker, G.M. (1961) *The Management of Innovation*, London: Tavistock.

Caluwe, L. de and Vermaak, H. (2004) 'Thinking about Change in Different Colours', in J. Boonstra (ed.) *The Dynamics of Organizational Change and Learning*, London: Wiley.

Capra, F. (1986) 'The concept of paradigm and paradigm shift', *Revision*, 9, 11–12.

Capra, F. (1996) *Het Levensweb*, Utrecht: Kosmos-Z&K (I gratefully acknowledge the translation of this text by colleagues in the Netherlands).

Carnall, C.A. (1976) *Diagnosis for Change*, Henley: The Management College.

Carnall, C.A. (1982) *The Evaluation of Work Organization Change*, Farnborough: Gower.

Carnall, C.A. (1986) 'Toward a theory for the evaluation of organisational change', *Human Relations*, 39, 745–66.

Carnall, C.A. (2004) 'Change Architecture', in J. Boonstra (ed.) *The Psychological Management of Organization Change*, London: Wiley.

Casse, P. (1979) *Training for the Cross Cultural Mind*, Washington, DC: Society for Intercultural Education.

Castells, M. (1996) *The Rise of the Network Society*, Oxford: Blackwell.

Chandler, A. (1962) *Strategy and Structure: Chapters in the history of the American industrial enterprise*, Cambridge, MA: MIT Press.

Chartered Institute of Personnel Development (2003) *Reorganizing for Success: CEOs' and HR managers' perceptions,* London: CIPD.

Checkland, P. (1986) *Systems Thinking, Systems Practice*, Chichester: Wiley.

Checkland, P. and Howell, S. (1998) *Information, Systems and Information Systems*, Chichester: Wiley.

Checkland, P. and Scholtes, J. (1995) *Soft Systems Methodology in Action*, Chichester: Wiley.

Child, J. (1984) *Organization*, London: Harper and Row.

Clark, J. (1995) *Managing Innovation and Change*, London: Sage.

Clark, K.B. and Fujimoto, T. (1991) *Product Development Performance*, Boston, MA: Harvard Business School Press.

Clark, T. and Clegg, S. (1998) *Changing Paradigms*, London: Harper Business.

Collins, J. (2001) *Good to Great: Why Some Companies Make the Leap . . . and Others Don't*, New York: Harper Collins.

Cooper, G. (1981) *Psychology and Managers*, London: Macmillan.

Cooper, G. and Hingley, P. (1985) *The Change Makers*, London: Harper and Row.

Cope, M. (1996) 'The use of stage events to mobilise change', paper presented at the Academy of Human Resource Development, Minneapolis.

Cummings, T.G. and Huse, E.F. (1989) *Organization Development and Change,* 4th edition, St Paul: West.

Dalton, M. (1959) *Men who Manage*, New York: Wiley.

Darwin, J., Johnson, P. and McAuley, J. (2002) *Developing Strategies for Change*, Harlow: Pearson Prentice Hall.

D'Aveni, R.A. (1994) *Hyper-competition*, New York: Free Press.

Dawson, P. (2003) *Organizational Change: A Processual Approach*, London: Routledge.

Deal, T.E. and Kennedy, A.A. (1982) *Corporate Cultures*, Reading, MA: Addison-Wesley.

de Vries, K. and Miller, D. (1984) *The Neurotic Organization*, New York: Jossey-Bass.

de Vries, M.F.R. (1980) *Organizational Paradoxes*, London: Tavistock.

Doz, Y.L. and Prahalad, C.K. (1991) 'Managing DMNCs: a search for a new paradigm', *Strategic Management Journal*, 12, 4.

Dubin, R. and Spray, S.L. (1964) 'Executive behaviour and interaction', *Industrial Relations*, **3**, 99–108.

Ellinor, L. and Gerrard, G. (1998) *Dialogue*, New York: Wiley.

Emery, M. (2004) 'Open Systems Theory: Implications for Development and Learning', in J. Boonstra (ed.) *The Dynamics of Organizational Change and Learning*, London: Wiley.

Emery, M. and Purser, R.E. (1996) *The Search Conference*, San Francisco: Jossey-Bass.

Emery, F. and Trist, E.L. (1963) *Organisational Choice*, London: Tavistock.

Ernst, D. (1994) 'Inter-firm networks and market structure', University of California, Berkeley, BRIE Research Paper.

Felix, E. (2000) 'Creating radical change: Producer Choice at the BBC', *Journal of Change Management*, 1 (1), 5–21.

Fiedler, F.E. (1967) *A Theory of Leadership Effectiveness*, New York: McGraw-Hill.

Forrester, J.W. (1969) *Industrial Dynamics*, New York: Wiley.

Foucault, M. (1970) *The Order of Things*, London: Tavistock.

Foucault, M. (1972) *The Archeology of Knowledge*, London: Routledge.

Foucault, M. (1977) *Discipline and Punish: The Birth of the Prison*, New York: Pantheon Books.

Foucault, M. (1980) *Power/Knowledge*, Brighton: Harvester.

Foucault, M. (1986) *The History of Sexuality*, Harmondsworth: Penguin.

Fraher, A. (2004) *A History of Group Study and Psychodynamic Organizations*, London: Free Association Books.

French, W.L. and Bell, C.H. (1995) *Organization Development*, 4th edition, Englewood Cliffs: Prentice Hall.

Friedman, Milton (1972) *Studies on the Quantity Theory of Money*, Chicago: University of Chicago Press.

Fritz, R. (1996) *Corporate Tides*, San Francisco: Berrett-Koehler.

Fromm, E. (1944) *The Fear of Freedom*, London: Routledge.

Fukuyama, F. (1995) *Trust: The social virtues and the creation of prosperity*, London: Hamish Hamilton.

Furze, D. and Gale, C. (1996) *Interpreting Management*, London: International Thomson Business Press.

Galbraith, J.W. (1977) *Organizational Design*, Reading, MA: Addison-Wesley.

Gardner, H. (2004) *Changing Minds*, Boston, MA: Harvard Business School Press.

Ghosal, C. (2002) 'Saving the business without losing the company', *Harvard Business Review*, 80 (1), 37–46.

Ghosal, S., Gratton, L. and Rogan, R. (2002) *The Transformation of BP*, London: London Business School.

Gilbert, X. and Strebel, P. (1989) 'From innovation to outpacing', *Business Quarterly*, Summer, 19–22.

Goffee, R. and Jones, G. (1996) 'What holds the modern company together?', *Harvard Business Review*, November–December.

Goffee, R. and Jones, G. (1998) *The Character of the Corporation*, London: Harper and Row.

Goleman, D., Boyatzis, R. and McKee, A. (2001) 'Primal leadership: the hidden driver of great performance', *Harvard Business Review*, 79 (11), 42–51.

Gordon, W.J. (1961) *Synectics*, London: Harper and Row.

Gouillart, F.J. and Kelly, J.N. (1995) *Transforming the Organization*, New York: McGraw-Hill.

Gould, M. and Campbell, A. (1987) *Strategies and Styles: The role of the centre in managing diversified corporations*, Oxford: Blackwell.

Gratton, L. (2000) *Living Strategy*, Harlow, Essex: Prentice Hall.

Greenly, D. and Carnall, C.A. (2001) 'Workshops as a technique for strategic change', *Journal of Change Management*, 2 (1), 33–46.

Greiner, L. (1972) 'Evolution and revolutions as organizations grow', *Harvard Business Review*, July–August.

Grundy, T. (1994) *Strategic Learning in Action*, London: McGraw-Hill.

Grunig, R. and Kuhn, R. (2001) *Process-based Strategic Planning*, Berlin: Springer.

Habermas, J. (1974) *Theory and Practice*, London: Heinemann.

Hackman, J.R. and Oldham, G.R. (1976) 'Motivation through the design of work', *Organizational Behaviour and Human Performance*, 3, 12–35.

Hall, R. (1980) *Organization*, New York: Wiley.

Hamel, G. (1996) 'Strategy as revolution', *Harvard Business Review*, July–August.

Hamel, G. and Prahalad, C.K. (1994) *Competing for the Future*, Boston, MA: Harvard Business School Press.

Hampden-Turner, C. (1996) *Charting the Corporate Mind*, London: Basic Blackwell.

Handfield, R.B. (1995) *Re-engineering for Time-based Competition*, London: Quorum Books.

Handy, C. (1983) *Taking Stock*, London: BBC.

Handy, C. (1984) *Organizations*, 2nd edition, Harmondsworth: Penguin.

Hannan, M.T. and Freeman, J. (1983) *Organizational Ecology*, Boston, MA: Harvard University Press.

Hansen, M.T. and van Oetinger, B. (2001) 'Introducing T-shaped Managers: Knowledge Management's Next Generation', *Harvard Business Review*, vol. 79, no. 3, March, 107–116.

Hastings, C. (1993) *The New Organization*, London: McGraw-Hill.

Hart, A. (1997) 'Team Midwifery', Brighton Health Care NHS Trust Research Report.

Harré, R. (1984) *The Philosophies of Science*, Oxford: Oxford University Press.

Hellreigel, D., Slocum, J.W. and Woodman, R.W. (1986) *Organizational Behaviour*, 4th edition, St Paul, MN: West.

Hersey, P. and Blanchard, K. (1988) *Organizational Behaviour*, New York: Prentice Hall.

Hersey, P., Blanchard, K. and Johnson, D. (2000) *Management of Organizational Behavior: Leading Human Resources*, 8th edition, Upper Saddle River, NJ: Prentice Hall.

Hickson, D.J., Butler, R.J., Cray, D., Mallory, G.R. and Wilson, D.C. (1986) *Top Decisions*, Oxford: Basil Blackwell.

Higgs, M. and Rowland, D. (2001) 'Developing change leaders', *Journal of Change Management*, 2 (1), 47–66.

Higgs, M. and Rowland, D. (2005) 'All Changes Great and Small: Exploring Approaches to Change and its Leadership', *Journal of Change Management*, vol. 5, no. 2, June, 121–152.

Hofstede, G. (1968) *Cultures Consequences*, Harmondsworth: Penguin.

Homer-Dixon, P. (2000) *Ingenuity*, New York: Alfred Knopf.

Horne, J.H. and Lupton, T. (1965) 'The work activities of middle managers', *Journal of Management Studies*, 12, 14–33.

Hurst, D.K. (1995) *Crisis and Renewal*, Cambidge, MA: Harvard Business School Press.

Itami, H. (1987) *Mobilizing Invisible Assets*, Cambridge, MA: Harvard University Press.

Jacobs, R.W. (1994) *Real Time Strategic Change*, San Francisco: Berrett-Koehler.

Jacques, E. (1952) *The Changing Culture of a Factory*, New York: Dryden Press.

Jameson, B.J. (1984) 'The reception of politics into management development', unpublished PhD thesis, Henley-Brunel University.

Janis, I. (1972) *Victims of Groupthink*, New York: Houghton Mifflin.

Janis, I.L. (1989) *Crucial Decisions*, New York: Free Press.

Janis, I. and Mann, F. (1976) *Decision-Making*, New York: Free Press.

Johnson, G. (1987) *Strategic Change and the Management Process*, Oxford: Blackwell.

Johnson, G. (1988) 'Rethinking incrementalism', *Strategic Management Journal*, vol. 9, no. 1, 75–91.

Juch, B. (1983) *Personal Development*, Chichester: Wiley.

Judson, A. (1990) *Making Strategy Happen*, London: Blackwell.

Kanter, R. (1983) *The Change Masters*, London: George Allen and Unwin.

Kanter, R., Stein, B.A. and Jick, T.D. (1992) *The Challenge of Organizational Change*, New York: The Free Press.

Kaplan, R.S. and Norton, D.P. (1996) *The Balanced Scorecard: Turning Strategy into Action*, Boston, MA: Harvard Business School Press.

Kay, J. (1993) *Foundations of Corporate Success*, Oxford: Oxford University Press.

Keeley, S. (1988) 'Managing change at ABF', unpublished MBA dissertation, Henley-Brunel University.

Kelman, S. (2005) *Unleashing Change*, Washington, DC: The Brookings Institute Press.

Kingston, W.J. (1977) *Innovation*, London: John Calder.

Kirkpatrick, D. (1985) *How to Manage Change Effectively*, New York: Jossey-Bass.

Kirton, M.J. (1988) 'Adaptors and innovators', in Gronhaug and Kaufman (eds) *Innovation: A cross-disciplinary perspective*, Oslo: Norwegian University.

Kissinger, H. (1979) *The White House Years*, London: Weidenfeld and Nicolson.

Knights, D. and Morgan, G. (1991) 'Corporate Strategy, Organisations and Subjectivity: a critique', *Organization Studies*, vol. 12, no. 2, 251–273.

Kolb, D.A. (1984) *Experimental Learning*, New Jersey: Prentice Hall.

Kotter, J.P. (1978) *Organizational Dynamics*, Reading, MA: Addison-Wesley.

Kotter, J.P. (1988) *The Leadership Factor*, New York: Free Press.

Kotter, J.P. (1996) *Leading Change*, Boston: Harvard Business School Press.

Kotter, J.P. and Hesketh, J.L. (1992) *Corporate Culture and Performance*, New York: Free Press.

Landes, D. (1967) *Unbound Prometheus*, Cambridge: Cambridge University Press.

Lawler, E.E. (1978) *Motivation and the Work Organization*, Monterey, CA: Brooks Cole.

Lawler, E.E. and Bachrach, S.B. (1986) *Power and Politics in Organizations*, New York: Jossey-Bass.

Lawrence, P.R. and Dyer, D. (1983) *Renewing American Industry*, New York: Free Press.

Lawrence, P.R. and Lorsch, J. (1967) *Organization and Environment*, New York: Richard D. Irwin.

Lee, R. and Lawrence, P. (1985) *Organizational Behaviour Politics at Work*, London: Hutchinson.

Leroy, F. and Ramansanto, B. (1997) 'The cognitive and behavioural elements of organizational learning in a merger', *Journal of Management Studies*, 34 (6), 871–94.

Lewin, K. (1947) 'Action Research and minority problems'. In G.W. Lewin and G.W. Allport (eds) (1948) *Resolving Social Conflict*, London: Harper and Row.

Lindblom, C. (1959) 'The science of muddling through', *Public Administration Review*, 19 (Spring), 82–8.

Lipniack, J. and Stamps, J. (1994) *The Age of the Network*, New York: Wiley.

Lorange, P. and Nelson, G. (1987) *Strategic Control*, San Francisco: West.

Lorsch, J. (1970) 'Introduction to the structural design of organization', in P.R. Lawrence and J. Lorsch (eds) *Organizational Structure and Design*, New York: Irwin-Dorsey.

Lorsch, J. (1986) 'Managing Culture: the Invisible Barrier to Strategic Change', *California Management Review*, vol. 28, no. 2, 95–109.

Lukes, S. (1974) *Power, a Radical View*, London: Macmillan.

Lynch, R. (2000) *Corporate Strategy*, 2nd edition, Harlow: Prentice Hall.

Macpherson, C. (1962) *The Political Theory of Possessive Individualism*, Oxford: Clarendon Press.

Mansfield, R. (1986) *Company Strategy and Organizational Design*, London: Croom Helm.

Mant, A. (1983) *Leaders We Deserve*, Oxford: Martin Robertson.

Manzoni, M. (2000) Paper presented to E-HR 2000 Conference, London, 25–28 September.

March, J.G. and Olsen, J.P. (1976) *Ambiguity and Choice in Organization*, Bergen: Universitets Forlaget.

March, J.G. and Simon, H.A. (1958) *Organizations*, New York: Wiley.

Markides, C. (2000) *All the Right Moves: A Guide to Crafting Breakthrough Strategy*, Boston, MA: Harvard Business School Press.

Martin, J. (1995) *The Great Transition*, New York: American Management Association.

Masuch, M. (1983) 'Vicious circles in organisation', *ASQ*, 30 (1), 46–62.

McGrath, R.G. and MacMillan, I.C. (2000) *The Entrepreneurial Mindset*, Boston, MA: Harvard Business School Press.

Meadows, D.H. (1972) *Limits to Growth*, New York: Universe Publications.

Merkle, J. (1980) *Management and Ideology*, San Francisco: University of California Press.

Merton, R.K. (1940) 'Bureaucratic structure and personality', *Social Forces*, 18, 560–8.

Milborrow, G. (1993) 'Management development to the year 2000', paper presented to the Management Development Conference at Henley Management College, Henley, UK, 20 October.

Miller, D. (1990) *The Icarus Paradox*, New York: Harper Collins.

Miller, D. and de Vries, K. (1984) *The Neurotic Organization*, New York: Jossey-Bass.

Mintzberg, H. (1973) *The Nature of Managerial Work*, New York: Harper and Row.

Mintzberg, H. (1994) *The Rise and Fall of Strategic Planning*, Englewood Cliffs, NJ: Prentice Hall.

Mirvis, P.H. and Marks, M.L. (1992) *Managing the Merger*, Englewood Cliffs, NJ: Prentice Hall.

Moss Kanter, R. (2001) *Evolve: Succeeding in the Digital Culture of Tomorrow*, Boston, MA: Harvard Business School Press.

Munch, B. (2001) 'Changing a culture of face time', *Harvard Business Review*, 79 (10), 125–132.

Myerson, D.E. (2001) 'Radical change, the quiet way', *Harvard Business Review*, 79 (9), 92–104.

Newmann, J.E., Holti, R. and Standing, H. (1995) *Changing Everything at Once*, London: Tavistock Institute.

Nohria, N. and Berkely, J. (1995) 'The virtual organization', in Heckscher, C. and Donneellon, A. (eds) *The Post-Bureacratic Organization*, Thousand Oaks, CA: Sage.

Nonaka, I. and Takeuchi, H. (1995) *The Knowledge Creating Company*, Oxford: Oxford University Press.

Norburn, D. (1988) 'The chief executive: a breed apart', *Strategic Management Journal*, 10, 1–15.

Norlton, G. (1998) 'Creating an opportunity for positive change', MBA dissertation, Henley.

Ohmae, K. (1982) *The Mind of the Strategist*, New York: McGraw-Hill.

Orgland, M.Y. (1997) *Initiating, Managing and Sustaining Strategic Change*, London: Macmillan.

Ouchi, W. (1981) *Theory Z*, Reading, MA: Addison-Wesley.

Parry-Jones, R. (1996) 'A vision for the future', *European Business Journal*, Summer, 47–55.

Parker, M. (2000) *Organizational Culture and Identity*, London: Sage.

Pascale, R. (1990) *Managing on the Edge*, Harmondsworth: Penguin Books.

Peters, T. and Austin, N. (1985) *A Passion for Excellence*, New York: Random House.

Peters, T. and Waterman, R.H. (1982) *In Search of Excellence*, New York: Harper and Row.

Pettigrew, A. (1973) *The Politics of Organizational Decision-Making*, London: Tavistock.

Pettigrew, A. (1985) *The Awakening Giant: Continuity and change in ICI*, Oxford: Basil Blackwell.

Pfeffer, J. (1981) *Power in Organizations*, New York: Pitman.

Pfeffer, J. (1998) *The Human Equation*, Boston, MA: Harvard Business School Press.

Piercy, N.F. (2004) *Market-Led Strategic Change*, 2nd edition, Oxford: Heinemann-Butterworth.

Piore, M. and Sable, C. (1984) *The Second Industrial Divide*, New York: Basic Books.

Porter, M. (1985) *Competitive Advantage: Creating and sustaining superior performance*, New York: Free Press.

Prahalad, C.K. and Hamel, G. (1990) 'The core competence of the corporation', *Harvard Business Review*, 68 (3), 79–91.

Pressman, J.L. and Wildavsky, A. (1973) *Implementation*, San Francisco: University of California Press.

Putnam, R.W. and Thomas, D. (1988) 'Organizational action map: pay and performance', in R. Putnam (ed.), 'Mapping organizational defence routines', mimeo, Harvard Graduate School of Education.

Quinn, J.B. (1992) *The Intelligent Enterprise*, New York: Free Press.

Quinn Mills, D. (1991) *The Cluster Organisation*, New York: Wiley.

Revans, R. (1972) *Hospitals, Communication, Choice and Change*, London: Tavistock.

Rickards, T. (1985) *Stimulating Innovation*, London: Frances Pinter.

Rieley, J.B. (2001) *Gaming the System*, Harlow: Financial Times Prentice Hall.

Rifkin, J. (1995) *The End of Work*, New York: Putnams.

Roethlisberger, F. and Dickson, W.J. (1939) *Management and the Worker*, New York: Wiley.

Rogan, M. (2002) *The Transformation of BP*, London: London Business School.

Rogers, E.M. (1995) *Diffusion of Innovations*, 4th edition, New York: Free Press.

Rose, M. (1975) *Industrial Behaviour: Theoretical development since Taylor*, London: Allen Lane.

Roy, D. (1954) 'Efficiency and the fox', in 'Formal intergroup relations in a piece-work machine shop', *American Journal of Sociology*, 60 (33), 255–66.

Rubinstein, M.F. and Furstenberg, I.R. (1999) *The Minding Organization*, New York: Wiley.

Schein, E. (1965) *Organizational Psychology*, New York: Prentice Hall.

Schein, E. (1996) *Organizational Culture and Leadership*, 3rd edition, San Francisco: Jossey-Bass.

Schnattsneider, E.E. (1960) *The Semi-Sovereign People*, New York: Rinehart and Winston.

Schwartz, H. and Davis, S. (1981) Matching corporate culture and business strategy, *Organizational Dynamics*, no. 10, 30–48.

Scott, W.R. (1981) *Organizations: Rational, natural and open systems*, New York: Prentice Hall.

Senge, P. (1990) *The Fifth Discipline*, London: Random House.

Simon, H.A. (1957) *Administrative Behaviour*, New York: Free Press.

Smale, G. (1998) *Managing Change Through Innovation*, London: The Stationery Office.

Sofer, C. (1973) *Organizations in Theory and Practice*, London: Heinemann Educational Books.

Stacey, R. (1996) *Complexity and Creativity in Organizations*, San Francisco: Berrett-Koehler.

Stacey, R. (2003) *Strategic Management and Organisational Dynamics*, Harlow: Pearson Prentice Hall.

Stalk, G. and Hout, J.M. (1990) *Competing Against Time*, New York: Free Press.

Steers, R.M. and Porter, L. (1979) *Motivation and Work Behaviour*, New York: McGraw-Hill.

Stewart, R. (1977) *Managers and their Jobs*, London: Macmillan.

Stewart, R. (1982) *Choices for the Manager*, London: McGraw-Hill.

Stewart, V. and Chadwick, V. (1987) *Changing Trains: Messages for management from the Scot Rail Challenge*, Newton Abbot: David and Charles.

Strauss, G. (1963) 'Tactics of lateral relationships: the purchasing agent', *Administrative Science Quarterly*, 161–86.

Strauss, G. (1976) 'Organizational development', in R. Dubin (ed.) *Handbook of Work, Organization and Society*, New York: Rand McNally.

Strebel, P. (ed.) (2000) *Focused Energy*, Chichester: Wiley.

Sweet, T. and Heritage, V. (2000) 'How managers gain commitment to change', *Journal of Change Management*, 1 (2), 164–178.

Taylor, B. (1983) 'Turnaround – recovery and growth', *Journal of General Management*, 8 (2), 32–8.

Thornbury, J. (1999) 'KPMG: Revitalising culture through values', *Business Strategy Review*, 10 (4), 1–15.

Tichy, N. and Sherman, S. (1995) *Control Your Destiny*, London: HarperCollins.

Trist, E., Higgin, C., Murray, H. and Pollack, A. (1963) *Organizational Choice*, London: Tavistock.

Trompenars, F. (2001) *Riding the Waves of Culture*, 2nd edition, London: Brealey.

Turner, B. (1986) Sociological aspects of organizational symbolism, *Organization Studies*, vol. 7, no. 2, 101–117.

Van der Erve, M. (1994) *Evolution Management*, Oxford: Butterworth–Heinemann.

Vince, R. (1996) *Managing Change*, Bristol: Policy Press.

Vroom, V. and Yetton, P.W. (1973) *Leadership and Decision-Making*, Pittsburgh: University of Pittsburgh Press.

Walton, R.E. (1985) 'From control to commitment: transforming work-force management in the USA', in K. Clark, R.H. Hayes and C. Lorenz (eds) *The Uneasy Alliance: Managing the productivity–technology dilemma*, Boston, MA: Harvard Business School Publishing.

Watkin, J.W.N. (1970) 'Imperfect rationality', in R. Borger and F. Coffi (eds) *Explanation in the Behavioural Sciences*, Cambridge: Cambridge University Press.

Watson, G.H. (1993) *Strategic Bench-marking*, New York: Wiley.

Weick, K.E. (1979) *The Social Psychology of Organizing*, New York: Addison-Wesley.

Weick, K.E. (1991) *The Social Psychology of Organizing*, 2nd edition, Reading, MA: Addison-Wesley.

Weick, K.E. (1995) *Sensemaking in Organizations*, Thousand Oaks, CA: Sage.

Wheatley, M.J. (1992) *Leadership and the New Science*, San Francisco: Berrett-Koehler.

Wheatley, M.J. (1996) *A Simple Way*, San Francisco: Berrett-Koehler.

Whitehead, T.N. (1936) *Leadership in a Free Society*, London: Oxford University Press.

Whittington, R. (2001) *What is strategy – and does it matter?* 2nd edition, London: Thomson Learning.

Wiener, M.J. (1981) *English Culture and the Decline of the Industrial Spirit, 1850–1980*, Harmondsworth: Penguin Press.

Wilensky, H. (1967) *Organizational Intelligence*, New York: Basic Books.

Williamson, O.E. (1975) *Market and Hierarchies*, New York: Free Press.

Willmott, H.C. (1984) 'Images and Ideals of Managerial Work', *Journal of Management Studies*, vol. 21, no. 3, 347–368.

Wilson, D.C. (1992) *A Strategy for Change*, London: Routledge.

Woodward, H. and Buchholz, S. (1987) *After Shock: Helping people through corporate change*, New York: Wiley.

Woodward, J. (1965) *Industrial Organization: Theory and practice*, London: Oxford University Press.

Zinn, H. (1980) *A People's History of the United States*, London: Longman.

Index

Note: Page references in *italics* refer to Figures; those in **bold** refer to Tables; [CS] indicates a case study.

'360-degree' feedback/appraisal techniques 8, 52

ABB (Asea Brown Boveri) 33–4
ABF Ltd 158, 182, 183, 299, 314
  case studies 177–81, 295–9
accelerator effect 99, 334–5, 336
acceptability of change 286
acceptance of change, creating 189–90
access 231
accountability 9, 16, 28, 268, 304
achieved status 314
achieving objects 191
action
  supporting 155
action learning 68
action research approach 68, 71–2
action maps, Agyris concept 259
adaptability 148, 192, 332
adaptation stage in coping cycle *241*, 243
adaptive culture 223, 315
adaptive organization, changes needed
to achieve *141*
Airbus Industrie 58
alignment 5–6, 10
A.K. Rice Institute 82
alliances 31, 55
ambiguity, incapacity to tolerate, 121
ambition
  assessment of 99, 100
  in change 328–9, 336–7
  characteristics 329
  level of 95–7
ambition profile/assessment 5–7
anxiety, change-caused 238

architecture 5, 45, 94
architecture of change, effective 223
ascribed status 314
assessment of organizational effectiveness,
    techniques for 194–206
  functional analysis 195, **195–8**, 197, 205–6
  organizational diagnosis 201, **202–5**, 205–6
asset management, 'whole-life' approach to 342
attention, management of 148
attitude surveys 71
authority, as facilitating process 17
autocratic management style 178, 210
autonomy 230
awareness 177, *255*, 255–6

balanced scorecard 6, 8, 52, 116–18
  workshop to create 118
barriers to change 159
BBC 102, 277–8 [CS]
behavioural facilitation 86
behavioural skill 148
Ben & Jerry's (ice cream) 157
benchmarking 8, 46
  competitive 46, 175–6
  global 46
  strategic 46
  use by companies 175–6, 235
Benetton 101
'bet your company' culture 312
better performers, managerial behaviour
    towards 275
Bhopal disaster 321–2
bias, in conflict management 322
block busting 123–4, *124–5*, 135, 260

blocks to problem solving and change
120–6, 135
cognitive blocks 123
cultural blocks 122–3
emotional blocks 121–2
environmental bocks 123
limits to problem solving 124–6
perceptual blocks 121
working through 123–4
BMW 173
Body Shop 6
bold stroke 69
'bolt on, rah rah' management 185
bottom-up models of change 53, 54
Branson, Richard 149
break-through change 74, 98, 100, 102
strategic management of 93–104
break-through teams 48
Brighton Health Care NHS Trust [CS] 40
British Airways 7
British Army 173–4
British Petroleum (BP) 76–7 [CS]
cultural change at 32
British Petroleum Engineering (BPE) [CS] 57–8
British Telecommunications plc 7
broker 32
build-up to change 73–4
Bull (computer company) 30
bureaucracy 137
dysfunctional consequences 130
structure of 137
unintended consequences 130
business architecture 46
business capability profile 110–12
business needs 231
business process analysis 58
business process re-engineering 46, 48, 56, 58,
176, 254

CAC Consultants [CS] 133–4
Canon 96
capability 177, 255, 256
capture of learning 160
career management 263
cascade communication programmes 163
cascading 257–8
cash control 304
catalogue shopping 342
centralization, arguments for 18–20
centres of excellence 263
CEOs, view of managers 42
'chairman's rice pudding' 189
Chandler, A. 29

change accelerator 334–5, 336, 338
change agents 98, 260
change architecture 8–10, 254–79, 328, 335, 337
blocks 272–7
components of 329–30
performance characteristics of 330
change capability framework 328, 335–9
change champions 260
change coping cycles 240–4, 260, 300
change culture 332–3, 336, 338
change equation 210–13
change leadership 333–4, 336, 338
change programmes 7, 299–300
change readiness 281–3, 285–6
change readiness index 4, 7, 97
change theories
critical perspectives 78–92
traditional models 63–77
change timing 324
change workshops 163
'Changing Childbirth' [CS] 39–41
changing organizations 41–6
charisma 151
checklist(s)
creativity in problem solving 123–4
diagnosing change 222–3
managing change 284–5
choice
informed 332
organizational environments and 136–44
clarifying plans 286–7
clinical approach towards change 67–8
clinical rationality 126
closure programmes 176
cluster organization 54, 57
CNN 6, 45, 96
coercive power 319
cognitive blocks 123
cognitive skill 148
Cohen, Ben 157
collectivism 311
failure of 28
Colt Telecom 64
command and control mode, value-added
problems 112–13
commitment model 25–6, 27, 70
common platform 9
communication
direct 304
as facilitating process 17
informal 17
and management information systems 231
media of 21

communication cascades 9
communication skill 148
communitarianism 313
company track record of changes 284–5
competence models 52, 267
competition 173
competitive advantage, basis 46
competitive benchmaking 47, 175–6
competitive insulation profile 97
'complex man' model of human
    behaviour 209–10
complexity theory 70, 74, 84–9
compromise 302
conceptualizing process 70
concurrent engineering 101, 102
confidentiality 250
conflict
    learning involving 228
    as part of change 221–2, 246
conflict management 23, 320–4
    bias 322
    conflicting demands 322
    decision making 320
    external forces 322
    things that managers can do 322–4
    things that managers cannot do 320–2
    uncertainty 322
connectivity 94, 268, 334
consensus 302, 308
consistency 268
contagion models 65
contingency approach 80, 127
    and choice and organizational
        environments 136–8
    criticisms 140–1
    and leadership style 152–3, *152*, 319
    organization design, resources and
        complexity 138–40
    theory 137–8
contradictions, learning by exploring 228
control model 24, **25–6**
convergent systems 167, 332
conversations 163–4
coping cycle 240–4, 260, 300
    adaptation stage *241*, 243
    compared with ecocycle 165
    defence stage *241*, 242
    denial stage 240–2, *241*
    discarding stage *241*, 242–3
    internalization stage *241*, 243–4
coping with change 238–40
coping with organizational change 235–7
    rebuilding self-esteem 236–7, *236*

coping with process of change 244–9
    know others who can help 247–8
    know your situation 246–7
    know yourself 244–6
    working on self-esteem 248–9
core competence 6, 94
corporate culture 27, 35, 308–10
corporate leaders 149
    and explicit strategy 150
    as individuals 151–2
corporate politics 316–20
    and leadership 319–20
    managing 324–5
corporate transformation, strategies for 342–3
counterintuitive behaviour complex systems 131
counterpart 32
counter-rational behaviour 129–33
creative destruction 98, 100
credibility 334
crisis, management of 301–6
critical mass 335
critical perspectives 78–92
critical theory 81–3, 88
criticism, not accepting 123
cross-cultural skills 28
cross-functional teams 235
cultural blocks 122–3
culture characteristics 311
culture change 8, 43, 32, 332–3, 336, 338
culture models 307–25
customer primacy 332
customer service programmes 30
cycles of change 255–8, **259**
    beginnings stage 256, *257*
    focusing stage 256, *257*
    inclusion stage *257*, 257
cybernetics 84
cycle(s) of management **258**, 259

decentralization 18–19, 149
    arguments for 19–20
    for professionals 23
decision making 17–18, 320
    American and Japanese models 101–2
decision-support system 136
decisiveness 304
deeply held beliefs, learning through
        expression of 229
defence stage in coping cycle *241*, 242
deficient organization 137
de-layering 30, 176
delegating leadership style *153*, 154
delegation 19–20

delimitation of problem area 121
Dell Computers 6, 96
denial stage in coping cycle 240–2, *241*
depiction of organizations, traditional 52, *53*
deregulation 173
design systems 323
diagnosing 148, 189–223
diagnosis
  authenticity in 221–3
  see also organizational diagnosis
dialogue 163–4
diffusive learning 85, 87
dilemmas, learning by exploring 228
dilemmas of organization 18–27, 35
  centralization vs decentralization 18–20
  change vs stability 27
  efficiency vs effectiveness 21–2
  from control to commitment 24, 27
  global vs local 21
  professionals vs line management 22–4
dimensions of an organization's
    structure 136
direct communication 304
Direct Line (insurance) 6, 96
discarding stage in coping cycle *241*, 242–3
disinvestment 304
distinctive capability 5, 46, 94
divisionalized organizations 14–15, 16, 30
doing, learning by 47
dominant coalition 232–3
double-loop learning 48, 88, 99, 162
dynamic homeostasis 87
dynamic systems theory 87

early adopters 85, 86, 333, 334
easyJet 6, 96
ecostyle model 165
economies of scale 50
effective change, necessary conditions
    for *255*, 255–6
  awareness *255*, 255–6
  capability *255*, 256
  inclusion *255*, 256
effectiveness 21, 190
  efficiency and 21–2, 191–4
  measuring 190, 192–3
  strategy for 280–91
  techniques for assessment of
    organizational 194–206
effectiveness matrix *193*
efficiency 21
  and effectiveness 21–2, 191–4
Egan, John 149

Eisenhower, Dwight D. 274
emergent change model 73–6, 77
emergent strategy 83
emotional blocks 121–2
empathy 32, 231, 236, 249, 300
employee-management relations, in
    management models **26**
employment-creation programmes 131
employment assurances, in management
    models **26**
empowerment 41–2, 31, 176
energy for change *275*
engagement 278–9
enterprise engineering 100
entrapment 302
entrepreneurial mindset 99–100
entrepreneurial structure 13
entrepreneurship 48
environmental blocks 123
environmental change, effects 301
espoused theory 313
ethics, emphasis on 24
evaluation 70
evidence-based leadership 332
evolution 161
excellence
  books on 27–8, 141
  centres of 263
  in companies, characteristics 145
  leadership and 27–35
expansion of markets 305
expectations of change 283, 333
experience-based design 89
experimentation, learning based on 228
expert power 319
explicit knowledge 168, 342
explicit strategy 150
external focus 21
external forces, and conflict
    management 322
external pressures **226**

facilitative management style 300–1
failure
  of collectivism 28
  fear of 45, 158, 314, 323
  learning from 47
  study of 7, 301
  to use all sensory inputs 121
fantasy 122
fear of failure 45, 158, 313, 323
fear of freedom 158, 300
fear of taking a risk 121

Federal Express 6
federal structure 16
feedback 52, 65, 277, 288–90, 300, 311, 314
felt need 332
femininity 311
financial control 33
financial realism 29
First Direct (telebanking) 96
focus, as block to change 122
focusing on change 323
followers 64
followership 150
force field analysis 280–1
Ford 38–9 [CS], 166
    as learning organization 39, 161
formal organization 16, 52
frame resonance 64
freedom, fear of 158, 300
functional analysis questionnaire 195, **195–8**
    case study example 197, **197–9**
functional and professional advice 231
functional structure 14
functional tendencies *140*

gaming the system 99
garbage-can model 127
General Electric 97–9
General Motors 80–1, 91
generic multi-organizational change
        programmes 176
generic organization-wide change
        programmes 176
Glaxo 51
global benchmarking 46
global organization 21
Good to Great model 73
governance 9, 268, 331
grapevine 318
Greenfield, Jerry 157
group think 124, 302, 310
guiding coalition 276

Haagen-Daz 157
Harvey-Jones, Sir John 149
Hawthorne research 309, 310
Health Service Trust [CS] 215–20
heroes 157, 317
Hewlett-Packard 91, 276
hierarchy orientation 302
homeworking 55
horizontal focus 40
horizontal integration 39, 50
horizontal management *54*

hubris 124
human-centred model 7
'human' dimension of change 206–10
    'complex man' 209–10
    'rational-economic man' 207
    'self-actualizing man' 208–9
    'social man' 208
Human Genome project 277
human resources (HR) strategy 263
humour in problem solving 122

IBM 91
    right-first-time campaign 150, 156
Icarus Paradox 99
ICI 67
idea organizations 82
Ikea 6, 101, 340
imperfect rationality 127
implementability 4
implementation 7–8, *43*, 70, 136
implementation exercise 281–8
    managing change 284–5, 286–8
    readiness for change 281–3, 285–6
implementing change 66
    clinical approach 67–8
    critical perspectives 78–92
    emergent approach 73–6
    linear approach 68–72
    and organizational development 67–8, 71–2
    and systems theory 72–3
    traditional models 63–77
Implementation Index 96
implementation programme *262*
inappropriate or deficient organization 137
inclusion 177, *255*, 256
incremental change 102
incrementalism 124, 127
incubation of ideas, inability 122
independence (in networks) 58
individual behaviour 233
individualism 311, 313
ineffective leadership and change
        management, syndrome *44*, 45
ineffectiveness-effectiveness patterns **132**
informal communication 17
informal organization 16–17, 52
information
    lack of correct 123
    providing 250–1
information system, and structure of
        organization 136
information technology (IT) 22, 342
    barriers to implementation 159

informed choice 332
inner directed 313
innovation 5, 22, 64, 65, 155, 305
    strategy for 146
innovative organization 144–6
inspiring visions 96–7
integrated levels (in networks) 59
integrated organizations 31
integrated patient care (IPC) 40
integrating new practices and
    procedures 287
integration 71, 335
integration of knowledge sets 100–1
intellectual capital 58
intelligible information 236
interactive learning 88
interchangeability 231
interest groups 233–4
interfaces, managing of 28
internal focus 21
internal pressures **226**
internalization stage in coping cycle *241*,
    243–4
International Engineering 142–4 [CS], 210, 211,
    314, 318, 323
    functional analysis questionnaire 194,
    197–9, 197, 200
    leadership potential questionnaire **212–13**
    organizational diagnosis check-sheet
    and questionnaire **201–5**, 205–6
international expansion 305
internationalization 32
intrinsic motivation 23
intuition 122
investment and disinvestment 304
invisible assets 31, 150, 190
    failure to develop 24
involving people in change 251–2, 277–8
    advantages 252
    disadvantages 252
    factors affecting 252
irrationality, organized *125*
isolating the problem 121

Japanese companies 308
Japlin, Kao 169
job design 71, 73
job design principles, in management
    models **25**
job diagnostic survey 245
job rotation 21
Johari Window idea 68
joint ventures 32, 254

judging ideas rather than generating
    them 121–2
just-in-time manufacturing programmes 176

Kirton adoption-innovation (KAI) test 260
Kissinger, Henry 316–17
'know-all' bosses 123
knowing-doing axis 66
knowledge base 168–9, 191
Kodak 234–5
Komatsu 96
Kotter model of change 70–1
KPMG [CS] 9–10

lagging measures 277
language, incorrect 123
late adopters 333
leaderless syndrome **304**
leaders 149
    characteristics 151–2
    and emergent change model 74
    level 5 72–4
    and process of change 64, 66
    and situations 151–4
leadership 148–59, 300
    areas of competence 148–9
    change 333–4, 336, 338
    context of 154–6
    contingency approach 319
    and corporate politics 319–20
    evidence-based 332
    and excellence 27–35
    and human scale 158
    managerial performance 34–5
    managerial roles **34**, 36
    and managers 156–8
    strategy and structure 29–34
    and vision and strategy 150–1
leadership potential questionnaire 211, **212**
    analysis of development needs 211,
    212–13, 213
    case study example **211**
leading measures 277
lean production model 56
lean thinking 308
learning
    by doing 47
    by use 47
    and change 183–4, 258–61, 265–8
    diffusive 85, 87
    encouraging of through change 334
    from change 9, **227**, 228–9, 295–300
    from failure 47

interactive 88
and management performance 182–4
organizational 47, 50
stages of 258
strategic 260
as a transformational resource 342
learning-curve effect 240
learning loop 177, *177*
learning maps 8
learning organization 39, 47–8, 87, 160–71, 342
changing perceptions of organization 161–4
competence development in handling
change 169–70
convergence and 167–9
disciplines for 164–7
Ford as [CS] 39, 161
learning orientation 334
learning space 86
legitimate power 319
leverage 94, 99, 268, 334
Lewin model of change 70
linear approach 68–72, 74, 77
list making 146
living measures 277
local organization 21
London Underground [CS] 213–14
loyalty, changes in attitudes 42
Lufthansa [CS] 8, 270–1

McKinsey 341–2
management issues, focusing on 155
managed incrementalism 47
management in action 16–18, 36
management of attention 148
management autonomy 230
management of changing organization 184–5
management competence models 56
management of crisis and turnaround 301–6
management development
assessment of 211–12, **212–13**
facilitative management style as part of
300–1
managing change for 299–301
management of expectations 268, 333
management information systems 17
developments in 231
management of meaning 148
management models **25–6**
management organization, in
management models **25**
management performance and learning 182–4
effective organizational structures and
systems 182

effective team work 182
learning from changing 183–4
organizational change 183
management philosophy, in
management models **26**
management of self 149
management structures 13–16
divisional structure 14–15, 16
entrepreneurial structure 13
federal structure 16
functional structure 14
matrix structure 15
product structure 14
management of trust 148
managerial activities 156
managerial competence 73, 263
managerial performance 34–5
managerial roles **34**, 36
managerial skills for effective
organizational change 225–35
dealing with organizational culture 229–32
managing transitions 225–9
politics of organizational change 232–5
managing change 224–53
checklist for **284–5**
effectively 184–5
for management development 299–301
managing corporate politics 324–5
managing in different cultures 231
managing stress 288
managing transitions 225–9
mandarin, leader as 155, 157
mapping 110–16, 276
market-based approach to change 55
market-induced change 340–2
market leadership 98
market state 78, 82
market testing 31
masculinity 311
matrix management 15, 23–4
meaning, management of 148
mental models 165
mentor 32
merger/integration programmes 176
metanoia 161
methods of communication 21
Microsoft 5, 91
mind-set 50, 165, 314
mind-set shift 52, 55, 161, 162–3, 225, 266,
342, 344
monitoring performance 190–1
most respected co-workers 86, 87, 333
motivation process 70

multinational corporations 56
multi-organizational change
    programmes 176
multiple leaders (in networks) 58
multiple rationalities 233
mutually defeating interactions 221

NASA 85, 277
National Health Service (NHS) 51, 215–21[CS]
negotiation, personal 305
network organization 58–60
networks 53–4, 56, 263, 318
    organizing principles 58–9
    types 56
next steps programme 48
Nike 166
Nintendo 101
Nissan 279
non-adaptive cultures 315
Novartis 21

open-door policies, in management
    models 26
open-space events 8, 9
open systems theory 73, 74, 85
openness 231
opinion leaders 85, 86
organization design 139
    and functional tendencies 139, 140
    resources and complexity 138–40
organization-specific changes 176
organization-wide change programmes 176
organizational change
    coping with 235–7
    culture models 307–25
    evolution of theory of 91–2
    and management performance 183
    politics of 232–5
    and strategic convergence 326–39
organizational change cycle 260
organizational choice 27, 72–3
organizational climate 145
organizational culture 230–1, 308–15
    dealing with 229–32
    features of strong 317–18
    implementation of change 232
    managing in different cultures 231
    models of 311–15
organizational decline, signs of 301–2
organizational defences 49
organizational development (OD)
    and change implementation 67–8, 71–2
    literature 145

organizational diagnosis 201
    case study examples 214–21
    insightful 222
organizational diagnosis questionnaire 201,
    201–5, 205–6
organizational ecocycle 165
organizational effectiveness, sustaining
    120–47
organizational learning 47, 50, 160
    see also learning organization
organizational life cycle 166–7
organizational memory 87
organizational slack 86, 334
organizational structure(s) 309
    and strategy 29–34
    and systems 182–3
organizational syndromes 303–4
    leaderless 304
    paralysis 303
    personal style 303
    systems focus 303
    tight control 303
orientation 311
Oticon 167–8[CS], 321
out-of-touch managers 124
outcome-based consulting 266
outer directed 313
outpacing 101
outsourcing 31
ownership 285, 287

paradigm, definition 344
paradigm shift 162–3, 266, 344
parallel activities 102
paralysis syndrome 303
parochialism 124
participating leadership style 153, 154
participation 22
partnerships 39
patient-focused care (PFC) 40
PC World 342
people, as important asset/resource 9, 150
perceptual blocks 121
performance characteristics, of
    change architecture 330
performance expectations, in
    management models 25
performance gap 148
performance management 163, 274–5, 331
performance monitoring 9, 190–1, 277
'person culture' 312
personal experience, learning based on 228
personal impact 32

personal learning cycles 260
personal mastery 164–5
personal negotiation 305
personal responsibility and
    accountability 304
personal style syndrome **303**
Philips [CS] 315–16
Philips Lighting 276
Philips NV, Operation Centurion 33
pilot programmes/schemes 48, 156
planned approach to change 55
pluralism 313
political power model 128
political skills 316, **317**
politics of organizational change 232–5
positivism 81, 82, 83
postmodernism 81, 83–4
power 319–20
  social bases of 319
power culture 231, 312
power distance 311
pragmatism 159
primary cluster 115
privacy, protection of 250
privatization 173
problem orientation 333
problem solving
  blocks to 120–6
  humour in 122
  limits 124–6
  supporting 155
process benchmarking 46
process culture 312
process skill 148
product champions 22
product development 31
product (management) structure 14
productive reasoning 49, 135
productivity improvements 41
professional advice 231
professional rationality 234
professionals vs line management 22–4
profile of ambition 5–7
programmes of change 261–72
progress effect 240
project groups 2, 263
project structures 23–4
property management department
    (example) 229–32
psychological contract 67, 68
public sector, strategies for change in 305
public testing of issues and problems 231
purposiveness 127

quality improvement programmes 48, 140, 156
quasi-professionals 23

R&D, and budget cuts 21
radical change 97–103
rational behaviour, need for 135
rational-economic model of human
    behaviour 207
rationality 126–35
  clinical 126
  definition(s) 127–8
  hard 128
  imperfect 127
  multiple 233
  professional 234
  soft 127
readiness for change 281–90
  acceptability of change 286
  company track record of changes 281, 283
  expectations of change 283
  ownership of problem or idea for
      change 285
  top management support 285–6
readiness-for-change index 4, 7, 97
reality testing 226–7, 268
reason, and intuition 122
Reebok 166
referent power 319
relationships, building 263
relay assembly test room study 309–10
reputation 5, 46, 94
resistance to change 3–4, 39, 68, 238
resonance 331–2, 335, 337–8
resource-based view of strategy 6, 93–4
resource utilization 192
responsibility, personal 304
rethinking the organization 39
Reuters [CS] 341
reward policies, in management models **26**
reward power 319
reward systems 151
right-first-time programmes 48, 141, 156, 340
right-on-time delivery 340
risk aversion 121, 159
risk management 331
risk taking 21, 305, 311
  fear of 121
  learning encouraged by 229
  supporting 155
risky shift 124
rites and rituals 309, 317
role culture 230, 312
role modelling 318

rolling out 257
Rolls-Royce 156
Rover Cars 173
Royal Logistics Corps 173–4
rules of the game, changing 6, 38–9, 98, 108

Sainsbury Homebase 340
satisficing 124, 126
saturation 121
scaleability of workshop process 268
Schein, Ed 313
search conferences 8
secrecy 250
selection and training of staff 21
self, management of 149
'self-actualizing' model of human
    behaviour 208–9
self-assessment for change 288–90
    implementing changes **289**
    monitoring changes **289–90**
    planning changes **289**
    preparing for change **289**
self-deception 302
self-defeating strategies 221
self-esteem
    bases for building 248, 300
    effect of stress 238–9
    rebuilding of 236–7, *236*, 248–9
self-esteem effect 240
self-fulfilling prophecies 221
self-organization 84
self-reliant manager 32
selling leadership style *153*, 154
Senge, Peter 161, 164
sensitivity 299
sensory inputs, failure to use 121
sequential time 314
'set up to fail' syndrome 275
shared vision 165
simultaneous engineering 38
single-loop learning 48, 99
situational leadership theory 153–4, *153*
Skandia 58
skilled incompetence 132–3
skills, development in people 155
skills analysis 245
slogans 150–1
SmithKline Beecham [CS] 184, 225
sociability 314–15, *315*
social capital 52, 55
social influence 65, 87
'social' model of human behaviour 208
social movements 64, 65, 89–90
social paradigm 162

socio-technical systems model 7
soft rationality 127
solidarity 315, *315*
Solutions approach 335
specific vs diffuse 313
stability, versus change 27
stakeholders 70, 82, 174, 327
    engaging 9
Starbucks 96
status 314
stereotyping, as block to change 121
strategic alliances 32
strategic assets 46
strategic benchmarking 46
strategic business units 29, 41
strategic change 3–11, *174*
strategic control 33
strategic convergence 329–39
strategic credibility 83
strategic innovation 6
strategic learning 260
    and action *261*
strategic management of change 93–104,
    269–70, *269*, 271–2
strategic planning style 33
strategic vision 42
strategies
    for change 172–85, **226**
    for corporate transformation 340–4
    formation of 175
    inflexible use of 123
    and structures 29–34
strategy forums 8
strategy talk 81, 82–3
stress, change-caused 47, 238–9, *239*, 245–6, 306
    managing 288–90
strong cultures 310
superuser concept 170
supply chain management 52, 340
support
    lack of 123
    top management's 285–6
support cluster 115
sustainability 5
Swatch 6
symbols 309
synchronic time 314
syndrome of ineffective leadership and
    change management *44*, 45
synectics 123
synergy 28
systems crisis, overcoming 149–50
systems dynamic approach 73
systems focus syndrome **303**

systems theory 71, 72–3
systems thinking 164

taboos 122, 130
tacit knowledge 163, 168, 314, 342
task culture 230, 312
Tavistock Institute of Human Relations 72,
    82, 83
Taylor, Ann 170
team learning 165
team work 23, 182
technical uncertainty profile 99
telephone banking 96, 342
telling leadership style 153, *153*
theory E and O change 69
tight control syndrome **303**
time, giving 251
time-based competition approach 45
time-based management approach 31
time-based product development
    strategies 176
time to market 31
timing 166
    effective management of 156, 323–4
tipping point 65
top-down models of change 53
top management, support by 285–6
total quality management/programmes 30, 48,
    100, 176, 254, 308
tough guy/macho culture 311
Toyota lean production model 56, 308
Toys R Us 342
tradition 324
    as block to change 122–3
traditional depiction of organizations 52, *53*
traditional models 63–77
    clinical approach 67–8
    emergent approaches 73–6, 77
    linear approaches 68–72, 74, 77
    systems theory 72–3
trained incapacity 121
training
    and budget cuts 21
    and development, focused 263
    and organizational change 235, 287–90
transformational change 97–103
transformational leadership 48, 149
transformational resource, learning as 342
transforming the organization 37–60,
    45, 46–9
transparency 268, 278, 333
trust 52, 150
    emphasis on 24
    management of 148

turnaround 132, 304–6
    management features affecting 304–5
    strategies 305

uncertainty 238, 322
    avoidance 311
unemployment 51–2
unifying consequences 96
Union Carbide Corporation 321–2
universalism 313
use, learning by 47

value added 8, 53, *53*, 59
value-added clusters 114
value-added contributions 114–15
value-added design 110, 112, 343
value-added organization 49–58, 107–19
    balanced scorecard 116–18
    business capability profile 110–12
    changing rules of the game 108
    mapping the value flow 114–16
    techniques 109–18
    Value-added metric 112–13
value-added problems of command and
    control mode 112, 114
value chain 31
value creation 99
value of people and ideas, and learning 229
value stream re-invention 101
values 317
    emphasis on 24
    setting and sustaining 155, 323
vertical integration 38–9, 50
vicious circles 97, 275
virtual organization 31, 51, 55, 79
    characteristics 55
virtuous circle of change 125
visibility 334
vision influencing 168
vision and strategy, and leadership 150–1
visioning the future 44, 276
voluntary links (in networks) 58

Walt Disney Company 94
warning signs of structural problem 301
Waterstones 342
weak cultures 310
weak performers, managerial behaviour
    towards 275
Wilkinson Sword [CS] 263–5
work-hard/play-hard culture 311–12
Work Out Programme (General Electric) 98, 99
work streams 330
workshops 118, 235, 268